THE GREA

The Circus Strongman who Discovered Egypt's
Ancient Treasures

STANLEY MAYES

TAURISPARKE
PAPERBACKS

Published in 2003 by Tauris Parke Paperbacks
an imprint of I.B.Tauris & Co Ltd
6 Salem Road, London W2 4BU
175 Fifth Avenue, New York NY 10010
www.ibtauris.com

In the United States of America and in Canada distributed by
Palgrave Macmillan, a division of St Martin's Press
175 Fifth Avenue, New York NY 10010

Cover Illustration: Giovanni Battista Belzoni. Drawn on stone by M. Gauci
and lithographed by C. Hullmandel. (Coloured by Stylorouge).

ISBN 1 86064 877 0

A full CIP record for this book is available from the British Library
A full CIP record for this book is available from the Library of Congress

Library of Congress catalog card: available

Printed and bound in Great Britain by MPG Books Ltd, Bodmin, Cornwall

To My Daughter
DAPHNE

CONTENTS

PREFACE page 11

ILLUSTRATIONS

PLATES

ILLUSTRATIONS

ILLUSTRATIONS

ILLUSTRATIONS IN TEXT

Grateful acknowledgment is here made to the City Museum, Bristol, for
permission to reproduce Belzoni's drawing of Abu Simbel and to the
Griffith Institute, Ashmolean Museum, Oxford, and the Bankes family of
Kingston Lacy, Dorset, for permission to reproduce another drawing of
Abu Simbel from the Bankes MSS. (both facing page 145). The Brockedon
portrait of Belzoni (facing page 256) is reproduced by permission of the
National Portrait Gallery. The Finsbury Public Library is thanked for
allowing the reproduction of a Sadler's Wells play-bill in its possession
(page 41). All other illustrations are reproduced by courtesy of the Trustees
of the British Museum.

PREFACE

MY OWN interest in Belzoni goes back several years and grew out of a much earlier interest in ancient Egypt. Belzoni began to fascinate me in the way that that other pioneer of archaeology, Heinrich Schliemann, always has done. But whereas the German's place in the pantheon of great men was assured by his discovery of Troy and his excavations at Mycenae and Tiryns, it seemed to me that the Italian's achievement had never been properly recognized. Popular books on Egyptology devoted a few pages to him, but concentrated on the more flamboyant aspects of his character and career; they were also, in general, inaccurate. On the other hand professional Egyptologists were justifiably too busy catching up with the arrears of conservation, cataloguing and publication accruing over the last seventy years to be much concerned about an 'unscientific' collector of antiquities whose operations were carried out just twice that length of time ago.

Giovanni Battista Belzoni was born in Padua in 1778, the son of a poor barber. Poverty and the Napoleonic Wars drove him to England, and for ten years he wandered through the fairs and theatres of the British Isles, playing a pantomime giant at Sadler's Wells, performing feats of strength and conjuring tricks and arranging scenic effects with fountains and cascades of real water. He was tall and immensely strong; 'the handsomest man (for a giant) I ever saw' was Sir Walter Scott's verdict on him. In the year of Waterloo Belzoni arrived in Egypt, bent on persuading Muhammad Ali to adopt a new type of water-wheel for the irrigation of the country. The project failed and Belzoni was stranded. It was then that he undertook, on behalf of the British consul, to bring down from Thebes the colossal granite head of Ramses II which is now in the British Museum. During the next three years Belzoni excavated the buried temple of Abu Simbel, discovered six royal tombs in the Valley of the Kings, opened the Second Pyramid, found the lost city of Berenice, and by his efforts secured for the British Museum a superb collection of Egyptian antiquities. He died at the age of forty-five trying to reach the mysterious city of Timbuktu and to solve the problem of the Niger.

The question was, Could Belzoni be regarded as anything more than a freak, a 'character', a romantic adventurer whose Egyptian years were only an episode in a short but eventful career? What were his real motives in devoting himself so energetically and so single-mindedly to a succession of herculean tasks in Egypt? Was he any better or worse than his contemporaries who engaged in the mad scramble for antiquities at the beginning of the nineteenth century? How much did Belzoni know of Egypt's past? Did he understand the significance of his discoveries or see where they might lead? In short, what was his contribution to Egyptology?

It is not easy to find the answers to these questions in Belzoni's own *Narrative*. Hastily put together, all offers of help refused, this sprawling, inconsequential account of his work in Egypt baffles as much as it entertains. We move in an almost uncharted world of nameless ruins and confused mythology. Belzoni died before the decipherment of the hieroglyphics had made any real progress. The tangled clues in his book need gathering into strong strands if they are to sustain a claim to greatness.

It is true that Belzoni enjoyed a brief fame in his own day. He was lionized in Regency London as a great and intrepid traveller; as a foreigner he was approved of for his devotion to the British interest. But he soon became a myth. The man of flesh and blood, with all his schemes and hopes, passions and perturbations, was turned into a pasteboard hero—the very model of a self-made man, a smug epitome of patience and perseverance. Dickens embalmed him in a phrase: 'The once starving mountebank,' he wrote, 'became one of the most illustrious men in Europe!—an encouraging example to those, who have not only sound heads to project, but stout hearts to execute.'

No biographer disturbed that mid-nineteenth-century interment. The centenary of Belzoni's death passed in 1923 with only some slight effusions in Italian journals and periodicals. His fellow-countryman, Camillo Manfroni, expressed the hope that someone with a knowledge of the material in the British Museum would undertake a life of Belzoni. In the last twenty-five years a number of letters have come to light in Italy and been edited by various hands. But it was clear that the chief sources for a life of Belzoni must be in Britain.

Not all, however, are in the British Museum and even the material that is there is widely scattered. The first task was to clear away the Victorian rubbish that buried the giant Belzoni as a mountain of sand had engulfed the colossi of Abu Simbel. (Even the articles on Belzoni in *The Dictionary of National Biography* and the latest edition of the *Encyclopædia Britannica* were full of inaccuracies.) Then when almost every statement made about Belzoni after 1830 had either been rejected as false or held in suspense for further scrutiny, a search was begun among old newspaper files, contemporary periodicals, theatre records and reminiscences, collections of playbills and other trivia preserved in scrap-books and miscellanies, for traces of Belzoni's passage through the fairs and theatres of the British Isles. The harvest might have been better, but enough was gleaned to show the kind of world Belzoni moved in during the formative years of his life, the sort of man he was and the ambitions that he cherished.

For Belzoni's Italian background and his relations with his family by far the most valuable source has been the letters published by Prof. Luigi Gaudenzio in *Giovan Battista Belzoni alla luce di nuovi documenti* (Padua, 1936). The other Belzoniana published by Manfroni and Bellorini have helped to fill in some of the gaps.

But it is Belzoni's contribution to our knowledge of ancient Egypt, still more the impetus that he gave to the study of its civilization, that are the *raisons d'être* for this book. Fortunately his *Narrative* could be checked by reference to the published journals of more than a dozen travellers who met him in Egypt. Turner, Burckhardt, Richardson, Irby, Henniker, Edmonstone, Pearce, Fitzclarence, Cailliaud, D'Athanasi, De Forbin, De Montulé, Finati—all show different facets of Belzoni's personality. My chief regret is that I have not been able to consult the MS. journal of Alessandro Ricci, the doctor who worked so long and laboriously on Belzoni's behalf in the tomb of Seti I; the journal is, I believe, still in Cairo. The first volume of *Il Corpo Epistolare di Bernardino Drovetti*, published by Giovanni Marro in 1940, has been of the greatest help. This scholarly edition of part of the vast Drovetti correspondence is a rich mine of information about the European community in Egypt, as it revolved around the influential French consul during the early years of the nineteenth century. Again I am sorry that I have not been able to search for further traces of Belzoni among the hundreds of letters still unpublished. But it is good to know that Professor Savina Fumagalli of Turin University has taken over the task which Professor Marro left unfinished at his death.

It was not enough however merely to straighten out Belzoni's tangled narrative and to supplement it from the letters and journals of his contemporaries. That might have provided an entertaining story, but it would not have answered my main purpose. I have tried therefore to relate Belzoni's work on each site in Egypt to what was known of it before his day and broadly what has been discovered since. A good deal of the pleasure in writing this book has come from the effort to trace the history and provenance of Belzoni's main finds. The results are given in an Appendix that may add a little to the reader's interest when he sees the objects themselves in the British Museum.

Work on my book was already well advanced when I learnt that two other books about Belzoni were on the way. They appeared almost simultaneously. I hope I am being fair to Mr. Maurice Willson Disher if I say that in *Pharaoh's Fool* he has seen the interest which Belzoni created in ancient Egypt rather as an exotic ornament of the Regency period he knows so well than as the beginnings of a new science. Mr. Colin Clair on the other hand in *Strong Man Egyptologist* was prevented by the size and scope of a 'pocket' biography from doing more than concentrate on a single figure 'in close-up'. My own book is as long as these two together. At the risk of diffuseness I have moved backwards and forwards in time to show something of the way in which Egypt impinged upon the West both historically and politically. And the rivalries of the French and British for influence in Egypt could not be separated properly from the cut-throat scramble for antiquities.

Many people have helped with this book. I am grateful especially to Mr. Colin Clair for so generously placing at my disposal the results of his own researches into Belzoni's life which lack of space prevented him from using. I would also particularly like to thank Professor Luigi Gaudenzio of the University of Padua and Professor Savina Fumagalli of the University of Turin for all their courteous help and for the gift or loan of books.

My thanks are due to all those who have given me permission to quote from material in their possession: Sir John Murray, K.C.V.O., D.S.O. (various Belzoni letters); Sir Thomas Kendrick, K.C.B., Director and Principal Librarian of the British Museum (relevant passages in the Minutes of the Trustees and the Museum's Letter Books, as well as records in the Department of Egyptian Antiquities); the Master of the Rolls (F.O. and War Office papers in the Public Record Office); Dr. F. S. Wallis, Director of the City Museum, Bristol (a letter in Mrs. Belzoni's notebook); and the Librarian of the Guildhall Library, London (MS. material on Bartholomew Fair).

Others who have helped me in my search for Belzoni and whose kindness I now acknowledge are: Miss Lucia Paravicini, Librarian at the Italian Institute, London; Signor Girolamo Bonsembiante, advocate, of Padua; Mr. George Nash of the Enthoven Theatre Collection, Victoria and Albert Museum; Mr. Raymond Mander; Miss Sybil Rosenfeld; Professor Ernesto Scamuzzi, Superintendent of Egyptian Antiquities at Turin; Miss Rosalind Moss and Miss Barbara Sewell of the Griffith Institute, Ashmolean Museum, Oxford; Mr. Leslie Grinsell, Curator in Archaeology, The City Museum, Bristol; Dr. Philip Corder, Assistant Secretary of the Society of Antiquaries of London; and Quatuor Coronati Research Lodge No. 2076.

I owe a special debt of gratitude to University College, London and in particular to Professor Walter Emery and the Librarian of the College for allowing me to borrow books on Egyptology from the Edwards Library. Indeed, but for the kind encouragement which Professor Emery and Dr. A. J. Arkell gave to my amateur interest in Egyptology some years ago, this book would never have been written.

I received great help from the National Library of Rome, which sent me books on loan through the National Central Library. I would like to thank both these institutions, as well as Mr. Swanton of Beckenham Public Library and the Staff of the Westminster and Finsbury Public Libraries. Of the London Library I can only say that it was indispensable.

Of course, the British Museum itself is really the second hero of this book, in spite of the animadversions passed upon it in Chapter XV. I am very grateful to the staffs of the Reading Room, North Library, Print Room, Department of MSS. and Newspaper Library at Colindale. I am also indebted to Mr. I. E. S. Edwards and Mr. T. G. H. James, Keeper and Assistant Keeper of Egyptian Antiquities, for allowing me to browse through their records and search the cellars of the Museum for Belzoni finds that are not at present on exhibition.

Egyptologists and Orientalists may not altogether approve my spelling of ancient and modern Egyptian names. In both cases I have tried to be as consistent as possible, with some deliberate exceptions. When the Greek form of an ancient Egyptian name is much more familiar than the native spelling, I have not hesitated to use it; thus Cheops is preferred to Khufu. For expert advice—not always taken—on the transliteration of modern Egyptian names I am indebted to Mr. A. E. H. Paxton; in general, I have followed the system used in the 1929 edition of Baedeker's *Egypt*, except in the case of some pure Arabic names.

Lastly, I would like to thank Mrs. Emma Lewis for valuable help with my Italian correspondence and Miss Dorothy Evans for her excellent typing of my manuscript.

London, August 1958   STANLEY MAYES

CHAPTER I

*Tell me, Muse, of that man, so ready at need, who wandered far
and wide, after he had sacked the sacred city of Troy, and many were
the men whose towns he saw and whose mind he learnt, yea, and
many the woes he suffered . . .*

HOMER, The Odyssey, translated by Butcher and Lang

*My native place is the city of Padua: I am of a Roman family,
which had resided there for many years. The state and troubles of Italy
in 1800, which are too well known to require any comment from me,
compelled me to leave it, and from that time I have visited different
parts of Europe, and suffered many vicissitudes.*

BELZONI, Preface to Narrative of the Operations, etc.

IN the early months of 1803 Charles Dibdin Junior was getting
together a company for Sadler's Wells. For the past three years he
had been author, producer and stage manager—for an inclusive
salary of two guineas a week—at the little summer theatre that lay over
the fields towards Islington. Now by a stroke of luck he was also part-
proprietor. The previous season had not been very good. In fact, Mr.
Siddons—husband of the great Sarah—and three of his four copartners
in the Wells had decided to sell out. Negotiations were already in train
when Dibdin discovered what was afoot. He approached his employers
and asked if the deal had gone too far for them to withdraw. Siddons
assured him it had not. Richard Hughes, who acted as general manager,
told him it only needed youth, professional experience and a spirit of
enterprise to make the Wells as prosperous as it had been before. The
upshot was that Charles Dibdin and his younger brother Tom[1] bought
Siddons's quarter share for £1,400, borrowing the money to pay the
first instalment; William Reeve, the theatre's musical director, and Bob
Andrews, the scene-painter, took another quarter share; a third was
divided between Mr. Yarnold and Mr. Barfoot, two gentlemen of means
living in North London; and Richard Hughes kept his own quarter
share. Thus at the age of thirty-four Charles Dibdin Junior, a former
pawnbroker's assistant, became the moving spirit of Sadler's Wells. In
the course of a long professional life, both here and at other minor
theatres, he wrote and produced over two hundred popular entertainments. They ranged from plays and burlettas through pantomimes and
harlequinades to the most elaborate spectacles on real water. Of these

17

2

fugitive pieces little remains but a scatter of songs and a few truncated texts. Yet, oddly enough, Charles Dibdin was destined to introduce to the public in this first year of the new management a personality whose own eventual contribution to culture was to be so solidly monumental. For among the performers engaged at Sadler's Wells in the spring of 1803 was a certain Giovanni Battista Belzoni.

Most of the men in the previous year's company had been taken on again. First and foremost there was young Joe Grimaldi, who in the last couple of seasons had begun to found 'a *New School* for Clowns', as Charles Dibdin says in his *Memoirs*. 'The present mode of dressing Clowns and painting their faces', he points out, 'was then invented by Mr. G.' Grimaldi was now given a three-year contract 'at a high and rising salary'; probably it was less than ten pounds a week. (Dibdin himself by his new contract received only four guineas a week in summer and three in winter; he was, however, allowed a house rent-free in the Wells yard.) Next in importance was Jack Bologna, a splendid, spirited Harlequin now at the height of his powers. He had come to England nearly twenty years before as a small boy in his father's family troupe of acrobats. Jack's brother Louis was still with him. Then there was 'Jew' Davis, a coarse-grained comic given to playing crude practical jokes on the foreign members of the company, and a number of other useful but undistinguished performers. Dibdin realized that the Wells must offer bigger salaries if it was going to attract more talent. Eventually he was able to secure the services of Mr. Townshend from the Theatre Royal, Covent Garden, for twelve pounds a week. He was to play most of the leads this season until his conduct both on and off the stage became so impossible that his contract had to be cancelled. Mr. King, a popular singer and Harlequin, also came to the Wells from Covent Garden at this time. Other new comers included the eccentric Mr. Bradbury of the Royal Circus, famous for his antics on the stage with a live pig; Signor Cipriani, a clever mime and burlesque dancer; and the youthful Master Menage, an expert in 'skin work', i.e. animal parts, who had scored a great success two years before as the Monkey in *Perouse, or The Desolate Island*.[2]

The 'female department', as the age so inelegantly called it, seemed to be less in need of new talent than the men, though Wheeler, the stage-doorkeeper of the Wells, recorded that 'the manager's wife, Mrs. C. Dibdin, could bear no rivalry, and a song encored would dismiss the Lady singing it from ever singing it again, and at the end of the season from the theatre'.[3] In 1803 the twenty-odd ladies of the company were apparently augmented only by the three Dennet sisters—a singer and two dancers—and by little Miss Gayton, a nine-year-old child, whose skipping-rope hornpipe was soon to be so popular with audiences at the Wells.

Such was the world into which Belzoni walked one day soon after his arrival in England. We are not told how he came to meet Charles Dibdin, though the latter says in the *Memoirs* that his prompter, Morelli, was the man 'to whom all the Italian Minstrels and gymnastical performers used to apply, on their arrival in England, as to a House of Call, and he brought them all, first, to me'. Certainly the original Pandean Band, which started a new vogue that summer for the Pan-pipes, came to Dibdin's notice through the efforts of Morelli. It is very likely that the prompter performed the same service for two more of his fellow-countrymen—the brothers Belzoni.

Francesco throughout remains a pale simulacrum of Giovanni Battista, but the two together in the flesh must have been a remarkable sight. According to Cyrus Redding,[4] a Cornish journalist who met them both some years later, Giovanni was 'full, if not over, seven feet in height'. Redding was a tall man himself—he claimed to be six foot one —and he says that he looked short beside Giovanni. He thought Francesco was six foot three or four. Probably there is some exaggera-tion here. A Spanish passport issued to Giovanni in 1812 merely gives his height as 'over six feet'.[5] John Britton says that he was registered in the books of the Alien Office as six feet six inches.[6] A search at the Public Record Office has failed to reveal this entry. However, in the absence of any conclusive evidence, we may take this last reference as likely to be near the mark. What earned Belzoni the epithet 'gigantic' was not mere inches of height so much as the magnificent proportions of his body. Broad-shouldered, deep-chested, long of limb, with a noble head carried splendidly erect upon a strong neck, he moved as gracefully as a ballet dancer amongst ordinary shuffling humanity. And that though Cyrus Redding allowed he had one leg slightly in-kneed.

Belzoni was a very handsome man; the existing portraits of him leave no doubt about that.[7] His strong aquiline features give him an air of great nobility, whether he is seen full-bearded and mustachio'd or with the lower part of his face clean shaven, whether he is in Regency cos-tume or dressed *à la Turque*. The mouth is large and sensitive, the nostrils delicately formed, the eyes full of a mild compassion that still does not hide their fire. 'Blue eyes, fresh complexion,' says the Spanish passport, but the beard, we know, in later years was black. There is a gentleness about the face, a quiet, natural dignity, a sense of strength in repose. His manner was modest and unassuming. Those who knew him best spoke of his great good temper, and indeed his whole life was eloquent of his patience and perseverance. That he could also be jealous and suspicious of others is not surprising. He was too ready to expect the best of his fellow men, and when they fell short of that to believe the worst.

What commended Belzoni to the manager of Sadler's Wells was his fine handsome address and above all his great strength. Probably the young giant—he was just twenty-four—demonstrated this in the simplest possible way, by letting as many men as could clamber upon him. The human load was limited only by their difficulty in holding on; Belzoni stood or walked about as though the men were kittens. Whether he had yet invented the piece of apparatus that allowed him to carry eleven persons at once is not clear; perhaps it was made for him here at the theatre. All that we know from Dibdin's *Memoirs* is that he engaged the two brothers. Giovanni was to give a weight-lifting exhibition and play any suitable parts that could be devised for him in pieces which had to provide scope for all the varied talents of the company. A Giant, a Cannibal Chief, a Wild Man of the Woods—it must have seemed to Dibdin there were many possibilities for a man of Giovanni's physique and appearance, even if his English at this time was very broken or practically non-existent. Francesco would be a supernumerary and make himself useful where he could. There is no record of his appearing in a part this season, though subsequently, Dibdin says, he 'performed as a Mime, on the Wells Stage, Lebrun's Passions[8] to music, in a very masterly and impressive manner; but it was *caviare* to John Bull, and we soon withdrew it'.

What had brought these two young Italians to England in the middle of 'the phoney peace' with Napoleon? . . .

Originally the family came from Rome, but for many years the Belzonis had been settled in Padua, where the boys' father, Giacomo Bolzon—to use the North Italian corruption of their name—made a modest living as a barber. He and his wife Teresa, a big, sad woman who suffered from chronic headaches,[9] had a hard struggle to bring up their four boys and at the same time help their even less fortunate relatives. (The story that Giovanni was the fifteenth addition to his parents' family is late and unlikely, though it may reflect some attempt to reckon up the various aunts, cousins, daughters-in-law and grand-children that eventually became dependent on the barber and his four sons.)[10] They were a happy, united family. The fortunes of one were the fortunes of all. And if economic necessity sometimes drove them apart, love and affection as often brought them together again.

Giovanni Battista Belzoni—Giambattista or Gio Batta, to give him the familiar diminutives—was born in Padua on 5 November 1778.[11] Little is known about his childhood and early youth. There is the usual apocryphal story that he ran away from home after reading an exciting

adventure story—in this case a translation of *Robinson Crusoe*. Cyrus
Redding gives a more circumstantial account of an episode that he must
have heard about from Belzoni himself. It seems that Giovanni had
never even been out of Padua till he was thirteen years old. Then one
day his parents decided to give the family a treat. They closed the
barber's shop, where Giovanni now helped his father, and went off into
the country to picnic at the hermitage of Ortono, on a pleasant hill near
the warm springs that feed the baths of Abano. The strange volcanic
beauty of the place—lush grass, bare rocks and teeming vines—made
a deep impression on the town-bred boy. When Giovanni returned to
Padua, the bright dream over, the barber's shop disgusted him. A day
or two later, still haunted by the beauty of the countryside, he stole
away from the house with his young brother Antonio to find the
delectable spot again. The way was longer than they thought, the roads
hot and dusty. Presently they overtook a cart going to Ferrara. The
driver offered them a lift and they gladly accepted. But when they
reached Ferrara, almost fifty miles away, the man demanded payment
and, as they had no money, took some of their clothes instead. The boys
were now committed to a much bigger adventure than they had planned
at first. For Giovanni, as soon as the urge to get away had asserted itself,
the goal was Rome. There he knew that his family had its origins in a
romantic past; there was the city of whose wonders he had heard his
parents speak so often; there he might escape for ever from the boredom
and drudgery of the barber's shop. For Antonio, only nine, the adventure had already gone too far. Presently he broke down and began to
cry. Giovanni's own desire to go on was not so strong as his compassion
for his brother. Together they returned to Padua.

Three years passed before Giovanni was able to realize his dream of
going to Rome—this time with his family's blessing and consent. At
sixteen the handsome young giant could no longer be kept tethered to
a barber's chair. His ambitions were high but as yet undefined. He had
had little formal education. To the end of his days he never learnt to
spell either in his native Italian or in the English of his adoption. But
he showed a certain mechanical aptitude and an interest in science, and
it must have seemed that there was more chance for a bright lad in the
bustling, thriving streets of Rome than in the quiet backwaters of
Padua.

The times were not propitious. Even before Giovanni left home the
states of Northern Italy had begun to feel the grinding pressure of the
French military juggernaut. In March 1796, when the seventeen-year-
old boy was just beginning to taste the sweets of independence in Rome,
a young Corsican general of artillery was given command of the French
army in Italy. In less than a fortnight he had thrown back the armies

of Austria and Piedmont and imposed his own terms on the King of
Sardinia. During the next few months, with a series of crushing blows,
Bonaparte carried the war right into Austrian territory. Milan fell,
Mantua fell, and soon the road to Rome lay open. Early in 1797 the
Pope was forced to accept a humiliating truce, and before the summer
the ancient republic of Venice had signed her own death-warrant. A new
Cisalpine Republic came into being and the 'liberated' states of
Northern Italy found themselves saddled with a French army of occu-
pation. Finally in February 1798 the Pope went into exile and the
French entered Rome.

The sequence of events in Giovanni's own history is somewhat less
clear. Certainly the French invasion of Rome unsettled him badly and
caused him to change his plans. But we do not know how far he had
progressed with his study of hydraulics, which he says interested him
at this period. Perhaps this only meant that he had some job of work
among the fountains of Rome, making or repairing the pipes for these
ingenious *jets d'eau*. According to one account, he was boring an artesian
well when the French entered Rome.[12] This may have been in a
monastery, for at one point he decided to become a monk and began
to prepare himself for admittance to the Capuchin order.[13] Belzoni's
brief autobiographical notes in the Preface to his *Narrative* suggest that
these were the studies which the French so rudely interrupted.

We need not place too much credence on the story that Giovanni
turned to the monastic life because he had been crossed in love.[14] It is
hard to believe that a young man of his energetic habit and restless
temperament would seek consolation in the cloister. Much more likely
is the explanation hinted at by Belzoni himself, that he was trying to
make good the gaps in his education. And this is not at variance with
the reason given by Redding that 'he had no means of support, and
became a monk out of necessity'. There may also have been the idea in
his mind that he could take refuge in a monastery till the storm of war
was over. Belzoni had no wish to be pressed into the French army, and
his size and appearance made him all too obviously an ideal fugleman.

But the unsettled state of the country proved chronic and even the
monasteries were no longer safe from Napoleon's soldiery. Giovanni
made up his mind to try his fortunes abroad. With a *colporteur*'s pack
of religious images, rosaries and relics[15] to provide him with a living,
he took to the road and trudged north over the Apennines, over the
Alps into France. Here again the details are blurred. Redding says that
after visiting Paris he returned to Italy in 1800. Finding the situation
no better he set off again and this time went to Holland.[16] Evidently
the prospects there seemed better, for after another visit to his home
he went back to Holland, taking with him his brother Francesco.

Giovanni says little about his life at this time. In the Preface to his book he writes: 'My family supplied me occasionally with remittances; but as they were not rich, I did not choose to be a burthen to them, and contrived to live on my own industry, and the little knowledge I had acquired in various branches. I turned my chief attention to hydraulics, a science that I had learned in Rome, which I found much to my advantage, and which was ultimately the very cause of my going to Egypt.'

Giovanni can hardly have set the Zuider Zee on fire with his skill in hydraulics. Indeed, his friend Redding admits that the Dutch seemed to know more about the subject than the young Italian expected. Perhaps, as so often happens with those who are thwarted in their secret ambitions, Belzoni was obliged to lay claim to more qualifications than he possessed simply in order to have an opportunity to practise the craft of his choice. But it is true that when he came to write the Preface to his book nearly twenty years later he was anxious to give himself a respectable bourgeois background. So his early scientific pursuits were emphasized, and all reference to weight-lifting and other ignoble exhibitions was rigorously excluded.

In fact, we know now that during their stay in Holland the brothers supported themselves mainly by petty trading in and around the port of Amsterdam. There is a letter written jointly by the two young men—apparently the only one to survive from this period—which gives an idea of their precarious existence.[17] It shows their devotion to each other and the eagerness with which they looked for news from home. The grammar and spelling are very odd; the paper is torn and smudged. Yet through the simple, commonplace language shines a sturdy Italian independence—symbol of a spirit abroad in Europe that Napoleon was not going to quench.

The letter is undated, but from the reference to All Saints' Day— 1 November—and the mention of the brothers' imminent departure for England it would seem to have been written towards the end of 1802.

'Carisimi Gienitori,' says Giovanni, as one who would write 'Dere Pairents——' (Inevitably the rough homespun texture of his Italian and the idiosyncrasies of his spelling must disappear in translation.) 'Dear Parents, I got your letter on All Saints' Day, and am very sorry about the trouble you have had, but also very glad to know that I shall soon be able to get my goods. I promise you I will soon repay the merchant who endorsed the bill, so that the money will be refunded and everything settled . . .' Evidently Giovanni has had to borrow. He goes on to say that after being ill for more than two months he has now quite recovered and will be able to work again as soon as he has his stock-in-trade. He is glad to hear that his mother's headaches are better, but annoyed with his father for suggesting that he does not know how to look after himself properly. 'I've taken nothing but Peruvian bark powder, Peruvian bark extract, Peruvian bark essence,' he says indignantly. Francesco has been with him day and night and the good, kindly people in whose house they have been staying are patience itself. Giovanni explains that he caught the fever in a village to which he had gone with other traders to attend a fair.[18] There was practically an epidemic there and some of the others were still ill, but Francesco fortunately had escaped. 'He's as fat as a pig,' he adds by way of compliment to his brother. There is a word more about business. He asks his parents to tell Signor Bernardi that his boxes have never arrived. If he will send another lot before Giovanni leaves for England, he will do what he can. Then back to the family. So young Antonio is going to get married? Giovanni wants to know more about it. He makes a joke about his brother's drinking habits and wonders whether he is going to marry a rich wife. Then with lots of kisses and affectionate embraces for all the family he signs himself: 'Vostro filgio Gio Batta Belzoni'.

To this Francesco adds a brief postscript. He assures his parents that Giovanni is quite well again, but he admits that the illness has cost them a lot of money. He too is all agog to hear more news of Tonio's intended marriage.

Soon after this letter was written and probably in the early part of 1803 Giovanni and Francesco came to England. They left a Continent dominated by Napoleon for a country divided against itself. The Treaty of Amiens, signed in March 1802, had brought only an illusory peace to a Britain wearied by nine years of war. In the months that followed, thousands of English tourists flocked to France, anxious to see what was left of the *ancien régime*, eager to quiz the new Paris fashions, and curious to catch a glimpse of the little sallow-faced man who had made all Europe tremble. Some of the more naïve were dazzled by the splendid efficiency of the State machine and the First Consul's smile for the gullible English. Why should they worry if Bonaparte wanted to bring the rule of law to other less enlightened countries? Britain was an island, and the narrow seas were her bulwark. So long as she was able to trade with the rest of the world, did it matter much what happened on the continent of Europe?

Yet there were others who came back from France shocked and disturbed by the ruthless militarism of the new order. The absence of all free discussion, the muzzling of the press, the subservience of the intellectuals, above all the miasmatic presence of the secret police filled liberal-minded Englishmen with disgust. The old Whig Opposition leader, Charles James Fox, whose sympathy for the ideas of the

Revolution had more than once made him suspect, now told Napoleon to his face that all government which existed by force alone was oppressive and evil.

It was unfortunate that England's well-being at this time depended on the prescriptions of 'Doctor' Addington. When George III in a moment of mad lucidity forced Pitt to resign over the question of Roman Catholic emancipation, Henry Addington—'that mass of conciliation and clemency', as someone once called him—became Prime Minister. Peace at almost any price was the 'Doctor's' policy. To achieve it he had given up all England's colonial conquests, except Ceylon and Trinidad, in return for a vague assurance that the *status quo* in Europe would be preserved. Ten days after the signing of the Peace Treaty Addington abolished Pitt's wartime measure of an income tax. In the next few months drastic cuts were made in the armed forces. And across the Channel Bonaparte smiled as he watched a nation of shopkeepers prepare their own ruin.

Throughout the summer and autumn of 1802 Europe's dictator outmanœuvred the English at every turn. He had already sent a task force to the West Indies and alarmed the United States by claiming part of Louisiana. Before long French officers were arriving in India to scheme with native princes for the expulsion of the English. In Europe the First Consul tightened his stranglehold on Italy and refused to withdraw French troops from the puppet Dutch Republic. He intervened in Germany and embroiled Austria and Prussia, so that there should be no concerted action against him. Then, while the English looked on helplessly, in October he raped Switzerland.

If there were any illusions left about the purity of Napoleon's intentions, this cynical extinction of Swiss liberty finally dispelled them. When Lord Whitworth went off to Paris in November as the new British ambassador, he was instructed by the Foreign Secretary, the lugubrious, long-necked Lord Hawkesbury, who looked 'as if he had been on the rack three times and saw the wheel preparing for a fourth', to acquaint the French Government with His Majesty's determination 'never to forego his right of interfering in the affairs of the Continent on every occasion in which the interests of his own dominions or those of Europe in general may appear to him to require it'. This 'forcible Feeble' negative was as far as the Foreign Office was prepared to go at the moment. Yet even the 'Goose' Addington, afraid to say bo, realized it was impossible now for Britain to give up Malta, as the terms of the Peace Treaty required, unless she was willing to sacrifice all her influence in the Mediterranean and endanger her Eastern trade. Whitworth had been in Paris only a fortnight when he informed the Foreign Secretary that 'the acquisition of Egypt is the object which the First

Consul has most at heart, and that to which our utmost attention should be directed'. As proof he cited the pretended 'trade mission' of Colonel Sebastiani to North Africa and the Levant. Two months later, when the Colonel's provocative report on the state of Egypt was published in *Le Moniteur* and picked up by the English press, all London knew that Napoleon's aim was to re-occupy Egypt and set himself astride Britain's vital trade-route to India and the Far East. The four thousand British soldiers waiting to be evacuated from Egypt would not be able to stop him. Only if Malta remained in British hands could the Mediterranean be kept open.

Resentment had grown strong against French provocation, complaisance turned to obstinacy. Yet now that the Government had taken a stand on Malta, it became terrified that public opinion might push it over the edge into war. The 'Doctor' still huddled the humiliating rags of the Peace about him, even though they no longer covered the nakedness of his policy. Fox cheerfully renounced war and urged the Government to honour its obligations. (It was one of the ironies of the situation that Britain could now be held up to obloquy as the violator of the Peace. If from many countries in Europe 'answer came there none' about the real infractions of the Treaty, it was only because Napoleon, like the Carpenter with the Oysters, had 'eaten every one'.) Meanwhile the younger Tories under Canning schemed to bring back Pitt. He, like another Cincinnatus, pottered about the gardens of Walmer Castle and bided his time. Lord Grenville and his friends spoke of England's lost prestige and clamoured urgently for war. Between talk of appeasement and calls for action, the people did not know where they were. Few realized as clearly as Castlereagh did that war was inevitable; that waiting for Europe to rise in revolt was mere self-deception; that every month of delay and vacillation gave Napoleon the time he needed to prepare for fresh conquests.

Such was the situation when the two Belzonis arrived in England. The total population of Great Britain was then about ten millions. London had some nine hundred thousand inhabitants. Its western boundary was Park Lane—once Tyburn Lane till its more fashionable residents found the name too grim. Oxford Street was a broad, airy avenue, flanked on either side by fine squares and ending at Tyburn turnpike. Beyond in open country lay the little hamlet of Bayswater, famous for its tea-gardens. Paddington itself was rural and remote; in the distance the cupola of its new church rose above the tops of venerable elms. From there the New Road ran through fields and nursery gardens past Tottenham Court to the pleasant village of Islington. North of High Holborn the houses of the new rich advanced in a planned and orderly procession, overrunning Bloomsbury and Russell

Squares and pushing on to Tavistock. Yet one could still walk from Gower Street to Hampstead through fields and country lanes. There were cows and dairy-maids even in Portland Place. South of High Holborn lay Covent Garden with its theatres and market, its coffee-houses, taverns, bagnios and brothels spreading down through a maze of mean streets to St. Clement's and the Strand. Already there was talk of removing Temple Bar because it hindered the flow of traffic between Westminster and the City. It was often quicker and more convenient to go by water or to cross and re-cross the river by the bridges. There were still only three at this date—Blackfriars, Westminster and old London Bridge.

It was an age of great prosperity for the London tradesman. The rapid growth of the capital, the increase in the number of manufactured goods, the restrictions on foreign travel during nine years of war and the delay in social reform, all contributed to the rise of a comfortable shopkeeper class with few pretensions to taste or education. Its amusements were mainly drinking and card-playing, but it was also fond of the theatre. And here the supply of popular entertainments was never equal to the demand.

By the Licensing Act of 1737 Covent Garden and Drury Lane were the only two theatres in London that were allowed to present legitimate drama. (An exception was made some thirty years later when Samuel Foote, the comedian, broke his leg in a fall from a horse belonging to the Duke of York and, on the Prince's intercession, obtained a patent to open the little theatre in the Haymarket during the summer months. As the other two patent houses were winter theatres, this did not affect their monopoly.) In 1752 an Act 'for regulating places of public entertainment' gave local magistrates the power to grant annual licences to minor theatres and halls for singing, dancing, and the performance of burlettas. A burletta was defined as 'a drama in rhyme, which is entirely musical'. In other words, so long as the actors did not speak dramatic dialogue in prose but sang or delivered their words in a form of recitative, they were within the letter of the law. This gave enterprising managers a great deal of scope. When John Palmer staged an elaborate pantomime-spectacle at the Royalty Theatre in Wellclose Square, Whitechapel, in 1786, the proprietors of the patent theatres were seriously alarmed and took steps to have the theatre closed. It opened again with a more modest pantomime, but this time Delpini the clown was unlucky enough to *speak* the words 'Roast beef!' without a musical accompaniment. Palmer was charged with contravening the Act. The magistrates found there was no case; whereupon the indignant patentees had the magistrates removed from office. Such was the strength of vested interests. Sheridan, as Member of Parliament, did not hesitate to speak out strongly against bills intended to license theatres whose existence would affect him as manager of Drury Lane.

Although the monopoly of the patent houses was not finally broken till 1843, the minor theatres gained ground steadily. The Act of 1788 allowed four of these places of entertainment—Sadler's Wells, the Royalty, Astley's Amphitheatre and the Royal Circus—to 'continue exhibiting performances of singing, dancing, pantomime and music'. By the turn of the century the royal theatres were fighting a losing battle. Even the most prolific playwright could not keep them going with new pieces and long runs were unknown. Revivals with names like Kemble and Siddons were always a draw, but leading actors and actresses were apt to find provincial tours more profitable. Sometimes the most successful piece of the season was a pantomime, and here the minor theatres could compete on equal terms. Moreover they filled their bills with popular variety acts—jugglers, rope-dancers, acrobats, strong men, performing dogs and horses and every novelty that an ingenious management could devise or discover. Their appeal to the London tradesman and his apprentice was simple and direct.

Of the four minor theatres that existed at the beginning of the nineteenth century, Sadler's Wells was by far the oldest. In the year 1683 Mr. Sadler, a surveyor of highways and the owner of a 'Musick House' at Islington near the reservoir known as the New River Head, discovered in his grounds a medicinal spring which had once belonged to the Priory of Clerkenwell. He was quick to see its commercial possibilities and, in order to attract custom, laid out gardens round the well, engaged a pipe and tabor band for dancing, and stationed a damsel with a dulcimer in an artificial glen to play for those who felt romantic. Under his heirs and successors other entertainments were added: clowns, tumblers and rope-dancers soon made their appearance; interludes and pantomimes were performed. In 1765 the original wooden 'Musick House' was pulled down and a more solid structure took its place. Tom King, the actor who created the part of Sir Peter Teazle in *The School For Scandal*, became lessee of the Wells in 1772, and under his management the status of the theatre greatly improved. The elder Charles Dibdin began to write for it and the nobility bestowed its patronage. Sadler's Wells was now the principal home of pantomime in England, while from time to time it would delight the public with some startling novelty. One such was the presentation in 1783 of a play, *The Deserter*, acted entirely by dogs;[19] it helped the management to clear £10,000 that season. In the 1780s a number of famous Continental performers appeared at the Wells—Dubois, the celebrated clown; Redigé, a superb acrobat billed as the Little Devil; and his mistress, La Belle Espagnole, who danced with swords fastened to her feet and an egg under each.

These all came to stay. Under their tutelage grew up the young Bolognas, Richer, the rope-dancer, praised by Hazlitt as 'matchless in his art', and Joe Grimaldi, who in the year 1800 made his first appearance as Clown and ushered in a new era of pantomime at Sadler's Wells.

CHAPTER II

Need I fear
To mention by its name . . .
Half-rural Sadler's Wells?
                    . . . here more than once
Taking my seat, I saw (nor blush to add,
With ample recompense) giants and dwarfs,
Clowns, conjurors, posture-masters, harlequins,
Amid the uproar of the rabblement,
Perform their feats.

WILLIAM WORDSWORTH, The Prelude, 1805 [1]

CHARLES DIBDIN JUNIOR had got together his company for the summer of 1803. Probably, if he ran true to form, he then began to consider the writing of his pieces. He was a prodigiously fast worker. It was not unknown for him to begin the composition of a two-act burletta on Friday morning and have it ready for presentation to the public by the following Monday evening. A cynic might say that this was obvious from the sorry doggerel that has survived, but in fairness one must ask whether the impact of a modern musical play could be judged in a hundred and fifty years' time merely by reading its lyrics in cold print. Dibdin seems to have had the magic Harlequin touch capable of transforming the crude elements of song, dance, mime, scenic effects and stage tricks into something theatrically alive and compelling. Only in this way can we explain his successful management of the Wells for so many years.

The theatre was licensed to open on Easter Monday and the season usually lasted until the first or second week of October. Dibdin decided to concentrate on essentials this year and not attempt any ambitious stunts like the previous year's pony races. These had been organized with the starting-point and finishing-post actually on the stage. There were large doors at the back of the theatre that gave directly on to the Wells yard and commanded a view of the main gates and the open country beyond. But the races proved to be too big a draw. People living in houses nearby complained that their fences were broken down by boys climbing up to watch. The footpath along the New River that ran beside the theatre was blocked with excited spectators. Eventually the magistrates intervened and the races had to be stopped.

For the opening something was needed to mark the change of management. Perhaps a song by the company on the theme of 'new brooms' would meet the occasion. Of course, it would have to be topical and glance at the political situation. Then there might be a melo-drama, an operatic piece that would count as a burletta—preferably something founded on recent fact, a story that had caught the popular imagination. That could be followed by a 'serious' pantomime. This must give plenty of scope to Grimaldi. The programme had to end with

'THE PATAGONIAN SAMPSON'

a traditional harlequinade, for which a new theme, scenery and tricks would be required. Also somewhere in the evening's entertainment there must be room for a special gymnastic exhibition by Signor Belzoni.

Dibdin always liked a touch of the exotic. He had a friend at the

British Museum in the Reverend Thomas Maurice, an Orientalist who sometimes gave him ideas for original presentation.[2] Once at the scholar's suggestion the title of a show was advertised in Greek. On another occasion Arabic script was used on a poster. Whether Maurice's erudition was called in now is more than we can say, but Dibdin evidently felt it was wasting an opportunity to present Belzoni merely as 'the Italian Hercules' or 'the Roman Giant'. Instead he decided to bill him as 'the Patagonian Sampson'.

It is a great pity Giovanni in later years was so ashamed of his life in the theatre that he left not one word about his experiences at this time. Dibdin had chosen the story of Jack the Giant-Killer for his opening pantomime, and Giovanni, of course, was to play the Giant. Easter Monday fell that year on 11 April and probably rehearsals began towards the end of March. We may think of Belzoni and his brother striding out each day over the fields to the theatre. At the stage door they would exchange a word with Wheeler, its tall, gangling guardian, whom Dibdin described as 'an original being in every respect; he walked more like an automaton than a living being, something in the manner one would imagine that a pair of Tongs would walk; and talked, Ye Gods, how he would talk!'

Inside, the theatre seemed like a dark, empty shell, lit only by a few wax candles whose flames flickered in the constant draughts and sent great shadows scurrying up over the circle of open boxes and the gallery high above them. The stage was large for so intimate a theatre—ninety feet from orchestra pit to the back wall and almost fifty feet wide. Yet it must have seemed too small for the vast activity going on all over it at a rehearsal. Whatever piece was being taken down stage, you could be certain Bob Andrews and his men were busy in some corner putting the finishing touches to the scenery. In another Garland, the machinist, would be testing the operation of a 'trick'—perhaps a haystack that turned into a cart or a cottage that became an elephant. Here Jack Bologna would be practising his leap through a brick wall. Over there Grimaldi would try to perfect an eccentric dance routine. Some of the actors would still be conning their lines, others arguing with Mr. Smithyes or Mrs. Robinson over the shortcomings of their costumes. 'Jew' Davis would have the usual knot of men around him listening to his low stories. Mrs. Dibdin would be avid for any scandal about the prettiest Miss Dennet. Down in the orchestra pit Mr. Reeve sat at the piano and encouraged his fellow-musicians to greater efforts, while over all presided the amiable genius of Charles Dibdin, whose task it was to produce order out of this chaos.

When it came to Giovanni's turn, he would quietly and unassumingly go through his Strong Man act, lifting successively heavier weights till

1. OLD SADLER'S WELLS AND THE NEW RIVER, 1813

2. A SCENE FROM 'PHILIP QUARLL'

Sig. Belzoni. the Patagonian Sampson as he appeared at Sadlers Wells
Theatre on Easter Monday 1808 carrying Seven Persons to represent a Pyramid

3. BELZONI'S HUMAN PYRAMID

he came to his last and most impressive feat—the Human Pyramid. The harness he wore for this weighed one hundred and twenty-seven pounds. It consisted of an iron frame fitted with ledges on which ten or twelve members of the company could perch themselves till the whole looked like some huge human candelabrum. Then delicately, Agag-like, holding a flag in either hand, Belzoni would walk round the stage with three-quarters of a ton of humanity dependent from his broad shoulders. When he came down to face the footlights there were no tortured muscles visible, no agonizing look on his handsome face. The beauty of Belzoni's performance lay in the ease with which he accomplished it.

Yet afterwards he must have been glad to escape from the dusty, dim-lit stage to the fresh spring air outside. There were tall graceful poplars along the edge of the New River that would have reminded Giovanni and Francesco nostalgically of home. Beyond the theatre, the grassy banks sloping down to the water were already pied with wild flowers. There were always boys fishing in the cut who must have goggled at the young giant and his brother as they walked along, talking earnestly in liquid Italian of their hopes and plans. The New River Head was only a stone's throw away—a large reservoir of irregular shape with an inner basin surrounded by a circular, tree-lined walk. From here seven-inch wooden pipes conveyed fresh water to all parts of the metropolis. Giovanni with his interest in hydraulics may well have persuaded the New River Company's engineer to let him look at the two steam-engines and the wheel that raised the water to a higher level for the benefit of the inhabitants of Pentonville, Tottenham Court Road and a great part of Marylebone. Certainly he would have admired the ingenuity of that enterprising Welshman, Sir Hugh Myddelton, who nearly two hundred years before, in the reign of the first King James, had brought London a water supply from Hertfordshire by an aqueduct thirty-seven miles long.[3]

Pleasant as the spring may have been in England that year, the clouds were gathering fast on the international horizon. On 18 February Bonaparte had sent for Lord Whitworth and talked to him for two hours with his elbows on the table. He enumerated all the provocations he had received from England; the chief was the refusal to evacuate Egypt and Malta. The presence of four thousand British soldiers in Alexandria, said the First Consul, was not a protection to the country but a challenge to him to invade. He would rather see the English in the Faubourg St. Antoine than remaining in Malta. Yet he still wanted peace; he insisted he had nothing to gain by going to war with England. Whitworth could hardly get a word in edgeways, but he gamely stuck to his brief.[4]

Early in March troop movements were noticed in the neighbourhood of the French and Dutch ports. George III sent a message to both Houses of Parliament recommending the adoption of appropriate defence measures. The Commons voted ten thousand additional seamen for the navy and ordered the militia to be embodied forthwith.

On 13 March an extraordinary scene took place at the Tuileries, where Whitworth had gone to introduce some English visitors to Madame Bonaparte. In the presence of a large assembly the First Consul made a violent attack on the English ambassador. 'We've fought for fifteen years already, but you want to fight for another fifteen. You force me to it.' Lord Whitworth protested, but Napoleon strode away. 'The English want war,' he said in a loud voice to the Russian ambassador, 'but if they are the first to draw the sword I will be the last to sheathe it. They don't respect treaties. We must cover them with black *crêpe.*'

In London the Government could not make up its mind for how long it wanted to hold on to Malta. There was a great willingness to trust to the 'chapter of accidents'—to let matters take their course, in the belief that they might turn out to be just as bad, if not worse, for the other side. Napoleon was not ready to fight yet, but he could not afford to let the English keep Malta. He even offered them another island by way of compensation—Crete, Corfu or anything in the Eastern Mediterranean. The English turned down every suggestion. They were incredibly stubborn. It was Malta or war.

But if the Addington Government was now going to show itself strong by refusing to budge, the people of England were not disposed to face the discomforts of war before it was absolutely necessary. Above all they were not willing to forgo the pleasures of the first holiday in the year. Those who could afford it still planned to spend Easter in Paris. At home the spas, the gardens and the summer theatres were preparing for a brisk trade. The new man-milliners now so evident in the neighbourhood of Bond Street were ready to launch their spring creations. *The Times* of 2 April observed that the most fashionable colours were pink and pea-green and that straw hats with dome crowns were now becoming general. The Panorama in Leicester Square announced the last week of 'Lord Nelson's Tremendous Battle of Copenhagen'—to be succeeded by a magnificent new exhibition entitled 'A View of Paris'.

On Easter Sunday morning *Bell's Weekly Messenger* sounded a note of doom in its editorial. 'Terrible, indeed, would be the necessity of a war. To fight to restrain French ambition?—Has it not grown from war, and flourished from disaster?—Surely Mr. ADDINGTON, whose peaceful politics have been the theme of everyone's panegyric, will never adopt a system which has so dreadfully failed in the hands of his predecessor . . . England, already bending under the weight of a too extended Colonial dominion, can have little ambition for an inheritance of perpetual slaughter and invincible rebellion. . . .'

But the choice between peace and war was not England's. Already Napoleon had begun to lay his invasion plans. And that very night of Easter Sunday he came to a momentous decision that changed the course of world history.[5] He would cut his losses in the West, give up the vast territory of Louisiana to the Americans—for a price—and tip the scales of Empire to the East—to Egypt and beyond.

Easter Monday was fine and bright. From an early hour the tradesmen and their families, the shopkeepers and apprentices, were abroad in their holiday best, determined to enjoy themselves. By the late afternoon, when they had eaten and drunk to repletion, they were ready to be entertained. Crowds began to converge on Astley's and the Royal Circus, and those who preferred more rural surroundings set out for Sadler's Wells.

The doors opened at half past five and the performance began at half past six. Servants were allowed to keep places for their masters till half past seven, and at half past eight the public were admitted at half-price. The performance was over about eleven. That meant a late walk back across the fields—an adventure which might be attended by danger on dark nights. Footpads often lurked behind the hedges to attack and rob the citizen with a well-lined purse. It was usual for the Wells to provide patrols and to draw attention to the nights of full moon. This year there was something even more reassuring in their advertisements: 'For the convenience of the Public, the Proprietors have put on additional Patrols in the Field leading from the Wells to Town, also a quantity of additional Lamps in the said Field, and in the Avenues to the Theatre by Permission of the NEW RIVER COMPANY.'

Eighteen months earlier the auditorium of Sadler's Wells had been completely rebuilt and its shape altered from square to semicircular. The alterations, says Dibdin, were not made before it was necessary, 'for it was, I think, the dirtiest and most antique Theatre in London'. Private boxes like those at Drury Lane were installed, but at first they were not very satisfactory. Further changes were made before the 1803 season opened so that the management could proudly state in its bills: 'The Private Boxes in the lower part of the Theatre have been totally altered from last Season, and are now perfectly calculated to accommodate the Nobility, Gentry and Families in the most eligible manner.' A seat in a box cost four shillings, in the pit two shillings and in the gallery a shilling.

There was one other attraction about the Wells this season which gave it a pull over its rivals. Some years before it had been the practice to serve drinks at reduced prices. Dibdin now revived this custom and was much criticized in the press for it. He offered the public the choice of red or white wine, imported in cask and bottled in the theatre, and advertised it in the following way:

NEW SADLER'S WELLS

———

New Proprietors

New Management

New Performers

New Pieces

New Music

New Scenery

New Dresses

New Decorations

and

OLD WINE

at 1*s. per pint* ! ! !

By half past six on Easter Monday, when the curtain was due to rise on the first night of the season, the audience had been warmed into a mellow and expansive mood. The house was filled to capacity, and it held over two thousand. The orchestra under Mr. Reeve had played a succession of popular airs against a sustained hubbub of talk and laughter. Suddenly there was an expectant hush. (There were no lights to dim, and throughout the performance the members of the audience were visible to each other as well as to the actors.) Then the curtain rose and the orchestra struck up the opening number—'New Brooms!'

> Brooms! Brooms! Who buys my brooms
> The money in no waste consumes;
> My brooms are new, and Sirs, I ween,
> You'll all allow 'new brooms sweep clean'.

It was not very witty, but as the Broom Man sang it it was neat enough to make the audience smile in anticipation of good things to come. When he reached the last verse he had the whole house with him.

> France taught with air balloons to rise,
> 'To sweep the cobwebs off the skies,'
> But let them sweep what e'er they please,
> 'Tis Britain only sweeps the seas.
> Brooms! Brooms! Who buys my brooms?

And then suddenly—the moment the audience had been waiting for—the short sturdy figure of Grimaldi was on stage in the character of Sir John Bull, poking fun and defiance at his neighbours across the Channel.

That put the house in a thoroughly good humour and they were now ready for the first main dish of the evening, *Fee! Faw! Fum! or, Jack the Giant Killer*. Those who had read the playbills carefully or bought the pantomime 'book'—on sale in the theatre, price one shilling, with a synopsis of scenes and the words of the songs—knew that Jack was played by Master Menage, the popular juvenile from Covent Garden, that the Giant was a new comer, Signor Belzoni, making his first appearance in England, and that their favourite Joe Grimaldi was the Giant's Dwarf. There were seven scenes in the pantomime and the dialogue (or recitative) was apt to go like this:

THRUMBO THE DWARF: Oh what a feast for Giant Grumbo!
TWO MONSTERS: Thanks to the valiant Hurlo Thrumbo.
THRUMBO: He'll eat him up—
JACK (*invisible*): No, he won't! No, he won't!
THRUMBO: Who the deuce is that?
1ST MONSTER: Do you know?
2ND MONSTER: I don't.
THRUMBO: The Giant Grumbo to dinner will come,
    And he'll eat 'em up with a fee! faw! fum!
JACK: The Giant Grumbo to dinner may come,
    But that (*snapping his fingers*) and a fig for his fee! faw! fum!

How much Belzoni had to say or sing beyond his 'Fee! Faw! Fum!' is not on record, but we know that the pantomime contained a number of 'combats' and a 'combat dance' arranged by Jack Bologna. Dibdin and his associates would hardly have failed to make the most of Giovanni's fine physique and natural stage presence in a piece like this.

The interval that followed gave a chance for further refreshment, and up in the gallery the fat man Wren would raise his stentorian voice as soon as the curtain was lowered. 'Come, ladies, give your minds to drinking!' was invariably his earnest exhortation. Wren was one of the characters of the Wells, and the management must have found him a great asset.

The next item on the programme was announced as a new Burletta Spectacle entitled *Edward and Susan; or, The Beauty of Buttermere.* This was a highly topical piece founded on fact of the kind now regarded by the popular Sunday press as its own special province. Six months earlier, Mary Robinson, daughter of the landlord of the Char Inn at Buttermere and, by virtue of the chivalrous tradition in these matters, a local beauty, had been tricked into marriage by a notorious swindler called John Hatfield, who wooed her under the name of Hope. Coleridge took up the cause of this lady of the Lakes, deluded by false Hope, and wrote to *The Morning Post* about her. Mary soon became a national heroine and even a subject for literature and song. A fund was opened for the Beauty of Buttermere and Dibdin promised a benefit performance. Hatfield was hanged the following September—actually for falsely assuming the privilege of an M.P. and sending his letters through the post free. Mary afterwards married a respectable farmer and lapsed into decent obscurity.[6]

We are fortunate in having a candid criticism of this piece by no less a person than Mary Lamb. She and her brother Charles made up a party to go to the theatre about the beginning of July. The programme had changed since the opening night, but *Edward and Susan* was still in the bill. On 9 July Mary Lamb wrote to Dorothy Wordsworth:[7]

'We went last week with Southey and Rickman and his sister to Sadlers Wells, the lowest and most London-like of all our London amusements—the entertainments were Goody Two Shoes, Jack the Giant Killer, and *Mary of Buttermere*! Poor Mary was very happily married at the end of the piece, to a sailor her former sweetheart. We had a prodigious fine view of her father's house in the vale of Buttermere—mountains very like large haycocks, and a lake like nothing at all.' (So much for Bob Andrews's scene-painting, which Dibdin thought as good as any in London!) 'If you had been with us, would you have laughed the whole time like Charles and Miss Rickman or gone to sleep as Southey and Rickman did?'

Poor tragic Mary Lamb! Did *she* laugh or weep at the fortunes of her namesake? Within a week of writing this letter her own delicate hold on reason had loosened once more and, as Charles told Rickman, Mary was 'again steering without card or compass'.

None of this little literary party at the Wells have told us what they thought of *Jack the Giant Killer* or of Belzoni's appearance as Pero in

Goody Two Shoes or of his performance as 'the Patagonian Sampson'. But perhaps Dorothy Wordsworth persuaded William to go one night —if, indeed, he needed any persuasion, for he was fonder of the theatre than he really cared to admit and often visited the Wells at this period. Certainly he must have seen Belzoni. But his reflections, as he set them down later in *The Prelude*, were more concerned with his own state of mind than with the actors on the stage.

> Nor was it mean delight
> To watch crude Nature work in untaught minds . . .
> To have, for instance, brought upon the scene
> The champion, Jack the Giant-Killer: Lo!
> He dons his coat of darkness; on the stage
> Walks, and achieves his wonders . . .
> The garb he wears is black as death, the word
> '*Invisible*' flames forth upon his chest.

Wordsworth was naturally much affected by the story of Mary Robinson, whom he knew well. He was also interested in the way in which

> dramas of living men,
> And recent things yet warm with life

were translated to the stage, though he deprecated their over-popular treatment by the Dibdins and other dramatists. As he told Coleridge in *The Prelude*, he considered a 'domestic incident',

> Such as the daring brotherhood of late
> Set forth, too serious for that light place—
> I mean, O distant Friend! a story drawn
> From our own ground—the Maid of Buttermere.

The poet was still preoccupied with his thoughts of Mary Robinson when he left the theatre. Perhaps he did not appreciate Belzoni's performance as the Patagonian Sampson, which usually followed *Edward and Susan*. Perhaps the subject seemed to have no moral significance. . . . But we have wandered far enough with Wordsworth; we must go back to the first night.

Strong Man acts were still comparatively rare at that date, though already some exponents of the weight-lifting art had discredited their skill with the crude deceptions which they practised upon the public. Giovanni—to judge by the reports of those who saw him at the Wells and elsewhere—was patently genuine. Unfortunately there is no record of the feats he exhibited other than the Human Pyramid. That was always the most memorable part of his performance, whether because the audience sometimes assisted or because it was essentially a demonstration of one man's physical superiority over his fellows. The iron frame was no more than a mere adjunct necessary—though itself it weighed more than a hundredweight—to give Giovanni's human load a minimum foothold.

On the first night at the Wells he seems to have had the co-operation of a squad of supernumeraries. R. H. Norman's water-colour drawing (see plate facing page 33) shows Belzoni supporting eleven bewhiskered gentlemen uniformly dressed in Oriental costume—white trousers and white tunics girdled with red sashes. (Their youthful, even feminine, appearance is probably due to the artist; Richard Norman[8] was a better Pantaloon than painter.) Four of them stand or sit each side of Belzoni on the projecting apparatus, while the other three, with Prince of Wales's feathers on their heads, are perched on a ledge behind his back. One can imagine the exclamations of astonishment from the tradesmen and their wives—the open-mouthed wonder, the neglect of drinking—as the Pyramid formed up. When the last man was in position Belzoni took a flag in either hand. Then with slow and stately steps he began his progress round the stage. As he came down to the footlights carrying his colossal burden—a splendid figure in leopard-skin tunic and red gladiator boots—the audience roared their approval. Giovanni Battista Belzoni had made his successful *début* in England.

The evening's entertainment ended with a harlequinade. For this Dibdin had written a new comic pantomime which he called *Fire and Spirit; or, A Holiday Harlequin*. The many changes of scene showed—appropriately enough for an Easter Monday audience—a number of places of holiday resort around London. These included Chalk Farm, Richmond Hill, Greenwich Park and the Blackwall Wet Docks. There was also a representation of the new Paddington Canal with a passage boat on it. Another scene had as its setting the Horns Tavern at Kennington. By a remarkable coincidence Mr. Townshend, the leading man, had recently become the licensee of that popular public house. Before the season ended Dibdin had cause to regret he had allowed such blatant advertisement.

The plot of *Fire and Spirit* has not survived, but we know it involved Harlequin and Columbine, Pantaloon and Clown in a wild harumscarum chase from one end of London to the other. Sadler's Wells had a very able machinist in a man named Garland. He not only devised the traps and pivoting panels through which Harlequin made his celebrated leaps, but he was also responsible for the tricks by which a piece of scenery suddenly changed into something quite different before the

SADLER's WELLS.

Under Patronage of his Royal *Highness* the Duke of Clarence

Monday May, 9th, 1803, *and following Evenings.*

A new Dance composed by Mr. Bologna Junr called

BLACK and WHITE:

The much admired Burletta Spectacle called

Edward and Sufan.

(The laft Week it will be Perform d)

Edward, Mr. TOWNSEND,

Firft time, an entire new Serio Comic Pantomime, with new Mufic, Scenery, Dreffes, and Decorations, called,

Philip Quarll:

Or, the Englifh Hermit

The Mufic compofed by Mr. REEVE, and the Overture accompanied by the Pandean Minftrels.

Principal Characters.——Philip Quarll, Mr. GRIMALDI, Beaufidellee, *(His Monkey)* Mafter MENAGE, Pirate, Captain, Mr. BOLOGNA, Junr. Black Chief, Signor BELZONI, English Lieutenant, Mr. KING, Pirate Boatswain, Mr. SMITH, Black Leaders of Tribes, Meffrs CIPRIANI, L. BOLOGNA, BANKS, and HARTLAND, And the Lady, Mad: St AMAND,
English Sailors, Pirates, Savages, &c. by the reft of the Company,
After which the wonderful Performance of the

Patagonian Sampfon.

The Evenings Entertainments to conclude with the comic Harlequinade called,

Fire and Spirit.

Harlequin, Mr. BANKS—Clown, Mr. GRIMALDI—And Colombine, Mad. St: AMAND,
The Burletta-Spectacle, Serio Comic, and Comic Pantomime, written &c. by Mr. C. Dibdin,
Junr.—And the Scenery by Mr. Andrews

Boxes 4s Pit 2s—Gallery 1s—with Unadulterate! Wine at only 1s the Pint,.
Doors opened at half paft Five, begin at half paft Six, Places kept till half paft Seven—Places for the Boxes may be taken of Mr. D'Cleve, at the Box Office of the Wells, every Day from 11 till 2. Books of the Songs to be had at the Wells.

On Monday next a new Burletta Spectacle, called LITTLE RED RIDING HOOD, or the WOLF ROBBER, in which Mifs DE NET will make her firft Appearance at this Theatre:

B. HUGHES Printer, 156 White-Crofs-Street, St Lukes:

A SADLER'S WELLS PLAYBILL, 1803

astonished eyes of the spectators. The machinist's greatest skill was often required for the Transformation Scene. On this occasion, as the playbills tell us, the pantomime finished with a Magical Cataract. To devise an illusion of falling water with only candlelight for illumination called for the combined skill of scene-painter and machinist as well as for the co-ordinating genius of a producer like Charles Dibdin.[9]

There was no doubt that the new season had opened with considerable *éclat*. The notices in the press were all favourable. *The Times*, getting into its stride by Wednesday morning—perhaps because its critic had been conscientious enough to stay till the end of the entertainment—wrote: 'Sadler's Wells on Monday and last night was literally a bumper. The decorations are extremely elegant, and the improvements many. The performances are calculated to please all tastes, and the performers were nearly all new, and all acquitted themselves to the entire satisfaction of the audience. Townshend is a sure card to the concern; Grimaldi, King, Cipriani, Menage, Davis, and Smith, who has a most excellent bass voice, were greeted with the universal plaudits of the audience, and the Patagonian Sampson excited every expression of wonder. The music and scenery were highly approved. The wine seemed to go off briskly, the best proof of its being good.'

But, however well the season might begin, a constant effort was needed to keep full houses at the Wells, especially in a summer like that of 1803 when the weather was not particularly good. The opening bill might last for a month but after that there must be changes in the programme. So almost at once Dibdin and the company had to begin work on new pieces. On 9 May *Edward and Susan* entered its last week —though it was revived later—and a 'serious' pantomime, *Philip Quarll*, was given its first performance. This was based on an imitation of *Robinson Crusoe* published in 1727 under the arresting title, *The Hermit; or, The Unparalleled Sufferings and Surprising Adventures of Mr. Philip Quarll, an Englishman*.[10] As Dibdin pointed out in a programme note, 'the History of Philip Quarll, who lived a solitary life on an Island inhabited only by Monkies, is too generally known to require much elucidation in this brief sketch; but as Quarll's life afforded little scope for Pantomimic Expression, a little liberty has been taken with the Fable, and other actors besides Quarll introduced; and he is represented as having a Son, a circumstance not in his life'.

Quarll was played by Grimaldi, a serious part for him. Beaufidelle, his faithful monkey, was impersonated by the agile Master Menage. There was a Black Chief (Belzoni) and a Pirate Captain (Jack Bologna). The piece opens with Quarll and Beaufidelle finding a chest full of useful articles washed up on the beach. 'Comic incident of the imitative Character of Monkies'. Then the scene changes to another part of the island. The Blacks land from a canoe and go off on a hunting expedition. There is a storm and a pirate ship is wrecked. The Pirate Captain comes ashore with a Lady prisoner (Mme St. Amand). They meet two of the Blacks who attempt to seize the Lady. The Pirate kills them, but the Lady escapes and the Pirate goes in chase. Enter now Belzoni, fierce and formidable as the Cannibal King. Much pantomimic dismay on his part at the sight of his men slain. He sends his solitary follower for reinforcements.

Next Grimaldi is seen sitting outside his hut and writing up his journal with constant interruptions from the Monkey. Suddenly the Lady appears—to their mutual astonishment. The Pirate Captain and the Black Chief arrive on the scene and a general scuffle ensues for possession of the Lady. Belzoni, alas! is soon slain. From now on there is a series of running fights, captures, escapes and rescues, in which Quarll's life is saved, first by the Monkey and then by the Lady. Finally an English ship arrives, the Pirate Captain is liquidated—in fact, he jumps into the sea—and the young Lieutenant in charge of the shore party is discovered to be Quarll's own son. 'The Curtain drops during the picture of astonishment, gratitude and joy formed by the several characters.'[11]

Philip Quarll did well, but *Little Red Riding Hood*, put on the following Monday to replace *Edward and Susan*, turned out to be a flop, even though it had Joe Grimaldi in the part of Rufo the Robber. Perhaps the time of its birth was inauspicious. A few hours before the first performance Parliament had been told that Britain and France were recalling their ambassadors. Two days later England was at war.

Yet there could only be relief now that the long months of indecision and uncertainty were over. Few people seriously thought that the conflict could have been avoided. A wave of patriotic feeling surged through the country, making itself felt in cheerful, defiant ditties, scurrilous rhymes and rude, derisive cartoons—all aimed at Napoleon. There was no more fervid British public than a Wells audience, and the company —English, French and Italian as they were—responded to the people's mood and gave them what they wanted.

Throughout May and June Belzoni continued to exhibit his feats of strength each night as the Patagonian Sampson and to appear as the Black Chief in *Philip Quarll* or occasionally the Giant in a revival of *Jack the Giant Killer*. Of his relations with the other members of the company we know nothing. By nature Giovanni was gentle and unassuming, and unless 'Jew' Davis provoked him with crude horseplay, it is unlikely that he made any enemies.

Some time in June Dibdin told a correspondent that they were 'preparing as an Experiment an Exhibition of Hydraulics by way of change and variety'.[12] This was brought into the repertory on 27 June under the title *Fire and Water*, and the playbills announced that Jack Bologna was in charge. Whether Giovanni helped back stage with what must have been an impressive display of fountains and coloured fire; whether he was able to provide the technical knowledge and skill that Bologna needed in devising his spectacle; or whether it was only here that he began to acquire the rudiments of that science which he later professed to have studied in Rome—these are questions that must remain unanswered. We know that eventually Belzoni had his own exhibition of hydraulic experiments. Probably he learned something of the subject at the Wells.[13]

A strange serio-comic accident happened to Belzoni one night, if we are to believe John Britton, the antiquarian and topographer, who helped Charles Dibdin to publish some of his songs and became acquainted with Belzoni in 1803. According to him, Giovanni had reached the climax of his act as the Patagonian Sampson and was parading round the stage with his 'pyramidal group' when 'the floor gave way, and plunged him and his companions into the water beneath. A group of assistants soon came to their rescue, and the whole party marched to the front of the stage, made their bows, and retired behind the scenes.' It is odd that Dibdin makes no mention of this incident. The water under the stage can only have been an overflow from the springs said to exist there; it was not until the following winter that the vast tank was constructed for Dibdin's famous aqua-dramas. This circumstance alone throws some doubt on the story.[14]

The last pantomime of the season was *Goody Two Shoes; or, Harlequin Alabaster*, in which Belzoni for a time appeared as Pero or Pierrot, a great lubberly lumpkin with very little to do. Harlequin was played by Jack Bologna, Columbine by Mme St. Amand, and Clown by Grimaldi. The fairy-tale 'opening' occupied only one of the fourteen scenes. The plot provided for an alabaster figure that came to life as Harlequin—a splendid fellow of kingfisher brilliance wearing 'red for affection, blue for constancy, yellow for a pleasant mood, brown for fortitude'; but his face was black 'to show all creatures of perfection lack something'. With a touch of his magic sword he woke the sleeping Columbine, who instantly fell in love with him. Their bliss was brief; almost at once they were surprised by Columbine's would-be father-in-law. The lovers fled and the harlequinade had begun.

It was here that Dibdin excelled in inventiveness and his scene-painter and machinist so ably abetted him. The chase led first to 'A House of Entertainment'. There was some comic business of bill-sticking, but soon the lovers were in flight again. They reached the North Foreland Lighthouse, where a topical note could be introduced—

'French Balloons, or Aerial invasion, frustrated by Harlequin'. Scene V showed a Fairy Pavilion—'Clown's exaltation—Go carts—Escape of the Lovers'. They came to St. Michael's Mount in Cornwall and there was an episode with gypsies in which Clown was caught stealing. At this point Dibdin brought on little Master Davis to sing a new song, 'Bony the Bantam Cock', which was designed to produce mock groans of terror, ironic cheers and ribald cock-crowings for the 'pocket' dictator he impersonated. The harlequinade continued through a series of changing scenes till the lovers reached St. James's Park. There, set prominently on stage in front of a back-cloth showing St. James's Palace and the Mall, were two sentry-boxes and a large gun. Mr. Smith (in the character of a lamb-seller) sang a song that declared: 'If the French are all *Lambs*, Bonaparte's a *Black Sheep*.' At the end of the scene the diminutive Napoleon was taken prisoner ('Bonypart pocketed') and at a touch of Harlequin's magic sword—prophetic moment for Belzoni!—the gun and the sentry-boxes turned into a crocodile and a couple of Egyptian mummies. The pantomime ended in 'Regions of Utopia'.[15]

Goody Two Shoes had its first performance on 20 June. The Lambs and their friends saw it the following week. The piece was still being revived as late as 27 September, but the part of Pero was then played by Mr. Willis: Belzoni had left the Islington theatre. Probably his last appearance at Sadler's Wells was on Saturday, 9 July, when he performed his feats of strength as the Patagonian Sampson and also acted in *Philip Quarll* and *Goody Two Shoes*. The date suggests that he had reached the end of a three months' contract which began on Easter Monday. If so, one wonders why it was not renewed, since his act was popular, and this was proving to be the most successful season at the Wells for several years. Was Belzoni's talent perhaps too limited for pantomime and burletta? Or did his innate restlessness drive him to look for a change of scene?

Whatever the reason for his leaving the Wells, early in September the Patagonian Sampson was again drawing large crowds—this time at Bartholomew Fair.

CHAPTER III

. . . that ancient festival, the Fair,
Holden where martyrs suffered in past time,
And named of St. Bartholomew . . .

> *What a shock*
> *For eyes and ears! what anarchy and din,*
> *Barbarian and infernal,—a phantasma,*
> *Monstrous in colour, motion, shape, sight, sound!*

WILLIAM WORDSWORTH, The Prelude, 1805

IT is said that the founder of Bartholomew Fair was once an entertainer himself. According to the story, Rayer (or Rahere) was jester to King Henry I and an excellent juggler before he repented of his frivolous life at Court and set off on a pilgrimage to Rome. There, during an illness, he vowed that if he recovered he would build a hospital for the poor. Later St. Bartholomew appeared to him in a dream and pointed out the exact spot he had chosen for the project in the suburbs of London beyond Aldersgate. On his return Rahere obtained a grant from the king and in 1123 founded St. Bartholomew's Hospital and Priory in the open space known as Smithfield. He himself became the first Prior. But the old conjuring tricks were hard to forget and many were the miracles wrought by Rahere to the credit and benefit of his pious foundation.[1]

One of the privileges he conferred upon himself was the right to hold an annual three-day fair in August. Primarily this was for the sale of Flemish cloth, brought over in the summer months from Ghent and Bruges and Ypres. The merchants were allowed to set up their stalls within the precincts of the Priory in return for the payment of an appropriate toll. Though cloth was the staple of Bartholomew Fair, other commodities soon began to appear on stalls rigged up outside the Priory among the elms and ponds of West Smithfield. And from the very beginning mountebanks, tumblers, jugglers, mummers, dancers and ballad-singers frequented the Fair whose site had always been for Londoners a place of popular recreation.

In time, when English cloth became as good as Flemish and could be bought all the year round, the need for the original Cloth Fair disappeared, but the general trade continued. By the end of Elizabeth's reign even this had declined and the serious purpose of the Fair was forgotten; goods were still bought and sold, but the shows and entertainments were now the main reason for its existence.

Ben Jonson has given us an unforgettable picture of the Fair in all its sleazy, greasy detail. Ursula, the fat pig-woman, Joan Trash, the gingerbread-seller, and the bawds, bullies, whores, cutpurses, 'getpenny' showmen and hucksters of *Bartholomew Fair* are too well known to need more than a mere mention here. By Pepys's day the place had become more fashionable, though it was scarcely more respectable. The Restoration turned the Fair into a carnival and extended the three days' riot to fourteen. It was now that the authorities began to be worried about the effects of this annual saturnalia, with all its attendant drunkenness, debauchery, violence and crime. The first hint of the Fair's possible suppression came in 1678, but it took nearly another two hundred years to get rid of so popular an institution. The eighteenth century saw a massed descent of the actors on Bartholomew Fair. It was worth the trouble of fitting up a booth or the expense of hiring a room in an inn when a play might be presented for a fortnight or more. But actors were still rogues and vagabonds and the corrupting influence of the theatre was more feared by the authorities than the delinquency of the mob. Again and again the City fathers tried to confine the Fair to three days; again and again the noisy, sprawling monster burst its bonds.

The reform of the calendar in 1752 moved the opening of the Fair from 23 August to 3 September.[2] In 1803—the year Belzoni made his first appearance at Smithfield—that happened to be a Saturday. In the morning, following ancient usage, the Lord Mayor went in semistate to proclaim the Fair. Leaving the Mansion House shortly before eleven, he drove in his gilt coach westwards to the great grim pile of Newgate, where he paused and drank the customary 'cool tankard' with the Keeper of the gaol. (Perhaps in this agreeable encounter there was a hint to those who might abuse the freedom of the Fair.) Then the procession turned north towards Aldersgate. Presently it stopped and the Lord Mayor left his coach and walked through to the gateway between Cloth Fair and Smithfield—the traditional place of proclamation. But the Fair had already been opened—no less traditionally—at midnight on Friday by a wild and hooligan mob, whose ringleaders had gathered earlier in 'The Hand and Shears' for a long and riotous evening. As the clock of St. Bartholomew's struck twelve, the moving spirits sallied forth into Cloth Fair, roaring with drink, ready to lead a crowd now some hundreds strong up and down the rows of booths facing each other across the cattle-pens and into the narrow lanes around Smithfield. There they hammered on doors, knocked down those who were unwise enough to open to them, pulled the women's skirts over their heads, and beat and robbed any whom they found unprotected in the street. It was an old-established custom of the Fair, and the organized toughs who systematically broke the peace they had just illegally and prematurely proclaimed were known to all Londoners as 'Lady Holland's Mob'.[3]

Peace descended on Smithfield for a few hours after the mob had done its work—but peace only of a relative kind. Long before it was light the dealers and traders, the roundabouts men, the side-show proprietors and owners of booths, who had kept out of the way while the riot was on, were hard at work trying to make up for lost time. By eleven all was ready for the Lord Mayor.

More than two-thirds of the licences granted for Bartholomew Fair in 1803 were issued to small dealers in haberdashery, toys and gingerbread.[4] Their stalls were set up round the edge of Smithfield, facing the houses; those who came late overflowed into Giltspur Street, Cock Lane and the other approaches to the market, where tenure was precarious and there were constant complaints of encroachment. The central space on either side of the cattle-pens was reserved for the main attractions of the Fair. Here the same familiar names were seen year after year; Saunders's Tragic Theatre, Pidcock's Menagerie and Gyngell's Grand Medley were among the 'regulars' at this period.

According to Thomas Frost, a Victorian journalist who collected stories of the old showmen from people who had known them personally, it was Gyngell who first presented Belzoni to the public at Bartholomew Fair.[5] Dan Gyngell seems to have been a quiet, gentlemanly sort of man with considerable skill as a conjuror. At one time he worked with a widow named Flint, and both of them travelled for some years in a show run by Flockton, who left it to them when he retired. A bill of 1795 advises visitors to Bartholomew Fair that they will find 'the Widow Flint and Gyngell, at Flockton's original Theatre up the Greyhound Yard, Smithfield'. Here Gyngell exhibited conjuring tricks and showed his virtuosity on the musical glasses; his wife sang; there was a puppet-show of Italian *fantoccini* and one could still see Flockton's famous musical clock, 'a curious organ, exhibited three times before their Majesties'. Originally it was said to have contained nine hundred moving figures, but Gyngell claimed only just over half that number.

Later the showman moved out of the Greyhound Yard into a more prominent position in the market. He borrowed a title from another veteran named Jobson and soon 'Gyngell's Grand Medley' became a familiar sight at the Fair. It is shown (with the name mis-spelt) in one of two coloured prints by Rowlandson published in 1799. Gyngell's name is not in the list of showmen who were granted licences at Bartholomew Fair in 1803. This gives only the barest details—the surname of the licensee, a rough indication of the kind of show he was presenting and the amount he paid for the licence. It appears from the

list that in 1803 there were two rival shows of 'Wild Beasts' exhibited
by Pidcock and Appleby, as well as Salter's 'Baboons'. Morgan had a
'Little Man' and Haynes a 'Large Fish'. (There is no mention of
'Giants' or 'Strong Men' in the list, and in fact the newspapers particularly regretted the absence of Big O'Brien, the Irish Giant, that
year.) There was also 'Rope Dancing' in the Exon booth and 'Tumbling'
presented by Briggs. Cunningham had 'Clock Work' and Meeson his
'Phantasmagoria'. Lastly, the showman Saunders had two exhibitions,
listed as 'Horsemanship' and 'Play Acting'. Ellar, the well-known
Harlequin who afterwards worked with Belzoni in Ireland, said he saw
him in 1808 performing in Saunders's booth at Bartholomew Fair 'in

BOOTHS AT BARTHOLOMEW FAIR

4

the character of the French Hercules'. Gyngell had his own show that year, but possibly in 1803 he was sharing a booth with Saunders and the licence was taken out in one name only. No showman would wish to give the authorities an excuse for raising the cost of his licence.

Apart from the shows there were, of course, the 'rides'. In the days before steam made possible a more violent and vertiginous agitation of the human body, the pleasure-seeking public had to be content with the basic motions of the Ups-and-Downs, the Roundabouts and the Swings. Of these the first evolved later into the Big Wheel; the other two have survived, almost unchanged, beside the newest mechanical 'rides'. Rowlandson did not hesitate to show the effect of the swings on too queasy stomachs; to make matters worse he put in the same corner of the picture the grinning negro pieman who had now replaced the monstrous Ursula.

Wordsworth—more sensitive soul!—also frequented Bartholomew Fair about this time and described the scene in *The Prelude*. In imagination he looks down upon the crowd from some showman's platform:

> Below, the open space, through every nook
> Of the wide area, twinkles, is alive
> With heads; the midway region, and above,
> Is thronged with staring pictures and huge scrolls,
> Dumb proclamations of the Prodigies;
> With chattering monkeys dangling from their poles,
> And children whirling in their roundabouts;
> With those that stretch the neck and strain the eyes,
> And crack the voice in rivalship, the crowd
> Inviting; with buffoons against buffoons
> Grimacing, writhing, screaming,—him who grinds
> The hurdy-gurdy, at the fiddle weaves,
> Rattles the salt-box, thumps the kettle-drum,
> And him who at the trumpet puffs his cheeks,
> The silver-collared Negro with his timbrel.
> Equestrians, tumblers, women, girls, and boys,
> Blue-breeched, pink-vested, with high-towering plumes,—
> All moveables of wonder, from all parts,
> Are here—Albinos, painted Indians, Dwarfs,
> The Horse of knowledge, and the learned Pig,
> The Stone-eater, the man that swallows fire,
> Giants, Ventriloquists, the Invisible Girl,
> The Bust that speaks and moves its goggling eyes,
> The Wax-work, Clock-work, all the marvellous craft
> Of modern Merlins, Wild Beasts, Puppet-shows,

All out-o'-the-way, far-fetched, perverted things,
All freaks of nature, all Promethean thoughts
Of man, his dulness, madness, and their feats
All jumbled up together, to compose
A Parliament of Monsters. Tents and Booths
Meanwhile, as if the whole were one vast mill,
Are vomiting, receiving on all sides,
Men, Women, three-years' Children, Babes in arms.

Such were the surroundings in which Belzoni found himself on 3 September 1803. If he felt a need to be reticent about his appearances at Sadler's Wells, how much more ashamed he must have been of being exhibited like a freak at Bartholomew Fair! Fortunately there exists the unimpeachable record of one who saw him there and actually volunteered to be part of his Human Pyramid. The writer was John Thomas Smith, author of *Nollekens and his Times*, Keeper of Prints and Drawings in the British Museum, and an inveterate talker. (He once showed his etching of Nelson's funeral procession to the beautiful Emma Hamilton, who promptly fainted and fell in his arms; 'and, believe me, reader, her mouth was equal to any production of Greek sculpture I have yet seen'.)

The gallant and gossiping John Thomas sets down his adventure under the date 1803 in *A Book for a Rainy Day; or, Recollections of the Events of the Years 1766–1833*. It is worth quoting in full:

About this time, in order to see human nature off her guard, I agreed with a good-tempered friend of mine, one of Richard Wilson's scholars, to perambulate Bartholomew Fair, which we did in the evening, after taking pretty good care to leave our watches at home. Our first visit was to a show of wild beasts, where, upon paying an additional penny, we saw the menagerie-feeder place his head within a lion's mouth.

Our attention was then arrested by an immense baboon, called *General Jacko*, who was distributing his signatures as fast as he could dip his pen in the ink, to those who enabled him to fill his enormous craw with plums, raisins, and figs. The next object which attracted our notice was a magnificent man, standing, as we were told, six feet six inches and a half, independent of the heels of his shoes. The gorgeous splendour of his Oriental dress was rendered more conspicuous by an immense plume of white feathers, which were like the noddings of an undertaker's horse, increased in their wavy and graceful motion by the movements of the wearer's head.

As this extraordinary man was to perform some wonderful feats of

strength, we joined the motley throng of spectators at the charge of
'only threepence each', that being vociferated by Flocton's successor
as the price of the evening admittance.

After he had gone through his various exhibitions of holding great
weights at arm's-length, etc., the all-bespangled master of the show
stepped forward, and stated to the audience that if any four or five
of the present company would give by way of encouraging the 'Young
Hercules', *alias* the 'Patagonian Samson', sixpence apiece, he would
carry them all together round the booth, in the form of a pyramid.

With this proposition my companion and myself closed; and after
two other persons had advanced, the fine fellow threw off his velvet
cap surmounted by its princely crest, stripped himself of his other
gewgaws, and walked most majestically, in a flesh-coloured elastic
dress, to the centre of the amphitheatre, when four chairs were placed
round him, by which my friend and I ascended, and after throwing
our legs across his lusty shoulders, were further requested to embrace
each other, which we no sooner did, cheek-by-jowl, than a tall
skeleton of a man, instead of standing upon a small wooden ledge
fastened to Samson's girdle, in an instant leaped on his back, with
the agility of a boy who pitches himself upon a post too high to clear,
and threw a leg over each of our shoulders; as for the other chap, (for
we could only muster four,) the Patagonian took him up in his arms.
Then, after *Mr. Merryman* had removed the chairs, as he had not his
full complement, Samson performed his task with an ease of step
most stately, without either the beating of a drum, or the waving of
a flag.

I have often thought that if George Cruikshank, or my older friend
Rowlandson, had been present at this scene of a pyramid burlesqued,
their playful pencils would have been in running motion, and I
should have been considerably out-distanced had I then offered the
following additional description of our clustered appearance. Picture
to yourself, reader, two cheesemonger, ruddy-looking men, like my
friend and myself, as the sidesmen of Hercules, and the tall, vege-
table-eating scarecrow kind of fellow, who made but one leap to
grasp us like the bird-killing spider, and then our fourth loving
associate, the heavy dumpling in front, whose chaps, I will answer
for it, relished many an inch thick steak from the once far-famed
Honey Lane market, all supported with the greatest ease by this
envied and caressed *Pride* of the *Fair*, to whose powers the frequenters
of Sadler's Wells also bore many a testimony.

George Cruikshank did, in fact, commemorate Belzoni's appearance
at Bartholomew Fair. He was commissioned to do so by Smith himself

for a book on remarkable characters. But Smith died before it could be published. The engraving shows the incident just described. And according to *A Descriptive Catalogue of the Works of George Cruikshank* by G. W. Reid the cheerful face in profile on Belzoni's right belongs to 'Rainy Day' Smith.[6]

We have already noted some of the other attractions of Bartholomew Fair in 1803. The principal wild beast show was Pidcock's Royal Menagerie, which had its permanent home in Exeter Street, off the

CRUIKSHANK DRAWING OF BELZONI

Strand. 'General Jacko with his regiment of monkies' was always a popular draw, though sometimes they got out of hand. (In 1809 the Court of Pie Powder[7] had to give judgment in the case of Minerva v. a Baboon; the lady in question, a fellow-performer, alleged assault and was awarded damages.) Bills which have survived show there was the usual assortment of monsters, including a two-headed calf and another that was double-bodied. Haynes's 'Large Fish' was billed as 'the Nondescript', and its owner claimed that this 'surprising inhabitant of the watery kingdom was drawn on the shore by seven horses and about a hundred men. She measured twenty-five feet in length and about eighteen in circumference, and had in her belly when found, one thousand seven hundred mackerel.'

One can imagine Belzoni's feelings at having to compete with this fishy monster. The noise of the rabble milling round the booth, the strident voice of the barker, the indignity of standing up there on the platform before a gaping, ribald crowd while the showman went over his points, and the sheer drudgery of twenty or more performances a day must have been almost more than his sensitive nature could bear. Fortunately, it lasted only three days. But the prospect beyond was one of more appearances at smaller fairs, less money perhaps for the same exertions, and a slow metamorphosis into a mere beast whose usefulness would not outlive his brute strength.

The alternative was to devise his own exhibition. To a man with Belzoni's urge to self-improvement and desire for respectability even the fairs offered an opportunity for combining instruction with entertainment; there was greater scope still in permanent halls and theatres. Exhibitions of Phantasmagoria—the first had arrived in England only in 1801—hydraulic experiments (for which he considered he had a special aptitude), panoramic views of great beauty and interest such as could be seen in Leicester Square, unique collections like the Cabinet of Wax brought over to London the previous year by a certain Mme Tussaud, with lifelike models of leading figures in the French Revolution—all these had a scientific character that lifted them above the vulgar shows of bearded ladies and two-headed calves. A man of taste and refinement might properly devote himself to instructing the public by means of such edifying demonstrations. There was room too for ambition.

But for the moment Giovanni Belzoni was still at Bartholomew Fair, lifting heavy weights all day long, allowing anyone, drunk or sober, dirty or clean, to clamber over him, rubbing shoulders with vice and depravity, yet sometimes also mixing with greatness. Crime flourished in the Fair in the absence of any effective police force. In 1801 a mob of thieves and pickpockets surrounded some well-dressed women and

tore the clothes from their backs. In 1807 a juvenile gang was brought
to trial at the Guildhall for their activities during the Fair. Their leader
was a fifteen-year-old boy and the ages of the others, boys and girls,
ranged from ten to fourteen; they were sentenced to long terms of
imprisonment for stealing toys, which they had disposed of through a
sausage-seller named Perfect.

Yet about the time that Belzoni exhibited his feats of strength at
Bartholomew Fair, another youngster was appearing first in Saunders's,
then in Richardson's show. Like Master Menage, he was good at
animal parts. He tumbled about in a monkey skin, danced on the tight-
rope, threw flip-flaps and rode the horses. Between the acts he would
often amuse himself and the other performers by reeling off speeches
from Shakespeare or Sheridan. He was known as Master Carey, though
the showmen sometimes called him 'King Dick'. The public knew him
later as Edmund Kean.[8]

About this time, too, a passionately patriotic newspaper, *The Anti-
Gallican*, published a programme for a booth at Bartholomew Fair, 'the
whole to conclude with a Farce, called HARLEQUIN EVERYWHERE'. In
it, said the paper, 'Signior NAPOLEONE will exhibit a singular piece of
activity, comprised in a HOP, STEP and JUMP, from *Italy* to *Egypt*, from
Egypt to *Paris*, and from *Paris* to the *Coast of England*'.

It was a good jest at that moment.

CHAPTER IV

Mr. Belzoni was doomed, like some of the noble animals of lower nature, to bear upon his colossal frame not fewer, if we mistake not, than 20 or 22 persons. Thus he has been seen at the Cork and Cove theatres lifting up this human weight of individuals strapped around his hips, shoulders and neck, and moving across the stage as stately as the elephant with the Persian warriors.

The Gentleman's Magazine, 1821

SOON after Belzoni arrived in this country he took himself a wife. Sarah Belzoni was a remarkable woman in many ways. For nearly twenty years she was Giovanni's faithful companion in his wanderings through Europe and Africa. Yet, devoted as she was, Sarah did not cling. If she was bored with what Giovanni was doing or interested in something else, she went her own way and joined him later. Equally, he had no compunction about leaving her behind if she was likely to be an encumbrance. Quite early in their married life she must have given up all idea of having a home and children. But there was nothing mannish or unnatural about her, though often she had to wear men's clothes and live among men in strange, uncomfortable places. On the contrary, Sarah showed a great interest in the lives of the women she met in Egypt and Palestine. She had a keen, observant eye and a woman's quick understanding. Her remarks are sometimes spiced with an agreeable kind of malice but, in spite of language difficulties, the Arab women felt her sisterly regard and generally treated her with respect. She was left a widow when she was just turned forty. For a time she struggled to keep her husband's name before the public eye, to see that he received even posthumously some of the recognition he deserved. But it was not easy. She lived on for almost half a century after Giovanni's death and finally died obscure and forgotten, a mid-Victorian old lady.

There is no record of Sarah's first meeting with Belzoni; we do not know her maiden name or anything of her antecedents. Indeed the early references to her are so meagre and contradictory that they are almost worthless. *The Dictionary of National Biography* states—on what authority it is not known—that Belzoni's 'personal charms soon brought him an English consort of Amazonian proportions, and the gigantic pair set about earning their living'.[1] Charles Dickens, writing in his own *Household Words* in 1851, described Mrs. Belzoni as 'a pretty, delicate-looking, young woman'. According to the same author, Henry Salt, the future English consul general in Cairo and Belzoni's patron and employer in Egypt, first met the young couple when they were performing in the streets of Edinburgh. Salt befriended them, says Dickens, and secured an engagement for them 'at a liberal salary' in Astley's Circus in London. Here Giovanni appeared as Hercules and carried twelve men on his arms and shoulders, 'while Madame, in the costume of Cupid, stood at the top, as the apex of a pyramid, and waved a tiny crimson flag'.

It is to be feared that Dickens was allowing his imagination to carry him away as it did when he and his father so disastrously 'edited' Grimaldi's *Memoirs*. Giovanni, it is true, did appear at Astley's Amphitheatre in 1805, but then it was with a troop of Indians, the engagement lasted only three weeks, and the billing was not such as to suggest 'a liberal salary'. In any case, Belzoni was already a familiar figure in London and could hardly have been recommended as a new discovery. To clinch the matter finally, we know that Salt was out of the country from the middle of 1802 till the end of 1806.[2]

What then are we to make of Sarah's character and appearance and the part she played in Giovanni's early life? Cyrus Redding, who knew her well, says that there was 'nothing remarkable in her person or manner', but that her own 'Trifling Account' at the end of her husband's book showed that 'she was somewhat above the average of her sex and station'. Presumably he meant by that that she was more intelligent than most women he knew of the lower middle class. As Redding was particularly interested in recording—even if inaccurately—the heights of Giovanni and his brother, it seems clear that Sarah was not unusually tall. Certainly there is no suggestion on Redding's part that she ever engaged in weight-lifting, though she may well have helped her husband with the other entertainments that he devised.

Most of the references speak of Sarah as an Englishwoman, but the article on Belzoni in that useful compendium, *The Book of Days*, published in 1863-4, says that he married in Ireland. The same source tells us he was in that country in 1809 and again in 1812; he could also have been there earlier. James Curtin,[3] the lad who travelled out to Egypt in service with the Belzonis, was Irish—though Giovanni found him in Edinburgh—and he seems to have been especially devoted to Mrs. B. Was she then Irish, too? There is no real evidence on this point. Yet there are some aspects of Sarah's character, as it emerges from the pages of her husband's *Narrative* and her own 'Trifling Account'—the independent spirit, the obstinate devotion, the wry humour, the occasional flashes of temper, above all, the understanding of Giovanni's deep brooding ambitions—that suggest more the Celt than the Saxon.[4]

At any rate Sarah was only about twenty when she married Belzoni, and he was four or five years older. She must have been very much in love with this handsome young giant, so mild and gentle in his ways, yet so consumed by his passion to succeed. From the start she would have learnt to accept all kinds of discomfort and inconvenience as they travelled about the country, following the big fairs or, when the chance offered, playing a provincial theatre circuit. They were never long in one place; always new audiences beckoned them on; variety was the essence of the world to which they belonged. There were probably few towns in the British Isles with a theatre or hall of sorts in which Belzoni did not make at least one appearance during the next ten years.

It was a decade of slow but significant change. Though England was locked in a life-and-death struggle with Napoleon, new forces were already at work shaping the destinies of the nineteenth century. In the year 1800 a Mr. Cartwright had organized 'A Grand Display of Philosophical Fireworks, by Inflammable Air', at the Lyceum Theatre in the Strand. Four years later there were lectures and demonstrations at the same theatre to illustrate 'the wonderful discovery of refining Smoke, to make it burn more brilliant than wax'. In 1805—the year of Trafalgar —some London streets were lit by gas for the first time. In 1810 the National Light and Heat Company was launched with a capital of one hundred thousand pounds.

Steam, too, was in its infancy. In 1802 Richard Trevithick had been granted a patent 'for Methods for improving the construction of Steam Engines, and the Application thereof for driving Carriages, and for other purposes'. In 1803 Fulton's steamboat appeared on the Seine. By 1811 the first locomotive was in use at a South Wales colliery.

Electricity was a new toy. In the year that Belzoni appeared at Sadler's Wells *The Times* reported some interesting experiments carried out on the body of a newly-hanged murderer. These showed that 'the eminent and superior powers of *Galvanism*' were 'far beyond any other stimulant in nature'. *The Times* understood that the galvanic process had also been used 'in several cases of insanity, and with complete success'.

Telford and Macadam were just beginning their great work on the roads of England. From London to Dover was still a very long day's journey even at the best time of the year. In winter the roads around the capital were often impassable because of mud. Travellers to the north were warned to be prepared for any emergency after Manchester. There were few good roads in East Anglia. In Devon and Cornwall there were only bridle-paths where you would look for highways.

Such was the England in which Giovanni and Sarah began their travels. There are many gaps in the story of their wanderings, and sometimes we lose sight of them for months or even a year or two on end. Yet, up and down the country, in old newspaper files and faded scrap-books, there must still be traces of their passage. Forgotten little theatres and public halls, ancient inns and dingy assembly rooms may yet preserve some unsuspected record of a performance by Belzoni.

Both 'Rainy Day' Smith and Thomas Frost agree that, after the close of Bartholomew Fair in 1803, the Patagonian was seen at Edmonton, exhibiting feats of strength in a field behind the Bell Inn. There is also a tradition that Belzoni appeared this year at Camberwell Fair, which was held in August; he might have gone there from Sadler's Wells. There were other fairs too in the London suburbs—Peckham and Tothill and Charlton Horn Fair—that might have offered employment to the end of October. But we can only surmise what happened. Giovanni disappears now into the great maelstrom of itinerant entertainers and only surfaces occasionally in some turbulent eddy or quiet backwater.

What seems very strange is that Belzoni never went back to Sadler's Wells. Charles Dibdin says in his *Memoirs*: 'This Gentleman after he left us, went to Lisbon, where he performed; and a few years afterwards, called on me at my house, at Sadler's Wells; and told me he had come expressly to England, to engage performers for Lisbon: after which interview I never saw him . . .' But it was not until 1812 that Belzoni went out to Portugal; he returned to England for a short time early in the following year.

What should have attracted Belzoni to Sadler's Wells in Dibdin's second year of management was the inauguration of the Aqua-drama. With great secrecy, during the winter of 1803-4, the whole stage of the Wells was ripped up and a vast tank installed beneath. It was almost ninety feet long from front to back and varied in width from ten to twenty-five feet. When finished, it was filled with water to a depth of three feet by means of an Archimedes screw placed on the bank of the New River.

Dibdin's plan was no less than to present the Siege of Gibraltar—still fresh in people's memories after more than twenty years—as a magnificent stage spectacle *with real water*. Shipwrights and riggers were brought in from Woolwich Dockyard to construct model men-of-war on a scale of an inch to a foot. They were to be exact replicas of ships of the line down to the smallest detail of rig and armament. Bob Andrews painted an enormous drop scene that showed the English Grand Fleet drawn up in line of battle against the combined fleets of France and Spain. Finally, to make full use of the new element, a number of men and boys were engaged who were prepared to swim about in the water to represent the drowning enemy before they were rescued magnanimously by gallant Jack Tars.

What a chance for Belzoni, the earnest hydraulician! It is hard to

believe that he had no hand in this, yet there is no reason to suppose
that he did. Dibdin says specifically in his *Memoirs* that his senior
partner Mr. Hughes suggested the idea, from having understood—how
true this is, Dibdin says he does not know—that if Fawcett and Co.[5]
had taken over the theatre they intended to avail themselves of the
nearness of the New River and introduce real water into their produc-
tions. The very note of doubt that Dibdin expresses about his rivals'
intentions makes his explanation the more plausible. He could hardly
have forgotten it if Belzoni had provided the inspiration; and if he
merely wanted to deny him the credit he would surely not have invented
a story and then thrown doubt on it himself.[6]

We cannot therefore hail Belzoni—much as we should like to do—as
the originator of a new kind of stage spectacle that now captivated
London in the way the Dog Drama had done—and lasted so much
longer. There was no lack of suitable material in the years that followed
Trafalgar. Stirring battles at sea, ocean tragedy, lighthouse epics, even
mill-stream melodrama—all relied for their success on the same element
—real water. For a time the term Aquatic Theatre gave the Wells a
unique character. With the water as well as the wine, no wonder things
went swimmingly for the younger Charles Dibdin.

But if Giovanni did not invent the Aqua-drama, at least he had been
at the Wells when they first introduced 'an Exhibition of Hydraulics',
and though it was presented by Jack Bologna, Belzoni may have had
more to do with it than we can prove. Certainly in the New Year (1804)
he was presenting his own version of this fountain display under the
same title, *Fire and Water*, at the Royalty Theatre in Wellclose Square.
John Astley, son of Philip who owned the Amphitheatre near the
southern end of Westminster Bridge, had taken the East End house
for a short Christmas season. (The family had had a run of bad luck:
Philip had not long escaped from internment in Paris, where he had
gone during the short-lived Peace of Amiens; and the Amphitheatre
had been burnt down on the eve of Belzoni's first appearance at
Bartholomew Fair.)

On Boxing Day John Astley opened at the Royalty with a special
holiday bill that included Belzoni's act set to music: 'the Patagonian
Sampson, whom Mr. Astley has engaged for six Nights, will go through
his surprising Feats of Strength, accompanied by a Groupe of Savages.
During the above most extraordinary exercise, the five Pandean
Minstrels, from Vauxhall Gardens, will execute various Martial Pieces
of Music, each Person at the same time playing on two Instruments.'[7]

The show proved popular and its run was extended for another week.
Then on 9 January Belzoni was given a chance to do what he so much
preferred to his Strong Man act, not because it was less arduous but

because it was more scientific and therefore respectable. He was allowed to bring forward 'a most curious Exhibition of Hydraulicks'—whether the same or an improved *Fire and Water* we have no means of telling. But the chemically red flames and the leaping liquid jets were a great joy to Londoners east of the Tower. They came in their hundreds, not for one week but for two, to see the magic of the man who set water on fire and fire upon water.

That was not Belzoni's only connection with the Astleys. Young John quickly rebuilt his father's circus on the South Bank and renamed it 'Astley's Royal Amphitheatre of Arts'. The horses were still the main attraction, but Drama and Variety continued to add their quota of excitement and suspense. A programme that Astley put on about a year later included a Grand Spectacular Divertisement showing the Garter ceremony at Windsor Castle, a revival of an old popular melodrama and a harlequinade. But that was not enough—even with the horses— and the untiring impresario went on to inform his patrons that 'Mr. Astley, Jun. ever anxious to bring forward an Exhibition that may tend to contribute to the amusement of the Public, has engaged for a few evenings, Signor BELZONI, who, with a troop of Indians, will, for the first time at this Theatre, go through various surprising Herculean Exercises!'

Belzoni's engagement lasted for three weeks—from 13 May to 1 June. At the end of the first week a Sunday newspaper wrote: 'What with the attractions of the grand Spectacle of the *Castle of Otranto*, the sur-prising *Horsemanship* of the *Equestrian Roscius*, the almost more than human feats of *Strength* of the astonishing *Troop of Indians*, led on by the *Giant Belzoni*, the magnificent national production of the *Windsor Installation*, and the inimitable Harlequinade of "Laugh and Lay Down", the *Royal Amphitheatre*, Westminster Bridge, has nightly over-flowed with company during the whole of the last week; and we may venture to say, that, as the whole of these performances are to be repeated to-morrow evening, the house will be found to exhibit a crowded audience in every part of it.'

The 'puff' seems laboured, and perhaps the show was not as good as it sounded. At any rate, in the third week Belzoni's name disappeared from the bills, leaving only the anonymous Indians. A month later Astley introduced a completely new pantomime into the programme. The final scene showed 'a splendid Temple with Cataracts'. O forecast of Philae! Was that the prophetic handiwork of the future Egyptologist, or had our hydraulician already hurried on?

We now lose sight of Giovanni for more than three years, unless, as Mr. Willson Disher thinks, he walked on as a captive giant at Drury Lane in 1807.[8] He seems to have been back at Bartholomew Fair in

1808, and perhaps he appeared there regularly. According to *The Book of Days*, Ellar the Harlequin and younger contemporary of Grimaldi observed 'in some unpublished notes' that he saw Belzoni that year 'performing in Sander's Booth at Bartholomew Fair, in the character of the French Hercules'. Unfortunately those notes have disappeared. The Bartholomew Fair records show that in 1808 Saunders was licensed only to exhibit a display of horsemanship; the previous year he had a play and booths. Ellar may have been mistaken in the date but, as we have already seen, the evidence of the licensee lists is not conclusive.

Tom Ellar, who was once described by a critic as 'quicksilver in convulsions, or an electric eel in a St. Vitus's fit', made his first important appearance at the Royalty Theatre in Wellclose Square on Easter Monday, 1808. Five years later he was junior Harlequin at Covent Garden and doubled for Jack Bologna in the difficult jumps after the latter broke his collar-bone. Later he went to the Wells. He had a long and brilliant career, but in his old age the public forgot him. He fell on bad times and was even reduced to earning a few coppers by a pitiful caper or a tune on his guitar in the pubs of the East End. Thackeray once wrote of him: 'Our Harlequin Ellar, prince of many of our enchanted islands, was at Bow Street the other day in his dirty, faded, tattered motley—seized as a law breaker for acting at a penny theatre, after having well nigh starved in the streets, where nobody would listen to his guitar. No one gave him a shilling to bless him: not one of us who owe him so much.'

Tom Ellar's notebook, quoted by *The Book of Days*, also gives us our next glimpse of Belzoni. In 1809 both were engaged for a pantomime— *The Mountain Witches; or, Harlequin Miller*—at the Crow Street Theatre, Dublin. Ellar played Harlequin, Columbine was a very pretty young girl, Betsy Dyke, who afterwards became the wife of the poet, Thomas Moore, and Belzoni's job was 'to superintend the last scene, a sort of hydraulic temple', which evidently involved an ingenious display of fountains. For some reason—whether because of the difficulties of the theatre or the ambitious nature of the performance—Belzoni was over-anxious. As a result, the elaborate hydraulic machinery went berserk. Water poured into the orchestra pit and soaked the musicians. Tom Cook, the first violin, ducked under the stage with his fellow-performers, 'leaving Columbine and myself, with the rest', as Ellar says, 'to finish the scene in the midst of a splendid shower of fire and water'. The audience must have been delighted. Ellar does not say what the management thought of Belzoni after this, but no doubt his colleagues forgave him. The Harlequin pays him a warm tribute: 'Signor Belzoni was a man of gentlemanly but very unassuming manners, yet of great mind.'

There is much more evidence of Giovanni's activities in 1810.

Amongst other things he visited Perth, Edinburgh and Plymouth, and exhibited or took part in a great variety of entertainments. *The Gentleman's Magazine* for April 1819 mentions in a biographical note 'feats of strength, and experiments in hydraulics, musical glasses and phantasmagoria'—and all at Edinburgh. Frost in *The Old Showmen* and Smith in *A Book for a Rainy Day* say that Belzoni appeared in the second title-role in Tom Dibdin's *Valentine and Orson*—again in the Scottish capital. At Perth Belzoni seems to have risen to even greater heights of virtuosity. At Plymouth he merely exhibited feats of strength.

The chronology is uncertain, but probably the Scottish tour lasted some months. There was a northern theatre circuit consisting of Perth, Aberdeen, Montrose, Arbroath and Dundee. Normally a stock company visited each in turn and an individual performer like Belzoni would do the same. But the only record we have of him on this circuit comes from Perth. The drama in that enterprising city suffered a severe setback in 1809. At the end of the season a touring company was performing *Macbeth* one night in the Glovers' Hall Theatre, when suddenly, it is said, as the murdering Thane reached the line, 'This is a sorry sight', the gallery collapsed and three hundred people were buried under broken timbers and *débris*. Miraculously no one was killed, though a large number were injured. The citizens of Perth missed their theatre, and when the Grammar School building in St. Anne's Lane presently became vacant it was turned into a playhouse. The New Theatre opened on 2 May 1810 with Mrs. Glover from Covent Garden in George Colman's comedy, *The Jealous Wife*. But the public was still nervous after the accident and at first the houses were very thin. Casual performances of plays and a ballad-opera—*The Duenna*—were given during the early summer. Then, towards the end of June, the theatre opened for one night to present Signor Belzoni in a variety entertainment. After exhibiting a number of feats of strength he carried a pyramid of seven men round the stage. This was well below his best effort. And perhaps it was to make up for such shortcomings that he also played airs on the musical glasses that night.

It was hardly a performance to make history. Yet the people of Perth must have taken a fancy to Belzoni and he seems to have liked Perth. We find him appearing as an actor in two pieces presented at the St. Anne's Lane theatre on 15 October of that year.[9] One was a patriotic opera, *The English Fleet in 1342*, and the other an afterpiece called *The Jew and the Doctor*; Belzoni's parts are not known.[10] The following week brought Perth a theatrical event of the first importance in those days—a visit from Mr. and Mrs. H. Siddons, Sarah's son and daughter-in-law. Henry Siddons had recently taken over the management of the Edinburgh Theatre, and in the autumn of 1810 he and his wife made a

Scottish tour. At Perth they presented *As You Like It*, *Much Ado About Nothing*, *King Henry IV* and two performances of *Hamlet*. There were also some minor afterpieces and Henry's own composition, *Time's a Tell-Tale*. On the Monday after they had gone Belzoni took the theatre again for three days. Greatly daring, after the feast of Shakespeare the week before, he undertook to play the title-role in *Macbeth, King of Scotland*. This may have borne little resemblance to the play that Shakespeare wrote. We know the liberties taken with the Bard at that time. Elliston turned *Macbeth* into a burletta, and when he presented *Othello* at the Surrey some wag placed a laundry notice outside the theatre, MANGLING DONE HERE.[11] That was in London, in the Blackfriars Road. . . . But that on Scottish soil—only a few miles from Birnam Wood and Dunsinane—Giovanni Belzoni should play Macbeth seems almost incredible. Physically he must have been superb. But it would be charitable to hope that not too much of Shakespeare's text was left to the mercy of his still limited English.

Macbeth was followed the same evening by a pantomime piece, *The Algerine Pirates; or, The Rock of the Seven Capes*. It was produced by Belzoni, who also played the part of Goth, the chief pirate. On Tuesday Sheridan's *Pizarro* was given, and perhaps followed by the pirate piece. On Wednesday there was a further change of programme; Allan Ramsay's pastoral comedy, *The Gentle Shepherd*, was presented together with *Obi; or, Three-fingered Jack*, a rumbustious melodrama.[12] Belzoni took this night as a benefit.

That was his last recorded appearance in Perth. Whether he went to Edinburgh earlier or later in the year is a matter of doubt. Possibly he was engaged by Henry Siddons for the part of Orson, which he is said to have played in that city. *Valentine and Orson*, in the version then current, was a romantic Drama Spectacle devised—for 'written' is hardly the word—by Charles Dibdin's brother Tom for Covent Garden in 1804. The plot was based on a mediaeval romance. Valentine, in love with a princess, seeks to prove he is of noble birth and goes off in search of his brother Orson, who has been brought up in the wilds and suckled by a she-bear. The production at Covent Garden was described as 'one continued scene of unmitigated splendour'. Combats, banquets, processions, pageantry, a minimum of dialogue and a great deal of dumb show combined with the peculiar fascination that 'wild man' parts had at this time to ensure the play's success. Orson was a most exhausting role. Grimaldi, who often played it, would sometimes stagger off the stage after the curtain had dropped, gasping for breath, his face contorted with pain. Belzoni was a much fitter man and his great stamina sustained him. But even he found the part had unexpected hazards.

In the play, Orson's retreat is discovered when hunters shoot the bear and she withdraws into her cave. Presently Orson appears and fights the man who has wounded his foster-mother. Then the poor faithful creature comes out to die, and Orson has a most affecting scene. At Edinburgh, at least, there was no clever 'skin work', but a real live bear. The brute seems to have been of somewhat uncertain temper and Giovanni, for all his strength, had to guard against sly and vicious attempts to bite. On one occasion all his efforts to placate the animal failed. He dared not get into a clinch with her, and the death-bed scene was demonstrably lacking in proper affection. This was not good enough for the gallery. Indignant Scots voices urged Belzoni to show more feeling. ('Gie yo' puir auld mither a wee kiss, mon.') Giovanni was not going to risk it that night. Perhaps when cajolery failed he even cuffed the bear gently to make it behave. That was more than the audience could stand. They hissed and booed till the curtain was brought down on the unfilial scene.[13]

Of the 'phantasmagoria' which Belzoni is credited with having shown in Edinburgh there seems to be no record. This genus of entertainment had been popular for nearly a decade. On 4 September 1801 a London newspaper wrote: 'The Phantasmagoria, or Optical and Mechanical Exhibition, we understand is arrived in England. . . . The Visionary Illusions, representing the Phantoms of Absent and Deceased Persons, are said to surpass anything of the kind ever offered to the Public inspection. We are not yet acquainted with the particulars, but from what we have heard, and its great success on the Continent, our expectations are very sanguine. The workmen have been busily employed this month past in erecting a theatre for the representation, at the Lyceum, Strand, where it will shortly open.'

Philipstal's Phantasmagoria descended on London like the first kinematograph, the first talkies and the first 'wide screen'. Essentially it was a kind of magic lantern show. Faces of the famous were thrown upon a black screen in a darkened hall; they grew in size till the more nervous members of the audience called out in alarm; then they receded, dwindled, dissolved, and their place was taken by others. There was also an animated skeleton and a 'spectre' which was considered 'educational' in that it helped to dispel the belief in ghosts. Certainly M. de Philipstal's show packed the lower theatre in the Lyceum, while Lonsdale's sober 'Ægyptiana' in the large hall above was shown to almost empty houses. Mark Lonsdale, who was Charles Dibdin's predecessor as stage manager at Sadler's Wells, lost heavily on this highbrow exhibition, which tried too soon to interest the public in the unfamiliar land of Egypt. Its earnest and slightly muddled purpose may be judged from its advertised attractions: 'Part I—A Review of the

Arts, Manners and Mythology of Ancient Egypt. Part II—A Sketch of Modern Egypt. Part III—A View of Society and Manners, in modern Egypt. Ending with L'Allegro and a scenic view of the Imagery of the Poet.' Strange company for Milton!

In due course M. de Philipstal went on tour—for a while in partnership with Madame Tussaud, though their exhibitions remained separate.[14] Other kinds of 'phantasmagoria' soon followed and spread throughout London and the provinces, causing a crop of ugly new names to appear in the entertainment world. The Lyceum always seemed their spiritual home. In 1804 its Pantoscopic Theatre exhibited 'a great variety of Optical Eidothaumata', which included 'some surprising Capnophoric Phantoms'. In 1805 the larger theatre was taken over by Messrs. Schirmer and Scholl, Professors of Physic, for their Ergascopia—an exhibition of 'Musical, Mechanical, Aerostatic, Acoustic and Optical Novelties'. On the very same day Jack Bologna, having tired of hydraulics, opened the lower hall at the Lyceum with another exhibition, which was announced to be 'upon the same elegant plan of Mr. de Philipstal'. It also included some ingenious automata, such as the Marvellous Swan and the Turkish Conjuror. Bologna was at pains to point out that *his* exhibition had nothing to do with the German show upstairs in the larger theatre, which was 'illuminated by *refined* Gas, alias Smoke, to the annoyance of the company'.

Belzoni's restless, inquiring mind could hardly fail to be interested in these scientific novelties, and at some date he added 'phantasmagoria' to his repertory of entertainments. He still continued to act in plays, perform on the musical glasses, conduct experiments in hydraulics and exhibit feats of strength. According to *The Gentleman's Magazine*, he repeated in Ireland and the Isle of Man the performances he had given in Edinburgh.

Some time, however, in 1810—possibly in the early part of that year —Belzoni, his wife and his brother, Francesco, were all in Plymouth. Cyrus Redding, who was then editor of a local newspaper,[15] met them there when Giovanni became involved in a dispute with Foote,[16] the manager of the theatre, over the terms of his contract. In Redding's view, 'Foote wanted to screw the Italian too hardly in his bargains'. Belzoni's manner was mild enough, but if he thought somebody was trying to cheat him, all the passion of his Southern temperament was roused. He went to Redding, as a man who wielded the powerful weapon of publicity, and told him what had happened. The editor was sympathetic, felt he had justice on his side, and arranged the matter to Giovanni's satisfaction. He saw him perform at the theatre in his Strong Man act, 'supporting eight men when he stood upright, and even raising himself upon his toes. Two men sat astride upon his shoulders, an iron girdle with pendant stirrups held others, and he managed to support one or two with his hands.'

Redding was always warmly partisan where Belzoni was concerned. 'I have no doubt,' he says, 'he was right in his subsequent dispute with Salt in Egypt.' He calls him 'a plain, straightforward, single-minded man', and sums him up as being 'temperate, strong, mild-humoured and kindly, his manners marked by great suavity, his judgment sound, his frame capable of great fatigue, to which must be added, a very unassuming deportment, bravery, order, and perseverance'.

There was as yet in 1810 no sign that Belzoni had looked outside the world of the theatre and the fair-ground for the realization of his ambitions. That he was ambitious is clear enough. He aimed at mastering as many of the showman's arts as possible. Conjuring now became one of his new interests, and *The Book of Days* preserves the text and lay-out of a handbill distributed by Giovanni in Cork early in 1812. It read as follows:

Theatre, Patrick Street
CUT
A Man's Head
OFF!!!
AND PUT IT ON AGAIN!

This present Evening MONDAY, Feb. 24, 1812
And positively and definitively the LAST NIGHT

SIG. BELZONI

RESPECTFULLY acquaints the Public, that by the request of his Friends, he will Re-open the above *Theatre* for one night more—i.e. on MONDAY, Feb. 24, and although it has been announced in former *Advertisements*, that he would perform for Two Nights—he pledges his word that this present Evening, will be positively and definitively the last night of his Re-presentations, and when he will introduce a FEAT OF LEGERDEMAIN, which he flatters himself will astonish the Spectators, as such a feat never was attempted in Great Britain or Ireland. After a number of Entertainments, he will
CUT
A Man's Head Off!!
And put it on Again!!!
ALSO THE
GRAND CASCADE.

This 'definitively' last night may have been only the usual showman's language, but it is possible that by February 1812 Belzoni had made up his mind to go abroad. Although England was now the country of his adoption and he had an English wife, the long war years had put a restraint upon his movements that must have grown more and more irksome. He had wandered up and down the British Isles like a great caged animal in a booth at a fair. The threat of invasion had passed—even before Trafalgar—but then Napoleon had tried to starve England into submission. To tighten the screws of his Continental System he had invaded Spain and Portugal. The sudden revolt of the Spanish people gave him his first check and showed that Napoleon was not invincible. Soon a British force of 30,000 was fighting in the Peninsula. But after the death of Sir John Moore at Corunna and the withdrawal of the British army, the situation seemed hopeless again. It was not until the winter of 1811-12, when Napoleon was preparing to march against Russia, that the tide really turned. Early in 1812, as the finest French regiments were being drafted out of the Peninsula, Wellington advanced from his base in Portugal and captured Badajos and Ciudad Rodrigo. By the summer Madrid was liberated, and the French had gone from the south of Spain.

Some time during that year Belzoni was in the Peninsula. This seems clear from his own statement that after nine years' residence in England he went to Portugal, Spain and Malta. *The Gentleman's Magazine* for April 1819 says that he was engaged by the manager of the São Carlos Theatre, Lisbon—the date is not specified—to appear in *Valentine and Orson*. (This was probably *not* Dibdin's version.) Later, according to the same authority, Belzoni acted at the São Carlos in 'the sacred drama of Sampson'. A much later source, C. L. Brightwell's *Annals of Industry and Genius* (1863), says that Belzoni played Samson at Lisbon during Lent. There is, therefore, some reason to suppose that Giovanni left Ireland soon after his last appearance at Cork and was in Lisbon before Easter 1812. But, as we shall see, his engagement at the São Carlos Theatre could have been *one* or *two* years later.

Among the Belzoni papers published by Professor Luigi Gaudenzio in 1936[17] there is the Spanish passport already mentioned, which was issued to Giovanni in Cadiz on 12 December 1812. This gave him permission to go to Gibraltar, accompanied by his servant, James Curtin. An endorsement dated 27 January 1813 shows that they afterwards went to Malaga.

There is no mention of Sarah on the passport, which at first is surprising. But Giovanni was not yet on his way to Egypt and, in fact, he now returned to England. Perhaps this first Peninsular trip was only exploratory and he went back to fetch Sarah. Or he may have thought it was too dangerous to take her out there immediately. Certainly there was good reason to be cautious. Madrid only enjoyed a brief spell of freedom before it was captured again by the French and Wellington was forced to fall back on Portugal. Whatever the true explanation may be, less than a month after calling at Malaga, Belzoni was back once more in England—exhibiting at Oxford!

We owe our knowledge of this fact to a communication in *Notes and Queries* for 16 July 1864. The writer, who signed himself I.W., explained that a few days before, while turning over the papers of a friend who had died, he had come upon a handbill issued by Belzoni during his visit to Oxford. He himself had seen the performance advertised in the bill and after the lapse of over fifty years could still remember the Italian—'his lofty stature, his youthful, pleasing, and even genteel appearance, which caused much speculation in my mind as well as in that of others, who and what he could be, and how such a person could be a mere *conjuror and showman*'.

Belzoni gave his performances at the Blue Boar Inn, St. Aldate's. The first was on Monday, 22 February. Evidently it went down so well with the largely undergraduate audience that Giovanni decided to give another performance on the following Friday. After the customary reference to dyarchical indulgence ('By Permission of the Rev. the Vice-Chancellor and the Worshipful the Mayor'), the announcement went on to say that 'SIGNOR BELZONI, Strongly impressed with a due sense of gratitude for the very favourable reception he has experienced from the Noblemen and Gentlemen of the University, humbly returns his most sincere thanks, and respectfully begs leave to acquaint them, that on the above Evening he will repeat his Novel Performance, when no exertion shall be wanting to render it worthy of their notice.'

Indeed, he gave them everything he could. The show lasted two and a half hours. It began with 'THE GRAND SULTAN OF ALL THE CONJURORS', who undertook to 'disclose the manner in which some of the most intricate tricks are performed in the Art of Legerdemain'. After this and a change of costume Belzoni played English, Irish, Scottish and Italian airs on the musical glasses. Next he introduced 'his celebrated Scene, the Delineations of LE BRUN'S PASSIONS OF THE SOUL'. This was presumably the mime, performed to music, which Francesco acted at Sadler's Wells and the audience found too highbrow. Does it mean that Francesco took part in the Oxford performance, or had Giovanni incorporated the act in his own repertoire? The next item in the programme suggests that the brothers may have appeared together. 'THE ROMAN HERCULES' displayed 'several striking Attitudes, from the most admired antique Statues; amongst others, The celebrated Fighting Gladiators; With interesting Groupes from the Labours of Hercules,—

The Instructions of Achilles,—and other Classical Subjects, uniting Grace and Expression with Muscular Strength.' Surely Giovanni would have needed the help of others for these poses, and Francesco had almost as fine a physique as his brother.

One of Belzoni's feats of strength on this occasion was to lift a fourteen-pound firelock by the muzzle and hold it at arm's length with an extra two pounds' weight on the butt. This *seems* less remarkable than, in fact, it was. The weight-lifting display ended with Giovanni carrying a pyramid of seven men. Were they the brawniest undergraduates present?

Finally Giovanni announced 'a Grand and Brilliant Display of OPTICAL ILLUSIONS (never performed here) entitled the AGGRESCOPIUS' —what a word!—'Which S.B. has brought to the greatest perfection. The Objects which are represented in this Optical Illusion will change their postures, and so far will they seem animated to the Spectator, that some of them will actually change their countenances.'

We can imagine the hot, smoke-laden, candle-lit room at the Blue Boar packed with undergraduates, some of them only too ready to take advantage of the performer and spoil his show. I.W. says that on the night he was there a party of drunks tried to get one of their number to put out the lights. 'Belzoni, turning round and observing this, said very quietly and civilly, "Sir, I will trouble you not to meddle with the candles." ' Dr. Johnson could have done no better, and the would-be disturber of the peace was instantly quelled.

This is Belzoni's last known appearance in England as an entertainer. Before he left again for Portugal and Spain he called on Charles Dibdin and told him that 'he had come expressly to England, to engage performers for Lisbon'. Whether, in fact, Giovanni did take back any performers to the São Carlos Theatre we do not know. But Sarah was with him now, and the faithful James Curtin, and together they visited Lisbon and Madrid and probably other cities in the Peninsula. *The Gentleman's Magazine* says that, after appearing in Lisbon, Belzoni performed before the Court at Madrid. This may have been on his first visit in 1812. More likely it was in the early part of 1813 before the unwanted Joseph Bonaparte was chased off his throne. In the autumn and winter of that year the British finally pushed the French back over the Pyrenees. Germany was freed as far as the Rhine. Napoleon's Empire was rapidly shrinking, and soon Castlereagh would go to the Continent to direct the last phases of the war in Europe.

When next we meet Giovanni it is November 1814. Napoleon has abdicated and is safe—or almost safe—in Elba. Giovanni and Sarah have arrived in Sicily. At Messina he can look across the narrow Straits to his beloved Italy, which he has not seen for over twelve years. On

26 November—three weeks after his thirty-sixth birthday—he writes a loving letter to his family.[18] Though the style is still artless, the spelling (in the Italian) has somewhat improved.

Dear Parents,
I hope this finds you in good health, as it leaves me and my wife, we arrived here safely thank God after a long sea voyage, that is from Spain, where I wrote to you from Madrid asking you to write to me at Barcelona, but as we did not go there, I have not received your letter, so I ask you now to give me a prompt reply, direct to Malta where we are going from here, and from there to Constantinople, and then to see dear Italy again.

There is as yet no mention of Egypt. Constantinople is the goal—a city famous throughout the ages for its love of popular entertainments. On great occasions the Sultan would order public festivities that lasted for weeks on end. Innumerable conjurors, wrestlers, rope-dancers, acrobats, animal trainers and firework makers were needed to fill these mammoth variety bills, and the Sultan was never averse to using foreign talent. There was the English gunner Webb in the days of Elizabeth I who once made a Noah's Ark containing thirteen thousand fireworks for the Sultan Murat III.[19] In the nineteenth century Mr. Brock was called in to superintend the pyrotechnics at the Porte.[20] But for many years the chief devisers of the Sultan's fireworks and illuminations came from Bologna—so near to Giovanni's home. He may well have thought that his own specialities—fountains and cascades, illusionary decapitations and 'phantasmagoria', not to mention his feats of strength—would appeal to the Turkish mind and perhaps make his fortune. Yes, it was certainly worth while to go to Constantinople.

The rest of the letter was made up of anxious inquiries about the family: 'Tell me everything, especially about my poor mother's headaches, tell me if my brother Francesco has arrived yet, as I think he must be with you now since he left England for Italy about a year ago and if he has not arrived he must come soon, so write quickly, and tell me how things are with you and my brothers; please do tell them to write to me.'

Before Giovanni had time to post this letter at Messina, he received one written by his parents to Francesco, who had sent it on to him from London. It told him that his mother had been taking a course of baths at Battaglia near their home, but not whether they had had any effect on her migraines. He learned also that his sister-in-law—Antonio's wife—had borne her first child after ten years of married life. Giovanni added in a postscript to his own letter: 'That puts Antonio one ahead of me, as I have been married about twelve years and have had no children, nor would want to have any, as they would be a complete hindrance to my travels. However I must say, God's will be done.'

The news from home—old though it was—prompted Giovanni to write much more than he had at first intended. He was still greedy for details of the intimate family life that now seemed so strange and remote. 'Tell me how you are managing, how you are at home, how much rent you pay and whether you all live together or apart. Is Antonio still a follower of Bacchus? I suppose not, now he is a father, he must remember that if I once called him poor old man as a joke now I shall call him one in earnest.' So he rambles on. 'Tell my aunts that if they wake up early in the morning and write me a couple of lines, I shall be very grateful. If ever that Don Quixote of a brother of mine, that knight errant, Francesco, turns up with you, tell him I am like Orlando Furioso, and when I meet him I will give him the right treatment, but it will be a big bear-hug of pure and brotherly love, which is the way we always treat modern knights errant. I want to punish him for not writing to me at Lisbon as we had arranged in London, I want to make him eat chicken and polenta for three days, and join him too, it is twelve years since I tasted it. . . .'

He was very homesick, but it was no use; there was no future for him in his own country. Something in his parents' letter—something, it must have been, about the Austrian occupation of his homeland by the forces under Count Starhemberg—wrung from him the heart-felt cry: 'Poor Padua! Poor Venice! I see everything in ruins. Let's hope to God they will soon return to the old ways!'

So Giovanni sadly turned his back on Italy and crossed over to Malta. Six months before, the island that had meant so much to Napoleon— for which he had gone to war before he was fully prepared—had passed by the Treaty of Paris 'in full right and sovereignty to His Britannic Majesty'. Almost a year earlier Sir Thomas Maitland—a tough, pugnacious, dominating personality known to everyone as 'King Tom' —had been appointed Governor and Commander-in-Chief. He was now firmly laying the foundations of a new administration as quickly as the aftermath of plague would let him. For in the eight months between May 1813 and January 1814 Malta had been visited by the worst epidemic of bubonic plague that she had known since the seventeenth century. Five thousand people died, trade was paralysed, and the administration almost bankrupted. Only the most rigid fortress discipline was able to save the island.

Giovanni's intention, we have seen, was to go to Constantinople, and Malta was only the first stage in his journey. However, he stayed there nearly six months. Probably he performed at the little Manoel Theatre in Valetta, a *bijou* playhouse built in 1731 by a Grand Master of the Knights; now one of the oldest theatres in Europe, it still keeps much of its eighteenth-century charm, though it has been turned into a cinema. But the most important event of Giovanni's stay in the island—and perhaps the turning-point of his whole career—was his meeting with Captain 'Ishmael Gibraltar'.[21]

The man with this romantic-sounding name was an agent of Muhammad Ali, that former Albanian tobacco merchant now founding a new dynasty in Egypt. Ismail—as we should properly call him—was on the look-out for Western technicians who might be recruited into the Pasha's service. Muhammad Ali wanted engineers and industrialists —men to introduce new manufactures, new processes and new methods to replace those that had been employed in Egypt for hundreds, even thousands of years. Giovanni talked eagerly and confidently of his skill in hydraulics. Clearly Egypt's greatest problem was irrigation. He could build an improved type of water-wheel that, copied and reproduced throughout the country, would revolutionize the whole economy. . . . Constantinople was forgotten; Egypt was now the land of promise, beckoning him on. Here was the chance Giovanni had been waiting for all his life, to turn his scientific knowledge to some serious purpose. He seized the opportunity with both hands.

They left Malta on 19 May 1815—Giovanni, Sarah and the Irish lad James. They carried a collective British passport, made out for Alexandria, and a joint health certificate that declared there was no 'suspicion of Plague or Contagious distemper whatsoever' in Malta and its dependencies. Giovanni was stated to be a native of Rome and his age was given as thirty-two; in fact, he was four years older. Sarah, according to the same document, was twenty-nine, but Boase's *Modern English Biography*, which says that she died in 1870 at the age of eighty-seven, would make her thirty-two or thirty-three at the time of her visit to Egypt. The lad James, on the evidence of the health certificate, was only nineteen.

They sailed in the brig *Benigno* (Master: Pietro Pace), slipping out under the frowning fortifications of the Grand Harbour—past the white, terraced houses climbing steeply up the rock—to the waters of the open sea. Perhaps the master's name was a good omen—and the ship's, too—for the voyage was uneventful. Three weeks after leaving Malta they sighted the ruined 'Arabs' Tower' of Abusir[22] on the low desolate coast to the west of Alexandria. Off Marabout Island they picked up a pilot to guide them through the dangerous reefs and shoals that blocked the approach to the Old, or Western Harbour. Till lately this had been reserved for Muslim ships; Franks had to use the New, or Eastern Harbour, though it was strewn with rocks and half choked with rubbish. Between them stretched the narrow neck of land on which the Pharos had once stood; now a dilapidated fort and tumbled blocks of stone marked the site of the World's Wonder.

If Belzoni, with memories of Rome, expected noble ruins and antique splendour, Alexandria must have been a sad disappointment. He saw only a small dirty water-front with narrow unpaved streets leading off it, some rows of blind-eyed houses and a dozen shabby mosques poking their fingers at the sky. To the right of the town—a conspicuous sea-mark—rose the solitary Corinthian column known for generations as 'Pompey's Pillar'. On the left, near the shore of the Eastern Harbour, stood a granite obelisk—one of 'Cleopatra's Needles'. (Another lay on its side, invisible from the ship.) Needless to say, none of these had anything to do with the Egyptian queen or the Roman politician.[23]

But Giovanni was not thinking of antiquities at the moment. The weather was oppressively hot, especially at night. The *khamsin*[24] was raging and the sultry desert wind blew in turbulent oven-blasts through the ramshackle town and over the ships in the harbour. It brought with it the stench of death. For when the pilot came on board he had told them that Alexandria was full of plague.

CHAPTER V

UNTIL the end of the eighteenth century the average Englishman's ideas of Egypt were mainly derived from Shakespeare, Plutarch and the Bible. In the popular mind there was a composite picture of Joseph amassing vast quantities of corn in granaries shaped like pyramids, Moses calling down plagues of frogs, boils and lice upon a stubborn king, Pompey being murdered as he stepped ashore and Cleopatra drifting on the Nile in a golden barge with purple sails and silver oars. Two hundred years ago the educated Englishman had also read Herodotus and Pliny and had at least a nodding acquaintance with Strabo and Diodorus Siculus. He accepted, without much questioning, the ancient view of the Egyptians as a people of great wisdom who lived under a megalomaniac ruler, devoted a large part of their lives to preparing for death, were organized in rigid castes and did most things differently from everybody else. The secret of their writing had long been lost; their history was known only where it coincided with that of Greece and Rome. On the other hand scholars and divines could still study the growth of monasticism in Egypt. For a time during the fourth century A.D. the Thebaid with its large population of saints and ascetics had drawn more pilgrims than Jerusalem. In the end schism and heresy had taken Egypt out of the main current of Christianity. The Arab Conquest dropped a veil over the country, and the memories of Saladin and the Crusades were not memories of Egypt. But from the days of the first Elizabeth a steadily increasing number of English travellers visited the Levant. Many of them wrote books when they returned, and their observations on Egypt—often no more profound than one would expect from tourists—were added to their countrymen's already existing notions.

For example, there was Mr. Lawrence Aldersey, who spent a fortnight in Egypt in 1586[1] and was shown the sights of Cairo and Alexandria by the only Englishman to welcome him there—Thomas Rickman, 'master o' the Tyger' and husband of Shakespeare's 'rump-fed ronyon'.[2] There was the Reverend William Biddulph, a goatish cleric who became chaplain to the Levant Company and in 1609 published an account of his travels in Egypt and other countries of the Middle East under the fragrant pseudonym of Lavender.[3] George Sandys, youngest son of the Archbishop of York, a poet and one of the founders of Virginia, recorded his impressions of Egypt in *A Relation of a Journey begun An: Dom: 1610.* These men were not specialists. They had a boundless 'Jacobethan' curiosity and an insatiable appetite for marvels. They were as much interested in the pigeon post and chicken incubators of Cairo as in the pyramids of Giza or the mummy pits of Saqqara.

Later there were other kinds of traveller—men like John Greaves, Professor of Astronomy at Oxford, who wrote his learned *Pyramidographia* in 1646; antiquarians and naturalists such as Thomas Shaw, who visited Egypt in 1721 and was praised by Gibbon for his powers of observation; and explorers with a mission, like James Bruce of Kinnaird, whose travels (1768–73) were mainly directed towards discovering the source of the Nile.

These men learnt more about Egypt than their predecessors, but they were not concerned to relate what they found to the broader story of Egyptian civilization. Nor, for that matter, were the travellers from France, Italy and Germany who were moved to visit Egypt in the seventeenth and eighteenth centuries. It was left to a Dane, Frederik Ludvig Norden, to attempt the first systematic survey of the country undertaken in modern times.

Norden was only twenty-nine when King Christian VI of Denmark commissioned him to explore and report on Egypt. He landed at Alexandria, went up the Nile to Aswan, tried to reach the Second Cataract, but got no further than Derr. He returned to Denmark and came to London in 1740. There he helped to found the Egyptian Club for gentlemen who had travelled in Egypt. Interest in the subject was growing. The following year he published *Drawings of some Ruins and Colossal Statues at Thebes in Egypt, with an account of the same in a Letter to the Royal Society.*[4] Norden died in 1742. His journals were published posthumously and appeared in an English translation in 1757.

One night twenty years earlier, as Norden was travelling up the Nile, he was passed by an English clergyman returning towards Cairo. Richard Pococke[5] had not gone beyond Philae, but he covered a good deal of ground. He was persevering and tried hard to discover the forgotten site of Memphis. Gibbon complained that Pococke too often confused what he had seen with what he had been told. But his *Observations on Egypt*, which was only part of a much larger work, *A Description of the East, and some other countries* (1743), stimulated interest as much as Norden's drawings.

There were, of course, commercial contacts with Egypt. Since 1580, when English merchants received for the first time a grant of capitulations from the Porte for trade with the Levant,[6] they had tried to maintain a consul in Cairo or Alexandria. It was not always easy. There never was the volume of trade with Egypt that passed through Aleppo and Iskandarun. Moreover, by the eighteenth century, Turkey's control over Egypt was only nominal. There was still a Turkish Pasha in Cairo, but the real power lay in the hands of the district governors, the Mamluk Beys,[7] whose mutual antagonisms kept the country in a constant state of upheaval and revolt. The Beys were intolerant of all Europeans. They and their xenophobic followers used such methods of intimidation against the Franks—the name given to all Europeans in the Levant— that the majority of foreign traders were compelled to leave Egypt. Warren Hastings had been one of the first Englishmen to realize the importance of Egypt's position on the trade route to India, and in 1775 he initiated a treaty of commerce with Muhammad Bey. But because of the unsettled state of the country it was never implemented. The French were not much better off than the English. Between 1770 and 1785 the number of French business houses in Cairo fell from fifteen to three. The French consul, Magallon, was obliged to move to Alexandria. The British consul, Baldwin, had to leave the country altogether. 'I do not conceive,' he told his superiors in 1798, 'that Egypt can be much longer tenable by the Franks.' Ten weeks later Napoleon landed near Alexandria.

The French were always more realistic than the English over Egypt. Ever since the loss of their possessions in India they had looked enviously at the Nile valley as a source of compensation and a springboard for re-conquest. When Turkey sickened and grew feeble and the nations of Europe dreamed of partition, France thought first of Egypt. Louis XVI sent officers and experts to survey the country and judge its military strength. The Revolution gave the Beys a short breathing-space. But in 1798, while Baldwin was bemoaning the fate of the Franks, Magallon suggested to the Directory that the best way to destroy British power in the East was to invade Egypt.

The details of the campaign do not concern us here. Napoleon entered Cairo in triumph on 24 July 1798 after the Battle of the Pyramids. Eight days later Nelson destroyed the French fleet in Abukir Bay at the so-called Battle of the Nile. In another fortnight the army of *savants* that Napoleon brought with him settled down to its peaceful conquest of Egypt. The Commission of Arts and Sciences—soon to be organized as the Egyptian Institute—included fifty-two assorted engineers, eleven surveyors, eight surgeons, seven chemists, six interpreters; five architects, five designers and five printers; four mineralogists, four astronomers and four economists; three botanists, three zoologists, three pharmacists, three painters and three archaeologists;

two writers and two musicians; an engraver and a sculptor; and seven pupils from the Polytechnic. For the next three years they collected and classified fauna and flora, measured temples, described antiquities, copied inscriptions, surveyed canals and inquired into industries. Napoleon—before he deserted them—set questions to be answered by three- or four-man teams of experts: How could the local type of oven be used to bake the army's bread? Was there a substitute for hops in beer? (Those who remember an Egyptian war-time brew with its strange flavour of onions will appreciate the importance of this question.) Was it possible to purify the water of the Nile? Windmills or watermills—which were better? Could gunpowder be manufactured in Egypt? What improvements might be made in the law and administration?[8]

When the French army in Egypt finally surrendered in 1801, General Hutchinson stipulated that everything collected by the Egyptian Institute should be handed over to the Allied Command. He was strongly supported in this by William Hamilton,[9] a diplomat-antiquarian on the staff of Lord Elgin. The French scholars and scientists were naturally incensed. Geoffroy Saint-Hilaire, a brilliant young naturalist and the future rival of Cuvier, told Hutchinson plainly: 'We shall not obey. We shall burn our treasures here with our own hands. History will judge. You will have destroyed another Alexandrian library!'

Hutchinson relented. The *savants* returned to France with their notebooks and portfolios. The great work of publication began in 1808, languished through the worst of the war years, and was not completed till 1825.

But though the French were able to keep the greater part of their collections intact, a few valuable pieces did change hands.[10] One of these was a broken slab of black basalt found in 1799 by a French working party not far from the Delta town of Rashid, which Europeans call Rosetta. The slab was inscribed with three different scripts. The first was a hieroglyphic writing and the last was Greek; between them was something presently identified as a cursive form of the hieroglyphics. In October 1801, after considerable difficulty, Major General Turner obtained possession of the slab and sent it home to London, where it was deposited for a while with the Society of Antiquaries. A year later this key to the eventual decipherment of the ancient Egyptian language—the Rosetta Stone, as it now came to be called— was placed on public exhibition in the British Museum—just about the time that Belzoni arrived in London to draw his own curious crowds.

The news that there was plague in Alexandria was enough to alarm anybody. Belzoni decided that his own little party had better stay aboard the *Benigno* till he had some reliable information. Fortunately, on the day after their arrival, two European gentlemen came alongside the brig and told them that the plague was abating. They would have to go into quarantine in any case; so, without more ado, Sarah and Giovanni and the lad James went ashore and picked their way carefully through the garbage-strewn streets to the French *wakala*, where they were to lodge. This was simply a Turkish khan—a kind of building once universal throughout the Levant and still to be found in use today in towns like Yannina and Nicosia.

The only entrance was through a gateway opening on to a large courtyard. A staircase gave access to a wooden gallery that ran round the courtyard at the height of the first floor. Leading off it were a number of separate rooms, each occupied by a family. The ground floor was used for stores and stabling. It was a convenient arrangement in many ways, giving protection against both thieves and disease. A single guard at the gate could keep out strangers. In time of plague food was dropped into a large jar of water at the entrance and left there for half an hour; there was no contact between the bringer and the receiver. Warm bread was especially dangerous, even to touch; loaves mounted up outside till they were stale and safe.

The Belzonis and their servant were admitted to the *wakala*. They were given food and strict injunctions not to touch anything from outside, unless it had first been passed through water. Then they were left alone. For three or four days no one came near them. . . . It was just as well, for almost at once they were taken ill. It was more than 'gippy tummy'—that first plague of Egypt to afflict the modern visitor; there was vomiting too. Giovanni took the greatest care to conceal their sickness from the other inmates of the *wakala*. He knew it would be said they had caught the plague while passing through the town; imagination would stop at nothing less. Panic would spread; they might even be turned out. It was better to suffer in silence.

So they made themselves as comfortable as they could on the bare wooden floor of their room. Gradually the sickness wore off and they recovered their strength and cheerfulness. They began to make contact with their neighbours along the gallery. There were even some amusing creatures to watch in the courtyard below: a family of ostriches—the two old birds and four young ones—a pair of grotesque spoonbills and two Numidian cranes who indulged in elaborate courtship and gracefully-danced minuets.

News came in from the outside world. It seemed the plague was worse in Cairo. In Alexandria it was mainly the Turkish soldiers who were affected. They died like flies—twenty a day—in their tented camp outside the walls. The Arabs were apparently immune, though they took no precautions. But the death of a single European was enough to throw the whole Frank quarter into a turmoil. A Roman Catholic monk had died just before the Belzonis arrived.

Giovanni was told of the Arab belief that the plague would end with the rising of the Nile. This was expected at Cairo in a few days' time— on 18 June.[11] Alternatively, said the Greeks, the plague might last till St. John's Day—the 24th—but in no case longer. Giovanni's own belief was that very hot weather checked an epidemic as much as the cold; now that the *khamsin* had stopped the temperature was below eighty degrees.

The 18th came—a Sunday. A Greek priest died and a lay brother was taken ill at the Roman Catholic convent. For the Franks cooped up in plague-stricken Alexandria these two events marked the day. But over in Europe, at a little village in Belgium, a whole era was ending. A French army was flying in retreat, routed and broken. Napoleon had met his Waterloo.

The plague had diminished by the 24th and Giovanni was now able to make some contacts in the town. There were several consulates in the European quarter. Colonel Missett, the British consul general, had been in Alexandria, with one interruption, since 1803. At the end of the first English occupation of Egypt he was left behind to keep an eye on Turk and Mamluk and see that the French did not return. William Hamilton put it in splendid Foreign Office language: Missett's job was 'to convey to the British government authentic information of the events which should take place in Upper and Lower Egypt during those contests for dominion which it was foreseen must ensue between the Mamalukes and the Turks, when either party should no longer be overawed by the presence of our army; and when they should lose their recollection of the wholesome counsel of the British commander, given as it had been to them from the most upright and disinterested views; and supported by a calm, conciliatory, and dignified conduct'.

Unfortunately, after the Peace of Amiens the French appointed their own agent—a Piedmontese named Drovetti. For years the two men were rivals. They repeated the old pattern of Anglo-French relations that had existed two hundred years before when Elizabeth's first ambassadors to the Sublime Porte vied with the envoys of Henri III and Henri IV for the Grand Signior's favour. Only in this case each man looked forward to the occupation of Egypt by his own country, and to that end backed a rival Bey. When the Sultan recognized Napoleon as Emperor after his great continental victories of 1805–6, the English decided to re-occupy Alexandria. Missett brought in his Mamluk faction and Drovetti fled to Cairo. But the Mamluks were already a spent force and Missett failed to appreciate the growing strength of Muhammad Ali. The second English occupation was short-lived. Missett retired to Italy at the beginning of 1808 and stayed there three years. When he was posted to Egypt again for a second tour of duty the Mamluks had gone and Muhammad Ali was firmly established in power. Missett himself was now a helpless cripple, paralysed in all his limbs, though he was only about forty. He retired at the end of 1815—a few months after Belzoni's arrival in Egypt.

Bernardino Drovetti was a much tougher character than the urbane and cultivated English colonel, whose political judgment was so frequently at fault. This able, adventurous Piedmontese had studied law before he joined the army. Picked out by Napoleon for promotion, he became in 1801 chief of staff of the Piedmontese Division and later in the same year military judge in Turin. He was then only twenty-five. In 1802 he was sent to Egypt to be vice-consul in Alexandria. Later he was appointed consul general for France in succession to Mathieu Lesseps, father of Ferdinand who dug the Suez Canal. In 1814, when Piedmont became part of the Kingdom of Sardinia, Drovetti kept his nationality and lost his official status. But his influence with the Pasha was still great. The news of Bonaparte's escape from Elba encouraged him to think that the French flag would soon fly again over his consulate. Officially he was not reappointed consul general till 1821, but his position as France's representative was never challenged.[12]

Drovetti was to play an important part in Belzoni's life during the next four years, but we know little about their first meeting, except that the former consul general gave Giovanni some letters of introduction to people in Cairo. Why he got them from Drovetti rather than Missett —as he travelled on an English passport—is not quite clear. He may well have thought that the energetic Piedmontese—a fellow-Italian, after all—was likely to have more influence than the crippled English colonel presiding over his seedy *salon*. Moreover he had enjoyed Drovetti's hospitality in the French *wakala* and may have been thrown much more into his company. And perhaps too he had heard that a machine for raising water had recently arrived from England as a present from the Prince Regent; if so, he could hardly expect the British consul to give his blessing to a rival enterprise.

The Prince Regent's gift was the answer to a long-standing request from the Viceroy of Egypt and the subject of as pretty a piece of correspondence on the whims of princes as is preserved in the Public Record Office in London.[13] Three years before Ernest Missett had forwarded to the Government a letter from the Pasha, in which he spoke of the problems of irrigation and said that, having heard of ingenious new inventions in England, he would like to have 'a little steam-pump to try, and another machine that could be driven without the help of fire'.

Missett, endorsing this request, wrote: 'From what the Pasha had heard of the powers of steam engines, he was very anxious to procure one on a large scale; but on my representing the great expense with which it would be attended in a country which produces no kind of fuel, and where there are no workmen capable of keeping it in repair, he has given up the idea of having one for use, but still retains a wish to see upon what principle it is constructed.' As for the other machine, Missett thought that 'a preference should be given to a pump worked by means of horses'. And he added that it would be 'necessary to send some intelligent person with a couple of assistants to superintend the erecting of the two machines'. Muhammad Ali had already professed his willingness to go to any expense and to pay the money through his agent at Malta.

To the British Government, which was continually being plagued by the Pasha to allow him to send Captain Ismail 'Gibraltar' in one small corvette round the Cape of Good Hope to the Red Sea, a toy steam-engine seemed a much safer thing for him to play with than dreams of Eastward expansion.[14] Accordingly Lord Bathurst, Secretary of State for War and the Colonies, promised to accede to the request and then forgot all about it. He was reminded on a number of occasions by Colonel Missett and others that the Pasha was getting impatient, and at last action was taken. In February 1815—nearly three years after the original request—a Mr. Allmark arrived in Alexandria with a model steam-engine and a larger pumping machine. But by this time the Pasha was busy with his campaign against the Wahhabis and the present had to await his return.

There was every reason therefore for Giovanni to make haste to Cairo. As soon as word came that the plague there had almost ceased and that the Frank houses were open again, he decided to go. They might have gone by camel the fifty odd miles to Rosetta and taken a boat from there up the Nile. But as they heard there were many pilgrims for Mecca waiting at Rosetta for transport to Cairo, it seemed better to make sure of a boat by getting it at Alexandria. Eventually they agreed to hire a small one-masted *jerm* for two hundred and twenty-five piastres—less than six pounds—and to share the cost of the journey with a young gentleman from the Foreign Office named William Turner.

Turner, who came from Yarmouth, had gone out in 1811 at the age of eighteen or nineteen to join the staff of the British ambassador in Constantinople. Before returning home he went on a long and pleasant duty tour of the Middle East. After visiting Cyprus, Rhodes, Beirut and Palestine, he arrived in Alexandria about ten days before the Belzonis. There he stayed with Colonel Missett and, like him, showed a pretty fair contempt for the plague. He was still very young—only twenty-two—athletic and well-educated. He had been brought up on the classics and also spoke modern Greek and Italian. He once tried to swim the Hellespont and engaged in a correspondence on the subject with Lord Byron. He had a bright, inquiring mind and a great gift for setting down his impressions in an easy, readable way. He was the first of a dozen travellers who met Belzoni in Egypt and left some record of the encounter.[15]

Turner says that Belzoni told him he had 'devoted the last twelve years of his life to the study of mechanicks'. By now Giovanni may almost have convinced himself that this was true, so ardently did he desire to be recognized as a 'scientist', so clearly did he see success beckoning him in Egypt, so resolutely had he put the old life of the theatre and the fair-ground behind him. But young William Turner can hardly have been listening properly when he thought Belzoni said he had brought with him a machine that would raise water from the Nile 'without the assistance of man or beast'. It is doubtful if Giovanni carried about with him more than the idea in his head. Certainly when the machine was built it was intended to be worked by an ox. But perhaps Giovanni was thinking of the great steam-engines at the New River Head and the wheel that raised water for Tottenham Court Road.

Boats for Cairo usually left at night so as to cross the dangerous bar of the Rosetta mouth at daybreak. The travellers had decided to start in the early hours of Saturday, 1 July. The moon rose at half past twelve; at one Turner called at the *wakala* to pick up the Belzonis. They sent their luggage ahead and followed with their two servants, Irish James and a Rhodian Greek named George.[16] The night was warm and there was not much wind, but outside the harbour they ran into a heavy swell. The waves slapped sickeningly under the shallow bows of the barge-like *jerm*. Soon all the travellers were feeling queasy. They were not sorry when the Arab *reis* told them through George that it was impossible to cross the bar with such a swell; they must either stop at Abukir or return to Alexandria. They chose the second course and landed in the New Harbour at a quarter past three.

The wind blew strongly all that day. On Sunday, when it dropped, the *reis* called for them and they set off again in company with a number of other boats, all bound for the Nile. In the early afternoon they dropped anchor in Abukir Bay, so as to time their arrival at the bar for the following morning. They went ashore and George cooked a picnic meal of fish which he had brought with him; an Arab goatherd gave them milk. In the evening they strolled along the edge of the sea, then wandered inland over the dusty, deserted plain, thinking of the noise and tumult of Nelson's great battle in the bay seventeen years before.

They found many whitening bones of men scattered over the plain, and Turner picked up a small cannon ball that had lain there undisturbed since the day it was fired.[17] They sailed away from this haunted spot at half past one in the morning.

At noon the next day they reached the Rosetta mouth of the Nile and crossed the shallow bar without incident. To the right, on the flat, sandy bank, lay a broken, abandoned *jerm*, one of those that had set out with them from Alexandria and had unwisely tried to enter the river in the dark. They stopped near a village to eat and afterwards rested under some palm-trees. Here Giovanni saw and heard for the first time the groaning, creaking *saqiya*, the Nile's immemorial water-lifting machine. A blindfold ox or a great purple gamoose—the water-buffalo—turned a flat wooden wheel that transmitted the power to another skeleton wheel rigged upright in the shallows. Round this was roped an endless chain of red or yellow pots that scooped up the water and poured it at the top of the circle into a trough made from a hollowed-out tree. The wooden shaft of the driving-wheel turned in a wooden socket, the cogs too were of wood, and none of the parts was ever oiled. The music of the *saqiya* is still one of the unforgettable sounds of Egypt. At times it fills the air with the hum of drowsy, opulent bees on a hot summer's day; at times it wails thinly over the water like a sad bagpipe lament.

The travellers set off again at four. The wind blew strongly from the north-west and the current was slack, so that the *jerm* moved up-stream at a steady speed of six to eight knots. Turner, assiduous with his journal, asked the name of every village they passed. The *reis* was horrified at such a useless expenditure of effort and urged him not to continue; there were, he said—with complete faith in the magic of large numbers—seventy thousand villages between the mouth of the river and Cairo.

Soon they came in sight of Rosetta, glimpsing it first over the fields where it stood surrounded by palms and gardens. After the arid wastes around Alexandria the lush greenness of the place delighted them greatly. The river in front of the town was crowded with sailing-barges like their own, mostly filled with Turkish soldiers who were being re-called to Cairo. Turner sent George ashore to find Mr. Lenzi,[18] the British agent. He came back quickly with a fellow-Greek, who conducted them to a house not far away from the quay. Later Mr. Lenzi himself appeared, dressed in a magnificent hussar uniform, with a short red coat. He said that there had been three cases of plague reported in the town that day and he must ask the visitors to consider themselves in quarantine. The house they were in was clean and commodious and it was entirely at their disposal.

Rosetta then had a population of some twenty-five to thirty thousand; it was twice as large as Alexandria. In the centre the tall, tumbledown, red-brick houses had projecting upper storeys that almost touched across the narrow, dirty streets. But on the outskirts there were some attractive villas with vines growing on trellises in front of them. Belzoni and Turner went for a walk before it got dark—taking care not to touch anyone in the streets—and they noted with pleasure the many orchards that surrounded the town, though there was as yet little fruit on the trees. They came back to a good supper and clean, comfortable beds. But there were no mosquito nets and the travellers were tormented all night by the *ping* and thrust of the troublesome insects.

The next day—Tuesday—they did not leave till after twelve. The *jerm* was being fitted with an awning of mats to protect them against the increasing strength of the sun and the heavy night dews. But the breeze still blew strongly from the north and they made good progress. For a while they found themselves sailing between fields of rice, corn and maize, with palms and other trees fringing the banks. By the next day the scenery had changed completely. There were scarcely any trees and little cultivation. They passed a number of squalid villages, mere clusters of mud huts, much less permanent than the strange mounds or tells that dotted the Delta landscape and testified to the site of ancient settlements. The Nile was now so shallow that frequently they ran aground. Whenever this happened, the Arab boatmen hauled their galabiyas over their heads without shame and dropped naked into the water to put their shoulders under the barge and heave it clear of the mud-bank.

The men in the party bathed, but poor Sarah could only stifle and swelter in her most unsuitable clothing. However, that night they stopped at a village where, says Turner, they found 'a delightful little garden, crowded with palm, pomegranate, lemon, orange, peach, apricot, pear trees, &c.; where we supped off our goose. The Arabs, to whom the garden belonged, sat by us during supper; and our lantern illuminating the trees with the stillness of the night, and our picturesque situation, formed altogether a complete scene of the Arabian Nights Entertainments'. Let us hope Sarah enjoyed it as much.

The following day the wind blew in great gusts, which sometimes threatened to capsize the *jerm*. The travellers breakfasted off coffee and eggs under a large spreading sycamore tree. They watched Arabs drawing water from a well with a basket slung between two ropes. Giovanni must have been appalled at such a primitive device, yet secretly glad to think of the advantages his wheel would bring. In the afternoon the heat was so oppressive that even the parrot they had on board began to gasp for air. Later they sent George ashore to buy food. He talked to some Arabs, who asked how long it would be before the English came to occupy Egypt. When he answered at random, 'Five or six months', they expressed their pleasure that it would be so soon.

Before daylight the next morning the travellers had passed the southern tip of the Delta, where the Damietta branch of the Nile forked away to the north-east. At half past seven they went ashore and had their first distant view of the Pyramids. They were now very close to Cairo. The banks of the river were bare and almost treeless, but there were more houses and these were of better appearance than any they had seen in the Delta villages.

Presently they rounded a point and came in full view of Bulaq, the lower port of Cairo. The narrow reach was crowded with craft of all kinds. Beyond the forest of masts they could see rambling stone warehouses and tall shabby mansions built to the water's edge. Between them was a labyrinth of dark, noisome alleys and bright, strident bazaars.

The *jerm* dropped anchor at half past nine in the morning. It was just five days since they had left Alexandria. Turner and Giovanni went ashore at once and pushed their way through a seething, jostling, shouting crowd of porters, boatmen, Turkish soldiers, veiled women, naked children, vendors of sherbet and yoghourt, water-carriers, sweetmeat-sellers, beggars and idlers. They tried to avoid falling over the piled bales of goods, the pyramids of pots and the patient, kneeling camels. When they reached an open space they hired a couple of donkeys and then, with the owners running beside them, rode off over the dusty plain to Grand Cairo. Turner was going to stay at the Convent of Terra Santa, where Colonel Missett had already written to secure a room for him. But the holy fathers could not receive a woman within their walls, and Giovanni was obliged to part company with the young diplomat and return to Bulaq. There he and Sarah and James were presently accommodated in a house belonging to Boghos Bey, Muhammad Ali's Minister of Foreign Affairs and Commerce.

CHAPTER VI

Misr without an equal, Misr the mother of the world.
Traditional Arab description of Cairo

Cairo is particularly ill-built, and a stranger on arriving, after having heard so much of 'Grand Cairo', can scarcely believe his own eye-sight when he finds himself in this miserable hole.
CAPTAIN JAMES MANGLES, R.N., in a letter home, 1817

FROM the ramparts of Salah al-Din's Citadel, set high on a limestone spur of the Muqattam Hills, the early nineteenth-century traveller in Egypt looked down upon a scene almost as full of bewildering contrasts as is the modern city of Cairo. Only where the eye now sees a solidly built-up area stretching from Abbasiya to Giza, from beyond Shubra to the other side of Old Cairo, with thickening tentacles of development reaching out to Maadi and Helwan, to Heliopolis and along the road to the Pyramids—in Belzoni's day the traveller saw the city spread compactly below him like a half-closed fan, an irregular quadrant, with himself at the radiant point.

Beyond the circuit of the walls were open fields, brown and dusty before the annual inundation, but after the cutting of the Canal[1] dam veined with runlets of life-giving water and soon lush with young green growth. To the north-west, a mile from the city, was the bustling port of Bulaq, the gateway to the Delta. To the right of it and beyond were the pleasant gardens of Shubra and the Pasha's summer palace on the Nile. In the other direction, south-west through a full turn of the quadrant, lay the port of Old Cairo, from which travellers set out for Upper Egypt and Nubia. Here once had stood the Roman fortress of Babylon. Behind it at al-Fustat the invading Arabs had established their city-camp and made it the first Muslim capital of Egypt. Now only mounds of rubbish marked the spot. In front of Old Cairo the garden-island of Roda was thick with palms and acacia and sycamore trees. The Nile stretched like a great guardian snake beside the city and its ports, while out across the desert the dragon's teeth of the Pyramids sprang up at Mena and Abusir, at Saqqara and Dahshur.

When the traveller dropped his gaze to the city below him, his first impression was of the great height of the buildings and of the narrowness of the streets between them. It was as if the sun's fierce heat had opened up deep cracks in an ant-hill. At the bottom of dark fissures, into which the light scarcely penetrated, human beings swarmed with

87

a strange, insect-like activity. Yet Cairo was not as vast or as populated
as report said. Belzoni noticed that, while the principal streets were
always crowded, elsewhere except in the bazaars there was an air of
desolation and decay. Mud-brick houses soon crumbled into dust and
there were piles of rubbish everywhere. Turner, busily collecting information for the Foreign Office, calculated that the previous year the
population had been about three hundred and fifty thousand. Of these
he reckoned thirty-five thousand had been carried off by plague in the
four months before his arrival. (He made no allowance for the natural
increase of the Arab.) There were very few Turks in Cairo, apart from
the military, only about five hundred Greeks—so the Greek Patriarch
told Turner—and not more than one hundred and fifty Franks.

The walls of Cairo—some seven or eight miles round—were un-
remarkable, but three of the city gates were fine specimens of Saracenic
architecture. It was said that there were over three hundred mosques
in the capital. The largest and oldest of them rivalled, if they did not
surpass, the most famous foundations in Constantinople. There was
the unique al-Azhar, immensely rich and piously endowed, whose sun-
lit, arcaded court has been the centre of Islamic learning for almost a
thousand years. At the foot of the Citadel stood the great fourteenth-
century *madrasa*[2] of Sultan Hasan, with its splendidly proportioned
dome and two unequal but superb minarets. There was the oldest
mosque of all, built by Ibn Tulun; the minaret had its staircase outside,
hung above the vast stone quadrangle. There were mosques with row
upon row of granite and limestone pillars, plundered from the lost
temples of Memphis. And there were others whose blind outside walls
suggested nothing of the cool sequestered beauty within. Franks for the
most part found the outward appearance of the mosques forbidding;
they were usually more impressed by the rich arabesque ornament of
the Mamluk Tombs that lay in the fold of ground behind the Citadel.

The traveller who approached the city from Bulaq entered by the
Gate of Ezbekiya, not far from the later site of Shepheard's Hotel. He
found himself at once on the edge of a large dusty depression which is
now covered by Ezbekiya Garden. In August or September, when the
Nile had risen to the required height of sixteen cubits, the dam of the
Canal at Old Cairo was cut and the liberated waters poured through
the great dry ditch that bisected the city. They swirled into the dust
bowl of Ezbekiya and turned it into a muddy lake.

There were some big private houses around Birket el-Ezbekiya, many
of them ruined and dilapidated since Napoleon had his headquarters
there. At the other side of the square the traveller plunged into a labyrinth of narrow, crowded streets. The widest only admitted the passing
of two loaded camels; the narrowest was no more than four feet across

at ground level and diminished to a crack above. There were no pavements and the dust kicked up by hundreds of scuffing feet and the hooves of hard-ridden donkeys choked and blinded the unwary traveller. Barbers, beggars, lepers, quack doctors, pregnant women, naked saints, jugglers, soldiers, negroes, fortune-tellers, versifiers and circumcisers jostled and thrust him forward, stridently making their claims and demanding a way through. There was constant danger of being run down or crushed against a wall by some silently-padding beast, snuffling at the first-floor windows. The camel-drivers and donkey-men screamed invective and warning together—'*Riglak! Shamalak!* Watch your legs! Look to your left!' and other, less innocent, expressions.

The Frank quarter was separated from the rest of the city by wooden gates at each end of its main street. These were always closed at sunset and kept locked altogether in times of plague or riot. Accommodation was limited, but few Europeans cared to lodge in the Arab part of the city, where houses were plentiful and rents low. If there was no room in the Frank quarter, it was safer and healthier to stay at Bulaq.

The house which Mr. Boghos had provided for the Belzonis was not all it might have been; in fact, it was so old and dilapidated that they expected every moment it would fall about their ears. The windows were boarded up with broken pieces of wood. The staircase was so rotten that there was scarcely a single whole tread left in it. The front door had no lock or fastening of any kind and could only be kept closed by having a pole placed against it. In every room—and the house was a large one—the ceiling sagged ominously. There was not a stick of furniture anywhere—nothing but a mat in one of the less dismal apartments. Sarah jokingly called it her drawing-room. Fortunately they had brought sheets and mattresses with them. A box and a trunk served as a table, and in the absence of chairs—which seemed unobtainable in this country—they sat on the floor. They had a few plates and knives and forks, which they had provided for the journey on the boat. James, greatly daring, went out and bought some cooking-pots on the quay.

Giovanni's immediate objective was to obtain an audience with the Pasha, so that he might explain to him why his own water-wheel was superior to any others. Boghos Bey—a shrewd, energetic Armenian, contemptuous of the slow Arab tempo of life—arranged this at once for the morning of Saturday, 15 July. There was only a week to wait and the time passed quickly enough. When the windows of the Bulaq house had been opened, an unrivalled panorama spread itself before the travellers' eyes, with figures constantly in motion. The house commanded an excellent view of the river and the landing-place. There was bustle and movement all day long, with boats for ever arriving and departing. Among the heterogeneous hordes of passengers two main streams could be distinguished, moving in opposite directions: Turkish troops returning from the Delta, truculent and trouble-making, and Moorish pilgrims from Mecca, who halted their caravans at the quayside and pitched their tents in any open space to wait for the next boat. These patient people spent hours, it seemed to Giovanni, just sitting, smoking, singing and saying their prayers.

Meanwhile Mr. Turner was making a brisk round of visits in Cairo. He called on Signor Bokty, an Italian engineer who had been appointed Muhammad Ali's Director General of Industry and was also consular agent for Sweden. He met the Patriarch of Alexandria, who received him 'with every distinction of pipes, coffee, sweetmeats, lemonade, incense, and rose-water'. But his main contacts were with Boghos Bey. The Minister had a well-furnished house in Cairo, kept a good table (European *cuisine*) and enjoyed all the comforts that the country could provide. He was, according to Turner, the most agreeable and liberal-minded Levantine that he knew. He was now Muhammad Ali's most trusted adviser at a salary of over £6000 a year. Yet only two years before he had incurred the full force of the Pasha's displeasure and almost lost his life. He had failed to provide his master with a certain sum of money by a particular day. Muhammad Ali, incensed, ordered his minister to be thrown into the Nile. He was already on his way to the river, bundled up in a sack and thrown across a donkey, when a fellow-Armenian, a merchant named Walmass, rescued him from the guards without much resistance on their part. They later reported that they had done their duty, and Boghos lay low for a while. When the next financial crisis came the Pasha began to regret his hasty decision. He was even heard to say that he wished Boghos were alive. This was the cue for those who were in the secret, and the Armenian was soon restored to favour. The guards were executed for their disobedience. . . . The story sounds pure 'Arabian Nights', but is vouched for, with only minor variations in the telling, by Turner himself, Dr. William Holt Yates, Robert Curzon, and other English travellers who met this redoubtable Foreign Minister.

Turner dined almost every night at Boghos Bey's, not merely for the sake of his good table, but because of the interesting company he was always likely to meet there. Another frequent guest at this time was Shaikh Ibrahim, a tall, handsome, emaciated man who looked far older and wiser than his thirty years. Few who met him—even Arabs—guessed, if they were not told, that he was a European. Yet John Lewis Burckhardt—to give him the Anglicized form of his name which he adopted when he came to England—was a member of a well-known family at Basle, though he himself was born at Lausanne. Like Belzoni, he found the whole course of his life changed by the Napoleonic Wars. His father, an army colonel, came near to being executed on a false charge of treason. The younger Burckhardt did well in his studies at Leipzig and Göttingen, but he could not settle to a career under the shadow of French dictatorship. In 1806 he came to London with a letter of introduction to Sir Joseph Banks, then President of the Royal Society and an active member of the African Association.[3] There was at that time some talk of making a new attempt to penetrate into the unknown interior of Africa by the northern route through Egypt and the Fezzan. Burckhardt offered his services and was given a commission in January 1809. He had already begun to study Arabic at Cambridge, but it was decided that he should go first to Syria to acquire there a thorough knowledge of the language and familiarity with Arab ways far from the scene of his intended operations. On the voyage out he stopped at Malta, where he assumed the character and dress of a Muslim merchant from India. For the next two and a half years his base was Aleppo, but he travelled widely in Syria, Palestine and the Lebanon. He lived with Arabs, studied their customs, mastered their language and became so proficient in expounding the Koran that he was able to pass as a *mawla* or 'doctor of divinity'. When asked by Arabs to speak in his supposed native language of Hindustani, he would lapse into an unintelligible flow of guttural Swiss-German.

In 1812 Burckhardt crossed the Sinai Desert and came to Cairo. A caravan was just about to depart for the Fezzan, but the traveller excused himself from joining it on the grounds that he was still insufficiently prepared for his mission, which was now specifically to cross the Great Desert into the countries of the Niger. The fact is that Burckhardt was drawn too strongly towards the centre of the Arab world to be really interested in its periphery. But he was an honourable man and told the African Association frankly of his intention to undertake a journey into Nubia before the setting-out of the next caravan to the West. His sponsors approved his determination to become thoroughly acquainted with Egypt before he penetrated further into Africa. So he had travelled up the Nile as far as the Third Cataract. Then another project had occurred to him and he had crossed the Nubian Desert to the Red Sea port of Suakin. He was now so far advanced on the pilgrim route to Mecca that he could not draw back. He crossed over to Jidda and at Taif in the Hijaz met Muhammad Ali, who was then campaigning against the Wahhabis. The Pasha had seen him before in Cairo and knew of his connection with England. He had him examined on his knowledge of the Koran by two doctors of the law. They pronounced him not only a true but a most learned follower of Islam. Burckhardt spent three months in Mecca, from September to November 1814, and did everything that was expected of a pious pilgrim. In January 1815 he went on to Medina to see the Prophet's tomb. There he was attacked by a fever that laid him low for three months. When he arrived back in Cairo on 19 June, two or three weeks before the appearance of Turner and the Belzonis, he was still weak and exhausted after months of sickness and privation. But he had done something that perhaps no Christian and no European had ever done before.[4] And he had not missed a caravan to the West!

Burckhardt's understanding of the Arabs might have made him as famous as any of his successors—Burton, Palgrave, Doughty, Gertrude Bell or T. E. Lawrence—had his life not been tragically cut short. Yet before he died he met Belzoni and passed on to him something of his own great passion for breaking new ground, for pushing human inquiry into the older and remoter parts of time and place. He had a vast encyclopaedic knowledge about the countries in which he had travelled and he was generous and modest to a degree.

One evening Turner planned an expedition to the Pyramids. Mr. Boghos promised him a tent and a military escort. And, being gregariously inclined, Turner invited Belzoni and Mr. Allmark—the man who had been sent out to install the Pasha's pumping-machine—to go with him.

They met at Allmark's lodgings in Old Cairo the following evening. A relative of Boghos Bey was to be their guide. After supper they crossed the Nile, riding in the moonlight through the sycamores of Roda between the two arms of the river. At Giza they were met by the escort. The party now consisted of Turner, Belzoni, Mr. Allmark, the Armenian guide and four servants, all mounted on donkeys; the Pasha's officer and three Turkish soldiers on horseback; seven donkey boys; and two camels for the baggage. They managed to get rid of three other Turkish soldiers, whose function apparently was to ride ahead of them with blazing *flambeaux*. As the moon was shining brightly, this seemed a little superfluous. But Turner accepted the statement that only three years before a Frank who visited the Pyramids without an escort of at least fifty men would have been killed or robbed by marauding Bedouin.

They left Giza at nine o'clock. For the first hour the road was good; for the second it lay through fields so cracked by the sun's heat that the donkeys constantly stumbled. They passed three small mud-brick villages. The dogs ran out to meet them long before they reached the silent houses and followed, baying in the moonlight, till they were far on the other side.

For the last half-hour they were riding on soft sand. Two of the

Pyramids had been before them all the way, their black and silver shapes standing out sharply against the indigo velvet of the night. They seemed to grow no larger, indeed even to dwindle as the travellers came nearer. It was only when they were very close that suddenly their mass loomed up and filled half the sky.

The tents were pitched at the foot of the Great Pyramid, and after another meal the camp settled down for the night. A cool breeze was blowing from the north and the travellers, not yet inured to Egypt's heat, were grateful for it. They fell asleep with its freshness gently touching their faces.

Soon after first light Belzoni and Turner were roused by an Arab who had come to conduct them to the top of the Great Pyramid. They scrambled up the giant cold grey steps in the opalescent dawn and reached the flat, broken surface at the summit in a quarter of an hour, just before five o'clock. Presently in that still, rarefied atmosphere they could hear the sound of cannon being shot off on the Citadel to greet the new day. At a quarter past five the sun came up in splendour from behind the Muqattam Hills, silhouetting the domes and minarets of Grand Cairo and tipping the distant Pyramids at Saqqara with bright gold. In a few minutes the sun's heat had dissipated the white mist lying in the valley and the Nile appeared as a dark metallic strip uncoiled between the bright green fringes of the cultivation. The river was still rising. In another month its waters would have spread out over the arid plain almost to the very foot of the Pyramids. The villages they had passed in the night and the little feathery clumps of palms would be islands in a vast lake; travellers would come all the way from Cairo by boat. Only the desert would still look the same, a wilderness of sand and rock stretching away as far as the eye could see to the north-west, west and south.

Presently a number of small black dots were seen streaming over the sand towards the little camp. They were Arabs from the nearest village bringing skins of water, milk, eggs and fruit for sale to the Franks. They swarmed round the tents like ants; then suddenly, with amazing alacrity, they were racing up the side of the Pyramid in the hope of selling half-a-piastre's worth of milk to the *khawagat* on the top. 'They were all of them,' says Turner, 'almost black in complexion, nearly naked, and looked lean and half starved; one would have sworn they were resuscitated mummies.'

At half past seven the travellers descended, taking more time and using more caution than they had done on the way up. After breakfast they explored the inside of the Pyramid. It must have been an uncomfortable experience for a man of Giovanni's size, for the first passage—the Descending Corridor—is less than four feet high, only three feet five inches wide, and slopes down at an angle of twenty-six degrees. But there was worse to come. Just before the junction with the Ascending Corridor the passage was then so choked with rubble that only a narrow gap was left between floor and ceiling. The travellers had to lie down flat and be dragged through by the long-armed, sinewy Arabs. At one point Belzoni stuck fast and for two or three minutes, in spite of all the sweating efforts of the Arabs in front of and behind him, he could not move either forwards or backwards.

Eventually they reached the burial-chamber and stood beside the empty lidless sarcophagus. The travellers measured it and made it three and a half feet wide, so that Turner concluded it could have been slid through the passages after the Pyramid was finished. But he was wrong. As Sir Flinders Petrie later showed, the sarcophagus is just about an inch wider than the lower entrance to the Ascending Corridor, and so must have been placed in position while the Pyramid was building.

Cheops' funeral chamber seems to have had an odd effect on some travellers. John Sanderson and his friends, who visited the place in 1586, lay down inside the sarcophagus 'in sport'.[5] In 1842 a band of earnest Germans sang the Prussian national anthem in the confined space of the chamber. On Christmas Eve one of them—the Egyptologist Richard Lepsius—planted a palm-tree in the sarcophagus and decorated it with candles and presents.[6] Turner and his party did nothing more absurd than firing their pistols, which must have made a deafening noise and an abominable smell. Then, rather thankfully, they groped their way through the smothering heat of the passages, only to find a miniature sand-storm in progress outside.

After dinner and a rest Belzoni and Turner walked round the Pyramids, pacing out the length of each side and speculating on their origin, purpose and method of construction. Giovanni's views at this time are not known, but there is no reason to suppose that he showed anything more than the ordinary intelligent tourist's curiosity. He must have noticed, for example, that there was no way into the Second Pyramid, and Turner may have remembered the positive statement of Herodotus that it had no underground chambers. But certainly Belzoni could not have guessed that within the next three years he would solve its mystery.

At a quarter past three the travellers mounted their donkeys and set off on the return journey. South-east of the Great Pyramid they stopped in a hollow among the sandhills to look at the Sphinx. Only its head and neck were visible above the sand; it waited for another of those periodical clearances, of which the earliest on record was undertaken by the Pharaoh Thothmes IV. To commemorate the event he set up a *stele* between the paws of the Sphinx about 1420 B.C. Other clearances were made in Ptolemaic and Roman times. Captain Caviglia carried out a similar operation in 1818 and for a while Belzoni, to his embarrassment, was mistakenly given the credit for it. The Sphinx had to be cleared again in 1886 and even still more recently in 1926; those who remember it in the early 1920s will have seen it much as Belzoni did in 1815.

The travellers reached Giza by half past five and were across the river before dark. Giovanni found Sarah waiting for him with her usual equanimity. James had nothing untoward to report.

Belzoni was to see Muhammad Ali on Saturday morning. To save him an unnecessarily early start from Bulaq Turner had offered him a sofa the night before in his own lodging at the Convent. Even so he was up in good time to meet Mr. Boghos, who was to present him to the Pasha. They rode along on their donkeys at the usual fast trot, Giovanni uncomfortably trailing his long legs in the dust and trying to avoid imminent collisions at every moment. Suddenly, in one of the narrow streets leading up to the Citadel, a Turkish soldier on horseback bore down rapidly upon them. As he passed Giovanni, whose tight-fitting clothes clearly proclaimed him a Frank, the Turk aimed a vicious kick at him. His stirrup had an edge as sharp as a knife.[7] It cut through Giovanni's thin pantaloons and laid open a two-inch triangular gash in the fleshy part of his right calf. Blood poured out of the wound. The soldier swore at him and rode on. Around them the normal pandemonium of the street continued. Mr. Boghos quickly summoned help and Giovanni was taken to the Convent of Terra Santa, where he was laid on Mr. Turner's sofa, much to that gentleman's astonishment.

But there was nothing unusual in such an incident. For centuries Turks had treated Franks in this uncivil fashion. It was even less surprising now in Cairo where the returning troops were ripe for mutiny. One of their main grievances was the introduction of a Western type of army drill. The mere sight of a Frank therefore was enough to convince any Turkish soldier that he saw before him the chief author of all his troubles.

As soon as his wound had been treated and bound up, Giovanni was taken back to Bulaq. Sarah was calm and unflustered. With James's help, she at once set about making him as comfortable as possible in that comfortless house.

Belzoni says it was a month before he could stand on his legs, but this is an exaggeration.[8] Still, it was a nasty wound and it kept him confined to the house for some time. Turner meanwhile went off to Sinai, to visit the Convent of St. Catherine. The day before he left he rode over to Shubra to see Mr. Allmark demonstrate the pumping-machine in the presence of the Pasha. It had already failed once. Now again, because of a badly wiped joint, it did not work as it should. The Pasha looked displeased; after all, this was a gift from the British Government. Mr. A. asked for another ten days to put it right, but his face plainly said: What can you do with such people? Turner's comment was: 'When government sends presents of this kind into barbarous countries, it is a pity they do not put them in the hands of a man who can either speak the language of the people, or is attended by workmen of his own. Mr. A. is an excellent mechanist, but no talent of his can give ability to Arab labourers, especially as he cannot speak a word to them except through an imperfect interpreter.'

Soon after this Belzoni had his audience with the Pasha. His *Narrative* tells us little beyond the fact that Muhammad Ali received him very civilly and inquired about his limp. When he was told the cause of it, he remarked that such things were bound to happen where there were troops. Giovanni goes on: 'I made an arrangement with him, and undertook to erect a machine, which would raise as much water with one ox, as the machines of the country with four. He was much pleased with my proposal, as it would save the labour and expense of many thousands of oxen in the country. . . .'

Muhammad Ali was born at Kavalla, a small seaport on the North Aegean coast, in 1769. It used to please him in later life to remember that he was born in the same year as Bonaparte and Wellington. He was probably of Albanian stock, though some said he had Turkish or even Persian blood in his veins. His father had commanded a small body of irregulars in the service of the local governor. After his death Muhammad Ali was brought up by the governor with his own son; at eighteen he married one of the governor's relatives. For a time he engaged in the tobacco trade, for which Kavalla is still famous. He had a shrewd head for business, and might have become a prosperous merchant. But in 1798, when the Porte was persuaded to take action against the French in Egypt, Kavalla was required to provide three hundred men. The governor's son commanded this contingent and Muhammad Ali went as his lieutenant.

The Turkish force was feeble and ineffective, so that Muhammad Ali distinguished himself all the sooner by his courage and ability and was rapidly promoted. It was the state of anarchy in Egypt in 1803—after the expulsion of the French and the British withdrawal—that gave the ambitious young officer his first political opportunity. The Mamluk Beys—or what was left of them—had retired to Upper Egypt, where they rivalled the Bedouin in their capacity for plunder. They could no longer keep up the numbers of their corps by recruiting Circassian or Georgian slaves, since Turkey had placed an embargo on the export of young boys to Egypt. But the Turks were unable to suppress the Mamluks altogether, and the Mamluks could not drive out the Turks.

Muhammad Ali could be fox and lion by turns, cunning or bold as the circumstances required. He played Mamluk against Turk, Albanian against Mamluk, Egyptian against Albanian. For a while he was content to seem, as Missett thought him, a tool of the Mamluks. Then suddenly he dropped them overboard. In 1805 he had himself elected to the Pashaliq by the Shaikhs and citizens of Cairo, and the Sultan confirmed him in his office. In 1807 he foiled Britain's second armed intervention in Egypt—an enterprise of which a contemporary writer said that if it was done in earnest it was not enough and if in jest it was too much. But though the heads of British soldiers were paraded on spikes through the streets of Cairo, Muhammad Ali realized that Britain might be very useful to him in his schemes for the future. There were bad harvests in Europe during the next few years. Muhammad Ali sold the British large quantities of wheat for their army in the Peninsula at four or five times the normal Cairo price. It was paid for partly in bullion, partly in munitions, and partly in goods of English manufacture. The treasury began to fill, the army was regularly paid, and Egypt for the first time looked towards the West.

But the Mamluks were still a potential danger. One day in 1811, on the eve of his war against the Wahhabis, Muhammad Ali invited the Beys and their followers to a ceremonial parade in Cairo. Some eight hundred of them accepted the invitation; splendidly attired, accoutred and horsed, they assembled on the high rock of the Citadel. They watched while the Pasha presented a robe of honour to his second son, Tusun, who was to lead the expedition against the Wahhabis. Presently Turks, Albanians, Mamluks all moved off down the narrow, rock-cut passage between the inner and outer gates of the Citadel. When the unsuspecting victims were fairly in the trap, the lower gate was closed. Then the troops in front and the troops behind hacked at the Mamluks penned between them. Others rushed to the walls and fired volley after volley into the struggling men below. Soon the rocky lane was a shambles. Only one man is said to have escaped the massacre—a laggard rider in the rear who turned and urged his horse clean over the battlements.[9] Later that year the Pasha's eldest son, Ibrahim,[10] annihilated another Mamluk band in Upper Egypt. After that only a few scattered remnants of the corps survived in Nubia.

Many Western minds were shocked by Muhammad Ali's ruthlessness, but they had to admit there was a certain irresistible logic about it. He could not risk a Mamluk *coup* while his own troops were out of the country. And if Egypt was to go forward on the course he had set

7

for her, the war against the Wahhabis could not be postponed. This puritan Muslim sect had lately gained control of the Holy Cities of Mecca and Medina. The Porte had called for their dislodging, but neither the Pasha of Damascus nor the Pasha of Baghdad had responded to the appeal. To the new ruler of Egypt it seemed that here was his opportunity to establish himself as leader of the Arab world.

Muhammad Ali found the Wahhabis a tough proposition. He recovered the Holy Cities and laid the keys of Mecca at the feet of the Sultan. But when he tried to push further into the interior of the Hijaz, he was repeatedly driven back—sometimes, ignominiously enough, by a female chief named Ghaliya. For a year and eight months Muhammad Ali took charge of the campaign himself. By the spring of 1815 he was getting the upper hand of the Wahhabis, but he could no longer remain absent from Egypt. There were ugly rumours of the Porte arming against him. He left his son to finish off the campaign and returned to Cairo in June.

Muhammad Ali was now forty-six years of age. His short, stocky figure had not yet begun to put on weight, nor had his face acquired that look of 'an old gray lion', which so impressed Curzon nearly twenty years later. Indeed Turner, when he saw him, thought he was thin, but no doubt this was the effect of hard campaigning in the Hijaz; the climate of Arabia left Burckhardt a gaunt scarecrow and caused more casualties among the Pasha's troops than did the Wahhabis themselves.

Most travellers remembered Muhammad Ali's eyes. He had a very penetrating gaze and his broad low brow contracted in deep vertical furrows when he was thinking hard. Turner, schooled to suspicion of the Oriental mind, noted his 'dark and designing countenance'. Even the Pasha's smile seemed sinister; it reminded him of Shakespeare's Richard III, with his power 'to smile, and smile, and murder while he smiled'.[11] But Muhammad Ali could be most affable towards Europeans when he liked. He would invite them to sit beside him on the divan and ply them with searching questions about the new industrial civilization of the West.

It is a pity there is no fuller record of Belzoni's meeting with the Pasha. However, a day or two after his audience Giovanni wrote to Bernardino Drovetti.[12] Addressing him as his 'true friend' ('*Stimatissimo Sig.^re e vero amico*'), he told the former French consul that his affairs now seemed to be making a good start. His Highness had received him '*con molto gentilezza*'. The Pasha had realized Belzoni knew something about hydraulics from the opinion he had passed on Allmark's pump. So, as he was not satisfied with the English machine, he had instructed Belzoni to make a full-scale prototype of his own irrigation-wheel. As for the financial side, Giovanni indicated that he was a little worried. They had told him to trust to the Pasha's generosity, but he knew, he said, that 'once the bird is in the cage they give no more thought to the snare'. However, he was going to make one of his cheaper models ('*una delle mie machine più inferiori*') which, with a single ox to work it, would easily raise as much water as five or six of the Egyptian wheels. Then, if the financial side could be satisfactorily arranged, he would build another machine that would not need an animal at all to operate it. (This idea never came to anything, so we cannot be certain what Belzoni had in mind. But perhaps already he dreamed of revolutionizing Egypt by the power of steam.)

Giovanni ended his letter with a reference to the loan of another ten dollars which he had had from Drovetti's agent—presumably M. Asselin de Cherville, the French consul in Cairo. He was a *vif* little man, according to Turner, a keen Orientalist and, it seems, a cheerful boon companion. Later in the month, on the Feast of St. Louis, he gave a party in the illuminated garden of the French consulate, which overlooked the Canal. To this party he invited '*tous les buveurs et les chanteurs les plus déterminés*'. They drank and sang till dawn.[13]

It was now that Belzoni had another of those unpleasant experiences that frequently befell the European traveller in Egypt. The day after he wrote his letter to Drovetti a disturbance broke out in Ezbekiya Square. Some Turkish soldiers, goaded to a sullen kind of fury by the new Frankish drill, began to demonstrate in front of the palace where the Pasha's women lived. They overturned a number of fruit-stalls and raided a few shops, but there was little more than that the first afternoon and the night that followed was comparatively quiet. However, Muhammad Ali read the portents and as soon as the trouble began he left his palace at Shubra and retired to the greater security of the Citadel.

The troops were emboldened by the fact that no disciplinary action had been taken against them. The next morning, before it was light, hundreds of them gathered in Ezbekiya Square. Soon after dawn they tried to rush the palace, thinking to find the Pasha with his women. When the guards drove them back, they turned off into the bazaars and began to break open shops and warehouses with characteristic Turkish thoroughness; they were followed at no great distance by a happy looting Cairene crowd. Several times during the day they assaulted the big wooden gates that kept them out of the Frank quarter of the city. But the Europeans were on the alert; they had manned their houses that abutted upon the Square and their first defensive shots killed two and wounded five or six of the insurgents. After that the Turks were a little more wary in their approach.

That morning Giovanni left the Bulaq house at an early hour to go up to Cairo. He was puzzled at once by the strange silence where usually all was noise and confusion. The boatmen were getting ready to leave, although they had no passengers. There were no strings of camels taking water to the city, no donkey-drivers quarrelling passionately over their 'fares'. The shops were closed and the mile-long road to the capital seemed utterly deserted. Half-way to Cairo, Giovanni met some soldiers lounging near a bridge over a canal. He thought it prudent to ignore them but, as he passed, one of the men pointed a gun at him and the others laughed at the idea of frightening a Frank.

When he reached the city the vast dusty bowl of Ezbekiya was empty. The mutineers had learnt that Muhammad Ali was in the Citadel and had gone up there to hurl defiance; the townspeople were in their houses. Giovanni made his way round the Square and came to the gates of the Frank quarter which, to his astonishment, were still closed. As he looked through a grille in the small door set in one of the gates, an anxious face peered out. It was Bokty, the Swedish consul general. At once he bombarded Belzoni with questions, but Giovanni knew less than anybody what had happened. Suddenly there was a commotion a few streets away and the sharp rattle of muskets. The door was quickly opened and Giovanni was pulled inside. Then for the first time he heard about the mutiny.

Giovanni had some business with Mr. Boghos. The Minister tried to persuade him to stay in the quarter, but Giovanni was thinking of Sarah, alone in the house at Bulaq except for James and an Arab servant. As soon as he could, he slipped out to the gates and with some difficulty got them to open the small door for him. There was now a good deal of firing going on in the streets. As Giovanni trotted into the Square on his little donkey, he saw some soldiers hurrying in the direction of the palace. Others, he realized, were coming towards him. In a few moments he was surrounded. One man seized the bridle of his donkey, another grabbed Belzoni by the collar. Then all at once hands were diving into his pockets and into the breast of his shirt. He let them have their way. They took his watch, his pocket-book and a handful of coins. What attracted them most, however, was a topaz brooch which Giovanni wore in the frill of his shirt. When he saw they were pleased with this, he smiled at them and began to edge away. They let him go without further trouble. He had lost his valuables and his passport, but he knew he had got off lightly.

For forty-eight hours Cairo was in the hands of the looters. Then, as the troops glutted themselves with the spoil of the bazaars, the raids became fewer. But sporadic street fighting continued for several days, the gates of the Frank quarter remained closed, and the Pasha stayed in

the Citadel for nearly a month. He realized the strength of the mutiny
and knew it had to burn itself out. According to Turner, only a quarter
of the twelve thousand troops in Cairo were loyal; of the disaffected
the worst were the fifteen hundred Albanians. Muhammad Ali sent
his Syrian cavalry against the rebels and drove them back almost
into Bulaq. Giovanni and Sarah watched the fighting from an upper
window of their house. There were very few casualties, however, and
what took the heart out of the mutiny was the knowledge that the
new European system of drill was being withdrawn and no proceedings
were being taken against the rank and file. A few senior officers lost
their heads; this, as Turner records, was 'done sparingly at Bulac, with
a machine like a chaff-cutter'. The shopkeepers and merchants, whose
losses were estimated at four million piastres [£100,000], were compensated out of the Pasha's own pocket. For all that, many Europeans
now left Cairo; those who remained continued to run the risk of being
shot at or assaulted in the streets, long after the mutiny was over.[14]
Muhammad Ali was learning he could Westernize his new Egyptians
only so far and only at their own pace.

On 14 August Belzoni wrote again to Drovetti, explaining that the
mutiny had delayed matters, but now it was agreed with the Pasha
that he should have a hundred Spanish dollars [£25] a month as a
subsistence allowance for himself, his wife and his servant. The question of his ultimate reward was still unsettled; the only answer he could
get was that he must trust to the Pasha's generosity. So far he had
received no more than five hundred piastres on account.

By this time Giovanni and Sarah had moved into the little house at
Shubra that was to be their home for the greater part of the next twelve
months. Actually it stood within the grounds of the governor of
Shubra's residence, but from it Giovanni had free access to the adjoining palace gardens, where he was to set up his machine. The gardens
occupied some thirty to forty acres; they had been laid out only five
years before—by Greeks, probably from the island of Chios—but
already they had an established look. There were cool shady groves of
orange and lemon, tall cypresses, trellis-covered paths screened with
trailing clematis and roses, and fragrant bowers of mimosa. Turner,
who once visited the place, complained of the dust underfoot and the
lack of anywhere to sit down. But to Giovanni and Sarah, after the noise
of Bulaq and the stifling heat of Boghos Bey's tumbledown tower, the
gardens at Shubra were a cool oasis of peace. And this was only,
Giovanni observed, because of the long line of water-wheels on the
Nile bank that never ceased turning; beside them, derelict in its shame,
stood the present of the Prince Regent.

Belzoni was eager to start work on his own machine, but there were more delays. Muhammad Ali's Chief Engineer was ill and they had to wait for his recovery. In the meantime Turner had come back from his expedition to Sinai and was anxious, before he left Egypt, to see the pyramids and mummy pits of Saqqara. He proposed to go with Allmark the engineer, and he—who bore no grudges—brought along Belzoni and his wife.

They set off by boat from Old Cairo at half past five on a Sunday afternoon in late August. A few hours later they were sailing over flooded fields on the west bank of the Nile. The moon threw a soft light on the water and the little palm-tree islands were dark tufts of shadow. In the distance they could see the strange six-tiered shape of the Step Pyramid, and beyond it the dark monuments of Dahshur. At eleven o'clock they stopped and settled down for the night on damp ground under some palms. Next morning they saw that the canal which led towards the Pyramids was not yet full enough to take their boat. So they found donkeys and set off over fields thick with rushes and thistles, which the *fellahin* were clearing before the inundation waters were turned in upon them.

For the last hour and a half they rode along a causeway between two reedy canals. Then they struck out across the cultivation to the desert's edge and the foot of the Step Pyramid. They knew nothing of King Zoser and his architect Imhotep;[15] to these tourists the great white pyramid with its six shelving steps was only another ruined monument to be climbed for the sake of the view. Afterwards they breakfasted in its shade. They decided not to visit the 'Catacombs', as the Arabs said a ladder and lights were necessary. But they sent one of the men to fetch the mummy of an ibis. After half an hour he came back with a long narrow earthenware jar sealed with a red clay stopper. The tourists were frankly incredulous when the Arab told them this was an 'antika' and contained the mummified body of a bird. They laughed at his crude deception—such jars were found in every village household. In anger the Egyptian dashed the vase upon the ground; then from the fragments he picked up a small tangle of mummy-cloth and what might have been the bones of a hawk, that mouldered into dust between his fingers. Giovanni at least was abashed, for he tells the story of their unbelief. Turner preserves a more dignified silence, but he says M. Asselin de Cherville, the French consul, told him he had broken open over two hundred of these jars and failed to find a mummy intact. Another gentleman in Cairo, he adds, did the same without even having the satisfaction of finding a single feather.

In the afternoon the party split up. Turner and Belzoni wanted to see more pyramids; Allmark and Sarah would go back with George to the boat. The disposition of the *entourage* was not effected without some difficulty. 'One of the Arabs,' says Turner, 'was so noisy and insolent, that we were forced to beat him well with our sticks, for we found all explanation and remonstrance utterly useless.'

Giovanni and Turner rode for an hour across the desert to the great brown and white stone pyramid at Dahshur, later supposed to be one of the two built by the Pharaoh Sneferu, the predecessor of Cheops, though this attribution is now in doubt.[16] The travellers scrambled to the top, hoping to find the entrance of which their Arab guides had spoken. But this was only a trick to delay them so that they should have to spend the night in their guides' village and disburse more *bakshish*. 'We beat them with our sticks,' says Turner, 'for these ingenious devices, and one of them ran away.' Then they went on to the Bent Pyramid[17] and picked up fine flints and pieces of cornelian from the desert round about it. They looked lastly at the black and shapeless mass of the southern brick pyramid at Dahshur; this is but the core of the monument built by Amenemhet III, the great Middle Kingdom Pharaoh whose other pyramid stands beside the Labyrinth at Hawara.

They set off back to the Nile. Giovanni was sorry he had not seen the mummy pits of Saqqara, but he makes little of this episode in his *Narrative*, for his mind was then on other things. However, he observed that the village of 'Betracina'—did he mean Badrashain or Mit Rahina?[18] —seemed to be near the very centre of ancient Memphis, which Petrie later estimated to be 'the size of northern London from Bow to Chelsea, and from the Thames up to Hampstead'. On the road from Badrashain to Saqqara, just before reaching Mit Rahina, Belzoni would have had on his right a vast sunken area later to be revealed as the site of the great temple of Ptah, one of the most important buildings in the capital. But of the glories of the ancient city Belzoni would have seen nothing in all that dreary expanse of sand and donkey-thistle. 'Noph shall be waste and desolate,' said the prophet Jeremiah, and his words had been made good.[19]

When Turner and Belzoni got back to the river they found the boat had gone; it had been agreed the others should wait till the moon rose at half past seven, and then push off if they had not arrived. Fortunately they were able to hire another boat and so reached Old Cairo only three hours after the first party. They spent the rest of that night in Allmark's house. In the morning they heard of fresh disturbances in Cairo; an Italian, Mr. Baffi, who made gunpowder for the Pasha, had been bastinadoed by the soldiers when they caught him in the street.[20] But Turner continued his sight-seeing, and the Belzonis went back to their house at Shubra. This was almost the last time they saw the young man from the Foreign Office, for he left Cairo at the end of the week to return to Constantinople.

The day he left—25 August—Belzoni wrote again to Drovetti. Something had happened to his relations with Bokty, the Swedish consul whom Muhammad Ali had made his Director General of Industry. Drovetti had evidently suggested that Giovanni should turn more to Bokty for advice on the furtherance of his plans. Belzoni wrote back saying that Bokty was not to be trusted; he was a double-dealing rogue. Moreover, he knew nothing about hydraulics, in spite of all his pretensions—witness his ridiculous efforts to put the English machine in working order. What grounds for complaint Belzoni had against the Director General of Industry it is not clear. But another letter written by Belzoni—on 11 November—shows that he did at least have words with Bokty over his alleged treatment of the unfortunate Baffi. Belzoni accused Bokty of encouraging another Italian chemist to take up the manufacture of gunpowder in opposition to Baffi, so playing off one candidate for the Pasha's favour against another. This led to a complete breach between the two men. Belzoni said he would not rely on Bokty any more, while Bokty protested to Drovetti that he had only tried to help everyone. Probably that was the truth of the matter: he promised more than he could perform and granted the same exclusive rights to more than one applicant.

Giovanni, however, was quite confident that he could manage without Bokty. Indeed, it was now he had what seemed to him a brilliant idea. In his letter of 25 August he told Drovetti he had noticed that a good deal of land was unproductive simply because it was beyond the reach of the Nile waters even at the height of the inundation. He suggested that the Pasha should be asked to lease some of this land at a reasonable rent for a period of four or five years. Giovanni carefully added that the agreement must be made before Muhammad Ali saw how easily and cheaply the land could be irrigated with the new machine, otherwise the terms would not be so good. It seems he had visions of himself settling down to farm for four or five years and making a fortune by the use of modern methods.

Drovetti's answer is not known, but Muhammad Ali was certainly far too shrewd to fall for a proposition like this, especially when it came from such a source. Turner records that he never lost an opportunity of buying up land, often at a price that was only a fraction of its real value. More than half, sometimes two-thirds, of the produce went to the Pasha. In the same way he had got control of all the new industries. Western technicians were brought in to run them, but they remained the Pasha's monopoly. Apart from the powder factory at Badrashain, there were manufactures of silk and indigo. There was also a project to start a sugar refinery in Upper Egypt, and perhaps a rum distillery as well; an Englishman named Brine had already arrived with ten assistants to begin work. The Pasha was interested in other possibilities too, and he was still curious about steam.

Belzoni saw him quite often. 'The Bashaw,' he notes, 'is in continual motion, being sometimes at his citadel, and sometimes at his seraglio in the Esbakie; but Soubra is his principal residence.' The palace at Shubra was small; most of the rooms were grouped round a large central *salon*, reached from the top of a broad handsome staircase. But the Pasha spent a good deal of time in the gardens. 'His chief amusement', Giovanni tells us, 'is in the evening a little before sunset, when he quits his seraglio, and seats himself on the bank of the Nile, to fire at an earthen pot, with his guards. If any of them hit it, he makes him a present, occasionally of forty or fifty rubies. He is himself an excellent marksman; for I saw him fire at and hit a pot only fifteen inches high, set on the ground on the opposite side of the Nile, though the river at Soubra is considerably wider than the Thames at Westminster Bridge. As soon as it is dark, he retires into the garden, and reposes either in an alcove, or by the margin of a fountain, on an European chair, with all his attendants round him. Here his numerous buffoons keep him in continual high spirits and good humour.'

There was an odd mixture of Arabian Nights and schoolboy japes about these entertainments. On one occasion a Court buffoon shaved off his beard, dressed up in Frank clothes and presented himself as a visiting European. He was questioned through an interpreter in Italian, French, German, Spanish; at each interrogation he looked more blank and uncomprehending. Finally, when the Pasha was beginning to lose his patience, the buffoon burst out in Turkish and his own familiar voice. Muhammad Ali was so delighted that he sent the man off to his Deputy with a large order on the Treasury. Fortunately the figure was so astronomical that the Deputy at once suspected a trick; otherwise he might have found that the Pasha's sense of humour was limited.

Belzoni had the freedom of the gardens and often came upon these buffooneries as he strolled about to take the air. One evening he found some senior palace officials wrestling with a strange piece of apparatus. It was one of two 'electric machines' which the Pasha, ever in search of novelty, had had sent out from England. The other was broken when it arrived; this needed assembling and no one—not even the Pasha's Armenian physician—knew how to do it. As soon as Belzoni appeared, the Turks appealed to him. He saw the machine was based on a simple variation of a voltaic pile. Quickly, without difficulty, he fitted the parts together. Then he looked round for a suitable victim. It must have been with a certain quiet satisfaction that he picked on a stolid Turkish soldier and beckoned him to mount the stool. The guard, unsuspecting, stepped up; Giovanni put the chain in his hand, charged the machine, and delivered a good sharp shock. The Turk leapt off with a cry of terror, as though he had seen an *afrit*. The Court roared with laughter.

Muhammad Ali thought it was a trick; he could not believe the man's action had been quite involuntary. Then Belzoni, greatly daring, took a chance. 'I . . . desired the interpreter to inform his Highness, that if he would mount the stool himself, he would be convinced of the fact. He hesitated for a while whether to believe me or not; however he mounted the stool. I charged well, put the chain into his hand, and gave him a pretty smart shock. He jumped off, like the soldier, on feeling the effect of the electricity; but immediately threw himself on the sofa in a fit of laughter, not being able to conceive how the machine could have such power on the human body.'

How long the voltaic battery continued to amuse is not on record. One wonders whether Giovanni was ever tempted to show Muhammad Ali any of the scientific tricks he once had in his repertoire. Did the 'Grand Sultan of All the Conjurors' try to impress the Pasha of Egypt with feats of Western legerdemain? We can be certain he avoided any 'professional' display. The past had been left behind; even in Egypt, where magic has always been popular, Belzoni had no wish to be taken for an itinerant conjuror, a 'galli-galli' man. Now not even parity of esteem with the *shaikh*-magicians who caused clairvoyant images to appear in a mirror of ink would have satisfied the former exhibitor of phantasmagoria.[21] But Giovanni's fine physique must have called forth the rough soldierly admiration of the Turks and perhaps in these casual encounters he was sometimes prevailed on good-humouredly to demonstrate his strength.

The Belzonis were not without entertainment themselves during their stay in Shubra. The house overlooked an open piece of ground which was a popular place for wedding celebrations and other festivities. Early one morning a tall pole with a pennant was set up in the middle of the square and glass lamps and lanterns were strung overhead. A large crowd gathered, for it was a marriage-feast of some importance and there were guests from other villages; these arrived in procession, waving flags and beating tambourines. The festivities began with music and dancing. The men formed two circles facing each other round the pole; one stood still while the other revolved, each man holding on to his neighbours' shoulders. They kept this up for hours, watched by the women who sat, with the bride among them, at a distance apart. Meanwhile three or four sheep had been roasting on spits. To go with them were vast quantities of boiled rice and dishes piled high with green egg-plant and 'lady's-fingers'.[22] For the drinking department, says

Giovanni, they had a team of boys to fetch water from the Nile in earthenware jars, but there was also a sly *raki* party going on in one corner for those who did not take the Prophet's injunction against strong liquor too seriously.

As it grew dark the lamps were lit and the company settled down in decorous groups for the evening's main entertainment. It began with dancing of a kind which, in Giovanni's words, 'has never been described, and all who see it properly must be excused from giving a faithful picture of it'. What Giovanni saw—and Sarah, too, if she was not too shocked to watch—was evidently a belly-dance 'by two well-known and distinguished performers' from the ranks of the *Ghawazi*. These were a class of professional dancing-girls, often confused by visitors to Egypt with the usually more refined and cultured 'Almehs' (*Awalim*), who were professional singing-women. These girls were always in great demand at weddings and bachelor parties; sometimes they were even hired out to entertain and instruct the inmates of a *harim*. European travellers were not quite as reticent about the dancers as Belzoni suggests, though they generally affected to disapprove. The Chevalier Sonnini, who used to watch them from the windows at the back of the French consulate as they performed on the dry bed of the Canal, said that their 'steps and jumps bear no resemblance to the dances of our countries. They consist chiefly of very quick and truly astonishing movements of the loins, which they agitate with equal suppleness and indecency, while the rest of the body remains motionless.'[23] Denon, another Frenchman, was impressed by the girls' capacity for hard liquor: 'These dancers swallowed large glasses of brandy as if it had been lemonade.'[24] Sir Frederick Henniker, visiting a Cairo night haunt in 1819, was struck by 'the magnificent appearance of some Levantine ladies' who competed with the professionals. 'The master of the ceremonies frequently made the tour of the room, demanding "becksheesh".' The girls danced 'with heaven in the eye', but their eye was always on the *bakshish*. The top professionals, according to Henniker, would not provide an evening's entertainment for less than two or three thousand piastres, i.e. £50 to £75.[25]

Dancing was not the only entertainment, however, at the Shubra wedding. There was a play with a comedy camel and a pilgrim going to Mecca, and an afterpiece featuring a Frank as a sort of clown. Belzoni gives both farcical plots in some detail, but never by a word betrays his own experience in the theatre.

The governor of Shubra[26] was a friendly soul who took a fancy to Belzoni and liked him to drop in for a chat over coffee and a smoke. He was one of the few Mamluks who had kept his head and his authority, a widely travelled man with a special interest in estate management.

Sarah won his heart by sending him a hot drink several nights when he was suffering from a chill. Later, when she was troubled by a pain in the side, he insisted on prescribing for *her*. He conferred with the *shaikh* of the mosque, who wrote out certain verses of the Koran on three triangular pieces of paper. Giovanni was told that Sarah must fasten one of these to her forehead and the other two to her ears. The *shaikh* also gave him a piece of sheepskin with a charm written on it, which was to be applied to the affected part. To the governor's great satisfaction Sarah was better in a day or two.

Giovanni sometimes steered the conversation round to the subject of his machine, but he found the governor completely uninterested. Why, indeed, should anyone want to improve on something that had worked successfully for generations—whether it was a charm to cure colic or a water-wheel for the irrigation? As the months went by, Giovanni saw he was making no progress. By mid-November, when he broke with Bokty, he had probably not even begun work on the machine itself. For some reason, too, he had lost touch with Boghos and had to ask Drovetti to find out whether the Finance Minister had written to the Pasha's Deputy about the matter. The corridors of bureaucracy were growing longer and longer. . . . However, at last the necessary permits were obtained, but then it was a question of supplies. From the start there was prejudice against the machine; Western improvements were not more popular than the European drill. Belzoni says the people he had to deal with were afraid that 'the introduction of such machines into the country would throw many of them out of work'. They were reluctant to supply him with labour or with the wood and iron he needed for the wheel. Even when he got them the quality was poor. It took him three or four months to construct his cumbrous bovine treadmill. And then he had to await the Pasha's pleasure.

In the spring of 1816 Muhammad Ali spent some weeks in Alexandria, where a magnificent house had been built for him on the site of the old Plague Hospital. Belzoni's water-wheel was finished while he was away, and even when he returned to Cairo—probably in June as the plague abated—he did not come at once to Shubra. At last, however, the fateful day of the test arrived. Muhammad Ali came down to the gardens 'with several connoisseurs in hydraulics'. The great wheel had been set up at the end of a row of six saqiyas that turned and groaned continuously. An ox stood patiently waiting. At a sign from the Pasha he was pushed and goaded up a ramp by shouting Arabs till he entered the revolving drum. Slowly, jerkily the wheel began to turn; water splashed out of the rising buckets—became a stream, a torrent, that poured through the irrigation channels which threaded the garden.

Giovanni anxiously watched the Pasha's face. Muhammad Ali looked at the new machine and then at the line of saqiyas. The Arabs in charge of them were lashing their beasts into a furious shamble and the whine of tortured timbers rose to an ear-splitting scream. The combined flow of water from the six saqiyas was almost twice the normal amount; even so it scarcely equalled the output of Giovanni's single plodding ox. Yet when Muhammad Ali had conferred with his experts he gave it as his judgment that the new machine was only as good as four of the old. This was demonstrably untrue, but it was still high praise. Giovanni felt he had passed the test with flying colours. Not even bad workmanship and bad materials could offset the soundness of his invention. But he saw from the scowling faces of the Turks that they did not like it. He knew they were reckoning how much they would lose in authority and prestige, if in future they needed to employ only one man and one ox where previously they had used four.

Muhammad Ali was in a quandary. He recognized the value of the new machine and saw its possibilities, but he also realized the strength of the prejudice against it. He was saved from the necessity of making a difficult decision by his own love of buffoonery and horse-play. He wanted to see what would happen if the ox were taken out of the wheel and a dozen or fifteen men put in its place. The Arabs, laughing and shouting like children, jostled their way into the drum. In a rash moment, the Irish boy James—thinking perhaps of roundabouts and 'ups-and-downs' at home—decided to get in with them. The wheel began to turn, the water poured along the channels and the Arabs shouted with delight. Then—as suddenly as they had jumped in—they all tumbled out. James was left in alone, his slight weight the only counterpoise to the mass of water overhead. Grindingly the wheel ran back; the boy was flung up and out like a stone from a sling. He fell in an awkward heap and lay there still.

If Belzoni, busy a few moments later with first aid for a broken leg, had looked round at the Turks, he would have seen an expression of relief and satisfaction on many faces. Here was the clearest sign that the Frank machine was no good; it had tried to kill a man. Not even Muhammad Ali Pasha could go against that.

CHAPTER VII

I met a traveller from an antique land
Who said: Two vast and trunkless legs of stone
Stand in the desert . . . Near them, on the sand,
Half sunk, a shattered visage lies . . .

PERCY BYSSHE SHELLEY, Ozymandias, 1817

IN those last weeks of waiting, before Belzoni's 'wheel of fortune' so disastrously turned against him, a new character had quietly appeared on the scene—one who was to play a decisive part in shaping Giovanni's future. Colonel Missett had at last prevailed on the Foreign Office to release him from his duties on the grounds of ill health. And in March 1816 Henry Salt arrived in Alexandria to take up the post of His Majesty's consul general in Egypt.

Henry Salt was born at Lichfield in 1780, the youngest son of a hard-working doctor with a large practice and a family of eight children. After a desultory education he was sent to London to study under a gentlemanly landscape painter named Joseph Farington. He became a student at the Royal Academy at the time when the young men of the Antique School were noted—in the words of Salt's biographer, J. J. Halls—for their 'idleness, vulgarity, and indecorum'. Salt was not happy there, and indeed in later life he could hardly pass Somerset House—then the home of the Academy—without shuddering at the recollection of his student days. Afterwards for a short time he was a pupil of Hoppner, one of the leading portraitists of the day. His mother's death and a long bout of illness interrupted this training and unsettled a never very stable character. At the age of twenty-one Salt found himself living in cheap lodgings off the Haymarket, earning a few guineas from his friends and acquaintance when he could persuade them to commission a portrait, but facing the future with no great enthusiasm and little hope of succeeding in a profession for which he had been so ill prepared.

A year or so before this, Salt's uncle had introduced him to George, Viscount Valentia (afterwards Lord Mountnorris). In 1802 Lord Valentia was planning a tour of India and the East. Salt on an impulse suggested he should go with him as his secretary and draughtsman. Lord Valentia was somewhat taken aback, but on reflection decided he might do worse than accept the offer. So in June of that year Salt set off on what proved to be a voyage of discovery, no less of his own potentialities than of some hitherto uncharted regions east and south of Suez.

They were away for nearly four and a half years. (That effectively disposes of the legend, perhaps attributable to Dickens or his father, that Salt befriended Belzoni soon after his arrival in England.) In India Lord Valentia and his *protégé* were cordially received by the Governor General, the Marquess Wellesley. He gave them facilities to see the country and commissioned Salt to make a number of sketches. Wellesley was particularly interested in the idea of promoting trade between India and Abyssinia. So in 1804 he arranged for Lord Valentia to explore the Red Sea coast of Africa in the cruiser *Antelope*. But the commander proved difficult and some of the crew deserted; one of them was a sailor named Pearce, of whom we shall hear again. Lord Valentia and his suite could do no more than return to Bombay with their mission unaccomplished.

Six months later they were given another ship and a more agreeable commander. At Massawa Salt left the *Panther* and went up-country in charge of a small party. He was entertained by the Ras of Tigré, who sent him clotted cream at midnight and presented his compliments at four in the morning. At his departure Salt was handed letters and presents addressed to the King of England by the Emperor of Abyssinia. Thus at the age of twenty-five the indifferent portrait-painter suddenly found himself possessed of an unexpected degree of initiative, an interest in Africa and its ancient civilizations and a taste for upholding the British flag in remote corners of the world. He had also improved as a landscape artist.

Back in London Salt wrote up his Abyssinian Journal, which was eventually published in Lord Valentia's *Voyages and Travels*. In addition he was kept busy preparing illustrations for his patron's book and the drawings for his own *Twenty-four Views*. Meanwhile the Foreign Office decided that the Emperor's letters and presents must be reciprocated. Salt, with his experience of the country, was obviously the man for the job. In 1809 he was sent out on a second mission with instructions from Canning 'to ascertain the present state of the Abyssinian trade', and to follow Lord Valentia's example 'in endeavouring, by every means in his power, to cultivate the friendship of the different tribes on the coast of the Red Sea', while being 'particularly careful not to engage an unnecessary number of attendants; nor to incur any other expense . . . than such as may be absolutely requisite'.

Salt was not allowed to visit the Emperor's Court at Gondar because of the troubled state of the country. But his friend the Ras of Tigré welcomed him like a long-lost brother and they had many convivial occasions together. The Ras was devoted to Salt. Months later he wrote to him in London, earnestly inquiring about his health. The letter was written in a mixture of modern Amharic and liturgical Geez, the classical language of Ethiopia. Translated, it read: 'How art thou, my dear Mr. Sawelt? I am most happy that thou hast returned safe. Heaven is with thee: earth is with thee. How art thou, Hinorai Sawelt? Peace be to thee, and may the peace of the Lord be with thee! Above all things, how art thou, my friend Hinorai Sawelt? . . .'

The British Government, if perhaps less lyrical than the Ras, at any rate seemed pleased with Salt's mission, though it produced no very tangible results. They gave him a thousand pounds for his services over the two years and the publishers F. C. and J. Rivington promised him a minimum of eight hundred pounds for his book, *A Voyage to Abyssinia*. Work on this kept him busy till the summer of 1814.

It was in the following April that he heard of Missett's resignation. Salt had passed through Egypt on his way home after his first visit to Abyssinia and nothing now seemed more congenial in prospect than the post of consul general in Cairo. There he would be able to indulge his antiquarian interests to the full, he could maintain contact with Abyssinia, and he would have the satisfaction of being his country's chief representative in a growing sphere of British influence. Salt at once began to canvass support; the Right Honourable Charles Yorke,[1] Sir Joseph Banks and the Viscount Valentia were all asked to write to the Foreign Secretary and put forward his name. The outcome was not long in doubt. In just over a fortnight Salt heard that Lord Castlereagh had approved his appointment.[2]

Salt was now thirty-five. He was tall and manly in appearance, but for one who had chosen to make his career in Africa and the Middle East his constitution was not particularly robust. Patchy health made him active and indolent by turns. He was given to sudden moods of optimism and equally sudden bouts of depression; the psychologists would call him now a cyclothymic type. As consul general he was an improvement on Missett; Muhammad Ali respected him, and his transference of the consulate from Alexandria to Cairo brought him nearer to the Pasha and made his status almost ambassadorial. But Salt's irresolution and his old habit of procrastination often robbed him of the initiative when faced with a man like Drovetti. Emotionally, he was rather immature. His long friendship with Lord Valentia was perhaps the most satisfying of all his personal relationships. Salt had a weakness for a pretty face, and the thought of Egypt and what his biographer calls 'the great want of reputable female society in that country' impelled him to seek a wife before he left England. He fell in love with a young woman in Birmingham; she had looks and money, but her father not unnaturally disliked the idea of his only daughter

4. A MOSQUE NEAR ROSETTA

5. GRAND CAIRO FROM THE CITADEL

6. HENRY SALT

7. BERNARDINO DROVETTI

8. JOHN LEWIS BURCKHARDT

9. GIOVANNI BATTISTA BELZONI

going off to Egypt and opposed the match. Salt did not give up hope for some time after he had gone abroad, but his own too honest descriptions of life in Cairo finally discouraged the girl herself. How far this personal disappointment affected his work it is hard to say, but it certainly cast a shadow over the prospect that had once seemed so bright.

Salt's other trouble was money. He had originally understood that the post was worth about seventeen hundred pounds; in fact, his salary was less than fifteen hundred. There were no allowance scales. Salt spent over two thousand pounds on his kit and the voyage out, yet by June 1816, when he had been in Egypt nearly three months, he had received not quite two hundred pounds of his salary. At first he stayed in 'a small tower at Boulak belonging to Boghoz Yusuff'—probably the same ramshackle building in which the Belzonis lived for a time. 'This house,' says Salt, 'was a perfect oven; the sun glaring full upon the only windows we had in front for ten hours, and the kitchen at the back supplying us with almost an equal quantity of hot air.' In August the Pasha gave Salt a requisition order for a house in Cairo. It was a large, rambling place, with coloured marble floors and painted ceilings in the principal rooms—the whole eminently suitable for a consulate, but in a very bad state of repair. By the end of the year Salt reckoned he had spent two hundred and fifty pounds on putting it in order and needed half as much again to finish the work. He had paid Colonel Missett four hundred pounds for furniture and the same sum had gone on other essential items to make the place habitable. Apart from this initial outlay there was fifty pounds a year to pay for rent. Then there was the upkeep of a minimum establishment consisting of a cook, a steward, two footmen and a gardener, two janissaries, three horses and their grooms, a camel to fetch water from the Nile, a bullock for the garden and the mill, a water-carrier, a washerwoman and an odd-job man. With the expenses of a London-based secretary on top of this, Salt realized that his total income would barely meet his outgoings. There would certainly be no opportunity to save. To make matters worse his salary then —in December 1816—was three quarters in arrears. Only the kindness of Samuel Briggs, the senior English merchant in Alexandria, saved the new consul general from acute embarrassment.[3]

Salt had plenty to occupy his mind during those first few months in Cairo. His official duties, however, were not particularly heavy. Mr. Lee, the Levant Company's consul in Alexandria, attended to the ships' captains and their problems. There was only a small English colony in Cairo, though an increasing number of foreigners sought the protection of the British flag. Politically there seemed to be nothing more urgent than the Pasha's often-expressed wish to send an Egyptian corvette round the Cape to Suez; Salt saw no harm in this and eventually Lord Castlereagh agreed that the British Government had no objection. The consul therefore was free to devote himself to the interest most near his heart, so far as his financial worries and disappointment in love would let him.

Before Salt left England Sir Joseph Banks had urged him to use the unique opportunities of his office to collect antiquities and curiosities for the British Museum, of which Sir Joseph was a Trustee. Salt had also promised to collect for his patron, who in 1816 succeeded to the title of Lord Mountnorris, and for his young son, the new Lord Valentia, who was interested in coins. Then William Hamilton was still at the Foreign Office as Under Secretary of State; his *Ægyptiaca*,[4] published in 1809, remained the most complete and accurate guide to the antiquities, apart from the Napoleonic *Description*. Salt looked forward to an agreeable correspondence with him on new discoveries in this field. Lastly, as if to set the seal of approval on all consular burrowings and excavation, Salt had been asked to look for other pieces of the Rosetta Stone and monumental inscriptions generally. A Foreign Office memorandum of August 1815 stated confidently that 'whatever might be the expense of the undertaking, whether successful or otherwise, it would be most cheerfully supported by an enlightened nation, eager to anticipate its Rivals in the prosecution of the best interests of science and literature'.[5] Salt was to learn from bitter experience how falsely optimistic that was.

But in March 1816 he was all eagerness to begin the search. Even as he landed at Alexandria he saw gangs of men levelling the mounds outside the walls as part of a scheme to improve the fortifications; 'hundreds of poor devils of Arabs and buffaloes' were 'removing heaps of rubbish from place to place without any system, and thus reducing one hill only to form another'. Salt was at first hopeful that 'some good might result from laying bare the antiquities concealed under these masses of ruins', but after examining the ground he decided that there was little chance 'of any valuable discovery resulting from their labours, as they seem to content themselves with merely breaking up the surface, and this they pulverize so completely with the rude machines employed on the occasion, that it must be something very hard indeed which can resist being broken to pieces by their clumsiness'.

On his way up to Cairo Salt stopped at Sa el-Hagar and saw there a granite sarcophagus which the *fellahin* had recently dug up. Later he wrote to Hamilton saying that he agreed with the latter's identification of the place as the site of the ancient Sais. He described and drew the sarcophagus and said that the inscription on it seemed to confirm Dr. Young's idea that Egyptian hieroglyphics were meant to be read from the side to which the animal and human figures looked. Thomas Young, author of *The Undulatory Theory of Light* and an extraordinary polymath, had retired to Worthing in the summer of 1814 to work on the decipherment of the Rosetta Stone.

Salt's letter was written on 18 June from that uncomfortable old house in Bulaq. The plague, true to form, had just ceased. Shaikh Ibrahim had come back a few days before, 'as black as a negro, from Mount Sinai'. And it was probably in the next day or two that he introduced to the consul general a gigantic Italian who claimed British nationality and said he had been badly let down over a contract he had had to build a water-wheel for the Pasha.

A strong bond of sympathy had been forged between Burckhardt and Belzoni in their irregular meetings during the previous twelve months. The two men had much in common. Both had been uprooted by the Napoleonic invasions. Both had come to England in their youth. Both were being driven by some compelling force, away from the known and familiar, towards the distant and unattainable. They had the same single-mindedness of purpose, the same disregard for physical comfort, the same urge to cover large tracts of country—both real and metaphorical—by their own unaided efforts. Burckhardt had been dedicated for years; Belzoni was just about to find the true direction of his life.

Three years before, on his first visit to Upper Egypt, Burckhardt had spent a few days in the neighbourhood of Thebes. On the west bank of the river, in a ruined temple which the French *savants*, following Strabo, called the Memnonium, and Diodorus Siculus knew as the Tomb of Ozymandias, he had seen a colossal granite head of great beauty. William Hamilton had described it in his book as 'certainly the most beautiful and perfect piece of Egyptian sculpture that can be seen throughout the whole country'. He and his companions, Captain Leake and Major Hayes, had been 'struck with its extraordinary delicacy' and 'the very uncommon expression visible in its features'.

The peasants of Qurna told Burckhardt that the French had tried to take the head away. Apparently they had even drilled a hole in the right breast of the statue, though whether to blow off the lower part of the bust with a charge or for the purpose of attaching a hawser it is not easy to say.[6] At any rate they gave up the attempt. The Young Memnon was left still smiling its inscrutable smile.

Burckhardt, though art and archaeology were not his primary interests, had often thought of trying to move the head himself. He suggested the Pasha might like to send it as a gift to the Prince Regent, but Muhammad Ali could not believe that the King of England's son would thank him for a mere stone. When William John Bankes, a Dorsetshire squire, former M.P. and friend of Byron's, came out to Egypt in the winter of 1815-16,[7] Burckhardt discussed the project with him. Bankes saw the head later during his visit to Upper Egypt, but nothing more was done about it.

Clearly, to move a block of stone weighing seven or eight tons, to transport it over soft sand and load it into a boat seemed to call for a degree of mechanical skill and the kind of tackle or equipment that it would not be easy to find in Egypt. Yet it is likely that when Belzoni first heard of the head his interest in it was only remote. He may have promised to do something about it one day, but for the moment he was too preoccupied with the water-wheel. The disastrous end to a whole year's endeavour woke him sharply to the realities of the situation. He had very little money left and was probably even in debt, for Burckhardt says he had five months' pay still owing to him. 'So much for the Pasha's encouragement of European artists. They are enticed into his service by his emissaries in the Mediterranean, but are soon left to bewail their credulity.'[8] Belzoni's position was indeed desperate. He had a wife to support and a boy with a broken leg to look after; there was small chance of employment in Egypt and no prospects elsewhere.

Then he remembered the head. We can imagine his rushing off to see Burckhardt, as soon as he heard of his return, and offering to go at once to bring the Young Memnon from Thebes. Burckhardt could not afford to finance the project alone; he had very little to manage on himself. The only man who could help—and indeed was bound to help Belzoni—was the new consul general. They went round to see Salt and put the proposition before him. He, as we have seen, had financial troubles of his own, but his credit was good and, after all, he had been asked to collect antiquities. He knew of the head from Hamilton's own book and he heard Shaikh Ibrahim's enthusiastic description. He was impressed by the Italian's engaging manner and complete confidence in himself. If the consul showed any hesitation it was probably because he had so many problems on his mind and did not want to be rushed into anything. But he presently agreed to the project and ten days later —on 28 June—Belzoni received his written instructions.

Giovanni's own account of his commissioning is not to be trusted. It was written after his quarrel with Salt, when relations between the two men had been strained to breaking-point by mutual jealousy and suspicion. Belzoni is at pains in *Narrative* to suggest that he had frequently discussed the project with Burckhardt and had told Salt, even before the failure of the water-wheel, that he would be 'happy to undertake the removal of the bust, without the smallest view of interest, as it was to go to the British Museum'. He says airily that after losing the Pasha's contract he found he had just enough money to make a trip up the Nile to Aswan and back. He hired a boat and then, as 'Mahomet Ali was always ready to give a firman [authority] to any one who asked for it', he casually asked the consul to get him one when he called to announce his departure. He goes on: 'It has been erroneously stated, that I was regularly employed by Mr. Salt, the consul-general of his Britannic majesty in Egypt, for the purpose of bringing the colossal bust from Thebes to Alexandria. I positively deny that I was ever engaged by him in any shape whatever, either by words or writing'. This was the first of several foolish quibbles into which Belzoni was led by his own passionate conviction that Salt had tried to steal the glory from him. When this denial appeared in print, Salt was driven to making 'A Plain Statement of Facts',[9] which, however, was not published until after his death. In it he says that 'the firmaun from the Pasha, for liberty of excavation, &c. expressly states Mr. Belzoni to be *a person employed by me*'.

The truth is that the instructions, on the business side, were remarkably vague. In the first place Giovanni was 'requested to prepare the necessary implements' for moving the head before he left Bulaq. He was then to proceed as quickly as possible to Asyut and there deliver his letters to Muhammad Ali's son, Ibrahim Pasha, or whoever might be left in charge of the government of Upper Egypt. He was to consult with Dr. Scotto, Ibrahim's private physician, about boats and workmen, and then continue his journey to Thebes.

Next came instructions about finding and identifying the head. It was not to be confused with another that was much mutilated. Belzoni was to 'spare no expense or trouble' in removing the head to the banks of the Nile. If necessary, he should wait for the river to rise before attempting to get it into the boat. On no account must he move the head if there was any serious risk of injuring it or losing it in the Nile. Then followed this paragraph:

> Mr. Belzoni will have the goodness to keep a separate account of the expenses incurred in this undertaking, which, as well as his other expenses, will gladly be reimbursed; as, from the knowledge of Mr. Belzoni's character, it is confidently believed they will be as reasonable as circumstances will allow.

Later Giovanni was to point triumphantly to the fact that there was no mention anywhere of payment for his services. That, he argued, was proof that he was not 'employed' by the consul. It was unfortunate for all concerned that a strict business arrangement was not made at the start. But Salt, no doubt, thought he was doing more than his duty by a foreigner who claimed British protection when he undertook to pay all his expenses for the next few months. Belzoni accepted the commission with a light heart and clearly did not think about the matter at all. The consul gave him a further thousand piastres—about £25—to buy what antiquities he could; it was not specified whether these were for Salt himself or for Lord Mountnorris or the British Museum. Belzoni thought—or later pretended to think—that they were all for the national collection. But he must have been excited at the prospect of finding himself with a free hand to excavate and carry away whatever he liked in a country so prodigal of its treasures. Boat-loads of statues and sarcophagi would soon come floating down the Nile—to end up in the British Museum bearing the name of Belzoni, who would be suitably enriched for his services to art and science. Giovanni, rising ebulliently out of the depression into which the fate of his water-wheel had thrown him, saw illusory fame and fortune once again within his grasp.

When Burckhardt wrote to Hamilton a few days later—the latter was also Secretary of the African Association—he told him that Belzoni had had 'proper machines' made at Bulaq for the transport of the head. Obviously he had not seen them, for the only equipment Giovanni was able to secure was of the simplest and most primitive kind. It consisted of fourteen roughly-squared baulks of timber, four rollers that were merely sections of palm-tree, and some palm-tree fibre ropes. This gear was placed aboard a boat at Bulaq—the cheapest Belzoni could hire. Probably it was a single-masted *kanjia* with a huge lateen sail furled to a thin antenna-like yard and a small raised cabin in the stern. It had a *reis* and a crew of five. Sarah was to go with Giovanni and there was the lad James, still recovering from a broken leg, and a Copt interpreter who had been in the French army and was over-fond of liquor.

They left Bulaq on Sunday, 30 June. As they slid past the ugly line of warehouses and the mouldering mansions of the rich, past the green gardens of Roda, the Coptic churches of Old Cairo and the kiosks of Giza, Giovanni must have felt he had been too long stifled in the oppressive air of Cairo. Seldom in his life had he spent twelve months in one place. When the crew ceased poling and the great white sail filled with the north wind and the boat skimmed like a swallow over the first broad reach beyond the city, we can imagine that Giovanni felt pure joy. This was life, this was movement, this was adventure.

Belzoni tells us little about the journey to Asyut. But we cannot suppose he was insensible to the fascinating scene that unwound itself on either side of the river, like Barker's Panorama in Leicester Square, for which Salt's sketches of Cairo had once been the inspiration. Each day was like another, and each day the living frieze of figures on the bank repeated itself—the lean, brown labourer with his hoe, naked but for a loin-cloth; the hard-featured women, be-henna'd and tattooed, with breasts flapping loose under their gaping galabiyas; slim young girls carrying water from the river in jars upon their heads; patient donkeys; scrawny, flea-bitten, disdainful camels; and the great purple gamoose.

On the evening of the fifth day they reached Manfalut. There they met Ibrahim Pasha, who was on his way to Cairo. Giovanni presented his letters, but was told to deliver them to the Daftardar Bey or Treasurer, who had been left in authority at Asyut. With the Pasha was Drovetti, the former French consul general. He had been making what was thought to be a final tour of Upper Egypt in order to complete his collection of antiquities. Salt saw the collection a few months later when he was visiting Alexandria. He knew Drovetti intended to dispose of it and tried to persuade him to offer it to the British Museum. Salt thought he was likely to ask three or four thousand pounds and in a letter to Lord Mountnorris he expressed his doubts whether the British Museum could afford such a sum.[10]

There is no reason to suppose that at the time of this chance meeting there was any bad blood between Belzoni and Drovetti. After all, it was not the fault of the Piedmontese that the water-wheel failed to satisfy the Pasha. Giovanni had in fact been generously helped by Drovetti, though he may have blamed him for not using his influence more to obtain some compensation for him. Giovanni writes coolly of this meeting in the knowledge of later events. He says Drovetti made him a present of a granite sarcophagus lid. The only snag was that it was still in a tomb at Qurna. Drovetti had not been able to get it out himself and Belzoni was welcome to it if he could. For cheerful good measure Drovetti added that the Arabs at Thebes were refusing to work.

The following afternoon the Belzonis arrived in Asyut, which lies about two hundred and fifty miles from Cairo. The Daftardar Bey was not there, but was expected to return in two or three days' time. Giovanni called on Dr. Scotto, Ibrahim's Genoese physician, and found him charmingly dissuasive. It would be difficult, he said, to get permits for the workmen, there were simply no boats to be hired and, after all, what was the bust but a mere piece of stone, not worth the trouble of taking away? Deprecatingly the doctor piled an enormous mound of obstacles between Giovanni and his goal, then bluntly told him not to meddle in the matter at all. What private vested interests Scotto had we do not know, but probably like most other European residents in the country he found the antiquities a profitable side-line.[11] Belzoni soon saw that he could expect no help from this quarter. He bade the doctor good-bye and began to make arrangements on his own.

Asyut was then, as now, the largest town in Upper Egypt. It was the point from which the slave caravans departed for the Sudan and the market to which they brought their human merchandise. It was here in 1814 that Captain Henry Light was offered 'a young well formed negress, about seventeen years old, for the trifling sum of rather more than fifteen pounds sterling'.[12] And that was just after most of a caravan had been lost in the desert. The year before, Mr. Thomas Legh, M.P., and his friend the Reverend Charles Smelt had found prices even lower. 'Girls whose virginity was secured by means more powerful than moral restraint were valued at 500 piastres . . . Female slaves who could not boast of this advantage were in general sold for 300 piastres; but if they had lived in a Frank family, and had learned to sew, wash, and wait at table, their value was estimated in the market at Cairo at 700 piastres.'[13]

Giovanni had time while he was waiting to explore the amphitheatre of hills behind the town. Here he saw some of the rock-cut tombs of the ancient Siowt, chief seat of the worship of Apwat, a deity akin to the jackal-headed Anubis, after whom the Greeks called the town Lycopolis—'Wolf-city'. Belzoni says that only two of the tombs were worth seeing. One of them must have been the tomb prepared for Hepzefa, governor of Asyut in the reign of Senusret I (c. 2000 B.C.). But Hepzefa died on foreign service in the Sudan and was buried near the Third Cataract. His unused rock-cut tomb is the largest we know of belonging to the Middle Kingdom. Denon thought it remarkably fine, though Belzoni found it 'decayed' and disappointing.

When the temporary modern governor of Asyut had returned— several days late—Giovanni showed him the *firman* from the Pasha. He at once gave him an order to the Kashif of Armant, the Turkish official who had jurisdiction over the *fellahin* of Thebes. The party set off again—their numbers now increased by a Greek carpenter from Asyut—and reached Dendera on 18 July.

The great temple of Hathor at Dendera—the Tentyra of the Greeks —impressed most nineteenth-century travellers on the Nile. 'I could not expect to find anything in Egypt more complete, more perfect, than Tentyra', was Denon's rapturous judgment, while to Hamilton and his companions, after seeing 'innumerable monuments of the same kind throughout the Thebaid', it seemed that they had now arrived at 'the highest pitch of architectural excellence that was ever attained on the borders of the Nile'. Modern taste is much more critical of this late Ptolemaic and Roman building that belongs to an age less remote in time from our own than it was from that of Cheops.[14] It is only in its mass and because of its excellent state of preservation that the temple of Dendera still impresses. Compare its sculptured reliefs with those of the temple of Seti I at Abydos, which are more than a thousand years older. The Dendera figures are clumsy and commonplace beside the delicately flowing lines of Seti's artists. But Belzoni's contemporaries had as yet no perspective of Egyptian art and architecture; they saw nothing remarkable in the few reliefs then visible above the encroaching sand at Abydos. Until the problem of the language was solved, until the world had some idea of the vast length of Egyptian history, men were understandably at a loss to appreciate the ancient civilization of the Nile. They could only say with Hamilton of the infinite sculptured scenes at Dendera that, while it was difficult 'to attach any distinct meaning to them', it was certain that they were 'the records of a great and learned and wise people'.

Within the limits of the knowable, what then did Belzoni know about ancient Egypt? We can be sure that he set out from Cairo with no great impedimenta of learning. It is equally certain that, three or four years later, when he came to write his book, he possessed a considerable knowledge of his subject. It is true that he fell into most of the errors of his time and some of his own suppositions were wildly absurd. But he had acquired a unique practical experience in the field and had more than a nodding acquaintance with the authorities. Salt, we know, had a set of the great French *Description de l'Égypte*—or, at least, as many of the volumes as were then available; Giovanni must have thumbed them over in the consulate. Then Salt would be bound to have a copy of William Hamilton's *Ægyptiaca*; Belzoni clearly knew it well. *Narrative* also shows his familiarity with Vivant Denon's *Voyage dans la Basse et la Haute Égypte*.[15] Earlier travellers that he mentions, whose works he may have found in Salt's library, are Norden, Pococke and Bruce. Of the ancients he seems to have been best acquainted with Herodotus; as he had no Greek, he was probably dependent either on the English version by Littlebury (1737) or on the French translation by Larcher, published in 1786. And at some time certainly during his travels Belzoni had in his possession D'Anville's map of Egypt.[16]

An hour's sailing beyond Dendera brought them to the busy, bustling town of Qena. This was an *entrepôt* for the trade with India *via* the Red Sea port of Qusair and a staging-point for pilgrims to Mecca. Here too was the manufacture of those large ochrous water-coolers that Giovanni and Sarah had seen so often arriving on the quay at Bulaq. Inverted and lashed together with palm-fibre ropes, the jars floated down the river, a buoyant, unsinkable raft. The firing of these pots was such a tricky business, according to Hamilton, that generally three hundred out of a thousand were broken. Sir Frederick Henniker observes that 'Kenneh is also famous for other frail goods, and is one of the very few places in Egypt where a Franc may see licensed ladies without being bastonaded'.[17]

They reached Luxor on 22 July, just three weeks and a day after leaving Cairo. Giovanni, who had made a creditable effort at describing Dendera, here gave up the unequal struggle. 'I beg the reader to observe,' he says, 'that but very imperfect ideas can be formed of the extensive ruins of Thebes, even from the accounts of the most skilful and accurate travellers. . . . It appeared to me like entering a city of giants, who, after a long conflict, were all destroyed, leaving the ruins of their various temples as the only proofs of their former existence. The temple at Luxor presents to the traveller at once one of the most splendid groups of Egyptian grandeur. The extensive propylaeon, with the two obelisks, and colossal statues in the front; the thick groups of enormous columns; the variety of apartments and the sanctuary it contains; the beautiful ornaments which adorn every part of the walls and columns, described by Mr. Hamilton; cause in the astonished traveller an oblivion of all that he has seen before. If his attention be attracted to the north side of Thebes by the towering remains, that project a great height above the wood of palm trees, he will gradually enter that forest-like assemblage of ruins of temples, columns, obelisks, colossi, sphynxes, portals, and an endless number of other astonishing objects, that will convince him at once of the impossibility of a description. On the west side of the Nile, still the traveller finds himself among wonders. The temples of Gournou, Memnonium, and Medinet Aboo, attest the extent of the great city on this side. The unrivalled colossal figures in the plains of Thebes, the number of tombs excavated in the rocks, those in the great valley of the kings, with their paintings, sculptures, mummies, sarcophagi, figures, &c. are all objects worthy of the admiration of the traveller, who will not fail to wonder how a nation, which was once so great as to erect these stupendous edifices, could so far fall into oblivion, that even their language and writing are totally unknown to us.'

Belzoni had time for no more than a cursory glance at Karnak and Luxor before he crossed over to the western side of the Nile. A track led across the cultivation in front of the two seated Colossi on the plain. These once monolithic statues of Amenhetep III, now cracked and eroded or crudely restored, are almost all that is left of that Pharaoh's magnificent mortuary temple. Merenptah, the son and successor of Ramses II, aping his father's unfortunate habit of appropriating other men's memorials, used the temple as a quarry for his own. The statues survived, but the name of the Pharaoh was forgotten. Then somehow the Colossi came to be identified by the Greeks with the Homeric hero Memnon—son of Tithonus and the Dawn—who led his Ethiopians to aid the besieged Trojans and was killed by Achilles. In 27 B.C. an earthquake threw down the upper part of the northern statue; thereafter, till the Emperor Septimius Severus botched it up with sandstone blocks about A.D. 200, the figure was reputed to utter a gentle, melancholy sound at dawn—the vanquished hero saluting his ever-youthful mother. Tourists came from all over the Roman world to hear the 'vocal Memnon' and many of them recorded their remarks on the legs and feet of the statue.[18]

The Greeks added to the confusion when they gave the name 'Memnonium' to another mortuary temple—that of Ramses II—in which there were three colossal statues. So it was known to Strabo the geographer,[19] but Diodorus Siculus the historian[20] calls it the Tomb of Osymandias—which is a Greek corruption of User-maat-Re, one of the other names of Ramses II. Diodorus probably never saw the temple; however, his description of the first two courts is fairly accurate. He says that one of the colossal monolithic statues near the entrance was the largest in all Egypt. 'This piece,' he adds, 'is not only remarkable for its size, but admirable for the way in which it is cut and worked and for the excellent quality of the stone. Large as it is, there is not the slightest flaw or blemish to be found. It bears this inscription: "My name is Osymandias, king of kings; if any would know how great I am, and where I lie, let him surpass me in any of my works." ' Finally—to make confusion worse confounded—Diodorus appears to say that all these statues were made by Memnon of Syene!

We need not worry much about this mythical monumental mason of Aswan. The corrupt text of Diodorus merely conceals the statement that the statues came from the famous granite quarries near the First Cataract. All three represented the Pharaoh Ramses II, the Sesostris[21] of the Greeks. The largest now lies shattered and defaced as it did when Norden and Pococke, Hamilton and Denon saw it, toppled from its throne, in the ruined First Court of the Ramesseum. Originally the seated figure must have been about 57 feet high; it measured 22½ feet across the shoulders. The forefinger is 3½ feet long and a finger-nail 7½ inches. Yet in mere height the statue fell short of the two Colossi on the plain. They, when their crowns were complete, would have been nearly 70 feet high. The weight of each has been computed at around nine hundred tons, but Osymandias, it is claimed, would have tipped the scale at over a thousand.

Probably this statue, too, was thrown down by the earthquake in 27 B.C. The head and part of the body are still in one piece, but the face has been obliterated and the Arabs have cut mill-stones from the granite. Hamilton clambered over the ruin, 'not without great difficulty and danger', using the hieroglyphs on the arm for footholds. Denon thought that one of the feet, which was almost intact, might easily be taken away to give people in Europe some idea of the scale of these vast monuments.

The other two statues stood in the Second Court, flanking the grand central staircase that led to the Hypostyle Hall. Both were seated effigies of the king, smaller but hardly less majestic than the colossus in the forecourt. Now they lay shattered on the ground, dismembered like Osiris, their fragments intermingled. The right-hand head was badly mutilated; that on the left—lying face downwards, it would seem, in Norden's day[22]—had miraculously escaped injury except for its broken crown. This was the 'Young' Memnon, whose youthful beauty had fascinated the French and roused the admiration of Hamilton and Burckhardt. Other travellers, too, had looked at it in envy and wondered whether they could take it away. Captain Light in 1814 was only put off by consideration of the expense. 'There would have been no difficulty,' he says confidently, 'for the inhabitants were well disposed to assist me in any thing I wished to do, with the promise of reward.'[23]

Belzoni's first thought, as he entered the ruins, was to find the head. He had little time to spare for the colossus in the forecourt and none at all for the sculptured reliefs on the pylons and inner walls of the temple. The epic battle of Kadesh, Ramses charging the Hittite host, the enemy in full retreat across the river, and the poor King of Aleppo held upside down by his friends to get rid of the water he had swallowed during his ducking in the Orontes—these vigorous but repetitive scenes, boringly re-enacted wherever this vainglorious Pharaoh found a suitable expanse of wall, meant nothing, indeed could not mean anything to Belzoni and his contemporaries, who had never even heard of Ramses or of the battle of Kadesh.[24]

Yet the engineer in Belzoni could not fail to be impressed by the skill of the ancient Egyptians, who had floated a sixty-foot colossus down the Nile from Aswan and set it up here, with no other means than the lever and the inclined plane, in honour of Memnon—'or Sesostris, or Osymandias, or Phamenoph,[25] or perhaps some other king of Egypt; for such are the various opinions of its origin, and so many names have been given to it, that at last it has no name at all'.

Giovanni found the head of the Young Memnon lying, as he tells us, 'near the remains of its body and chair, with its face upwards, and apparently smiling on me, at the thought of being taken to England'. He was surprised at its beauty, but not at its size. And for the moment the practical aspect of the matter dominated all others.

Belzoni's first task was to establish himself on the site. A corner of a portico was walled off with loosely-piled stones to give Sarah and himself some privacy. Their things were brought from the boat and they quickly settled in. Giovanni says—perhaps a little too readily—that 'Mrs. Belzoni had by this time accustomed herself to travel, and was equally indifferent with myself about accommodations'. Poor Sarah, she had not much choice!

Giovanni then surveyed the ground between the temple and the river. The Nile was already rising fast—it was nearly the end of July —and he judged that in another month's time the inundation would reach the 'Memnonium'. The water would be too shallow to take a boat of suitable draught and, in any case, there was no tackle to lift the head over the side. He had to reach the bank, therefore, before the river rose above it. Any delay might mean the operation would have to be postponed till the following year.

Accordingly, while the Greek carpenter set about making a crude sledge or platform from the baulks of timber that had been brought from Bulaq, Giovanni went off to Armant—a town some twelve or thirteen miles south of Luxor—to arrange for the hiring of labour. The Kashif, or district governor, welcomed him 'with that invariable politeness which is peculiar to the Turks, even when they do not mean in the slightest degree to comply with your wishes'. Giovanni showed him the *firman* from the Daftardar Bey at Asyut. 'He received it reverently, and promised to do every thing in his power to get the Arabs to work; but observed that, at the present season, they were all occupied, and it would be better to wait till after the inundation of the Nile.'

That was only the first gambit in the Turk's repertoire. When Giovanni said he had seen many idle Arabs in the villages who would surely be glad of a chance to earn some money, the Kashif replied that they would rather starve than undertake such an arduous task without the help of Muhammad and the high Nile. Then, it was almost the time of Ramadan and the men would not work during the fast. Next, they were all working for the Pasha in the fields and could not be taken off the job. . . . Giovanni was very patient, and finally told the governor he would get the men himself. The Kashif said he would send his brother the next day to see if any men could be found. Giovanni answered that he would rely on this and promised the governor a present if he carried out the Pasha's orders. That ended the first game.

The following morning not one man turned up at the temple. Giovanni waited till nine o'clock, then mounted a camel and rode over to Armant. He found the Kashif unconcernedly giving directions for the building of a tomb for a local saint. Giovanni knew better than to utter a single reproach. He said he had come over for a coffee and a friendly pipe with the governor. Nothing loth, the Turk invited him to sit down. At the appropriate moment Belzoni produced a two-pound bag of coffee and a quantity of gunpowder. It was only when these had been gratefully accepted by the governor that Giovanni tactfully steered the conversation in the direction of the previous day's topic. This time he used a judicious mixture of threat and promise, and eventually the Kashif gave him a signed order for the Qaimaqam[26] of Qurna, instructing him to supply the necessary men. Giovanni delivered the order the same evening and awaited results.

But again the next day no workmen reported for duty. The Qaimaqam, a swaggering Albanian lieutenant-colonel, had for a long time been engaged in collecting antiquities for Drovetti. He was very off-hand when Giovanni went round to see him. There were no men available that day, he said; he would see what he could do the next day or the day after. It was all the more galling in that there were groups of Arabs hanging about the temple the whole time. They were only too willing to be taken on, but did not dare offer themselves for work without permission from the Kashif or the Qaimaqam. Finally—to add insult to injury—the governor of Armant sent over a soldier to inquire whether Belzoni still wanted any labour!

At last, on the Saturday morning, a few men came over from the Kashif. Others from Qurna quickly volunteered as soon as they saw that the work was permitted. Belzoni lined them up and told them they would get thirty paras a day, i.e. about fourpence-halfpenny, or half as much again as they were paid for their labour in the fields. (Seventy years later the standard rate of pay for labourers working under Quibell in the Ramesseum was still only two piastres, the equivalent then of fivepence.)[27]

The Arabs were convinced that 'Caphany'—the Granite One, as they called the Young Memnon—could not be moved. However, they had no objection to taking money from a crazy Frank who only wanted in exchange a large stone. There were some, of course, who said that there was gold inside it—the age-old Arab dream of hidden treasure. When they saw Belzoni writing in a notebook, they were sure he was working a charm to conjure it forth.

Giovanni's plan was very simple. The carpenter had made him a kind of open frame or grid by fastening together several baulks of timber at right angles. The first step was to lever up the head with poles so that the 'car', as Giovanni calls it, could be introduced beneath it. Then, with more levering from the other side, the head was slid into position on the car. How far Giovanni lent his own great strength to the task he does not say—he chose to be reticent on such matters—but we can imagine him perhaps seizing a pole from a group of ineffectual Arabs and reducing them all to astonished silence or bated cries of 'Mashallah!

Mashallah!' with a superb and easy display of force applied at the right spot. Then the process had to be repeated. The car, with the head firmly secured upon it, was raised at the front to admit a roller. Three more were introduced and the car was mobile. Four drag-ropes were attached to the frame and all was ready for the long haul to the river.

Indeed, that first day—Saturday, 27 July—the head moved forward several yards, and Giovanni sent off an Arab to Cairo with the news that Memnon had begun his journey to England. It must have been tricky work manœuvring him through the fallen stones and *débris* of the court. As the car advanced, inch by inch, two Arabs stood by to seize each roller the moment it became disengaged at the rear and so carry it round and lay it in the monster's path. The heat was terrific; it beat back from the stones of the temple till, in Giovanni's graphic phrase, the whole air was inflamed. He was too excited to think of the consequences of such exposure to the merciless Theban sun, and that night he began to suffer from heat-stroke. The portico he had chosen for their sleeping-quarters was far from cool and Giovanni spent a restless, disturbed night. But he was at work again early on Sunday morning, not sparing himself for a moment. That day they dragged the head clear of the temple and fifty yards further towards the river. Giovanni records that he had to break the bases of two pillars in order to get the car out. It is easy now to be too primly shocked at this. The aesthetic loss was slight and no archaeological evidence was destroyed. When the temple had already suffered so much damage, it would have seemed odd to scruple about causing a little more—especially with such a laudable object in view.

That night Belzoni was 'very poorly' indeed; his stomach rejected all food. When morning came he was too weak to stand. He had their possessions taken back to the boat in the hope that on the river at least the nights would be cooler. No progress was made that day, because Giovanni would not trust the Arabs to move the head without his supervision.

The grim struggle of the next few days is set down starkly in *Narrative*, which evidently at this point closely follows Belzoni's original notes.

On the 30th we continued the work, and the colossus advanced a hundred and fifty yards towards the Nile. I was a little better in the morning, but worse again in the evening.

On the 31st I was again a little better, but could not proceed as the road became so sandy, that the colossus sunk into the ground. I was therefore under the necessity of taking a long turn of above three hundred yards, to a new road. In the evening of this day I was much better.

On the 1st of August we still improved in our success, as we this day proceeded above three hundred yards. I was obliged to keep several men employed in making the road before us, as we went on with the head. The Irish lad that was with me, I sent to Cairo as he could not resist the climate; but what is singular, Mrs. Belzoni enjoyed tolerable health all the time. She was constantly among the women in the tombs, for all the Fellahs of Gournou make dwelling-places where the Egyptians had burial-places, as I shall have occasion to mention hereafter.

Poor James! Poor Sarah! It is difficult to know which to be the more sorry for. The boy must still have been feeling the after-effects of his accident and possibly the broken bone in his leg had not set properly. It was certainly a strange life for a lad who had entered the service of a strolling player, to find the crowded theatre and the noisy fair-ground now replaced by a silent, ruined temple, the friendly faces of London and Edinburgh exchanged for the dark, passionate look of the men who lived in the tombs. . . . Sarah of course was *heroic*. To endure the heat of Upper Egypt in August, to share the peculiar domesticities of the troglodyte women of Qurna, to have none of the amenities even a tour of the worst provincial circuit had provided, and to have a husband utterly indifferent to his own health and comfort, who took it for granted that his wife was equally tough—that was enough to make any woman wilt. Sarah not only stood up to the test but, as we shall see, took the greatest interest in the lives of the people about her. She was probably the first woman traveller in Egypt in modern times to penetrate so far south and she made the most of her opportunities. . . .

Belzoni's *Narrative* continues:

On the 2d the head advanced further; and I was in great hopes of passing a part of the land, to which the inundation would extend, previous to the water reaching that spot.

On the 3d we went on extremely well, and advanced nearly four hundred yards. We had a bad road on the 4th, but still we proceeded a good way. On the 5th we entered the land I was so anxious to pass over, for fear the water should reach it and arrest our course; and I was happy to think, that the next day would bring us out of danger.

But when Giovanni arrived on the site on the Tuesday morning there was nobody there except the guards and the carpenter. The Greek told him that the Qaimaqam had forbidden the *fellahin* to work any more for the Christian dogs. When Giovanni sent for the Albanian to demand

10. MOVING THE MEMNON HEAD

11. VIEW OF LUXOR

12. THE TEMPLE OF HORUS AT EDFU

an explanation, he was told that he had gone to Luxor. It was obvious what lay behind this manœuvre. In a few days' time the water of the rising Nile would reach the shallow depression where the head now rested. Once this happened the operation would have to be suspended for several months. That would give the French an opportunity to enter the field and the Albanian could expect a suitable reward from Drovetti.

There was no time to be lost. Giovanni crossed over to Luxor and sought out the Qaimaqam. He found him in an insolent, arrogant mood and the more he tried to cajole him with fair words and promises, the more impudent the fellow became. 'My patience was great,' says Giovanni, 'and I was determined that day to carry it to its utmost length: but there is a certain point, which, if exceeded, these people do not understand'. Finally the Albanian was foolish enough to lay hands on the Italian. Giovanni pushed him off and the Qaimaqam drew his sword. This was too much for Belzoni, who had suffered enough already from swashbuckling Albanians. He closed with the man, relieved him of his sword and a brace of pistols and pinned him against the wall with two great hands in the pit of his stomach. When all the breath and braggadocio had been squeezed out of him, Giovanni shook him like a rat.

That evening he arrived in Armant just before sunset. It was the time of Ramadan and the Kashif was preparing to break his fast with a large company of guests. He invited Belzoni to join them. A long carpet was stretched on the ground and the bowls and trays of food were placed on this. The meal began as soon as the sun had disappeared. Giovanni dipped discreetly in the communal dishes among the stretching arms and greasy fingers. Then, when pipes and coffee were served all round, he tackled the Kashif on the necessity of having workmen the next day.

The governor was bland but unconcerned. The *fellahin* had work in the fields for the Pasha and could not be spared. Next season, yes, the *khawaga* could have as many men as he liked. Giovanni rose to go; in that case, he said, he would get his labourers from Luxor. The Kashif remarked pointedly that Belzoni would have no need to fear on his night journey as he was armed with such *a fine pair of pistols*. Giovanni took the hint and promptly offered them as a present; probably they were the pair taken from the Qaimaqam. Then they sat down again and the Kashif put his hands on Giovanni's knees and said, 'We shall be friends.'

Giovanni left as soon as he had the Kashif's *firman* in his pocket. The boat travelled through the night and reached Qurna before dawn, after running against a submerged pier at Luxor and almost overturning. Giovanni sent at once for the Shaikh of Qurna and within an hour had the men back at work. That day they covered more ground than usual,

9

which Giovanni attributed to their being fresh after a day's enforced idleness. He was amazed at their energy, considering that it was Ramadan and they neither ate nor drank till after sunset.

On the following day—the 8th—the head was dragged clear of the danger area. 'On the 9th,' says Giovanni, 'I was seized with such a giddiness in my head, that I could not stand. The blood ran so copiously from my nose and mouth, that I was unable to continue the operation: I therefore postponed it to the next day.'

What a scene it conjures up! The sweating, half-naked Arabs hauling on the tow-ropes, chanting a work-song as the colossal head moved forward a few inches at a time; the endless shifting of the rollers under the car; the face of Memnon smiling inscrutably into the eye of the sun; and Giovanni standing there, overburdened with clothes, his head bursting in that terrible heat, anxiously watching every movement of the stone as it strained against its palm-fibre bonds, weighing the loss of time in every added yard against the risk of every unevenness in the path.

The end was undramatic, almost bathetic. 'On the 10th and 11th, we approached towards the river; and on the 12th, thank God, the young Memnon arrived on the bank of the Nile.' To celebrate the occasion and to show his appreciation, Giovanni gave each of his Arabs a bonus of sixpence.

During the next seventeen months, while the head was on its way to England, the story of Belzoni's activities slowly filtered through to a public that was becoming more and more interested in ancient Egypt. Towards the end of 1817 the wonder and speculation caused by travellers' tales of colossal statues broken in the dust, together with the news of the imminent arrival of a magnificent stone head for the British Museum, prompted a friendly contest between two poets on the theme of Osymandias. Horace Smith, a City business man, part-author of *Rejected Addresses*,[28] wrote a sonnet 'On A Stupendous Leg of Granite, Discovered standing by itself in the Deserts of Egypt, with the Inscription inscribed below'. It began:

> In Egypt's sandy silence, all alone,
>   Stands a gigantic Leg, which far off throws
>   The only shadow that the Desert knows.
> 'I am great Ozymandias,' saith the stone,
>   'The King of Kings; this mighty city shows
> 'The wonders of my hand.' The city's gone!
>   Nought but the leg remaining to disclose
> The site of that forgotten Babylon.

Horrified, the business man foresees a time when some primitive hunter, ranging

                                    through the wilderness
            Where London *stood*,

finds a huge fragment of stone

                                    and stops to guess
            What wonderful, but unrecorded, race
            Once dwelt in that annihilated place.

Shelley, transmuting the crude currency of the City to his own pure gold, avoided the grotesquerie of that 'Stupendous Leg'. But he had not seen the mild-eyed beauty of the Memnon when he wrote of a face

                                    whose frown,
            And wrinkled lip, and sneer of cold command,
            Tell that its sculptor well those passions read
            Which yet survive, stamped on these lifeless things,
            The hand that mocked them, and the heart that fed:
            And on the pedestal these words appear:
            'My name is Ozymandias, king of kings:
            Look on my works, ye Mighty, and despair!'
            Nothing beside remains. Round the decay
            Of that colossal wreck, boundless and bare
            The lone and level sands stretch far away.

CHAPTER VIII

*On the wall of the rock, in the centre of the four statues, is the figure
of the hawk-headed Osiris, surmounted by a globe; beneath which, I
suspect, could the sand be cleared away, a vast temple would be discovered, to the entrance of which the above colossal figures probably
serve as ornaments. . . .*

JOHN LEWIS BURCKHARDT, Travels in Nubia, 1819 [1]

I T had taken Belzoni only six weeks from the time he left Bulaq to
get the head of Young Memnon to the banks of the Nile. To a man
of his temperament it would have seemed almost indecent to go back
at once to Cairo, his commission fulfilled. Salt had impressed upon
him—and he had it in writing—that he must 'take care to engage a
proper boat for bringing down the head'. Well, there were none to be
had, says Giovanni, 'for they were all engaged, and mostly for the
Bashaw'. No doubt, if there had been the same urgency to take the head
down to Alexandria as there was to bring it to the Nile bank, Belzoni
would have found a way round the Pasha's priorities. But he was in no
hurry to get back to Cairo. In any case he had been instructed to collect
what antiquities he could. His brief was so wide that he might as well
make the best use of it. If a boat had to be sent from Cairo, that would
give him plenty of time to look round. He had worked hard enough
for the head; surely no one now would grudge him a little relaxation.

Such, we may suppose, was the general line of Giovanni's reasoning.
In *Narrative* he says with elaborate casualness and less candour:
'After having sent a courier to the consul about the boat, I thought I
could not employ my time better than in going up the Nile, as no extra
expense would be incurred. The boat which I had engaged might go
where I pleased. . . .' But Salt was paying all expenses, and Belzoni
could have dismissed a boat which he did not intend to use on the
return journey.

Before he left Thebes, however, he thought of the sarcophagus cover
which Drovetti had offered him, whether out of patronage or from some
perverse sense of humour. Behind the Ramesseum was a rocky tract of
land some two miles long, honeycombed with ancient tombs. Here for
generations the men of Qurna had lived among, and on the profits from,
their ancestral dead. They were a strange race of troglodytes, more
cunning and more independent than any other Arabs in the country.
'I do not know,' says Giovanni, 'whether it is because they are so few

132

in number, that the government takes so little notice of what they do; but it is certain, that they are the most unruly people in Egypt. . . . They have no mosque, nor do they care for one; for though they have at their disposal a great quantity of all sorts of bricks, which abound in every part of Gournou, from the surrounding tombs, they have never built a single house. They are forced to cultivate a small tract of land, extending from the rocks to the Nile, about a mile in breadth, and two and a half in length; and even this is in part neglected; for if left to their own will, they would never take a spade in their hands, except when they go to dig for mummies; which they find to be a more profitable employment than agriculture.'

The day after the head was safely brought to the river bank, Belzoni went with two Arabs to look at the cover of the sarcophagus that Drovetti had so admired but had not been able to get out. We know now that they belonged to the Pharaoh Ramses III; the splendid pink sarcophagus is in the Louvre and its cover in the Fitzwilliam Museum at Cambridge. But Giovanni makes no mention of finding them in the place from which they undoubtedly came: the elaborate rock-cut tomb of Ramses III in the Valley of the Kings, well-known to travellers then and for half a century before as 'Bruce's' or 'the Harpers' Tomb'. He speaks instead of going to a cave—'one of those holes that are scattered about the mountains of Gournou, so celebrated for the quantities of mummies they contain'.

Giovanni and his interpreter took off most of their clothes. Then, with two Arab guides, each man holding a candle, they entered 'a cavity in the rock, which extended a considerable length in the mountain, sometimes pretty high, sometimes very narrow, and without any regularity'. In places the roof was so low that they were obliged 'to creep on the ground, like crocodiles'. As they penetrated deeper into the mountain through a labyrinth of tunnels, Giovanni realized how much their safety depended upon their guides. Presently they came to a large chamber out of which opened a number of passages. After some whispered consultation the Arabs took one of the narrowest leading downhill. Belzoni began to have an uneasy feeling that all was not well. Certainly this was a burial-place, for there were skulls and bones all round, but no sarcophagus could have passed that way.

'This is the place,' said one of the Arabs, as they reached the bottom of the tunnel. Giovanni saw only a small opening at floor level, through which he knew he could never squeeze his own vast bulk. Against his better judgment he allowed the party to divide; one Arab and the Copt interpreter wriggled through, while the other stayed behind with Belzoni. For a time he could hear the murmur of voices gradually growing fainter. He waited patiently, uncomfortably, in the narrow tunnel. . . . Suddenly there was a distant, muffled crash and the Copt's voice was heard crying, '*O mon Dieu! mon Dieu! je suis perdu!*' Then all was silence. Giovanni called out to the interpreter, but there was no reply. He called repeatedly, but neither the Copt nor the Arab gave any sign of life. At last he decided he must go back the way he had come and try to get help. But his heart sank when the Arab who was with him said he had never been there before and did not know the way.

They scrambled back to the central chamber without much trouble. It was here their difficulties began, for neither could remember the passage along which they had come. Giovanni chose what he thought was the right one, but after walking for a long time they came to a dead end. The Arab sat down and at first refused to move, but Giovanni pulled him to his feet and dragged him back to the centre. The only course now was to try each passage in turn and to mark them as they did. Their candles were burning low, but Giovanni was afraid to put one out in case the other was extinguished by accident and they were left completely in the dark.

Some way along the second passage Giovanni heard a sound like the roaring of the sea at a great distance. He found it came from a small opening in the side of the tunnel. Fortunately they were able to squeeze through. As they stumbled along the noise grew louder and presently resolved itself into a babble of human voices—excited Arab voices—all talking together. In a few moments they walked out into the blinding sunlight.

The first person Giovanni saw in the crowd that clustered round them was the Copt interpreter. Quickly he told his story. The Arab who had gone forward with him had tumbled into a pit, and in falling put out both candles. It was then the Copt had cried out; but a moment later he had seen a tiny patch of daylight at the end of the tunnel. He had scraped away the sand and stones sufficiently to enable him to crawl out and then had gone to get help from the village for the man who had fallen into the pit.

The hole by which the interpreter had got out was quickly enlarged and Giovanni then realized why some of the Arabs were so agitated. They had deliberately blocked up this wide entrance and afterwards taken Drovetti, Belzoni and any other prospective customer for the sarcophagus by narrow, devious passages so that they could stipulate a large reward for 'discovering' the only way by which it could be brought out. Now the trick was exposed and it had cost one of their number a broken hip-bone. But that did not worry the men of Qurna.

Giovanni found that 'the sarcophagus was not in reality a hundred yards from the large entrance'.[2] He set several men to work at clearing the passage and then went off to spend a day or two exploring the open tombs in the Valley of the Kings. On the third day, on his return from the kings' tombs, he found that the Kashif of Armant had been up to his tricks again. He had come over to Qurna and seeing some Arabs working for Belzoni had had them arrested and sent off to the Armant gaol. The reason, as Giovanni later learnt, was that some of Drovetti's agents had just arrived with presents for the Kashif. When Giovanni saw him the governor maintained that the sarcophagus had been sold to the French. Giovanni pretended to be quite unconcerned and said he would be writing to Cairo about the matter.

The following Sunday Giovanni set off with Sarah on their voyage up the Nile. With them went the interpreter and the janissary; Curtin had gone back to Cairo and the carpenter had been discharged. Before leaving, Belzoni built a protective mud wall around the head of Young Memnon.

They reached Esna the next day. There Giovanni fell in with an old friend, Khalil Bey, who had recently been appointed governor of the upper provinces between Esna and Aswan. Khalil Bey had married a sister of Muhammad Ali and because of this family connection was largely independent of the Daftardar Bey at Asyut. He welcomed Belzoni warmly, and when he heard that he intended going up the Nile as far as Ibrim he wrote a letter of recommendation to the Kashif Husain, one of the three brother-chieftains who ruled in Nubia.

Giovanni briefly inspected all that could be seen of Esna's ancient temple, a Ptolemaic building with Roman additions, once sacred to the ram-headed Khnum. The temple stood in the middle of the modern town. The portico was choked with rubbish almost to the top of the columns and its walls were blackened from the manufacture of gunpowder out of the urine-soaked filth. The rest of the temple was quite inaccessible. Belzoni thought it 'a great pity that such beautiful edifices should be inhabited by dirty Arabs and their cattle'.[3]

A strong wind carried them on to Edfu. Here the best-preserved of all Egyptian temples lay smothered under an Arab village; the huts of the *fellahin* plastered the roof like wasps' nests and the excretions of man and beast seeped down to the sanctuary. Belzoni noted the vast artificial mounds that surrounded the city and guessed they might be productive of many antiquities. But already generations of *sabakh*-hunters had been at work, digging out the decayed residue of ancient brick that the *fellah* valued so much for its fertilizing properties. The temples might remain to be cleared of rubbish, but the city-mounds with their untold treasure of papyri and the simple objects of everyday life were steadily being destroyed.[4]

They passed through the narrow sandstone gorge of Silsila—the 'Mountains of the Chain', from which the Egyptians quarried so much of their building material from the Eighteenth Dynasty onwards. They saw the temple of Kom Ombo, threatened alike by the strong scour of the Nile current and by the insidious encroachment of the desert; the bright colours of the pigments still adhering to the reliefs excited Belzoni's wonder. Beyond Kom Ombo the sandstone changed to granite, the cultivation increased, and soon they saw ahead of them the pleasant heights of Aswan and the island of Elephantine.

Giovanni's first thought when they arrived was to seek out the Agha of Aswan, in order to procure a boat that would take him—at Salt's expense—above the Cataract into Nubia. But these were the last two days of Ramadan and nobody was disposed for business or negotiation. Giovanni wandered a little restlessly round the upper part of the town and admired the bird's-eye view of the river, where the dark granite islands like sleek elephants tossed the water into foam. When he returned to the boat he found the Agha and all his retinue seated on a mat under a clump of palm-trees close to the water. Giovanni at once invited them on board—or as many as the boat would hold. He treated them 'indiscriminately with coffee, and a small portion of tobacco each'. For the Agha there was a larger present of tobacco, soap and coffee, which was sent round to his house. In return he promised to let Belzoni have his own boat for the journey. There was less of a favour in this than the hope of making as much profit as possible out of the stranger.

Early the next morning Giovanni visited the island of Elephantine. He crossed the river in a primitive ferry-boat made of palm-tree branches covered with matting and pitched all over. It weighed about fifty pounds and supported nine persons—even when one of them was Belzoni!

Here, as at all other places where he stopped, Giovanni had a quick look round to see if there was anything easily portable—in the sense in which he understood the phrase. He records that he could not find 'the pedestal with Greek inscriptions, mentioned by Mr. Norden'. There was only 'a statue of granite, I believe of Osiris, about double the size of life . . . sitting on a chair, with some hieroglyphics on it, and its arms crossing the breast: but it was so mutilated that it did not appear worth taking away'. The upper part of what was evidently a companion piece to this had been removed by Hamilton. Belzoni must have seen here the still splendid remains of the temple of Thothmes III and the beautiful little shrine built by his great-grandson, Amenhetep III, for Khnum, the ram-headed god of creation and the Cataract; both of these were 'cannibalized' six years later by the Daftardar Bey to build a palace and a barracks at Aswan! Altogether Giovanni found the island 'pleasant enough', but he thought its charms had been exaggerated by other travellers. It was Denon in particular who became so lyrical about it when he arrived there with the French army of occupation. By contrast with Aswan, which on the second day of the occupation blossomed with 'tailors, shoe-makers, jewellers, French barbers with their poles, eating-houses, and *restaurateurs*, all at a fixed price', Elephantine, where Denon was stationed, became, in his phrase, 'at the same time my country house, and my palace of delight, observation and research'. Not only had it all the charm of a European landscape garden —with real, not sham, ruins—but the inhabitants were courteous and friendly in the extreme. They were of Nubian stock, black but not negroid, with slender, graceful bodies unencumbered by much clothing. That bold baronet, Sir Frederick Henniker, almost got into trouble here in Elephantine, trying to buy the wardrobe of a Nubian girl, which consisted only of a small leather fringe. He recalls with relish: 'I experienced considerable difficulty in the attempt, and even danger in my success.'

The Agha had promised to send along the captain of his boat. When he failed to do so Giovanni went to see him. The promise was repeated —and still not kept. Then the Agha appeared again and after some hedging said they must agree upon terms. Whereupon he asked for a hundred and twenty dollars for the hire of his boat—a figure so astronomical that Giovanni could not even consider it as a remote starting-point for the usual Oriental haggle. Instead he declared he would find a *reis* who knew the Cataract and get him to pilot the boat that was already at his disposal. The Agha protested that this was not allowed but Giovanni stuck to his guns. In due course he found a man who was willing to pilot them up as far as the Second Cataract and back for four dollars and a half. This brought the Agha's *reis* upon the scene. He said he was ready to leave the next morning, but he would not discuss terms; he left that to his master. Giovanni now threatened to abandon the whole project; he said he had no desire to incur enormous expense in seeing a country that had so little to attract him. The Agha at once became more reasonable. He offered his boat and a crew of five for an inclusive charge of twenty dollars. Giovanni clinched on this and arranged to move their baggage to the other boat the following morning.

While Giovanni was searching for a *reis* or poking about among the ruins of Elephantine, Sarah tried to create an atmosphere of goodwill by calling on the Agha's two wives. The one was old and extremely fat, but for that reason considered a great beauty; the other was young and, by Western standards, very pretty; and they lived in adjoining houses. Sarah describes how, when she visited the senior establishment, she was met at the door by the Agha himself, 'his wife, his sister, her husband, two young children, three old women, uglier than Macbeth's witches, and an old negro slave'. She was shown into a small yard and a plain deal chair was brought for her. The Agha went out and, while the Agha's brother-in-law made coffee, the women gathered round to examine her strange European clothing. When the coffee was brought Sarah indicated that she would like the Agha's wife to sit with her and drink a cup, but the man was plainly scandalized and, as soon as he could, locked the coffee-pot away. Sarah was then offered a pipe and smoked it for a while, as she had learnt to do in Egypt. When she put it down, one of the women took it up, but the man snatched it violently out of her hand and was only prevented from beating her by Sarah's expostulations.

Presently the Agha returned and, as a great treat, 'went to his treasury and brought out some dirty bruised grapes'. Sarah took the smallest bunch she could and kept them in her hands a long time before she could summon up courage to eat any. Then she produced her own presents for the women—some beads and a toilet-mirror. It was the largest looking-glass the women had ever seen and they fought over it like children.

Later Sarah watched while a meal was prepared for Giovanni and the Agha. It consisted of a dish of 'lady's-fingers' boiled in mutton broth and poured over bread, a little mutton and some minced meat mixed with rice and made up into balls. 'What other ingredients might be mixed,' says Sarah, 'shall by me be nameless; the cleanliness of this preparation I have not eloquence to describe: the horror I felt at the idea that I should be obliged to eat of it, was more than my English stomach could reconcile at that moment.' But there was no escape. Each dish was brought to Sarah before it was taken out to the men and the Agha's fat and greasy wife fed her literally with her own hands.

The following day, when Sarah received an invitation from the other wife, she was very loth to go. But, being a fair-minded woman, she did not wish to make any distinction between them. She found to her surprise a shy, pretty creature, who shrank away when her co-wife climbed upon the party wall to see what was going on. The younger woman offered Sarah some dates and a bag of grain and Sarah in return made her a small present of beads.

Before they left Aswan Giovanni gave the Agha a trifling *bakshish* and—at his special request—a bottle of vinegar. They boarded the other boat above the Cataract at night. Next morning Giovanni was up before dawn, eager to see the enchanting island of Philae, whose Arabic name Burckhardt quaintly translates as 'the social pleasures of Wodjoud'. To most nineteenth-century travellers Philae's light and airy temples, set among clumps of feathery palms, seemed the quintessence of Egyptian architecture. The building of the Aswan dam (1898–1902) doomed the island to drowning and there cannot be many alive who remember its loveliness. Yet none of the buildings on Philae was older than the fourth century B.C. The celebrated 'Kiosk', popularly known as 'Pharaoh's Bed', was built in the reign of Trajan (A.D. 98–118). Even an antiquary like Hamilton, who had helped Lord Elgin on his most famous—or notorious—enterprise, knew no better than to suppose that the 'Kiosk', being Egyptian, must be older than the Greek civilization, and thought therefore that the Greeks had little to add to this in order to produce their own finest examples of architecture. Such was the state of archaeological knowledge at the beginning of the nineteenth century.

Belzoni spent the rest of the morning exploring the island. He noted several large blocks of stone inscribed with hieroglyphics and—more important still—a red granite obelisk about twenty-two feet long that lay on its side near the water's edge in front of the great temple of Isis.[5] William John Bankes had considered the possibility of removing this monolith when he passed that way the previous November, but lacking proper equipment he had given up the idea for the time being. Yet he was curious enough to dig out the buried base of the obelisk, which had on it a Greek inscription more than twenty lines long.[6] It was a complaint from the priests of Isis at Philae to Ptolemy IX (146–117 B.C.) and his queen and sister Cleopatra that visiting generals, government officials and all their staffs and hangers-on expected full maintenance out of temple funds to the no small diminution of priestly perquisites. Bankes made a copy of the inscription. Later, in 1818, and some years before Champollion advanced a similar claim, this young Regency buck offered his own contribution to the decipherment of ancient Egyptian by identifying a cartouche on the obelisk—

—as the name of Cleopatra.[7]

Belzoni's subsequent adventures with the obelisk brought him into great danger of his life and were indirectly the cause of his leaving Egypt. But now, in August 1816, he was content to mark it down as one of the easier trophies to remove before he hurried off in search of other portable antiquities.

Few travellers before him had penetrated far into Nubia, and Sarah must have been the first European woman to do so for centuries. Pococke, Denon and Hamilton had all stopped at Philae. Norden went as far as Derr, one hundred and twenty miles above Aswan. In 1813 Thomas Legh and his companion, the Reverend Charles Smelt, reached Qasr Ibrim, three days' journey short of the Second Cataract, but 'received no encouragement to penetrate into a country where money

began to be of little use, and provisions very scarce'. A year later
Captain Light covered the same ground. Bankes, in 1815, pushed on
to Wadi Halfa. Burckhardt, of course, had gone much further, following the pilgrim road and the slave-trade routes deep into the Sudan
and rivalling the journeys of Bruce and W. G. Browne. But these were
the giants of African exploration and the curious traveller in Egypt
was seldom tempted to emulate them.

The Belzonis had their first alarming experience the day after they
left Philae. The captain and crew had gone ashore to buy provisions,
and a band of Nubian warriors armed with spears and shields of
crocodile-skin tried to commandeer the boat. They were driven off by
Sarah and Giovanni only at the point of a pistol.

Beyond the dark granite gorge of Kalabsha the travellers came to a
village of the same name. Here there was a temple in a good state of
preservation, approached by a stone causeway from the ancient quay.
The villagers surrounded the temple while the visitors were inside and
demanded money in threatening tones. But Giovanni refused to be
intimidated and stalked majestically through the crowd, while they fell
back in awe at his great height and commanding presence. Once outside he gave the villagers *bakshish* and promised them more in return
for antiquities. In this way he acquired several stone slabs bearing
Greek inscriptions.

Past Dendur with its temple dedicated by the Emperor Augustus
to two obscure local heroes; past Garf Husain, rock-hewn for Ramses II
by his viceroy in Ethiopia, where the Osirid columns—in Giovanni's
words—were 'adorned on the lower part of their bodies with curious
appendages, not unlike the tobacco pouches used among the High-
landers'; past Dakka, set in the midst of a once-fertile plain, where on
the walls of the sanctuary the Nile god Hapi with a woman's breast still
betokened plenty; past Maharraqa and its winding stone stair and the
figures of pagan gods overpainted with Christian saints, they sailed
deeper and deeper into the heart of Nubia.

Above Korosko the Nile turns north-west and, as the wind blew
mainly from that quarter and the current was now very strong, their
progress was slow. The banks were covered with thorn and acacia-trees
so that the boat could not be towed. The days were very hot, but the
nights surprisingly cold. It was here that Sarah began to indulge her
passion for keeping chameleons. At one time she had a collection of
fifty or sixty. She soon discovered that the little creatures were 'very
inveterate to their own kind' and would bite off each other's legs and
tails if they were kept together. 'One cameleon,' she says, 'lived with
me eight months, and most of that time I had it fixed to the button of
my coat: it used to rest on my shoulder or on my head.'[8]

On 5 September they reached Derr, the village-capital of Lower Nubia. Here Giovanni found one of the three brothers—Hasan, Husain and Muhammad—who ruled this part of the country between them. They were said to be descended from Bosnian soldiers sent there three hundred years before by the great Sultan Selim. For a time these local chiefs had lost their power to the Mamluk Beys, when the latter were obliged to retire into Upper Egypt and Nubia. But in 1811, after their last stand against the Pasha's troops at Qasr Ibrim, the Mamluks had fled still further south into the kingdom of Dongola, leaving the three brother-chieftains virtually in control of the country between the First and Second Cataracts, though they still owed a nominal allegiance to the Pasha.

Hasan Kashif, when Legh saw him in 1813, was a tall handsome man, apparently about twenty-five years of age; his manner was truculent at times, though he showed a certain rough good humour in his cups. (Finati,[9] who met him two years later while he was accompanying Mr. Bankes up the Nile, describes him as 'a gross, corpulent man, but much less dark than the usual hue of his countrymen'.) Hasan at first regarded Belzoni with great suspicion and inquired searchingly about his business. Perhaps he thought, as he had done with Burckhardt, that this was someone sent by Muhammad Ali to test his loyalty. Giovanni told him truthfully that he wanted to travel as far as the Second Cataract in search of antiquities. That would be impossible, said Hasan—not believing a word of it—for the people of the upper country were at war with one another. Then he proceeded to ask for coffee, soap, tobacco and gunpowder—in that order. Giovanni gave him all except the last. He also showed him the letter of recommendation to his brother Husain; Hasan's pointed comment was that it did not say where Belzoni was going. Giovanni saw that if he intended to travel any further up-country he must offer a handsome present. Accordingly he produced one of the cheap mirrors he had provided himself with in Cairo after inquiring about the tastes of the Nubians—proof, if that were needed, that even then his mind was a jump or two ahead of Consul Salt's. The Kashif was delighted with the glass. He 'was never tired of admiring his bear-like face', says Giovanni, 'and all his attendants behind him strove to get a peep at their own chocolate beauty'.

The travellers left Derr about noon on 6 September. After a few hours they passed the ruined Roman fortress of Qasr Ibrim, high on a bluff above the river. Here in the sixteenth century the Sultan Selim had left his garrison of Bosnian troops to moulder in peaceful oblivion; here three hundred years later the Mamluks had dispossessed their descendants and been themselves dislodged in turn by Ibrahim Pasha.

Two days more of difficult sailing brought the travellers to Abu

Simbel. This was the secret goal of Giovanni's endeavour. Three years earlier Burckhardt, on his lone pilgrimage south, had stopped here to look at a rock-cut temple hewn out of a cliff facing the river. Six colossal figures, flanked by other smaller ones, stood in niches formed by the enormous sandstone buttresses of the façade. In the centre was a doorway leading to a hall with six square goddess-headed pillars; beyond lay other chambers and the sanctuary itself.[10] Burckhardt had completed his inspection of the temple—which he judged to be of great antiquity—and was about to climb up the sandy slope that led to the desert plateau. Suddenly he noticed—a hundred yards or so to the south—the tips of what must be four even more enormous figures, almost engulfed by the river of sand that flowed down across the face of the cliff. The head and shoulders of one were still clear; another had its head broken off and the lie of the sand all but masked the jagged edge of stone; of the remaining two only the 'bonnets'—as Burckhardt and his contemporaries usually called the Double Crown of Egypt—were yet visible. 'The head which is above the surface', wrote Burckhardt in his journal, 'has a most expressive, youthful countenance, approaching nearer to the Grecian model of beauty, than that of any ancient Egyptian figure I have seen; indeed, were it not for a thin oblong beard, it might well pass for a head of Pallas.' In a letter to the African Association dated 1 July 1816 he commented on the resemblance between the colossi of Abu Simbel and the Young Memnon: 'The expression of the face is the same; perhaps a little more gravity is perceived in those of Nubia, but the incomparable serenity, and godlike mildness are remarkable in both.' And he added in his journal: 'On the wall of the rock, in the centre of the four statues, is the figure of the hawk-headed Osiris, surmounted by a globe; beneath which, I suspect, could the sand be cleared away, a vast temple would be discovered. . . .'

With such words as these Burckhardt, back in Cairo, had kindled Belzoni's imagination. The Italian—not unnaturally—was always impressed by size. Here at Abu Simbel, it must have seemed to him, were colossi worthy to rank with the shattered giant of the Memnonium and the seated figures on the plain of Thebes. Only they were buried under a mountain of sand that it would need a giant's strength to move. Yet under that mountain—so his friend Burckhardt believed—was a temple that modern eyes had never seen. Who knew what treasures it might not contain?

The size of the task when he saw it was enough to daunt even Belzoni. Ignoring the smaller temple altogether, he stumbled up the steep sandy slope to where the hawk-headed Re-Harakhte[11] marked the centre of the larger façade. Judging the buried figure to be more than twenty feet high and allowing room for a cornice and a frieze above the door,

Belzoni reckoned that the entrance to the temple could not be less than thirty-five feet below the surface. At every step his foot sank deep in the soft sand; as he lifted it clear the fine grains poured back into the shapeless print. Digging here, Giovanni reflected, would be like trying to make a hole in water. . . .

He was anxious to get to the village before nightfall; so, after a few rapid calculations in his notebook, he plunged down the slope again and boarded the boat. The village of Abu Simbel was only a short distance up-stream where the sandstone cliffs retreated and there was a patch of cultivation. Here Giovanni found a ragged group of rascality seated under the trees. When he asked for Husain Kashif, they pointed out a man of middling age who wore a white turban and a faded blue *galabiya*; that, they said, was Husain's son, Dawud Kashif.

A younger man pushed himself forward with a rough air of authority. This was Khalil, another of Husain's sons, whom the old man had cunningly promoted together with Dawud to the rank of Kashif—much to the indignation of his brothers, Muhammad and Hasan, who resented a diminution of their authority in favour of their nephews.

Giovanni's first exchanges with Dawud were not very encouraging. The Kashif laughed rudely when he said he had come in search of ancient stones: he had heard that tale before. A few moons ago, he declared, another Frank had come from Cairo in search of treasure and had taken away a large quantity of gold in his boat. Nor was Dawud much impressed by the offer of money. He and his people lived by barter. They had little faith in Muhammad Ali's piastres, till Giovanni convinced them by a sly dodge that the small bits of metal had value. He had previously arranged with the *reis* that if a man presented himself at the boat with a piastre he was to be given enough *dura*[12] to make him bread for three days. The trick worked, but Dawud was not slow to put his terms as high as possible. He said he would allow his men to work for four piastres a day. Giovanni eventually beat him down to two. He had even more cause to congratulate himself when he learnt that the traveller who had been that way some months before was none other than the great and influential Drovetti. Dawud said the Frank had given him three hundred piastres to open the rock while he went on up to Wadi Halfa. On his return the Kashif had handed him back the money intact; his people were not interested in the small pieces of metal and refused to work for them.

So far, so good; but Belzoni still needed permission from Husain Kashif before the work could begin. Though mostly peripatetic—according to Burckhardt, the old chief had twenty wives disposed about the country and visited each in turn—he had his principal establishment at Ashkit, a day-and-a-half's journey up the Nile. He was said to be there at that moment, but when the boat reached Ashkit he had already gone again. They were now so near Wadi Halfa that Belzoni could not resist the temptation to go thus far. His desire to get as close as possible to the Second Cataract almost led to disaster. The boat was caught in a sudden eddy and driven against a rock; it was only by a miracle that she was not stove in.

They came back to Ashkit on 15 September and found that Husain had returned. He was an old man approaching seventy, tall and erect, with an air of distinction about him in spite of the none-too-clean woollen shawl thrown over his head and the gaping holes in his shoes. He had a bodyguard of thirty men, some of them armed with matchlock guns and long swords, others with primitive spears and crocodile-leather shields.

The Kashif expressed surprise that Belzoni wanted to open the great cave in the rock at Abu Simbel. The old man himself was sure the entrance was concealed behind the ball on the head in the centre—by which he meant the solar disk of Re-Harakhte. But he maintained it would be very difficult to find a way in. When he saw Belzoni was so confident of success, he stipulated that if he found the temple full of gold he must give him half. To this Giovanni agreed on condition that, if he found only stones, they should all be his. So the bargain was struck.

But already in Abu Simbel the villagers had changed their minds. Although Belzoni now had a written authority from the paramount chief, they did not want to work. Eventually Dawud talked them round when he realized that he was likely to lose a substantial *bakshish*. But then the villagers, with all the stubbornness of a trade union, insisted that Belzoni should employ at least a hundred men. In vain he protested that thirty were more than enough. It was only when he threatened to abandon the whole project that they compromised on forty. They agreed to be at the boat before sunrise the next morning.

But the sun was high in the sky before the first volunteer appeared on the little beach. Giovanni philosophically set them to work as they came, getting them to draw away the sand from the centre of the façade just below the head of Re-Harakhte. They worked in pairs, using a kind of toothless wooden rake which one man pulled forward with a rope and the other drew back by its long handle. As a means of moving earth or sand on a level site it was remarkably effective. Here, however, the problem was to stop the slow unending avalanche of sand from the desert above. It bore down relentlessly on the place where they dug. Yet the first day the work went better than Belzoni had expected. At noon he gave the men some bread and lentil soup, which cheered them considerably; Dawud took his share with the others. At night Belzoni

13. DROVETTI AND HIS ENTOURAGE AT THEBES

14. THE FACADE AT ABU SIMBEL

15. GENERAL VIEW OF THE TEMPLES AT ABU SIMBEL

paid them what was due and told them to be early the next morning.
The travellers returned to the village to sleep.

On the second day the work again began very slowly. The men complained they were tired, and Giovanni had to promise them a rest the
next day. His own food supplies were now running low. He tried to buy
a sheep, but the villagers would not sell. He and Sarah had to content
themselves with a little boiled rice for their evening meal. Their stock
of butter was finished and milk was very scarce.

On the third day Giovanni complained to Dawud that he was not
keeping his part of the bargain. In particular, he refused to supply the
wood which Belzoni needed for palisades, though there was plenty in
the village. The trouble was that Dawud felt he had not yet received
a sufficient *bakshish*; he needed something like a brace of pistols to
make him well-disposed to the stranger. But as he grew more difficult,
so his younger brother, the sulky Khalil—in response to a suitable
inducement from Belzoni—became more accommodating. When the
villagers said they would not work unless their numbers were doubled,
it was Khalil who intervened and persuaded them to accept a ration of
grain instead.

In spite of this, on the fifth day, so many men turned up that it was
impossible to employ them all, since the work was concentrated at one
point. Giovanni was adamant in his refusal to pay more than he had
promised at first, so the men resolved the problem by dividing the same
sum among a larger number. Giovanni was astonished at the effect his
introduction of money into Abu Simbel had upon the local economy.
He discovered the reason no one would sell him a sheep was the difficulty of fixing the price. It was in Dawud's interest to keep it as low as
possible since *his* revenue was paid in sheep. But that would affect them
all in their exchange of sheep for *dura* with other villages. Finally it
was decided that the sheep should be 'given' to Belzoni, who would
offer a suitable present in return. Giovanni was equally concerned not
to establish a fixed rate of exchange in any particular commodity. So
he made the owner of the sheep a combined payment of soap, tobacco
and salt.

During the morning two of the men left their work and tried to board
the boat, intent on pilfering. Sarah was alone except for a small girl
from the village. But she confronted the men with a pistol and chased
them up the hill till they mingled with other villagers and their identity
was lost.

That night Khalil had all the wages money piled in a single heap on
the corner of an old shawl. Then, unable to restrain himself at the sight
of so much wealth—eighty piastres, no less—he flung himself on the
shawl and scooped up the lot. The workmen looked on at this blatant

embezzlement, but said not a word. Afterwards Giovanni congratulated Khalil on his superior magic in discovering treasure, but no doubt the irony was lost upon him. So did the love of money take firm root at Abu Simbel.

In less than a week Belzoni had cleared the sand to a depth of twenty feet in front of the figure of Re-Harakhte that stood in its niche between the jackal-headed staff User and the goddess Maat—the whole a rebus-signature of User-Maat-Re, Osymandias, the builder of the temple. To the right another colossal head and shoulders of the king had been un-covered; the ear alone was three and a half feet long. But Giovanni was less interested in the façade of the temple than in what he might find inside. By means of palisades of palm interlaced with saplings and brush-wood he had checked the fall of sand above the conjectured position of the entrance. Now he poured down water as close as he could to the rock and dug a small pilot hole in the wet sand, hoping to strike the top of the doorway. But by his own calculations he still had another fifteen feet to go. The task was too big to be completed with the means and in the time at his disposal. The head of Memnon had to be embarked before the Nile waters receded. And more urgent still was his own need of money—the very commodity that had been so despised but a week before.

Sarah was not sorry to go. Boiled rice and sour flat pancakes of *dura* bread were dismal enough fare, and there was not much even of these. She had borne the privations of this part of the journey with her usual stoic calm and had shown a genuine interest in the life and habits of the women. When the news spread that a Frank woman was on board, there was always great excitement among the female population. Sarah distributed cheap glass beads and was well content if she received in exchange a few antique cornelians. She called on Dawud Kashif's young wife and submitted to be half-undressed in order to gratify the women's curiosity about her clothes. They were puzzled by the intricate Frank costume—the man's coat and breeches, the many mysterious buttons, the feminine underwear. They were especially fascinated by Sarah's corsets and their remarks on these, she says, were 'extremely sensible'. (How this would have pleased Sir Frederick Henniker, haunted as he always was in Egypt by the sight of pendulous flapping breasts!) On the whole Sarah found the Nubian women more civilized and less demanding than their Arab sisters. But even *their* company palled after a while, and she looked forward to the return to Cairo.

Giovanni exacted a promise from Dawud that he would not allow anyone to touch the excavation till he came back again in a few months' time. Not that he placed much faith in this promise, but he guessed that the natural indolence of the villagers was even greater than their cupidity. They would not try to open the temple themselves, and he would keep a sharp look-out for any other European traveller in that region. That he had already aroused the jealousy of his rivals was clear from an incident that occurred only an hour or so after they had left Abu Simbel. A Turkish soldier on a dromedary delivered two threatening letters written in Arabic and signed (so Belzoni claims) with fictitious names. Both warned him to give up whatever project he had started in Nubia and return to Cairo. Giovanni was not the man to be intimidated in this way, but he saw plainly that there was trouble for him ahead.

At Philae Belzoni made a new appraisal of its portable antiquities. Besides the obelisk there were twelve sculptured blocks that had once formed part of a wall in a little ruined temple at the southern end of the island.[13] Pieced together they formed a charming scene of adoration— male and female figures bringing offerings to a god. Each block was three feet six inches long and three feet wide. As they were also two feet three inches thick they seemed to be too bulky to ship as they were. Accordingly Giovanni sent for the Agha of Aswan and gave him a hundred piastres to have the blocks cut down to six-inch slabs. It was further agreed that they should be embarked on the first suitable craft and sent down to Luxor. As for the obelisk, that would have to wait till the following season because of the difficulty of getting it down the Cataract. The Agha promised to arrange for a guard on the stones and was given four dollars for his trouble. He was to have another thirty dollars when the obelisk was safely removed.

The travellers were delayed again at Aswan through the cunning of the Agha. To keep the visitors in the town for a few more days, he hid all the available boats. Eventually Giovanni had to hire the Agha's own vessel at an exorbitant fee and in that they reached Luxor on 2 October.

The consul had arranged for Giovanni to draw money from a banker in Qena. Accordingly Belzoni hurried off there to replenish his purse. There was still no word from Salt about transport for the head, but on 8 October, while Belzoni was at Qena, a large boat appeared, heading up-stream. On board were two of Drovetti's agents—Jean Jacques Rifaud,[14] a tough little Marseillais, draughtsman, sculptor and energetic delver, and Frédéric Cailliaud,[15] a mild-mannered jeweller from Nantes with an interest in mineralogy and a taste for exploring. Giovanni inquired of the *reis* and learnt that the boat would be free after it had been to Aswan. He at once engaged it for the return journey to Cairo.

When he got back to Thebes he found the boat moored near the Young Memnon. The Frenchmen had probably been casting envious eyes at the colossal head that their fellow-countrymen had not been able to move. But now in the presence of Belzoni they belittled its value and importance in a way that made him choke with indignation. Worse still, they followed him to Qurna and told the Arabs that if they sold any more antiquities to the English they would all be bastinadoed by the Kashif of Armant. But even this was nothing to the malignancy of their dragoman, Giuseppe Rosignano, a Piedmontese. He drew Belzoni aside—so Giovanni says—and told him plainly that, if he continued his activities, there were those who would not hesitate to cut his throat.

However, in spite of this, Giovanni travelled up to Esna in the Frenchmen's boat to sign an agreement with the owners. They made so much of the risk involved in shipping such a heavy load and Giovanni was so anxious not to lose perhaps the only opportunity of getting the head away that season that he agreed to pay the extortionate sum of three thousand piastres (£75) for the hire of the boat to Cairo.

Half the amount was paid over at once. The janissary went up with the boat to Aswan to see to the loading of the reliefs at Philae and Giovanni returned to Karnak, where in defiance of the French he had already set a score of men digging among the ruins.

Belzoni's topographical details are never very precise and there are no names to guide us, but it is clear that the site he had chosen was within the precincts of the temple of Mut.[16] This lies to the south of the great temple-complex, at the end of the eastern avenue of sphinxes, and is surrounded on three sides by the waters of a Sacred Lake. Giovanni says he dug on the west side of the temple, away from the spot where the French had unearthed a number of statues at the time of their occupation, but there was to be trouble about this later. In a few days he found some twenty odd statues buried together in a hard compacted mass of rubble and brick. Most of them were black granite statues of the goddess Sekhmet,[17] the terrible lion-headed consort of Ptah, and six were quite perfect. In the same *cache*—for evidently the statues were not in their original position but had been hastily buried in some confusion—there was also a seated male figure in white limestone holding on its knees a shrine surmounted by a ram's head.[18] Belzoni was later persuaded to identify this as Jupiter Ammon, but the name on the base shows that it represented a weak and inconspicuous Pharaoh of the Nineteenth Dynasty, Seti II.

The prodigality with which successive rulers had endowed the great temple at Karnak should have left no room for jealousy among the early collectors of antiquities. Even at the beginning of this century the French Egyptologist Legrain was able to recover from the celebrated Karnak *Cachette*,[19] within a period of six months, no less than eight thousand bronzes and nearly five hundred stone statues. In Belzoni's day it was hardly possible to dig anywhere at Karnak without turning up some major antiquity.

Only money—or the lack of it—set a limit to Giovanni's acquisitions. He was expecting another remittance from the consul. In the meantime, while he waited for the boat from Aswan and the cash from Cairo, he crossed the river again to the western side and began to explore the desolate Valley of the Kings in the hills behind Qurna. Ancient writers had put the number of royal tombs as high as forty-seven, though only eighteen were known at the dawn of the Christian era. Hamilton found no more than ten accessible at the beginning of the nineteenth century; he agreed, however, that the site of several others could be determined by the chips and fragments of stone thrown up at the time of excavation.

THE GODDESS
SEKHMET

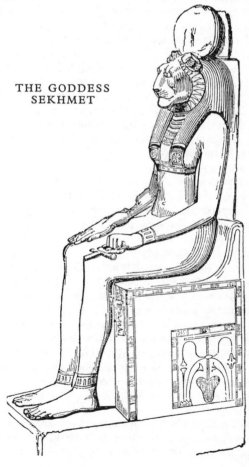

Giovanni pottered about at the far end of the Western Valley,[20] beyond the tomb of Amenhetep III which the French had discovered during their occupation of Egypt. He was particularly interested, as a water engineer, in the way in which, despite the rarity of rainfall in those parts, the rocks had been scoured by the action of mountain torrents. Casually he poked his stick into a heap of stones. It went deep —unexpectedly deep—meeting no obstacle. The following day Belzoni took a party of workmen to the valley, but could hardly find the spot again because his eyes were so troubled by ophthalmia. In a couple of hours the men had removed enough stones to uncover the entrance to a tomb. 'I cannot boast of having made a great discovery in this tomb,' says Giovanni with becoming modesty, 'though it contains several curious and singular painted figures on the walls; and from its extent, and part of a sarcophagus remaining in the centre of a large chamber, have reason to suppose, that it was the burial-place of some person of distinction.' It was in fact the tomb of Ai, the scheming priest who usurped the throne of Egypt after the death of Tutankhamun. The scenes painted on the walls have more in common with the tombs of the nobles than with those of other Pharaohs. Here is Ai, for example, fowling in the marshes like any other ordinary mortal out for a day's good sport. A man of common stock, he could not as of right command the pleasures of this life in the under-world; he needs must take them with him on the walls of his tomb.[21]

When the boat came back from Aswan the Philae reliefs were not on board, a cargo of dates had been loaded and the owners declared they could not undertake the conveyance of the head, though half the money had been paid already. Giovanni put it all down to the machinations of Drovetti's agents, and he was probably not far wrong. But the situation was suddenly changed entirely in his favour through a most absurd circumstance. A soldier arrived from the Kashif of Armant with a present of two small bottles of anchovies and two of olives. He also brought an invitation to a feast. Giovanni was puzzled at first by this apparent change of heart in his old and wily opponent. But he soon found out from the soldier that the Kashif was in a great rage with a certain Frank in Cairo, who had raised his expectations of a choice and valuable present and in the end had given him only these miserable small fish and a few worthless olives—fit only to give to another Frank. Giovanni guessed what pliant mood the Kashif must be in as a result of his disappointment and he determined to strike, as he says, 'while his mind was hot'.

He found the Kashif 'seated on a mat in the middle of a field, a stick fastened in the ground with a lantern attached to it, and all his attendants standing before him'. The Turk made a great show of compliments, offered Belzoni as many workmen as he wanted and would have had no objection to his taking away the two Colossi of Thebes, if he could have put them on his boat that night. The next morning he sat in judgment with a packed jury to hear Giovanni's case against the owners. The defendants were glad to get off with no more than the obligation to pay two-thirds of the extortionate sum they had charged Belzoni, for the hire of another boat. So the last obstacle was overcome and, with Drovetti's olives and anchovies now tipping the scale heavily against the French interest in antiquities, Belzoni prepared to take one of the richest cargoes of archaeological treasure down the Nile that that century had yet seen.

Embarking the head of Memnon called for another miracle of improvisation. It was now mid-November and the Nile waters had gone back some thirty or forty yards from the spot to which the head had been brought in August. There was a drop of eighteen feet from the bank to water-level. Giovanni's first task therefore was to build a ramp down which the head might be lowered. This took him two days, using a hundred and thirty men. Then he laid four palm-tree poles as a bridge between the ramp and the boat, taking care that the weight bore down upon the centre of the craft and not on the gunwale alone. A sack full of sand was slung across the 'bridge' to act as a brake if the head moved too fast and the further side of the boat was padded with mats and straw. Check-ropes, belayed round posts driven into the bank, steadied the descent. Slowly, inch by inch, the seven-ton granite mass was lowered on its car across the straining, bending palms; they groaned like a *saqiya* at the unaccustomed weight. The owners of the boat danced in an agony of despair. The workmen were apathetic: either the 'bridge' would break or the boat would sink; it was all one to them. Only Belzoni knew that he could not afford to make a mistake.

When the head was safely embarked the boat crossed over to Luxor. There it took on board the other antiquities that Giovanni had collected, including the statue of Seti II and the six finest figures of Sekhmet. Another sixteen were left behind for removal later.

For the past five or six weeks Sarah had lodged with an Arab family in Luxor, sharing an upper room, open to the sky, with six other women. It was the first time she had been left without an interpreter or a European, and she was mostly very wretched. She suffered from recurring bouts of fever and could hardly stomach the nauseating food that was offered her in all kindness. But her most alarming experience was a sharp attack of ophthalmia that coincided with Giovanni's. Her eyes became inflamed and discharged a virulent pus; the eyeballs were swollen and the lids would scarcely close, though the bright Egyptian light hurt intolerably. Sarah had nothing to bathe the eyes with but filtered Nile water. When the women saw this, they set up a loud cry and said it was bad for them; she must leave them alone. In twenty days her eyes might be better. If not, perhaps in another twenty. After that—well, *maalesh!* Never mind! . . . At the end of twenty days Sarah was quite blind; she thought she would never see again. *Maalesh! Maalesh!* At last the swelling went down but she could not lift her eyelids. Then the women boiled garlic in water and made her hold her eyes over the steam. After forty days—just as they had said—the visitation passed.

The Belzonis left Thebes on 21 November. Giovanni had had a recurrence of his ophthalmia and was obliged to spend most of the next fortnight in the darkness of the cabin. At Asyut he remembered to thank the Daftardar Bey for his letter to the Kashif of Armant. They reached Cairo at last on 15 December after an absence of five and a half months.

Salt had gone to Alexandria but had left full instructions with his secretary, Mr. Beechey. All the antiquities, except the head of Young Memnon, were to be deposited in the consulate. Belzoni professes that he found this distinction somewhat odd, since he thought he was collecting for the British Museum. But he did as he was requested and early in the New Year left Bulaq with the boat to take the head to Alexandria. At Rosetta it was landed and re-loaded upon a *jerm*, but this time Belzoni had proper tackle. At Alexandria the crew of a British transport helped him to get it ashore into a warehouse.

Burckhardt was full of admiration for Belzoni's achievement. As soon as he had seen the boat-load of antiquities at Cairo he wrote to Salt: 'Mr. Belzoni has succeeded beyond the most sanguine hopes you could entertain, and certainly done his utmost to execute his commission in full. He has brought, besides the head, seven statues, which will be a most valuable ornament to your future gallery.' Burckhardt clearly regarded Belzoni as being engaged, partly at least, in helping Salt to form a private collection. But two months later, when he wrote to William Hamilton about the Young Memnon, he said: 'Mr. Salt and myself have borne the expenses jointly, and the trouble of the undertaking has devolved upon Mr. Belzoni, whose name I wish to be mentioned, if ever ours shall, on this occasion, because he was actuated by public spirit fully as much as ourselves.'

Today the head of Young Memnon—Ramses II—occupies a commanding position in the Central Saloon of the British Museum's unique Egyptian Galleries. The names of Salt and Burckhardt are both inscribed upon the base, but there is no mention of Belzoni. Is it too much to hope that one day this will be changed?

CHAPTER IX

OWEN. — *How unfortunate, mamma! I wish that troublesome Mr. Drouetti would keep his agents in Alexandria, and not let them come to disturb Belzoni's plans.*

SARAH ATKINS, Fruits of Enterprise, 1821 [1]

BELZONI received one hundred pounds from Salt and Burckhardt for his services during the last six months of 1816. Each of them gave him twenty-five pounds on account of the head, and the consul added another fifty. What precisely this sum represented it would be hard to say. No doubt Salt felt it was the best he could do for his employee under the circumstances. In December 1816 his own consular salary was still nine months in arrears and he had already paid out over two hundred pounds to Belzoni for expenses. He may have thought the remuneration was a little inadequate, but it certainly never occurred to him that the antiquities were anything but his own property, to dispose of as he pleased.

Giovanni, on the other hand, was very reluctant to accept any payment that might imply a surrender of his rights—and these went beyond the mere question of ownership, though that was important and complicated enough. It was true the consul had given him money to buy antiquities. But most of what he had brought down to Cairo he had found for himself through his own powers of observation and knowledge of where to dig. . . . If Salt thought he could acquire a boat-load of statues for fifty pounds, might he not also claim the pieces now waiting for transport at Luxor and even those that had not yet been dug out of the *cache*? If Giovanni succeeded in bringing down the obelisk from Philae, was Salt going to offer him a paltry few pounds for something that would be a lasting ornament to any metropolis and make its donor's name famous? When the great temple at Abu Simbel yielded up its secrets, must the glory of discovery be shared with Salt?

How far these thoughts and fears had already taken root in Belzoni's mind we can only guess. But the seeds of suspicion were undoubtedly there. Nor were they discouraged from starting into growth when the consul—to make up for the inadequacy of the fifty pounds—told him he might keep two of the lion-headed statues for himself. (Belzoni afterwards sold them to the Count de Forbin[2]—Salt says for £175.) Salt was not an ungenerous man and in those early days he had a warm regard for Belzoni; when he wrote home to the public journals he gave full credit to his ability and achievements. But in his private dealings with Belzoni there was a blind spot that prevented him from seeing how much the Italian cared about *honour*. To *concede* him something that he already considered in one very real sense his own was to wound him deeply; it was worse than meanness or deliberate fraud. Salt failed to realize in time that he could not bind the genius of Belzoni as he hired a servant for his house. Had he only been able to make an imaginative but business-like arrangement at the beginning, the friendship of the two men would not have foundered in sordid quarrels and mutual mistrust.

For the moment, however, Belzoni's main concern was to get back as quickly as possible to Upper Egypt and Nubia. He could not bear the thought of Drovetti's agents having a free hand at Thebes. And he feared that if he stayed away too long from Abu Simbel some other enterprising traveller might open the temple before him.

Apart from the French there was only one such individual to watch, though he seemed fully occupied for the moment at Giza. Captain G. B. Caviglia[3]—his name in Italian means 'Belaying-pin'—was the Genoese master and owner of a merchantman sailing the Mediterranean under the English flag till some antiquarian quirk set him on the road to pyramid exploration. Leaving his ship at Alexandria when a suitable opportunity occurred, he arrived in Cairo on Boxing Day 1816, bent on making a thorough investigation of Cheops' Pyramid. With great courage and determination he climbed more than a hundred and twenty feet down the so-called 'well', proved its communication with the Descending Corridor, which he cleared of obstructions, and so solved a problem that had puzzled pyramidographers since the days of Pliny.[4] From this Caviglia turned to clearing the Sphinx of sand and excavating some of the *mastaba*-tombs[5] around the Giza plateau. Salt and Briggs— the liberal merchant of Alexandria—both supported him in his enterprise, and indeed the consul suggested that Giovanni might join forces with the sea-captain. But Belzoni was too much an individualist to work happily in harness with another so like himself, and he begged to be excused. 'I thought it would not be right,' he says in his *Narrative*, 'to attempt to share the credit of one, who had already exerted himself to the utmost of his power.' Under the condescending phrase we can sense the fierce pride that would brook no competition in the field he had chosen to make his own.

Perhaps Salt thought that if he could not keep Belzoni under his eye at Giza the next best thing might be to send someone with him to Thebes who would act as a restraining influence. At any rate he suggested that his secretary should accompany Belzoni on his next journey. Henry William Beechey[6] was the son of Sir William Beechey, R.A., and himself an artist of modest ability; Salt thought he might make copies of any interesting reliefs or inscriptions that were found, since he had no great opinion of Belzoni's talents in that direction. Giovanni was quite pleased at the prospect of the young man's company: 'I was fully satisfied that, after having weaned himself from those indulgences to which he was accustomed, he would make a good traveller.' Sarah was to stay in Cairo for a while—perhaps because she did not feel she could face another sojourn in Thebes so soon. Giovanni left her with the family of Mr. Cocchini, who acted as chief clerk in the consulate. James Curtin stayed too.

The party that set off up the Nile included a Turkish soldier, an Arab cook and a Greek employee from the consulate called Yanni Athanasiou. This ignorant and pretentious little man—who seems to have had none of the virtues and most of the vices of the Greek character —acted as Salt's interpreter and later as his agent, when he had broken with Belzoni. After Salt's death he came to England to supervise the sale of his collection and the preparation of the catalogue. This he published in 1836—under the Italian form of his name that he affected, Giovanni D'Athanasi—together with an account of his service in Egypt.[7] Even after the lapse of nearly twenty years he could not forget his jealousy of Belzoni. In his book he loses no opportunity of blackening the character of the man he succeeded. Sycophantic to Salt, he tries always to show Belzoni as a fool or a knave and himself as the real brains of the party. The very genesis of this second expedition up the Nile was due—in Athanasiou's version—to Belzoni's doubts as to whether he could succeed, and Salt's seconding of his most able lieutenants to the rescue.

It may have been now—unimpeded by a wife in European costume —that Giovanni first adopted Turkish dress. He makes no mention of this matter at all. Certainly during his first year in Cairo he revealed himself all too often as a Frank. But most Europeans found Oriental dress cooler and more convenient for travelling in Upper Egypt, though it was less accommodating—unless you stripped down to your drawers —when any physical effort was required. We need hardly doubt, however, that Giovanni had grown a full beard by this time, such as he is shown with in the portrait that forms a frontispiece to his book. Whether he also shaved his head the better to wear a turban we can only guess. But that, though a formidable step for a European, was a good way of keeping cool.

They left Bulaq on 20 February, provisioned for six months. But the cook, the janissary and the interpreter were so unaccustomed to economy that the food began to fail after a month and they were obliged to live on the country. In fact, the janissary was such a useless encumbrance and so insolent to his Christian employers that after a few days they sent him back.

There were strong southerly winds—unusual at this time of year—and the boat made slow progress. One evening they went to a village '*fantasia*' and Giovanni sketched the more modest of the dancers. At Minya, which they reached on 5 March, they paid their respects to Hamid Bey, the 'Admiral' of the Nile. He hinted something about a bottle of rum and they gave him two as an insurance against the boat's being pressed into 'national' service.

What was much more disturbing than this possibility was to find at the house of Dr. Valsomaki—a Greek who distilled his own hard liquor and ran a profitable business in 'antikas' and panaceas—two Copts dressed in Frank costume who turned out to be more agents collecting for Drovetti. They watched each other warily until Belzoni made an excuse for slipping away as quietly as he could.

The following day they reached the experimental sugar refinery which Mr. Brine had set up for the Pasha near Ashmunain, the ancient Hermopolis. There they learnt that Drovetti's agents were making a forced march to Thebes. Giovanni had visions of a host of renegade Frenchmen, Copts and Piedmontese converging on that pregnant plot of ground at Karnak from which he had taken the lion-headed statues. His mind was soon made up. Beechey could go on at his leisure in the boat, but he and Yanni would ride post-haste to Thebes. They hired a horse and donkey and left at midnight. Giovanni says that in the next five and a half days he had only eleven hours' sleep. The rest of the time was spent covering by horse, donkey and camel the two hundred and eighty miles to Karnak. Perhaps that was the beginning of Yanni's hatred of Belzoni.

Belzoni probably had much more cause to be annoyed with Yanni. Three months earlier, on his journey down the Nile, he had been most punctilious about calling on the Daftardar Bey and thanking him for his help. The Turk had then given him a letter, couched in a complimentary style and addressed to the British consul. When the time came for Salt to reply and he was thinking of sending a present to the Acting Governor of Upper Egypt, his interpreter—presumably Yanni—because he was too lazy to write a letter, assured him that this was not necessary. The results, for Giovanni, might have been disastrous. The Daftardar Bey was deeply offended and from then on bestowed his favour on the French. When Giovanni reached Luxor the Bey had already been there and instructed his doctor, a Piedmontese named Marucchi, to dig over the whole area where Belzoni had found the statues. It was said that the Bey intended to form a collection. But this sudden interest of the Turk in antiquities was merely a blind. In due course Drovetti's agents arrived to take possession of the finds, and Drovetti himself supervised their removal. It was some satisfaction to Belzoni that only four of the figures of Sekhmet now unearthed were really in a good state of preservation.

Giovanni lost no time in setting a small number of men to work on either side of the river. Then he hurried off to see the Kashif of Armant and show him his new *firman* from the Pasha. The Kashif was relieved to find that Belzoni had made no complaints about him in Cairo; evidently, he thought, his co-operation after the affair of the anchovies and the olives had outweighed his former defections. Now he came down to Qurna in person and gave the Qaimaqam strict orders to furnish Belzoni with all the help he needed.

Meanwhile, across the river at Karnak, Belzoni's workmen had begun to uncover a seated limestone colossus, nearly thirty feet high,[8] in the vast forecourt of the Great Temple of Amun, beyond the ram-headed sphinxes. He was anxious for the boat to arrive because he had in it some primitive but useful equipment; moreover he was in need of money—and Beechey held the purse-strings. As the rhythm of work slowed down, Belzoni found more time to look at the ruins. Though his eye was always searching for fresh places to dig, he was not insensitive to the grandeur of the great temple-complex at Karnak—big enough to swallow up ten cathedrals—a palimpsest in stone of nearly two thousand years of history yet unread. Sometimes he would wander through the petrified forest of those stupendous flower-headed columns in a state of exaltation. Then all the irritations of everyday life, the jealousy of rival collectors, the venality of the Turks, seemed trivial and remote. Of one such occasion he recalls: 'I was happy for a whole day, which escaped like a flash of lightning.' But he stayed late in the ruins that night, and disenchantment came when he stumbled over a stone in the darkness and broke his nose against another.

Drovetti's agents now arrived—the two Copts Giovanni had seen on the way up-river. They took over from the Piedmontese doctor and began to organize the work on a large scale. Soon almost the whole available labour force at Karnak was absorbed in the French excavations, and Giovanni could hardly raise a man. He was furious at finding himself thus impotent and saw it all as a gigantic conspiracy against him. His angry mutterings still echoed years later in *Narrative*. He did not blame the two Copts so much as 'those who had given them instructions, and others who were sent after them, consisting of European renegades, desperadoes, exiles, &c. People of this sort, under no restraint in any thing they do, were sent to obstruct my proceedings; and met with every encouragement from the Bey, and of course from his subalterns.'

When he could bear to wait no longer, Giovanni set off in a small boat in search of Beechey and found him at Qena, some forty miles below Luxor. It took them another three days to make their way upstream against a head wind. Then, armed with money and equipment, Giovanni plunged into the work again. But he still had difficulty in finding men at Karnak and was obliged to concentrate more and more on the western side of the river in the Thebes of the Dead.

The Arabs of Qurna were wily enough to show visitors only those tombs that had been open for a long time and were completely denuded of all that could be removed, except when they dramatically left a mummy or two *in situ*, in order to extract a larger *bakshish*. They also suspended their own private digging operations when strangers were about, and the signs by which they recognized the presence of a new tomb or a *cache* of mummies were a closely-guarded secret. It was only on this second and prolonged residence at Qurna that Giovanni was able to watch the Arabs at their work and learn something of their methods. They could not altogether hide them from him, and in time they came to respect the enormous bearded Frank whose superhuman strength they had seen demonstrated the year before and who now wanted to pay them for digging whether they found anything or not.

The burial-places in the long rocky tract behind the Memnonium ranged from elaborate mortuary chapels of the Theban nobles to caves and pits where the bodies of ordinary citizens were neatly stacked in criss-cross rows or piled pell-mell—'like macaroni cheese', as Giovanni's compatriot, Pietro Della Valle, had described the mummies at Saqqara two hundred years before.[9] In his day European travellers occasionally brought back some desiccated Egyptian as a scientific curiosity, but mummy—broken up and reduced to a fine powder—was chiefly valued as an item in the pharmacopoeia. John Sanderson, a factor in the Levant Company, who visited Egypt in 1586, shipped home over five hundredweight of mummy fragments for sale to the apothecaries of London, apart from various heads, arms and legs which he kept to show his friends and 'one little hand' that he gave to his brother the Archdeacon of Rochester.[10]

Later travellers sought whole mummies as souvenirs, but even when these were obtained intact there were often considerable difficulties in the way of getting them home, largely because of the superstitious fears of sailors about the presence of a dead body aboard ship. Colonel Missett presented William Turner with a very fine specimen before he left Egypt; *he* had had it from Captain Light, who acquired it in Qurna, as he relates in his *Travels*. The young diplomat packed the mummy in a double chest to make the contents less obvious. Then he addressed it to the British consul at Smyrna. In due course Turkish customs officials opened the cases and sent word to the consul that they had a large box waiting for him, which contained, so they believed, *the body of Napoleon*. How the consul reacted to this startling piece of news is not known, but he forwarded the box with great care to Constantinople. There a captain was found who had no qualms about a body so long dead and eventually Turner received the mummy safe and sound in England.

Mummies were the main object of Belzoni's searches among the tombs, not so much for their own sakes as for the rolls of papyrus that were often hidden in the wrappings or placed under the arms or between the legs. In this he was only following the example of the *fellahin*, who found that papyri commanded the best prices among the casual visitors to Qurna. They were light and easy to carry away—if they did not crumble to dust at a touch—and those found in the tombs usually contained extracts from *The Book of the Dead*[11] and were often beautifully illustrated in colour. Many of the richer tombs had been rifled in antiquity and everything of intrinsic value had gone; all that remained was the smashed coffins, the broken pottery and the trampled *viaticum* of the dead. But in others there was still a profusion of funeral furniture: Canopic jars[12] in sets of four that held the internal organs of the deceased; *shabti*[13] figures in wood or *faience* that would work for him in the under-world; amulets to protect him on his journey—the Eye of Horus and the Girdle Buckle of Isis, the Frog and the Flight of Steps, the Collar and the Head-rest, in agate, cornelian, turquoise, amber, porphyry and granite; scarabs—human-headed, heart-shaped, in all stages of evolution from the original beetle form; rings, necklaces, mirrors and combs, alabaster pots of eyebrow paint, toys and tools and all the loved familiar things that the dead had known in this world and might have need of in the next.

Belzoni evidently came across some burials which, if not intact, at any rate had not been much disturbed. 'It would be impossible,' he says, 'to describe the numerous little articles found in them, which are well adapted to show the domestic habits of the ancient Egyptians.' Nor does he give much account of the wall-paintings, 'as they have been so often described, particularly by Mr. Hamilton'. It is difficult to identify his discoveries merely from such details as: 'Here the paintings are beautiful, not only for their preservation, but for the novelty of their figures. There are two harps, one with nine strings, and the other with fourteen, and several other strange representations: in particular, six dancing girls, with fifes, tambourins, pipes of reeds, guitars, &c.'[14] Funerary feasts are a common enough subject in the Tombs of the Nobles.

At the other extreme from the small T-shaped chapels with their gay, colourful scenes of everyday life, were those so-called 'mummy-pits' that were in fact tunnels running deep into the mountain-side. They had been used for centuries to store the bodies of those who could not afford a private resting-place. Giovanni's description of them is rich in Gothic horror: how they would have provided him with a setting for his own earlier 'phantasmagoria'!

It needed strong nerves and physical stamina to enter these places. 'A vast quantity of dust rises, so fine that it enters into the throat and nostrils, and chokes the nose and mouth to such a degree, that it re-quires great power of lungs to resist it and the strong effluvia of the mummies. This is not all; the entry or passage where the bodies are is roughly cut in the rocks, and the falling of the sand from the upper part or ceiling of the passage causes it to be nearly filled up. In some places there is not more than a vacancy of a foot left, which you must contrive to pass through in a posture like a snail, on pointed and keen stones, that cut like glass.' Remember that Belzoni was six foot six or more in height and broad in proportion!

'After getting through these passages, some of them two or three hundred yards long, you generally find a more commodious place, perhaps high enough to sit. But what a place of rest! surrounded by bodies, by heaps of mummies in all directions; which, previous to my being accustomed to the sight, impressed me with horror. The black-ness of the wall, the faint light given by the candles or torches for want of air, the different objects that surrounded me, seeming to converse with each other, and the Arabs with the candles or torches in their hands, naked and covered with dust, themselves resembling living mummies, absolutely formed a scene that cannot be described. In such a situation I found myself several times, and often returned exhausted and fainting, till at last I became inured to it, and indifferent to what I suffered, except from the dust, which never failed to choke my throat and nose; and though, fortunately, I am destitute of the sense of smelling, I could taste that the mummies were rather unpleasant to swallow.'

Then comes the final horror. 'After the exertion of entering into such a place, through a passage of fifty, a hundred, three hundred, or perhaps six hundred yards, nearly overcome, I sought a resting-place, found one, and contrived to sit; but when my weight bore on the body of an Egyptian, it crushed it like a band-box. I naturally had recourse to my hands to sustain my weight, but they found no better support; so that I sunk altogether among the broken mummies, with a crash of bones, rags, and wooden cases, which raised such a dust as kept me motionless for a quarter of an hour, waiting till it subsided again. I could not remove from the place, however, without increasing it, and every step I took I crushed a mummy in some part or other. Once I was conducted from such a place to another resembling it, through a passage of about

16. THE BLACK AND PAINTED MEN

17. SETI IN THE PRESENCE OF THE GODS

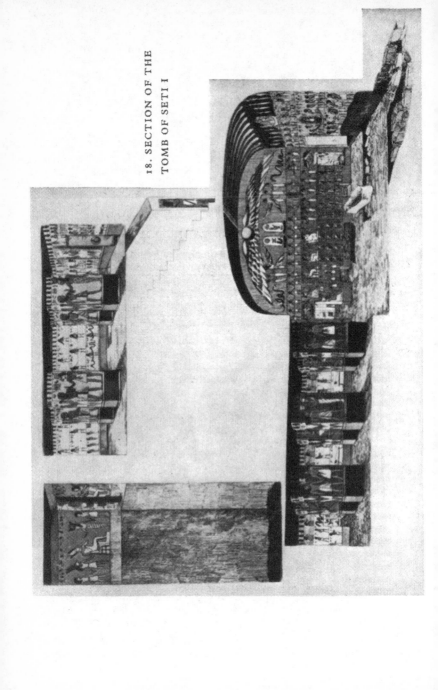

18. SECTION OF THE
TOMB OF SETI I

twenty feet in length, and no wider than that a body could be forced through. It was choked with mummies, and I could not pass without putting my face in contact with that of some decayed Egyptian; but as the passage inclined downwards, my own weight helped me on: however, I could not avoid being covered with bones, legs, arms, and heads rolling from above.'

Whenever Giovanni chose to stay the night at Qurna instead of returning to Beechey's little bivouac in the Temple of Luxor, he would lodge with some troglodytic family in a tomb. Usually it was one of the smaller mortuary chapels of the nobles. The doorway leading to the inner chamber would be walled up with mud, except for an opening just big enough for a man to creep through. Here the sheep were penned at night, strangely protected by the two jackal guardians of the tomb depicted over the doorway. The walls and ceiling of the outer chamber were blackened by smoke; plaster peeled from the three-thousand-year-old paintings. A clay saucer of rancid oil or mutton-fat fed a tiny flame. The only other furniture was a mat spread on the ground and a few crocks. Here Belzoni would hold court, seated cross-legged in the place of honour, while the Arabs brought him articles to sell and spun him tales of legendary treasure. In spite of their guile and cupidity the Arabs of Qurna were always friendly and hospitable towards Belzoni; 'whenever they supposed I should stay all night, they always killed a couple of fowls for me, which were baked in a small oven heated with pieces of mummy cases, and sometimes with the bones and rags of the mummies themselves.' Giovanni was astonished at the happiness of these people.

Sometimes he had a visitor from the outside world. On one occasion two fathers of the Propaganda—Capuchin friars from the Roman Catholic convent at Akhmim whom he had met on his first journey south—came to see the antiquities. Giovanni says he showed them everything—Karnak, Luxor, the Memnonium, the Tombs of the Kings —but 'the holy fathers, who had as much taste for antiquity as the animals that brought them', were quite unmoved. The only thing that roused them to exclamations of wonder was the discovery of a friend's name scrawled in charcoal on a wall.

The least welcome visitor was the Daftardar Bey. By the time he arrived, at the end of April, Belzoni had got his work well organized. At Karnak he had discovered another colossal head of red granite, finely polished and well preserved; it matched the colossal arm which he had already marked down for removal.[15] Both were now taken to his riverside dump at Luxor. Then there was the so-called 'altar with the six divinities',[16] so much admired by the French at the time of their survey. Belzoni took it—under the very eyes of Drovetti's agents—from the little temple of Mentu at the north-east corner of Karnak. With four large lion-headed statues of Sekhmet and the cover of the granite sarcophagus which Drovetti had so rashly offered him the year before, Giovanni now had enough antiquities to make a second boat-load.

The two Copts, furious at Belzoni's success and frightened at the possible consequences for themselves, hurried off to complain to the Daftardar Bey as soon as they heard he was in the neighbourhood. Muhammad, who was still piqued at the slight he imagined had been put upon him by the British consul, at once gave orders to the local Kashifs, Qaimaqams and Shaikhs that they should not allow the English any further facilities. As soon as Giovanni learnt this from the friendly Shaikh of Qurna, he went off to see the Bey and show him his *firman* from the Pasha. The Daftardar waved it aside and suggested—a little dangerously perhaps—that Muhammad Ali was in his dotage. Then curiosity moved him to come to Qurna where, in order to show his authority, he commanded the Shaikh to produce for him within the hour an untouched mummy. Incredibly, the man succeeded, but in spite of that the Daftardar, who wanted any excuse to intimidate the men who had worked for the English, had the Shaikh beaten till he was nearly unconscious. Giovanni threatened to write to Cairo to let the Pasha know how his orders were carried out by his own son-in-law. Whereupon the Daftardar saw he had gone too far and promised Belzoni an authority to procure workmen. But when the letter was read aloud days later to the assembled Arabs of Qurna, Giovanni realized that the Bey had double-crossed him. The order expressly forbade them either to work for the English or sell them antiquities; instead they were to offer everything they found to M. Drovetti or his agents.

Beechey sent the consul a full account of this affair, mentioning also another incident in which Yanni had been beaten by Arabs at Karnak. Salt replied on 12 May, saying that he had already seen Muhammad Ali and registered a strong protest. 'The Pasha,' he added, 'appeared much vexed and hurt at what had passed, and declared that he would write such a letter as should prevent any such treatment in future . . . I wish you, however, clearly to understand, that I do not agree with you in considering this to be a national insult, or as having anything to do with my Consular character. You must be aware that neither yourself, nor Mr. Belzoni, are at present engaged in any official employ; you are simply in the same situation as two travellers forming a collection, and are therefore only entitled to such reparation as any English gentleman would have a right to expect. It is absolutely necessary that this should be explicitly understood, for as you know I have no authority from Government for employing any person in such pursuits, and that I am bearing the whole expense and collecting for myself, you can only be considered as acting in a private capacity.' (As Beechey later told Salt's biographer that 'Belzoni was of so suspicious and dissatisfied a disposition, that it was in some respects difficult to keep on any terms with him', one wonders if the secretary risked an explosion by showing this part of the letter to Belzoni.) Finally the consul said: 'The affair of Yanni is chiefly to be attributed to your want of a Janisary to deliver you from this unpleasant predicament; I have therefore engaged the Albanian, who was with Mr. Bankes, in my service, and have sent him up to join you, and I would wish you, in consequence, to stay at Thebes until his arrival. I send you a small stock of medicines, some of the knives bought at Alexandria, some rice, tobacco, dried apricots, and wine. I have made arrangements with Cochini that you may have what money may be necessary. Say every thing kind on my part to Mr. Belzoni, and repeat my delight at the discovery of the head, vases and papyri.'

Beechey had evidently indicated that they were going on to Philae, as it seemed pointless now to remain at Thebes. By the time Salt's courier arrived they had gone, leaving Giovanni's collection on the quay at Luxor covered with earth and surrounded by a mud wall. At Philae there was an unpleasant surprise for Belzoni, which in his present mood made him mad with anger against the French. When he went to the little temple at the southern end of the island to look at the sculptured slabs he had left behind the year before, he found they had all been mutilated. Scrawled in charcoal on a stone were the jeering words, 'operation manquée' ('job spoilt'). Giovanni had no doubt where to lay the collective blame. Three of Drovetti's agents—Cailliaud, Rifaud and Rosignano—had gone up to Aswan in the previous October and prevented the slabs from being put aboard the boat. One of them must have done the damage at the same time. Of the three Cailliaud, the mineralogist, seemed to be the most respectable. But later Rifaud, the fiery little Marseillais, told Belzoni that it was Cailliaud who had mutilated the slabs with the little hammer that he always carried. Afterwards he retracted this statement and then again reaffirmed it. Psychologically we should expect the mineralogist to have been more capable of such cold-blooded treatment of stone than the sculptor and artist that we know Rifaud was. On the other hand the culprit may have been the unpleasant Rosignano.

However, it was no use crying over broken stones. Giovanni presently settled down to making a model in wax of the portico of the great temple of Isis, while he waited for the courier from Salt. He had set himself an extraordinarily difficult task, for already in May the thermometer sometimes stood at 124° F. and this was only because the mercury could go no higher!

When the courier arrived he brought the welcome news that Salt had at last agreed to Belzoni's repeated request that he should be allowed to complete his excavations at Abu Simbel. (Whether a flat refusal would have made any difference to Giovanni is a moot point.) But the consul still expressed his doubts about the existence of a temple and thought that the sculptured rock might prove to be no more than a façade.

The 'Albanian' whom Salt had now sent to go with the travellers as their janissary was a really remarkable character. Giovanni Finati[17] was born at Ferrara, only forty miles from Belzoni's own birth-place of Padua. Conscripted against his will into the French army, he was sent to Dalmatia and there deserted to the Turks. He became—nominally at least—a Muslim and adopted the name of Muhammad. In 1809 he went to Egypt and enlisted in the service of the Pasha. He was present at the massacre of the Mamluks, took part in the campaign against the Wahhabis, visited Mecca and was in Cairo again—though out of the army—at the time of the mutiny in August 1815. A month later he was engaged as interpreter by William John Bankes, who already had in his service a Frenchman from St. Domingo, an Arab and a Portuguese. This polyglot company set off up the Nile and, as we know, succeeded in reaching the Second Cataract. Finati had thus seen Abu Simbel and knew the local Kashifs. Afterwards he accompanied Bankes through Palestine and Syria and only left his service in June 1816, when Bankes went to Cyprus. Back in Cairo once more, with strong recommendations from Bankes and Burckhardt, Finati was marked down by Salt for future employment whenever an opportunity occurred. Nothing seemed more suited to his experience than the mission to Nubia.

A few days before his arrival at Philae two English travellers appeared in the island. The Honourable Charles Leonard Irby and James Mangles were both captains in the Royal Navy.[18] They had been friends since their early days together in H.M.S. *Narcissus*. Irby was nearly twenty-eight and Mangles three years older. The summer before they had set out on a post-war tour of Europe that had taken them further and further East and was to last four years in all. Both had a taste for adventure and exploring and, once they reached Egypt, they could do no less than go as far as the Second Cataract. Their arrival in Philae at this moment was a great stroke of luck for Giovanni. He knew the trouble he was likely to have with the Kashifs and their followers; four Europeans, it seemed to him, would command so much more respect than two. When he broached the idea of their joining forces Irby and Mangles were delighted; this was just the kind of enterprise they needed to give point to their travels. Moreover, as there was difficulty in finding a second boat to go up the Nile, that seemed to settle the matter.

For what was probably the first and last time the birthday of His Majesty King George III—the Glorious Fourth of June—was celebrated at Philae this year. Early in the morning the Navy ran up a flag on the highest pylon in the island. At noon they fired a salute of twenty-one guns. As they had only five fire-arms among them, this meant reloading till the barrels were too hot to hold. At night they let off another *feu de joie*. The natives were astonished that so much powder should be used and nobody killed.

On the following day Sarah arrived with James Curtin. Giovanni does not say whether he expected her or not, nor does she tell us why she made the journey. Perhaps she was anxious to see how Giovanni was faring after three months' absence. Perhaps she was bored or the plague drove her to leave Cairo. There was one other likely reason. Sarah was very eager to be present at the opening of the temple at Abu Simbel, and she may have known or guessed that Giovanni would soon be making his way there. So it was a great disappointment to her when she learnt that she was not to be included in the party. There was no room in the boat—so Giovanni said. Can it have been that he did not want Sarah with him on this occasion?

At any rate she was left sitting on a large quantity of luggage on the roof of the great temple of Isis, surrounded by a mud wall—like the collection at Luxor—and guarded against the Barabra[19] guards by James Curtin and her own stout heart. Sarah made what she cheerfully calls 'two comfortable rooms' of mud brick and, while James cleaned the silver (brought up for the use of Mr. Beechey) under the goggling eyes of the Arabs, she would casually handle a pair of loaded pistols. Every day the women came across from both sides of the Nile to see this wonder. They brought her eggs and onions and little 'antikas' in return for beads and small hand-mirrors.

The men left Philae on 16 June. In the party were the two naval officers, Beechey and Belzoni, Yanni, Hajji Muhammad (*alias* Finati) and an Arab cook. The crew consisted of five men—four brothers and their brother-in-law—and three boys, who were the sons of one or other members of the crew; the boat itself belonged to the boys' grandfather. From the start the travellers had trouble with this ingrowing family enterprise and particularly with the brother-in-law, Hasan, who was soon nicknamed 'the blue devil'.[20]

The Kashifs, Dawud and Khalil, were not at Abu Simbel when the boat arrived there, but the temple seemed undisturbed. Belzoni sent a message to the chiefs, and the travellers continued their journey up the Nile to Wadi Halfa. Here the crew staged a sit-down strike ashore in an attempt to get more money and the local inhabitants demanded *bakshish* for the view of the Cataract. Mangles pointed out that they were not charged for a sight of the travellers and so might consider themselves quits.

The boat returned to Abu Simbel on 4 July. Three days later a messenger on a camel came to see if this was really the party for whom Hasan had promised to open the temple. He went away satisfied that it was.

Another three days passed and then Dawud and Khalil appeared and squatted in their grass tents on the bank of the river. Giovanni had wisely sent them presents of turbans while he was in Cairo and this remembrance from afar had made a good impression; they were now in a most *receptive* mood.

They began to expatiate on the way in which they had resisted French attempts to seduce them from their engagement to the English. Giovanni cut them short by producing more presents. There was a gun for Dawud that had cost twelve pounds ten in Cairo, another turban and some trifles like soap, tobacco, gunpowder and coffee. For Khalil, the younger brother, the principal gift was a turban, but this was clearly a mistake. He wanted a gun too and went off to sulk in his tent when he saw that he was not going to get it. Giovanni could only placate him by giving him one of his own.

It was agreed that work should begin the next day, but fewer men turned up than had been bargained for, and even these were late. The temple—if such indeed it was—appeared much as it had done the previous September, though perhaps more sand had drifted into the hollow between the two central colossi. Re-Harakhte in his niche still strode boldly forward over the conjectured door, and high above him on the cavetto cornice the row of dog-headed apes sat facing the rising sun.[21]

The work went very slowly that day. The men sang a song that said Christian money was very good and they would get as much as they could. In the evening Giovanni made a bargain with the Kashifs that he would pay three hundred piastres for the temple to be opened, irrespective of the time it took. The Nubians thought they could do it in one day; Giovanni's party estimated three or four. About a hundred men appeared on the 12th and Dawud and Khalil took charge of operations, driving them hard all day. On the 13th there was much less enthusiasm. On the 14th they were too busy plundering a passing caravan of Moors to be interested in the temple. There was a desultory day's work on the 15th and that was the end of it as far as the Nubians were concerned. They had got their three hundred piastres, Ramadan began the next day, and the Franks were as far off reaching their treasure as they had been when they came.

Giovanni was not unprepared for this. That was why, independent though he was, he had welcomed the co-operation of two such stalwart young men as Irby and Mangles. All that he could hope for now from Dawud and Khalil was that they would stop their constant importunity for pipes, coffee-cups, knives, swords and anything else that took their fancy when they came aboard the boat. Before they left to go to Derr for the celebration of Ramadan, Belzoni told Dawud that the English would open the temple themselves, but that, faithful to their agreement, they would warn the Kashif just before they reached the door so that he could come to take his share of the gold. That afternoon, when all was quiet under the blazing eye of the sun, Giovanni left the crew asleep on the little beach below the temple and climbed up the burning white slope with his five helpers—Beechey, the two captains, Yanni and Muhammad. Stripped to the waist they set to, silently, to shift the sand.

An hour later some of the crew came up in astonishment to see the Europeans working without their shirts. They were even more surprised at the progress they had made. Presently, unbidden, they joined in and by the time darkness fell Mangles reckoned they had done about as much as forty of the villagers would have achieved in a whole day. Giovanni gave the boatmen two piastres each and the boys one, and promised this as a daily rate if they would work in the same way as the Franks.

For the next fortnight the Europeans rose each day before dawn, worked from first light or even earlier till about nine—when the sun became too hot—then continued again from three in the afternoon till the stars were out in the night sky. Yet this seeming routine was interrupted by every possible kind of distraction and excitement. Not all the twenty-two dog-headed apes from the cornice above them could have caused more mischief than the combined efforts of the crew, the villagers of Abu Simbel, a rival party from over the water and the spies and emissaries of Dawud and Khalil. Hasan—'the blue devil', as Mangles called him—tried to incite his brothers-in-law to mutiny and murder. Sometimes there were two, sometimes a hundred villagers demanding work. Two inferior Kashifs from Ibrim—but both better armed than Dawud and Khalil—came across from the eastern bank and offered their services but stayed to threaten. Dawud sent a spy to see who worked. Hasan chased Finati with a knife. The cook threw a kettle of water over a man who demanded money and was nearly killed by the enraged Nubian. There was a fracas between the villagers of Abu Simbel and the men from over the water. The workmen forged the pay-slips signed by Belzoni. Musmar—'Mr. Nail'—the old rogue of a foreman (self-appointed), tried to draw the wages of ten non-existent workers. The price of everything doubled. Tools disappeared, bread was stolen, the milkman was intimidated—and somebody sang, 'Nubia is a garden full of flowers'.

On Monday, 21 July, the diggers uncovered the right elbow of the statue to the north of the supposed site of the door. It gave them great encouragement, for it proved that the figures were seated, which meant they would not have to go so far down. But later the same day they came upon a rough projection from the wall that seemed to extend all the way between the two central figures; it suggested ominously that the temple had never been finished. Yet they continued digging, determined to find positive proof, one way or the other, about the existence of a door.

By the 30th the rough projection was found to be a cornice that had been badly damaged by a fall of stone and then crudely chiselled in an effort to reshape it. Below the torus moulding were hieroglyphs, finely carved. The travellers' hopes again rose high.

On the following day Giovanni drove in a row of palm-tree piles two or three yards from the cornice. Behind this palisade he poured a mixture of mud and sand to prevent the fine grains from running through. Then they began to clear the 'well' thus left, consolidating the sand with buckets of water from the Nile.

The sun was already setting behind the cliff when a small dark hole appeared in the rock; it was the broken upper corner of a doorway. The crew, who were working then with interest, began to shout, '*Bakshish! Bakshish!*', but Giovanni curbed their exuberance. They did not know yet how deep the sand might be within the temple. It was dusk by the time they had made the hole big enough for a man to crawl through. They could not see anything and, as the air inside was probably foul, Giovanni decided not to enter till the morning.

Perhaps too there was a flash of the old genius of showmanship in this decision, though Belzoni would never have admitted it. For, as the temple faced due east, Giovanni's observant eye must have noticed that the sun, when it rose, would cast its rays directly into the entrance and illumine the sanctuary beyond. There could be no more impressive moment for entering the shrine.

It was still moonlight on the morning of Friday, 1 August, when Giovanni and his companions climbed up the slope to the temple with candles in their hands. They had called to the crew to join them, but there was no response, although the men were awake. Presently, as they worked to enlarge the opening, they heard a commotion below, Hasan's voice roaring and the often-repeated word '*bakshish*'. Yanni went down to fetch a lamp and came back with a report that the crew were abusing them roundly and threatening to leave at once. When they saw this had no effect, they stumped up the hill, fully dressed in turbans and galabiyas—as they always were on these mutinous occasions—and armed with sticks, pikes, swords, daggers and a couple of rusty old pistols. There was a noisy altercation by the light of the flickering candles and the paling moon. Giant shadows danced over the figures of the colossi. The captain of the crew screamed in simulated rage and poured sand—for ashes—upon his head. Giovanni argued and expostulated. The bland, impassive features of Ramses II smiled secretly above them. And, while everyone else was engrossed in the dispute, Finati slipped through the hole like a lizard and was the first to enter the temple.

Suddenly they realized he had gone. The wrangling stopped immediately. One by one the travellers squeezed through the hole and slid down the slope of sand inside. They found themselves in a lofty pillared hall, where eight colossal figures of the king, Osirid in form, with crook and flail, faced each other in two rows of four across a central aisle. The square pillars at their backs were decorated with a series of brilliantly-coloured reliefs showing Pharaoh in the presence of the gods —Horus, Isis and Amun-Re, Harakhte and Ptah, Hathor of Thebes and Tum of On, ram-headed Khnum and ithyphallic Min. Vultures with outspread wings spanned the ceiling of the central aisle.

Beyond the hall and in line with the entrance was a smaller chamber with four square pillars; on them were scenes showing the king embraced by the gods. Beyond this again lay a narrow ante-chamber and then the sanctuary itself. As the travellers walked forward, crunching underfoot a black powdery substance which they afterwards judged to be decayed wood and holding aloft their candles to drive away the shadows, they could see in the depths of the sanctuary strange terrifying shapes. Even while they watched, the sun in majesty rose above the eastern horizon and threw a shaft of golden light along the main axis of the temple, dimming the pale candles. The splendour touched the four great seated figures ranged along the west wall of the sanctuary—mummied Ptah with his sceptre of life, power and stability; Amun-Re wearing his high plumed head-dress; Ramses himself, now admitted to the company of the gods, and hawk-headed Harakhte. Perhaps this was their first epiphany for a thousand years.

The sunlight did not last long in the temple, but with the aid of candles and torches Belzoni and his party were able to make a quick survey of the interior. The walls of the main hall were decorated with what he recognized as the exploits of the same hero he had seen so often represented in the Ramesseum, at Medinet Habu, and in the temples of Luxor and Karnak. Once again Ramses II boringly re-enacted his famous charge at Kadesh. Here on the north wall was the Egyptian army marching into Hittite territory, and Pharaoh dangerously far advanced with his favourite Amun division. The soldiers pitch their tents and relax unsuspecting behind the security of the stockade, believing the enemy is at Aleppo. But the Hittites have lured them into a trap. Two spies are caught and flogged and they reveal the truth. There is a hurried council of war—and then the attack is on. Single-handed in his chariot, Ramses cuts his way through a whole enemy brigade. Here is Kadesh on its hill above the Orontes and the Hittites in retreat and— last scene of all—Ramses and his officers counting prisoners and the severed hands of the dead.

Opposite, on the southern wall, is the hero again, gigantic in his chariot, firing arrows against a fort. But now with the fallen Asiatics are rows of negro and Nubian captives—a timely reminder to the local population.

Although none of the historical background was known at this time, it was evident to the travellers that here were the chronicles of a Pharaoh whose empire had stretched over many races of men. Giovanni and his companions were greatly impressed by the quality of the reliefs, and indeed he thought they were better, or at least bolder, than any he had seen in Egypt. But, apart from the satisfaction of having opened what was now seen to be the largest and finest rock-cut temple in Nubia, Giovanni's main quest was for antiquities that he could take away. Here the results must have seemed to him rather disappointing. He merely mentions that they found 'two lions with hawks' heads, the body as large as life; a small sitting figure, and some copper work belonging to the doors'.

Mangles, realizing in advance of his time the importance of recording the *exact circumstances* of an archaeological find, drew a plan of the temple on a scale of one twenty-fifth of an inch to a foot. On it he showed the position in which they found 'Part of a Monkey' or 'Half of Statue holding a Ram's Head'. Sorted out and pieced together, the sculptures amounted to a small pair of sandstone hawk-headed sphinxes, one perfect, the other slightly damaged; a cynocephalus monkey similar to those above the cornice but not so large; the upper parts of two colossal limestone statues, probably wives of Ramses II; and an odd little figure in painted limestone, kneeling and holding before it a curiously shaped pedestal on which is the ram's head of Amun. The small, sad face— Mangles thought it was a woman's—belonged, as we know now from the inscription, to Pa-ser, prince of Kash and governor of Nubia in the time of Ramses II.[22] These were all taken down to the boat. There was also a limestone torso of a male figure too decayed to remove. In the doorway leading to the second chamber they found a broken bronze socket for the pivot of a door. Traces of the wooden pivots still remained in the upper part of each doorway and there were other fragments of wood from temple furniture. 'Some of these,' says Mangles, 'appeared so perfect that we thought of bringing them away, but they mouldered at the first touch; we were, therefore, very careful in leaving what remained for the benefit of future travellers.' Mangles had in him more than the beginnings of a good archaeologist. But here were the problems of conservation all too clearly stated.

While Mangles and Irby measured and surveyed the temple inside and out, Beechey and Giovanni tried to get down on paper as much as they could of the scenes and inscriptions on the walls. But the atmosphere inside the rock was like that of the hottest and steamiest Turkish bath. The perspiration from their arms made their drawing-books so wet that they had to give up. So they contented themselves with strengthening the palisade in front of the entrance in the hope of keeping the sand at bay. On Sunday evening—after more trouble with Hasan —they managed to get the statuary aboard the boat and the crew were given a *bakshish* of forty piastres. Then early on Monday morning— 4 August 1817—they started on the return journey to Aswan.

Eighteen months later Beechey and Finati went back to Abu Simbel with Salt and William John Bankes. The party also included an Italian doctor named Ricci with a talent for drawing, and a young French draughtsman, Louis Maurice Adolphe Linant, who had been in the service of the Pasha. Under Bankes's able direction this team of amateur and professional artists tackled the problem of recording the reliefs and hieroglyphics in a most systematic way. The interior of the temple, says Finati, 'was lighted every day, and almost all day long, with from twenty to fifty small wax candles, fixed upon clusters of palm branches, which were attached to long upright poles, and, spreading like the arms of a chandelier, more than half way to the ceiling, enabled Mr. Bankes, and the other draughtsmen, to copy all the paintings in detail, as they stood, almost naked, upon their ladders'.

They also cleared the sand away completely from the most southerly colossus of the façade and discovered some female figures about its legs —giantesses even these—that were later to be identified as three of the reputed fifty-one daughters of Ramses II. When they measured Pharaoh himself they made him sixty-two feet from the base to the tip of his Double Crown. There were various Greek *graffiti* scrawled on the lower part of the legs which prompted Bankes to think that there might be even more on the statues nearer the entrance. So with great labour they shifted the sand from the second colossus and partly covered up the first again, because the Nile was too far away to dump the sand there. But they were rewarded by finding on the left leg of the headless colossus, near the doorway, an inscription chipped into the stone by a humorous Greek mercenary in the army of Psammetichus II (593–588 B.C.) and his comrade 'Axe'. This gave them a latest date for the building of the temple, but it was in fact nearly seven hundred years old when the Greeks passed that way; today we regard it as the over-blown achievement of a civilization already decadent after two thousand years of dynastic history.[23]

When they left Abu Simbel, Bankes's party had reduced the general level of the sand considerably, so that the visitor had a much better idea of the grand façade. A year later Finati passed that way again, now in the service of Sir Frederick Henniker, who, as he frankly admitted, was more interested in hunting and fowling than in Pharaohs and hiero-glyphics. However the baronet was not going to miss Abu Simbel. He found that in the course of twelve months the sand had completely covered up the entrance again and the men of Abu Simbel—who may have helped nature in expectation of a tourist trade—were prepared to dig it out again in twelve days if he employed thirty men. To call their bluff, Henniker forced in a pole with a sheet wrapped round it and made a kind of funnel through which he was able to slide into the temple. He had to reduce his 'habiliments', as he says, 'to a pocket-handkerchief', but he stayed four hours in that super-heated atmo-sphere, marvelling at the liveliness of the battle scenes. Getting out again through the sheet was a tricky business, for he had to work against the stream of soft sand that poured down into the entrance. Finati eventually pulled him clear, whereupon Henniker—who attracted oddity—found himself confronted by 'a Russian colonel very impatient and very angry at having been stopped. He went to the entrance, and returned immediately fully satisfied—the aperture was not large enough for him.'

If Giovanni ever read Sir Frederick Henniker's *Notes* he might well have taken offence at a couple of flippant phrases that seem like a direct 'dig' at Belzoni's fair-ground past. The colossi in front of the smaller temple, he says, are 'of such a size that a man who exhibits himself at three-ha'pence per foot would scarcely arrive above the knee', while the statues of the larger temple are 'equal to nine copies of the Irish Giant placed in a perpendicular line'. (O'Brien was a regular attraction at Bartholomew Fair round the turn of the century.) But Giovanni could hardly have been more delighted than by the words with which the baronet bade farewell to Abu Simbel—'contented to finish my journey in this part, with having seen *the noblest monument of antiquity that is to be found on the banks of the Nile*'.[24]

CHAPTER X

I have been very successful, as you may communicate to Mr.
Hamilton, in my researches in Upper Egypt; and above all, have
discovered a King's tomb, where the paintings are exquisitely beautiful
and fresh as on the day they were finished.

HENRY SALT in a letter to Mr. B.,[1] 1818

ON their way down river Belzoni and his companions met Dawud and Khalil. The latter plagued them with paltry presents in the hope of getting a better. The former protested his innocence of everything that had happened at Abu Simbel, even before the travellers made any complaint. But it was politic to keep on good terms with Dawud, now that he was the unofficial custodian of the temple. Giovanni therefore gave him some boots and looking-glasses for his wife.

There was more trouble now with the crew and, in particular, with Hasan. Once, after a violent scene, he drew his dagger and tried to stab Belzoni. Captain Irby had his hand badly cut in wresting the weapon away from him.

At Philae they found Sarah serene and unruffled on the top of the temple of Isis. They came down the Cataract in the Nubian boat and then thankfully paid off the crew and saw the last of them.

They reached Luxor in another boat on 17 August and installed themselves in the temple sanctuary. There was a letter from Salt saying that he intended shortly to come up the Nile to look at the antiquities. But Giovanni's first thought was to find out who was digging at Thebes, and where. The two Copts had gone and in their place were a couple of Piedmontese—Rosignano, with whom Giovanni had had an unpleasant encounter already, and a certain Antonio Lebolo, a former *gendarme* of Milan. Profiting by the absence of Belzoni, Drovetti's agents had turned their attention from the temples of Karnak to the tombs of Qurna, and had been pretty successful among the mummies. Giovanni was reluctant to work anywhere near these men, and partly for this reason, partly because of the hopeful indications he had found a few months before, he decided to concentrate on the Valley of the Kings.

Irby and Mangles spent a few days sight-seeing round the tombs and temples before they left for Cairo, and Giovanni was delighted to act as cicerone to such an appreciative pair. He found Mangles in particular a most enthusiastic admirer of his discoveries. He liked the company of these two cheerful young men, and they evidently respected him, even if, as Beechey said later, they thought he was more than a little mad. They had been through an exciting adventure together and that had established a bond.

When the captains had gone and Beechey had settled down to fill his drawing-book with sketches, Giovanni retired alone to the Valley of the Kings. He knew from his reading of Hamilton that at the beginning of the Christian era there were eighteen open tombs in the valley. Strabo, the Greek geographer who visited Egypt in 24 B.C., had said that about forty royal tombs existed beyond the Memnonium,[2] while his contemporary, the historian Diodorus Siculus, reported that the Egyptian priests of his day claimed to have records of forty-seven.[3] Giovanni counted ten or eleven that he thought might be classed as royal tombs and five or six that seemed to him to be 'of a lower order'. This agreed well enough with the ancient figure of eighteen and with Hamilton's own statement that in 1801–2 not more than ten were accessible, though the sites of several others could easily be determined.[4] The French *savants* who came with Napoleon listed eleven tombs already known and added a twelfth that they discovered in the remote and desolate valley which forms a kind of annexe to Biban el-Muluk, beyond it to the west.[5] This was the large and magnificent tomb that had once been for a short time the resting-place of Amenhetep III. Near it, in the Western Valley, Belzoni had discovered in the previous year the modest tomb of Ai. With this to encourage him, and believing—wrongly—that the Egyptians had first built royal tombs at Qurna and then gone further into the hills, Giovanni thought that the Western Valley might prove most productive. Little enough had been discovered in nearly two thousand years, but there was a strong and persistent tradition pointing to the existence of forty or more tombs. Hamilton saw no reason to discredit the view that a score or so still lay hidden in the hillside. He even added with touching but unfounded optimism that 'if, by the exertions of the curious and the liberal, they ever come to be explored anew, the sculptures and paintings in them must be untouched, and the tombs or sarcophagi themselves unhurt; for the greater part were certainly closed before the profane were allowed to enter and destroy'.

The Pharaohs of the Old Kingdom (*c.* 2800–2300 B.C.)—Cheops, Chephren, Mycerinus and the rest—relied mainly on the mass of stone in their pyramids to protect their tombs from violation by robbers; huge granite plugs and portcullises, masonry so exact that the joints in the casing-blocks were only one-fiftieth of an inch wide, reinforced their hopes of security.[6] But in this they were deceived, for the pyramids were all plundered, perhaps in the Dark Ages that followed the decay

of the Old Kingdom. In the Middle Kingdom (*c.* 2160–1785 B.C.)
Pharaohs like Senusret II and Amenemhet III tried to baffle the tomb-
robbers with a complicated maze of passages and chambers in the sub-
structure of their pyramids.[7] Yet this proved no more effective. By the
beginning of the Eighteenth Dynasty, which marked the rise of the
New Kingdom (*c.* 1580–1085 B.C.), there were probably few royal rest-
ing-places in all Egypt—*mastaba*, pyramid or rock-cut tomb—that had
not been rifled by the treasure-seekers. Their magnificence was their
undoing.

It was Thothmes I, the third king of the Eighteenth Dynasty, who
decided that in spite of the inconvenience to his spirit—which would
have to go down to his mortuary temple at Medinet Habu to receive
its offerings—his best chance of bodily survival lay in having a tomb
dug as unobtrusively as possible in some remote corner of the Libyan
Hills. His architect, Ineni, records on the walls of his own elegant little
tomb at Qurna how he thought he had complied with the royal wish.
'I was alone when I superintended the excavation of His Majesty's cliff-
tomb; no one saw and no one heard.' To make up for the inconspicuous
rabbit-hole of an entrance he concentrated on the interior decoration
and experimented with various kinds of plaster. Ineni was very pleased
with the result. But when the tomb of Thothmes I was discovered in
1899 there was little inside it apart from the broken fragments of a
sarcophagus.[8] In 1903 Howard Carter and T. M. Davies found another
sarcophagus bearing the name of this king in the tomb of his daughter
and successor, the masterful Queen Hatshepsut;[9] evidently at some
time—and probably during her reign—his body had been moved there
for safety. But still Thothmes was not secure. He was whisked away
again by panic-stricken priests in the Twenty-first Dynasty and hidden,
along with some forty other royalties, in a cleft of the rock at Deir el-
Bahari. For nearly three thousand years this remarkable *cache* remained
undisturbed. When at last it came to light in 1881 through the unusual
prosperity of a Qurna family that had been quietly living on this treasure
for the past six years, the coffin of Thothmes I was found to contain
the body of Pinezem II.[10] In the tomb itself Ineni's stucco has long since
fallen off the walls.[11]

Yet in spite of the lack of security in the Valley of the Kings, the
Pharaohs of the New Kingdom continued to be buried there. Pride got
the better of prudence and their tombs became more and more magnificent. The sarcophagi were immense; huge blocks sealed the imposing
entrances, which were then covered with *débris*. It was to no purpose.
The tombs of twenty-five Pharaohs have been found in Biban el-Muluk
or the Western Valley, and virtually all who reigned from Thothmes I
to the last Ramses of the Twentieth Dynasty are now accounted for.

Akhenaten, the heretic king, was buried at his capital of Amarna, and so probably was his successor, Smenkh-ka-Re. The only doubtful case is Thothmes II, but a small uninscribed tomb similar to that of Thothmes I has been presumed on good grounds to be his; certainly his coffin was found in the *cache* at Deir el-Bahari. Possibly a late Ramessid is missing, but it was under these weakling Pharaohs of the twelfth century B.C.—who all bore the name Ramses—that something like a state of chaos prevailed in the Valley of the Kings as a result of the tomb-robberies. In the reign of Ramses IX a commission was set up to investigate the scandal. From papyrus records of the subsequent trials and from labels on the coffins found at Deir el-Bahari we know how the gangs were organized and how the priests tried to foil them by switching the royal mummies from tomb to tomb. Ramses III was re-buried at least three times in this dynasty. Even Osymandias, King of Kings, had to be moved for greater security to the tomb of his father, Seti I. Later both were the uninvited guests of Queen Anhapu. They ended by being dumped—safely, if unceremoniously—in the *cache* at Deir el-Bahari.

Not one of the known burials in the Valley of the Kings was left undisturbed. Even the tomb of Tutankhamun was entered a few years after his death. But the thieves were evidently interrupted at their work and, though the rich and splendid furniture of the ante-chamber and its annexe was thrown about in confusion, little was taken away. The obscure entrance to the tomb, hidden under the remains of workmen's huts, kept it virtually intact until our own day.

After a careful survey of the Western Valley, Belzoni decided that there was only one likely place for a tomb. He had managed to get permission from the Kashif of Qus to employ twenty men. (This Kashif was now responsible for the area around Thebes since Giovanni's 'olives and anchovies' man at Armant had fallen foul of the Daftardar Bey and been dismissed.) Giovanni set the men to work digging at a spot about a hundred yards from the tomb of Ai. A little below the flinty surface they came upon some large stones. When these were removed a deep cutting in the rock was revealed. At the lower end was the walled-up entrance to the tomb. With a palm-tree laid across the cutting and another slung from it on ropes, Giovanni made a simple but effective ram. (We need not be too shocked at this; it was the only way to breach the rough wall of polygonal stones set in thick mortar, and no great harm was done, though Belzoni probably destroyed the clay or plaster seals that at a later date would have identified the occupant.) When he had squeezed through the gap, Giovanni found himself at the top of a flight of stone steps. At the foot were four coffins lying on the floor of the burial-chamber, bedded in cement, their heads towards the entrance. Beyond these were another four. All were painted and one of them was covered with a pall.

This was one of the two remaining tombs to be discovered in the Western Valley after those of Amenhetep III and Ai.[12] They contain no inscriptions and no names can be assigned to them, but they probably belonged to members of the Theban royal family at the end of the Eighteenth Dynasty. Giovanni unwrapped each of the mummies and noted that one of them had new bandagings over the old—a circumstance which, he says, showed 'that the Egyptians took great care of their dead, even for many years after their decease'. The painted linen pall on the principal coffin fell to pieces at a touch.

Giovanni had some satisfaction in finding mummies and coffins in their original position. But his hopes were centred much more on the objects that might be buried with the dead Pharaohs and he now inclined to the view—in which he was not far wrong—that the Western Valley was exhausted. Accordingly he turned his attention to Biban el-Muluk and, after splitting his workmen into small groups, set them to dig in several places at once. On the fourth day—9 October—they came upon the first tomb lying under the eastern cliffs of the valley. We can identify it now as the tomb of Prince Mentuherkhepeshef, Hereditary Prince, Royal Scribe, Son of Pharaoh, Beloved by Him, Chief Inspector of Troops.[13] He seems to have been the eldest son of one of the later Ramessid kings. The entrance to the tomb is large and imposing, with a long first corridor opening into a second. But it was never finished and the body was buried in a small pit under the limestone flags of the corridor. The plastering is very good and Belzoni says: 'The painted figures on the walls are so perfect, that they are the best adapted of any I ever saw to give a correct and clear idea of the Egyptian taste.' Modern opinion would agree that the scenes showing the young prince in the presence of the gods are executed with great delicacy; the colours are good and the wealth and luxury of the age are everywhere apparent.

The same day another group of workmen uncovered a second tomb not a hundred yards from the first. This must have been one of three unidentified tombs in a row that perhaps were built for relatives or favourites of Thothmes IV or Hatshepsut, who were buried near.[14] The tomb is uninscribed and undecorated and had been plundered in antiquity; a hole in the brick wall at the end of the first passage bore witness to that. 'After passing this brick wall,' says Giovanni, 'you descend a staircase, and proceed through another corridor, at the end of which is the entrance to a pretty large chamber, with a single pillar in the centre, and not plastered in any part. At one corner of this chamber we found two mummies on the ground quite naked, without cloth or case. They were females, and their hair pretty long, and well preserved, though it was easily separated from the head by pulling it a little. At one side of this room is a small door, leading into a small chamber, in which we found the fragments of several earthen vessels, and also pieces of vases of alabaster, but so decayed that we could not join one to another. On the top of the staircase we found an earthen jar quite perfect, with a few hieroglyphics on it, and large enough to contain two buckets of water. This tomb is a hundred feet from the entrance to the end of the chamber, twenty feet deep, and twenty-three wide.'

The following morning Beechey came over from Luxor with three visitors who had arrived the night before from Cairo; they were Colonel Stratton, Captain Bennett and Mr. Fuller. These were the first to see the new tombs and they were duly appreciative of Prince Mentuher-khepeshef. Giovanni was just about to take them over the hill to see the temples at Medinet Habu when word was brought to him that the workmen had found yet another tomb in the centre of the valley. Here, in a rough quincunx, were the five tombs which at that time formed the principal group in Biban el-Muluk; they belonged to the third, sixth and ninth Ramses, to Merenptah, the son of Ramses II, and to his obscure successor, Amenmeses. Almost at mid-point, hidden under the ancient workmen's huts and the outfall of *débris* from the tomb of Ramses VI, Tutankhamun's treasure was happily to add another to its thirty-two centuries of safe keeping in the earth. But only sixty yards away, near the tomb of Amenmeses, Belzoni's men had come upon the familiar outline of a rock-cut passage. He saw it would take a day to clear and his visitors promised to return.

The tomb that had been discovered was that of Ramses I.[15] His reign was brief and his tomb did not fulfil the promise of its impressive entrance. A broad flight of steps led to a descending corridor. Then came a second flight of steps, at the foot of which was the burial-chamber. On the left, over against the back wall, was a red granite sarcophagus containing two mummies. (Neither of these was the king's, for he, too, finished up in Deir el-Bahari.) In a corner of the chamber was a wooden *Ka* figure of the Pharaoh, almost as tall as Giovanni himself, advancing with one leg forward, its left hand holding an invisible staff of authority; only the nose was a little damaged. There was a similar statue, less perfect, in a small chamber at the side.[16]

The walls of the burial-chamber were adorned with paintings of the king in the presence of the gods. 'The ceiling was in good preservation,' says Giovanni, 'but not in the best style.' This was the earliest king's tomb then known in Biban el-Muluk. What Giovanni could not know was that its decoration marked the end of a stage in which the artists of the New Kingdom had progressed from simple outline paintings in the tombs to fully coloured figures like those in the temples. The next development—coloured reliefs—was soon to make its impact on an astonished world in the tomb of Ramses I's son and successor, Seti I.

The following day—a Sunday—the wind was unfavourable for Colonel Stratton and his friends to continue their voyage up the Nile. On Monday Giovanni arranged a little demonstration for them: 'I caused some spots of ground to be dug at Gournou, and we succeeded in opening a mummy-pit on that day, so that the party had the satisfaction of seeing a pit just opened, and receiving clear ideas of the manner in which the mummies are found, though all tombs are not alike. This was a small one, and consisted of two rooms painted all over, but not in the best style. It appeared to me that the tomb belonged to some warrior, as there were a great number of men enrolling themselves for soldiers, and another writing their names in a book.' This may have been the tomb of Thanuni,[17] Superintendent of the Military Scribes and Scribe of the Recruits, who lived in the time of Thothmes IV; his wife was a singer in the temple of Thoth.

Presently Colonel Stratton and his friends departed, taking with them Muhammad the janissary, *alias* Finati, who had been instructed by Salt to accompany them into Nubia. On Thursday Belzoni returned to the Valley of the Kings. He now made his men concentrate on a spot not fifteen yards from the tomb of Ramses I. At that point, where on the rare occasions when it rained in Thebes a torrent poured down from the hill above, Giovanni had noticed something that to his experienced eye suggested the presence of another tomb. The men from Qurna were convinced there was nothing there, but Belzoni kept them digging all that day and the next. On Friday evening the edges of a cutting in the rock appeared. There was a sudden spurt of interest. By midday on Saturday they had reached the entrance of the tomb, eighteen feet below the surface of the ground. From what could be seen of it, Giovanni judged it was one of the more important tombs in the valley. But the torrent had washed so much earth between the boulders in the approach cutting that the entrance, though not walled-up, was completely choked. Giovanni got the men to work away just under the lintel till there was room enough for Yanni, the smallest of the party, to wriggle through, stripped to his drawers. When he came back, after what seemed an intolerable length of time, he reported that the usual first corridor was half-choked with rubbish, that it sloped down to a flight of steps which descended to a lower corridor, and that this ended in a yawning pit. There were no mummies and no tomb-furniture, but the whole of the walls and ceiling were covered with splendid reliefs in colour.

Belzoni had discovered the most magnificent of all the tombs in the

Valley of the Kings. It was built for Seti I, father of Ramses II, whose monuments and memorials had so largely engrossed Giovanni's researches. Seti reigned about twenty years and died around 1300 B.C. His mummy is in the Cairo Museum, and there is an air of strength and nobility about that serene face, with its broad brow and high aquiline nose, that agrees with history's judgment of him as a great king. He was a fighter and carried war into Palestine and Syria in an attempt to recover the lost provinces of Egypt. But the Hittites were too strong for him and he was forced to fall back upon an uneasy armistice line south of Galilee. At home he was a diligent restorer of temples, but more modest than his son in recording his piety. His chief memorials above ground are the stupendous columns of the Great Hypostyle Hall at Karnak and the temples that he built for himself at Abydos and Qurna. Some of the sculptured reliefs in the temple at Abydos have a rare delicacy of line and colour, and it may be that Seti used the same artists for his tomb in the Valley of the Kings.

Thothmes I had been content with a rabbit-hole entrance, rough, undecorated steps and passages and a stuccoed burial-chamber with a single supporting pillar. Towards the end of the Eighteenth Dynasty some of the approach passages were also decorated and the entrance became more imposing. The tomb lengthened and its axis straightened and various devices were introduced to foil the robbers, who found that these developments favoured their trade. Meanwhile there were changes in the style of decoration. Thothmes III and Amenhetep II—kings of the mid-Eighteenth Dynasty—had adorned their tombs with simple outline drawings and texts from *The Book of That Which is in the Other World*. Ramses I, bringing in a new dynasty, gave the figures life and movement by filling them with colour. But to his son Seti is due the crowning achievement of building a tomb more than a hundred yards long and decorating it almost throughout with painted bas-reliefs.

As soon as the gap under the lintel had been made large enough, Beechey and Belzoni crawled through over the mound of rubble and earth. Their heads were at first very close to the sloping ceiling, and by the light of their candles they could see great vulture-shapes hovering above them with outspread wings against a background of stars. Only the upper part of the walls was clear of *débris*, but Belzoni observed that the painted reliefs and hieroglyphics began at the door. Later, when he measured the first corridor, he made it thirty-six feet two inches long and eight feet six inches wide.

They crept down the first long flight of steps into a weird underworld of the soul's night. Here on either side was the Sun-god in all his manifestations—white-crowned, bearded, plumed and horned, hawk-headed and *Ka*-handed, beetle-like and bald. At the foot of the steps knelt two graceful goddesses—Isis on the left and her sister Nephthys on the right. Above their heads were the jackal-guardians of the tomb. The texts from *The Litany of the Sun* that began on the walls of the corridor above ended here on the ceiling of the stairs.[18]

Cautiously now they traversed the second sloping corridor, mindful of the pit beyond. On the right the boat of the Sun journeyed through the fourth division of the under-world, the fourth hour of night. On the left it entered the fifth hour, drawn by seven gods and seven goddesses. And already the snakes had begun to appear.

They came fearfully through a doorway to the edge of the square pit. It was thirty feet deep and wider than the corridor behind. Above floor-level the walls were covered with painted or sculptured scenes: on either side the king between Isis and Horus, the king offering a cup to Hathor, the king before Osiris; facing them, Osiris with Anubis at his back.

But it was not these scenes that held Belzoni's attention now. Across the twelve-foot gap he could see a jagged hole in the painted wall, about two feet square. The light of the candles gleamed on strange shapes glowing in the dark beyond. This was not the end of the tomb, as Giovanni had at first supposed. Ramses I, building perhaps on a similar plan, had got no further than the end of the second corridor; there they made his burial-chamber. But in this tomb the chamber had become a pit and the wall at the back was intended to look like solid rock. The pit served a double purpose. It deceived, or at least impeded, intending tomb-robbers, and it acted as a sump for the water that occasionally coursed down from the torrent outside.

The trick certainly had failed. Sometime in antiquity a determined gang had battered through the plaster and stone of the walled-up opening, climbed down into the pit and scrambled up the other side. A palm-fibre rope still dangled from the hole opposite. Looking down, Belzoni saw at his feet another rope tied to a baulk of timber placed athwart the jambs of the door. It crumbled at a touch.

Any disappointment Giovanni felt that the tomb had been broken into was compensated by his excitement at the thought of what still might lie beyond. The reliefs he had seen already were enough to make this a major discovery. But for the moment he could not go forward and he had to return to the world above.

The following day they bridged the gap with two beams and Giovanni was able to cross over. He noticed that both the wood and the rope were in a much better state of preservation on the further side because the water had not reached them. Heaving his great bulk through the hole, he found himself in 'a beautiful hall, twenty-seven feet six inches by twenty-five feet ten inches, in which were four pillars three feet square'.

The pillars were adorned with figures of Pharaoh embracing or embraced by the gods. Isis, Horus, Hathor and Tum, Nephthys, Ptah, Anubis—they were all there, delicately chiselled and limned in deep ochrous reds, royal blues, bright gold and gleaming white. On the walls were the sinister coiled snakes of the under-world and the minor demons and deities of a monstrous mythology. Twelve gods drew on a twisted rope attached to a standing mummy. There was a row of mummies laid out on an elongated table that had a snake's head and a snake's tail. And—most interesting of all—there was 'a military and mysterious procession' in which the representatives of four nations marched: white men and black men, men in beards and kilts and tattooed, painted men.

Beyond this room was another chamber, down three steps. 'I gave it the name of the drawing-room,' says Giovanni, 'for it is covered with figures, which, though only outlined, are so fine and perfect, that you would think they had been drawn only the day before.' This was another device on the part of the ingenious tomb-builders to thwart the impious violators of the king's last peace. Appropriately enough, the wall-scenes show the tortures of the damned—lost souls drowning in the waters or roasting upside-down in a fiery furnace—while the boat of the Sun passes through the ninth, tenth and eleventh hours of the night, surrounded by serpents with wings and legs, disk-headed demons carrying darts and other creatures of a nightmare. But the designs here had only been sketched in—in red first with corrections in black; the sculptor had not yet begun his work. So it was hoped that the simple-minded thieves would suppose that the tomb was unfinished and had never been used for the burial of a Pharaoh. But the miscreants had tapped the walls all round and when they discovered that the fire-breathing cobras in the lowest register on the left gave out a hollower sound than the other weird denizens of the under-world, they had broken through into a corridor below that continued along the main axis of the tomb.

The corridor was properly approached by a flight of steps leading down from the previous chamber. When the burial was complete, the top of this staircase was sealed and made indistinguishable from the rest of the floor. But the thieves, once they had broken through from the 'drawing-room', presumably cleared the steps in order to make it easier to remove their loot.

We may imagine Giovanni now descending those steps. He had not made much of the scenes in the under-world. Nor would the scholars have done any better at that time. William Hamilton had said of the scenes in other royal tombs: 'The greater part of these representations relate to religious mysteries, and consequently our ignorance of these mysteries precludes every other explanation of them than what is fanci-

ISIS AND PHARAOH

ful and conjectural.' Until the key of the language was found and the
texts were translated, even the simplest concept of the soul travelling
in the Sun-god's boat across the heavens by day and through the terrifying under-world at night was beyond imagination.

If Giovanni did not understand the significance of these scenes, at
least he was aware of the excellence of the reliefs as works of art. And
indeed it seemed to him that the further he penetrated into the tomb
the better they became. The staircase was undecorated, but the jambs
of the doorway at its foot each bore on the inside life-size figures of Seti
and the goddess Hathor. Giovanni afterwards wrote: 'The female
appears to represent Isis, having, as usual, the horns and globe on her
head. She seems ready to receive the hero, who is about to enter the
regions of immortality. The garments of this figure are so well preserved,
that nothing which has yet been brought before the public can give a
more correct idea of Egyptian customs.' Or does he mean costumes?
'The figure of the hero is covered with a veil, or transparent linen, folded
over his shoulder, and covering his whole body, which gives him a very
graceful appearance. Isis is apparently covered with a net, every mesh
of which contains some hieroglyphic, serving to embellish the dress of
the goddess.' It was indeed a wonderful creation!

Beyond the door, on the left wall of the corridor, the king sat on his
throne before an altar, protected by a hovering vulture-goddess. Offerings were brought to his statues and the priests performed the ceremony
of Opening the Mouth, so that his mummy could breathe and eat and
drink; Giovanni thought this was 'the history of the hero divided into
several small compartments'. Then came another short flight of steps
and a few more yards of corridor, which presently widened into a
chamber. Here the reliefs were even finer; they showed Seti again in
the company of gods and goddesses and Giovanni named it the Room
of Beauties.

This room formed a kind of ante-chamber to the final glory of the
tomb-builder's art—a hall, slightly larger than the principal one above,
but with six pillars instead of four, opening upon a high vaulted chamber
that was set a step lower. Here, it must have seemed to Giovanni,
coming upon it for the first time, everything that had gone before
reached its consummation. Here were the snakes wreathed in fantastic
figures-of-eight, the sacred boat bearing the ram-headed god, the black
hours of night and the stars, the jackal-god and the mummy, winged
Isis and Nephthys, the sacrifice and the offerings, Horus and Hathor,
Osiris crowned and the divine Pharaoh himself. They glowed in their
rich colours like jewels in a case. . . . And then, as Giovanni came forward between the pillars, holding his candle aloft, he saw something
that must have made him catch his breath for its sheer loveliness—

THE GODDESS NEITH

something that lay, lambent as a pearl, under the dark blue vault—a great gleaming alabaster sarcophagus.

Nothing like it had ever been seen before. The usual material for stone coffins was granite, breccia or basalt, though limestone and quartzite were also found. They were massive, heavy and dull. This was a light, translucent shell, delicate and fragile, yet royal in all its proportions. The cover had gone and the sarcophagus was quite empty. But looking down upon it from his great height Belzoni could see how the sculptor who carved it out of a single block had shaped it slightly to the human form and the costume of the king—a swell for the thigh and heroic calf, a greater fullness for the folds of the head-dress. At its widest the sarcophagus was not far off four feet and it was more than nine feet long; the stone varied in thickness from two to four inches. Inside and out it was carved and inlaid with hundreds of tiny figures in blue paste that re-enacted the soul's journey through the underworld—an epitome of the whole tomb. In the hollow of the shell the goddess Neith, slim and bare-breasted, waited to receive the hero.

Below the sarcophagus and almost concealed by it, a short flight of steps led down into a tunnel. Later, when Belzoni had time to explore it, he found it was three hundred feet long—almost as long as the tomb itself. Describing it, he says: 'One hundred feet from the entrance is a staircase in good preservation; but the rock below changes its substance, from a beautiful solid calcareous stone, becoming a kind of black rotten slate, which crumbles into dust only by touching.' Giovanni went as far as he could even through this dangerous place, till his way was blocked by a fall from the roof and the accumulation of bats' dung. This showed clearly enough that the tunnel had once led to the open air, for the tomb was quite undefiled by these creatures. Probably it went right through the mountain to Deir el-Bahari, where in a bay of the Theban hills facing the river, Queen Hatshepsut, nearly two hundred years before the time of Seti I, had built her beautiful colonnaded temple. She had planned that her own tomb in the Valley of the Kings should run back so far under the mountain that the burial-chamber would lie almost below the shrine where offerings would be made to her spirit. But the tunnellers met bad rock and her tomb, which is seven hundred feet long, sweeps round in a great curve to avoid it. Perhaps Seti had had the same idea and thought he would make it easier for his *Ka* to pass from the burial-chamber through the mountain to his mortuary temple at Qurna. Belzoni says that 'at the bottom of the stairs just under the sarcophagus a wall was built, which entirely closed the communication between the tomb and the subterraneous passage. Some large blocks of stone were placed under the sarcophagus horizontally, level with the pavement of the saloon, that no one might perceive any stairs or subterranean passage was there.' They had been displaced so that the sarcophagus was balanced precariously over the hole. But whether this was the work of robbers or of the priests who entered the tomb at least twice—once to bring there the body of Ramses II and once to remove both him and his father to greater safety—it is impossible to say. Perhaps the priests carried the mummies in their wooden coffins through the tunnel to the tomb of Queen Anhapu. What is certain, however, is that robbers on one occasion used the main entrance. They broke the cover of the sarcophagus in getting it out and Belzoni found the pieces buried in the *débris* near the door.[19]

Apart from the tunnel, there were five rooms opening off the burial-chamber. Three of them were quite small—about eight feet by ten. The first room on the right showed Hathor as a cow straddling the sky with Re in his boat sailing under her star-spangled belly. The annexe opposite, with the king and his *Ka*, Anubis and the mummies and the great swollen serpents, Giovanni called the Room of Mysteries. Beyond this, on the left, was a much larger chamber with two pillars and a broad ledge running round three sides of it above a cavetto cornice. Giovanni gave it the somewhat incongruous name of the Sideboard Room and supposed that the ledge had been used to hold objects needed in the funeral ceremonies. The largest room of all was at the back of the vaulted chamber, behind the sarcophagus. It was over forty feet long and nearly half that in width. There were no reliefs or paintings in this room, but Belzoni found here the mummified body of a bull and an immense number of *ushabti* figures. The majority were of wood but some were of glazed ware in the magnificent Deir el-Bahari blue. These were not the only objects found in the tomb. 'On each side of the two little rooms,' says Giovanni, 'were some wooden statues standing erect, four feet high, with a circular hollow inside, as if to contain a roll of papyrus, which I have no doubt they did. We found likewise fragments of other statues of wood and of composition.'[20]

Belzoni was elated at his success. And indeed he had good cause to feel pleased. In twelve days he had found *four* new tombs in the Valley of the Kings. In the past year he had—almost casually—increased by one half the number known to the French at the time of their occupation. (It took a century more to discover the other fourteen identifiable tombs in Biban el-Muluk, and Howard Carter spent six fruitless seasons searching for Tutankhamun.) But for Giovanni the real satisfaction was all concentrated in this last splendid tomb and its magnificent sarcophagus. Nothing so fine had ever been found in Egypt before. The tomb of Ramses III ('Bruce's Tomb') and that of Ramses VI alone were comparable. But there the workmanship was much inferior and the painted reliefs—so long exposed to the bats and jackals of the valley and every scribbling, souvenir-hunting tourist—had suffered irreparable damage.

The news travelled fast by the Arab grapevine telegraph. Hamid Agha at Qena heard that a great treasure had been discovered and set off at once for Thebes with a troop of horse. As they rode into the Valley of the Kings the rocks re-echoed with the crash of their muskets. Had they come to take the place by storm? No, the Agha was all smiles and cordiality. Giovanni mustered up all the candles he could find and took him and his bodyguard on a tour of the tomb. He pointed out the superb figures of the gods and goddesses—Osiris in majesty, Isis gorgeously apparelled, a lovely profile of Hathor, the slim Nephthys. But the Agha was unimpressed. He showed him the snakes and demons. The Agha was looking elsewhere. He tried to interest him in the four races of mankind. The Agha was polite and abstracted. All this time 'his numerous followers were like hounds, searching in every hole and corner'. When they had been right through the tomb, Hamid dismissed his men and turned to Giovanni. 'Where have you put the treasure?' he asked with a bland smile. 'What treasure?' said Giovanni, smiling back and so confirming the Turk's suspicions. 'The treasure you found here. I have been told you found a large golden cock,[21] filled with diamonds and pearls.' Giovanni could hardly keep from laughing outright, but he assured the Turk with great solemnity that there was nothing like that. Eventually the Agha believed him and disconsolately turned to go. On their way out Giovanni asked him what he thought of the reliefs. Hamid gave them a quick glance. 'This would be a good place for a *harim*,' he said. 'The women would have something to look at.'

Meanwhile Henry Salt, having freed himself from consular duties for the time being, was preparing to make his long-anticipated visit to Upper Egypt. He had on his hands—pleasantly enough, for he was a social and gregarious man—the Earl and Countess of Belmore and their family and *entourage*. Apart from a considerable number of servants, this consisted of the forty-three-year-old Irish peer himself; his wife and cousin, Juliana; their two sons, Lord Corry and the Honourable Henry Corry, both in their teens; his lordship's brother, Captain Armar Lowry Corry, R.N.; his private chaplain, the Reverend Mr. Holt; and his physician, Dr. Robert Richardson, M.D. (Edinburgh), who was also the chronicler of the family's travels.[22] They had already visited Malta, Sicily, Italy, the Ionian Islands, Greece, Constantinople and Alexandria, and 'the noble traveller', as Richardson usually calls him, had set the Second Cataract as their next goal. They set out from Cairo on 28 October in three large roomy boats of the kind known as a *maash*, and Salt went with them. Proceeding by easy stages to give themselves time to look at the antiquities, they reached Thebes on 16 November and moored their boats by the great sycamore tree opposite Qurna. Two days before at Qena, Hamid Agha had told them of Belzoni's discovery of the New Tomb, and this was the first thing they wanted to see.

Their admiration of all they saw was music in Giovanni's ears. He warmed especially towards Lord Belmore and even pointed out to him a couple of likely spots in the valley where he might care to dig. The noble traveller found only two small mummy-pits—probably late interments—but at least it showed that Belzoni's method was not at fault. He got on well with Richardson, and the two argued together in a friendly way over the interpretation of some of the scenes. With Salt, however, in spite of his warm commendation of Belzoni's work, there was at once a feeling of constraint. Giovanni was jealous if anyone congratulated the consul. It seemed to him that the visitors paid too much attention to Beechey. Did they not realize even now that without Giovanni's expert eye to guide them they might go on digging for months and not find anything?

But there was another, deeper cause for the depression that now settled over him. Salt had brought bad news. Burckhardt was dead. For over two years the great Swiss traveller had been waiting in Cairo for the caravan that never came—the caravan that would enable him to make his long-premeditated journey across the Sahara through the Fezzan to Timbuktu and the country of the Niger. At last, word had come that among the pilgrims at Mecca was a party of West Africans who were expected to pass through Egypt on their way home in December 1817. Burckhardt had occupied himself during the two years in writing and putting his papers in order. He had sent off the last of his journals and a collection of Arab proverbs to William Hamilton.[23] He had heard that the colossal head of Memnon, after waiting for so many months in the warehouse in Alexandria, had left for England in a British transport. A few days later he went down with a sharp attack of dysentery. Dr. Richardson, who was in Cairo at the time, gave him all the attention he could, but Burckhardt's health had been undermined by self-imposed hardship and, in particular, by his experiences in Arabia. When he knew he was dying, he sent for Salt and made a final disposition of his little money and effects. 'Pay up my share of the Memnon head,' he said, and repeated it, as if he thought he had not contributed enough. There were small bequests to his servants, a thousand piastres for the poor of Zurich, and his Arabic manuscripts— nearly four hundred rare and precious volumes—to go to the University of Cambridge. Burckhardt died a little before midnight on 15 October —only a few hours before Belzoni began to dig on the spot where he made his greatest discovery. The Turks took the body of Shaikh Ibrahim and buried it with honour in their City of the Dead.

The news of Burckhardt's death was a bitter grief to Belzoni. Although Giovanni was six years his senior, he had looked up to him as to an older man and respected his integrity and single-mindedness, his dedication to a purpose and his disregard of self. He knew that Burckhardt had spent nine years preparing himself for a mission, feeling always that he needed some more experience, some other qualification, to ensure success. And then, at the very moment when his life's work was about to begin, to be struck down—Belzoni found words inadequate to express his emotions, but Burckhardt's death in his own hour of triumph must have touched him deeply. Perhaps even then, in the way he had once braced his body for a heavier physical load, he took upon himself, scarcely knowing it, the unaccomplished purpose of his friend.

But there were other more immediate reactions. Belzoni seems to have regarded Burckhardt as a protection against Salt's exploitation of him. Now he knew he was on his own, and his suspicions of the consul grew as he saw with what enthusiasm he talked about moving the sarcophagus to Cairo. Even his old hatred of the French was forgotten in a surge of indignation against Salt. He could afford to be magnanimous towards Lebolo and Rosignano, even though they had threatened his life and wrecked his work. He must have been more mollified still when Drovetti himself came to see the tomb on the Belmores' second visit. Richardson found the former French consul 'agreeable and intelligent', though he recalls with some amusement that he was the only Frenchman he ever saw in his life 'completely run out of the small change of compliment and admiration. He was so lavish of his civilities on entering the tomb, and every thing was so superb, magnifique, superlative and astounding, that when he came to something which really called for epithets of applause and admiration, his magazine of stuff was expended, and he stood in speechless astonishment, to the great entertainment of the beholders.' And, no doubt, to Giovanni's great satisfaction.

A few days later, when Lord Belmore's party had left for Aswan, and the valley had returned to its customary quiet, Belzoni began to address Salt in what the consul afterwards described as 'rather an ambiguous style'. He said, as Salt remembered the conversation, that 'it was time to think of his own interests; he had worked long enough for others, and desired to know how I intended to remunerate him'. Salt says in 'A Plain Statement of Facts', which he later wrote for his friends' information, that he told Belzoni he had always intended to allow him between three and five hundred piastres a month, according to circumstances, as a salary over and above his expenses. But, he had added, in view of Belzoni's success being far greater than was anticipated, he must con-

sider the matter further and give him an answer at another time. Salt
pointed out that so far he had had no return for all the money he had
expended on collecting antiquities, and his means were not large. What
he probably did not tell Belzoni was that his father had died in the
previous May and left him £5,000.

But the same day, as he saw Giovanni's unease, Salt came back to
the subject. He said he had decided to allow him a thousand piastres
a month—£25—retrospectively from the time he had left Alexandria
after depositing the head of Young Memnon. That was ten months
before. He also promised to give him whatever he could spare from
the antiquities.

Giovanni seemed satisfied for the moment. But about a week later a
chance remark by Salt, made in the presence of other English visitors—
probably Colonel Stratton and his friends returning from Nubia—
brought about an explosion. Salt had spoken of the length of time
Belzoni had been in his 'employ'. That was the word that struck the
spark. With eyes flashing fire, Belzoni denied that he had ever been
employed by Salt. He said he was working for the British nation, he
would be satisfied to go without reward, he was independent, and much
more like this. It must have been a very embarrassing scene. Salt felt
obliged to explain what remuneration he had promised Belzoni. The
visitors clearly thought it was reasonable and could not see why Belzoni
should want to deny an obvious fact. Giovanni retired hurt to lick his
wounds.

Salt was genuinely perplexed. He could not understand this attitude
of mind. As he told Belzoni when the visitors had gone and he tried to
talk him into a calmer mood, he looked upon him with the same high
regard that a gentleman would have for the architect whom he had
commissioned to build his house. All the merit belonged to the one, but
the other supplied the means and the house was his. The analogy was
lost on Giovanni. What man professionally employed was ever expected
to make brilliant and original discoveries on behalf of his employer?
Was there no one, now that Burckhardt had gone, who could see what
really mattered? Even Salt's assurances that he had always given Belzoni
full credit in his letters home failed to appease this perturbed spirit.

Yet how differently the young science of Egyptology might have
developed if one of Salt's letters written at this time had borne fruit!
M. Dacier of Paris, acting on a suggestion he received in a long communication from the consul, wrote impetuously to a young man then
teaching history at Grenoble—a young man interested in the problem
of the hieroglyphics, whose name was Jean François Champollion.
Dacier told him of the wonderful discoveries that were being made in
the Valley of the Kings by 'the Paduan giant', and urged him to go out

at once to join him. 'Alongside this giant you too will make giant strides and will find the key to the puzzle all the sooner.' But Champollion was too busy adapting for his pupils a system of mutual instruction invented by one James Lancaster, an educationist whom Belzoni met later at a social gathering in London. Hieroglyphs could wait, students could not, was the answer in effect given by the too-conscientious teacher. Ten years passed before Champollion saw Egypt. By then Belzoni was dead. But, with the key to the hieroglyphs now in his hands, Champollion celebrated a visit to the Valley of the Kings and honoured Belzoni's memory too with a birthday party in Seti's tomb for his five-year-old daughter. The *pièce de résistance* was to have been young crocodile *à la sauce piquante*; unfortunately it turned in the night.

Giovanni was still in a bitter mood when he set off for Cairo with Sarah, Yanni, James and a boat-load of antiquities. His instructions were to deposit the collection at the consulate and then return as soon as possible with equipment to remove the alabaster sarcophagus.

CHAPTER XI

A great nation like England should not miss the opportunity of making their own a man of such superior talents. He possesses, to an astonishing degree, the secret of conciliating the Arabs and literally makes them do what he chooses.

LT.-COL. FITZCLARENCE on Belzoni, 1818 [1]

SARAH BELZONI had made up her mind that she was not going back to Thebes. After her sojourn on the roof of the temple at Philae, she had stayed for a while with the Arab family at Luxor in whose house she had lodged before. But the husband had married a new wife and the old one was causing trouble. There were constant quarrels and fights, in which the first wife expected Sarah to take her part. When she refused to become involved, the woman set out deliberately to annoy her and even went to the length of putting something in her drinking-water to make her sick. Presently Sarah went to live in one of the tombs in the Valley of the Kings. But although this was quieter, it was not very congenial for a woman on her own. She did not like Cairo and, when an opportunity presented itself for her to go to the Holy Land, she grasped it eagerly and maintained it had always been her wish to see Jerusalem.

William John Bankes had written from Acre to ask Salt to send him back Finati. This was the chance. With Hajji Muhammad as their janissary, Sarah and James, both dressed as Mamluk youths, set off on their pilgrimage early in the New Year. They were delayed at Damietta and did not reach Jaffa till 9 March.

Giovanni had several things to do in Cairo, which took him longer than he had expected. He had decided that, if Salt must have the alabaster sarcophagus, he at least would show the world the New Tomb. He would take wax impressions of the reliefs and hieroglyphs, carefully note the colours and be prepared 'to erect a facsimile in any part of Europe'. The old habit of the showman was suddenly strong upon him. But to carry out this work he needed assistance. He was lucky in meeting at this time among his Italian friends in Cairo a young doctor from Siena named Alessandro Ricci. Ricci was a good draughtsman and interested in antiquities; he readily agreed to help Belzoni with his scheme.

But Giovanni also needed money. He had thought of sending the two lion-headed statues of Sekhmet, that Salt had allotted him, to his own native city of Padua. However, the Count de Forbin, Director General of the Royal Museums of France, was then in Cairo and he came to look over Salt's collection at the consulate. He made Giovanni an offer for the two statues and eventually Belzoni agreed to let them go for seven thousand piastres [£175], which he maintains in his *Narrative* was not a quarter of their worth, adding smugly: 'I never was a dealer in statues in my life.'

Giovanni says it was at this time he received several journals from Europe and found, to his great surprise, that all his discoveries and labours had been attributed to other people, while his own name was not even mentioned. 'I must confess,' he says, 'I was weak enough to be a little vexed at this; for, after such exertions as I had made in Upper Egypt, it was not pleasant to see the fruits and the credit of them ascribed to others, who had no more to do with them than the governor of Siberia, except as far as related to supplying me with money.'

This was most unfair, and when Belzoni wrote it his bitter feelings towards Salt had clouded both his memory and his better judgment. It is doubtful whether any journals mentioning Belzoni's discoveries had reached Cairo by this date. If there were any references in French publications they had not come from Salt. One of the earliest notices in English—if not *the* earliest—is to be found in the issue of *The Quarterly Review* dated January 1818. A tribute to Burckhardt includes a note about the Young Memnon—which had just arrived safely at the British Museum—and Belzoni is given full credit for its removal. It is clear that the editor had also received a communication from Giovanni himself enumerating his 'many new and curious discoveries'. Of these the most remarkable was said to be what Belzoni had now come to call the Tomb of Apis, from the fact that a mummified bull had been found in the last chamber; Apis, the sacred bull, was worshipped in Egypt from the earliest dynastic times and the memory of his cult had never been lost. Belzoni's letter, as quoted by *The Quarterly Review*, ends with a description of the alabaster sarcophagus, of which he says: 'No doubt, when I shall have it transported to England, as I hope to do successfully, it will be esteemed as one of the most precious treasures of which any European museum can boast.' On internal evidence this number of *The Quarterly Review* cannot have been in print before 22 March 1818.

What must have annoyed Belzoni, when at length the periodical did come into his hands, was the fact that he was confused with Caviglia. He had been at such pains to turn down Salt's suggestion that he should join forces with the enterprising captain, and now here he was credited with having uncovered the front of the Sphinx. So sensitive was Giovanni's *amour propre* that to have another man's successes attributed to him was almost as bad as having his own ignored or usurped by someone else. And he would not have been very pleased even when *The Quarterly Review* handsomely said: 'By the indefatigable labour of M. Belzoni and Mr. Salt, the British Museum is likely to become the richest depository in the world of Egyptian antiquities.'

Salt and Burckhardt had both done what they could to bring Belzoni's name before the public. Burckhardt had written to William Hamilton on 23 March 1817: 'If the British Museum is desirous to enlarge its Stock of Egyptian curiosities, this is the time; it may never find hereafter two Persons in Egypt equally fit and zealous to promote its views than are Mr. Salt and Mr. Belsoni—but the former is limited in his Expences & Mr. Belsoni has no pecuniary Resources whatever.' Salt, in a letter to *The Quarterly Review* (quoted in its issue of April 1818), had spoken of Belzoni's 'great talents and uncommon genius for mechanics', which had 'enabled him with singular success, both at Thebes and other places, to discover objects of the rarest value in antiquity, that had long baffled the researches of the learned . . .'

This was generous enough, albeit a little late, for the letter describes the tomb in the Valley of the Kings and so must have been written after Salt saw it in November 1817. Belzoni had got away to a good start with his own publicity, and early in 1818 a letter of his addressed to M. Visconti, an Italian archaeologist who held a post at the Louvre, was published in a French paper or periodical after Visconti's death in February. There it roused the wrath of Edmé François Jomard, engineer, geographer and archaeologist, a member of Napoleon's team of scientists and principal editor of the *Description de l'Égypte*.[2] Jomard wrote a scathing attack on Belzoni in the May issue of *Journal des Savans*. He ridiculed him for calling the lion-headed statues of Sekhmet 'sphinxes'. He pointed out—with truth—that the French had found, described and charted a large *cache* of these statues in the ruins of Thebes. Some of them had even been·for years in the British Museum, having been taken from the French at the time of their capitulation. And yet Belzoni pretended he had discovered them! (The Count de Forbin later made a similar charge, which Giovanni answered in his *Narrative*. The French, he said, had found their statues on the east of the temple, but he had dug on the west side in ground 'so strongly cemented together by time' that it could not have been disturbed for centuries. Moreover these statues were not uncommon; 'there were many others in various places', including some at Qurna.)

Jomard also poured scorn on the idea of calling the new discovery at Biban el-Muluk the Tomb of *Apis*. How many bulls' tombs there must be to bear witness to this cult! Moreover the tomb, said Jomard, was not the largest in the valley if it was only, as Belzoni claimed, three hundred and nine feet long. There were two others measured by the French that were three hundred and seventy-five and three hundred and fifty-one English feet in length.[3] As for the sarcophagus, *transparent comme une glace*, one must hope, for the advance of mineralogy, that it would soon be brought to Europe; then one might learn how a piece of alabaster nine feet seven inches long could be worked thin enough to be transparent as ice!

Even the head of Memnon was not immune from attack. Jomard asked if Belzoni had not seen the inscriptions on one of the seated Colossi in the plain which showed that this had always been the reputed Memnon. Perhaps he had taken away the head and shoulders of that statue? But no, there were many other colossal heads buried in the sand —one, in particular, in the monument of Osymandias, which the French had uncovered and left lying face upwards, quite easy to see. Although Jomard was ostensibly rebuking this inexperienced traveller for his fanciful and inaccurate use of the name Memnon, there was nothing here but chagrin that the French had lost so valuable a prize.

The Quarterly Review took up the challenge, not merely for Belzoni's sake, but because this was clearly a matter of national honour. 'Not content with claiming for his countrymen all the discoveries that are now making, and that may hereafter be made, M. Jomard appropriates to them all that have hitherto been made in Egypt.' What of Pococke, Norden, Niebuhr and Hamilton? asked the *Review*. It cheerfully counter-attacked and ended in triumph: 'Of M. Jomard's hostility towards M. Belzoni, or rather, we suspect, towards the English, under whose auspices he is prosecuting his discoveries in Egypt, the "Note" bears ample testimony throughout; the presumption of the writer is no less conspicuous; and the concluding paragraph exposes his ignorance in a matter in which he ought to have better informed himself, before he attempted to strip another of the laurels so justly his due. "The subterraneous temple of Ipsambul" [Abu Simbel], says the critic, "which M. Belzoni imagines himself to have discovered, had already been visited by many Europeans, *particularly by Mr. Thomas Legh*." It happens that M. Belzoni, so far from pretending to have *discovered* it, merely says, "I went to Nubia to *examine* the temple of Ipsambul"; and the only merit which he claims is that of having, "by dint of patience and courage, after twenty-two days persevering labour, had the pleasure of finding himself in the temple of Ipsambul, where no European had ever before entered." But it also happens that Mr. Thomas Legh not only did not visit Ipsambul, but was not within a day and a half's journey of it, and never once mentions its name.' . . .

The battle was on and Belzoni was its spearhead. And already by the

time these words were in print—in the early summer of 1818—he had
another tremendous discovery to his credit.

It was early in the New Year, soon after Sarah's departure, that
Major Moore arrived in Cairo on his way home from India with dispatches.[4] Giovanni was living at the consulate and doing the honours;
there were frequent visitors passing through and he began to enjoy his
new role of authority on the antiquities. As the major had a couple of
days to spare, Giovanni took him over to Giza and there, while they sat
on top of the First Pyramid, he 'descanted to him on the various opinions
entertained concerning the second, and what a pity it was, that, in an
intelligent age like the present, it had not been opened, so that the
interior remained quite unknown'. When they got back to Cairo,
Giovanni gave Major Moore some plans and descriptions of his discoveries to deliver to Lord Aberdeen, the President of the Society of
Antiquaries. After the major had caught his boat to Alexandria, Giovanni's mind still ran on pyramids and the possibilities of a new field
of exploration. Salt was out of the way at Thebes, where he would also
be useful in keeping an eye on the French. Caviglia had gone back to
his ship and there was no one now digging at Giza. . . . Supposing he
—Belzoni—were to find the entrance to the Second Pyramid. . . .

A day or two later he visited the Pyramids again with a party of
Europeans. While they explored the interior of the First, Giovanni
strolled round the Second and examined its stony flanks with a new
critical and searching eye. He had to pick his way over great mounds
of compacted *débris* that encumbered the base. On the north side—
where, if the Pyramid was like its neighbour, the entrance would
be—Giovanni was suddenly struck by an obvious and simple fact
that had never occurred to him before. 'I observed, that just under
the centre of the face of the pyramid the accumulation of materials,
which had fallen from the coating of it, was higher than the entrance
could be expected to be, if compared with the height of the entrance
into the first pyramid, measuring from the basis. I could not conceive
how the discovery of the entrance into the second pyramid could be
considered as a matter to be despaired of, when no one had ever seen
the spot, where it must naturally be presumed to exist, if there were
any entrance at all. I farther observed, that the materials which had
fallen exactly in the centre of the front were not so compact as those
on the sides; and hence concluded, that the stones on that spot, had
been removed after the falling of the coating. Consequently I perceived
the probability of there being an entrance into the pyramid at that spot.'

Secretly elated, he packed off Signor Ricci in the consul's boat with
a message for Salt that he had been detained by 'a little private business'

and would be setting out in a few days. He made a closer examination of the spot the next day and then bethought himself of the need to obtain a *firman*. With Yanni, he called first on the Kashif of Imbaba and found that he had no objection to Giovanni's digging at the Pyramids. Then, as Muhammad Ali was out of Cairo, he applied to his Deputy, who remembered him from the days of the water-wheel. Belzoni wanted Yanni to say that, as an intimate friend of Salt's, he desired to dig at the Pyramids. Yanni, with his curiously involuted Greek logic, thought that was dishonest and said, when he interpreted, that they were both servants of Mr. Salt, who were come, by order of their master, 'to make a slight excavation round the pyramids'. The *firman* was readily given on condition that no cultivated land was disturbed, and Giovanni at once made preparations for the dig.

Herodotus, who visited Egypt probably between 460 and 455 B.C., had said categorically that there were no subterranean chambers in the Second Pyramid. In this he was wrong, but he has also been misinterpreted. The emphasis—from the context—was on the word 'subterranean' and Herodotus did not say that the Pyramid was solid throughout.[5] Four hundred years later Diodorus Siculus repeated most of what Herodotus had said, but added that neither Cheops nor Chephren was buried in their Pyramids, though they had intended them to be their tombs. The same historian also recorded that the Second Pyramid had a way into it cut through one of the sides—presumably an attempt to force its secrets.[6] The elder Pliny—that dour Italian highlander with a magpie mind—found the Pyramids one of the most distasteful subjects he had to deal with among the twenty thousand facts in his *Natural History*. To him they were merely 'that idle and foolish exhibition of royal wealth' and he agreed with those who thought that the kings of Egypt had built them in order to squander their treasure and avoid leaving it to others.[7]

Pliny thus unwittingly gave encouragement to the view that associated the Pyramids more with treasure than with tombs. But the Oriental mind needed no such spur to the imagination. Masudi, a tenth-century Arab writer, quotes a Coptic tradition that the Pyramids were built before the Flood by a king who was warned of this impending disaster and placed in them the bodies of his ancestors, his treasures and the writings of the priests, which contained all kinds of wisdom. In the Second Pyramid there were repositories for weapons of war made of iron that would not rust, glass that would bend without breaking, and many potent drugs. Elsewhere Masudi relates the story that when the Caliph Harun al-Rashid was in Egypt he made an opening in the First Pyramid by means of fire and vinegar and with iron tools and battering-rams. After much effort he penetrated to a distance of twenty cubits inside the Pyramid and there was overjoyed to find a treasure that consisted of a thousand dinars of pure gold. But when the Caliph had reckoned up the cost of the operation he discovered it was exactly equal to the value of the treasure!

The same story is told of his son Mamun, who in fact probably did force a way into the First Pyramid by what is still known as 'Mamun's Hole'. It is doubtful if he discovered more than an empty sarcophagus. But a twelfth-century account[8] says that those who entered the Pyramid at this time found the image of a man in green stone. When it was opened it revealed the body of a man in golden armour ornamented with precious stones. A magnificent sword lay at his side and above his head was a ruby as big as an egg. The writer says he saw the case standing at the door of the palace in Cairo in the year 511 (A.D. 1133). No doubt it was a handsome anthropoid coffin of the New Kingdom or later.

These stories of buried treasure grew and proliferated in the glittering world of the Arabian Nights, but side by side with them in the Dark Ages over Europe a sober Biblical tradition prevailed. Sir John Mandeville, writing his *Travels* about A.D. 1360, said of the Pyramids: 'These are the Barns of Joseph that were made for to keep corn in for the seven barren years.' A century later the German traveller Breydenbach[9] dismissed this as fable and from then on the true character of the Pyramids began to be asserted.

M. Jean Palerme, secretary to the Duc d'Anjou et d'Alençon, the brother of France's Henri III, visited Giza in 1581 and left one of the first adequate accounts of the Pyramids in modern times. He explored the interior of the First Pyramid, but described the Second as a solid mass. Ten years later the Swiss naturalist Prosper Alpinus reported that the Viceroy of Egypt, Ibrahim Pasha, had intended to blow up Cheops' Pyramid by filling the well with powder, and was only dissuaded by the Venetian consul who told him it would endanger the city of Cairo. He thought the Second Pyramid had no entrance except by way of a subterranean passage that was supposed to lead from the bottom of the well in the First Pyramid.

Many European travellers visited and reported on the Pyramids during the seventeenth century—Sandys, Thévenot and Pietro Della Valle being chief among them. The first proper survey was made by an Oxford Professor of Astronomy, John Greaves, who published his *Pyramidographia* in 1646. Of the Second Pyramid Greaves said that the stones were not so large nor so regularly laid as those in the First Pyramid and he found the sides smooth and free of irregularities, except on the south. This last point is also made by Egmont (1709) and

Fourmont (1755), but De Caveri (1693) and Norden (1737) disagree
with them and describe the Pyramid as being dilapidated. It is therefore
difficult to be certain when the Second Pyramid lost the greater part of
its casing, but it would seem to have been at a period much later than
the First.[10]

Although the evidence of Western travellers from Herodotus onwards
is that the Second Pyramid had no known entrance—if, indeed, it had
any interior chambers at all—there was a strong Arab tradition that at
one time it had been open. Colonel Grobert of the Institut d'Égypte
mentions this in his *Description des pyramides de Ghizé*, published in
1801. Perhaps Belzoni, with his knack of picking up useful scraps of
information, heard of this persistent folk-memory and was strengthened
in his conviction that somewhere, in spite of all the failures to locate it,
there must be an entrance to the Second Pyramid.[11]

There were two points where it seemed a start might be made. On
the east side of the Pyramid were the remains of Chephren's mortuary
temple, from which a causeway descended towards the Sphinx and
ended at the so-called Valley Building—still buried at that date—where
the ceremonial washing and perhaps the embalming of the king's body
had taken place. Giovanni set forty men digging in the space between
the temple and the Pyramid; there he thought he would be certain to
come upon foundations and might possibly find some communication
between the two. The other spot he chose was in the centre of the north
face of the Pyramid, where on the analogy of its neighbour the entrance
was most likely to be. He paid the men—eighty in all—one piastre a day,
and had also engaged a number of boys and girls—at half rate—to carry
away the earth. His methods were beginning to approach those of a
modern dig.

The thin blades of the Arab hoes made little impression on the hard
amalgam of mortar and stone on the north side, but behind the temple
the men soon got down through forty feet of *débris* and uncovered a
pavement which clearly ran right round the Pyramid. The others had
to be encouraged by a reminder of the *bakshish* they would get when
the Pyramid was open to tourists. But as the days went by and they
broke their hoes on the unrewarding mass without finding any sign of
an entrance, they began to mutter '*Magnun, magnun*'; Belzoni, they
said, was mad.

On 17 February, after a week's fruitless effort, one of the workmen
found a chink between two stones in a lower course of the Pyramid; a
stick thrust in went more than two yards deep. That meant little, but
it encouraged the men to work harder and presently they discovered a
loose block in the face. When it was taken out, a rough cavity appeared

behind, choked with stones and sand. Giovanni spent three days clearing
this, and on the fourth found that more sand and stones were falling
into the hole from above. He traced it to what had seemed to be a
shallow surface cavity higher up the face. Probably this was the spot
referred to by Colonel Grobert when he said: 'This second pyramid has
been opened almost at the same height as the one we have just been
speaking about [i.e. the First Pyramid]. The passage leading down from
this opening is not very steep. It is choked with stones as it is seldom
visited. It would be impossible to get down into it now without a lot of
trouble and effort.' What is strange is that the French never tried.

Another two days' work clearing the lower cavity revealed a tunnel
that burrowed away into the heart of the Pyramid. It was obviously a
forced passage. Some of the stones had been cut right through; some
again had been taken out, leaving others perilously suspended overhead.
Disregarding the danger, Giovanni penetrated about a hundred feet
into this irregular burrow. Half-way along it another sap had been
driven down at a steeper angle towards the centre. Giovanni was only
deterred from exploring these tunnels to the very end by a nearly fatal
accident to one of his men. 'A large block of stone, no less than six feet
long and four wide, fell from the top, while the man was digging under
it; but fortunately it rested on two other stones, one on each side of him,
higher than himself, as he was sitting at his work. The man was so
incarcerated, that we had some difficulty in getting him out; yet, happily,
he received no other injury than a slight bruise on his back. The falling
of this stone moved many others in this passage: indeed, they were so
situated, that I thought it prudent to retreat out of the pyramid, or we
might have reason to repent when too late; for the danger was not only
from what might fall upon us, but also from what might fall in our way,
close up the passage, and thus bury us alive.'

So far Belzoni's operation had been conducted with reasonable
secrecy, but one afternoon he saw some travellers on the top of the
First Pyramid. They fired a pistol to attract his attention and he returned the salute. Presently the party descended the south-west angle
towards him. It proved to consist of the Abbé de Forbin, cousin of the
Count; the French vice-consul, M. Gaspard; the Father Superior of
the Convent of Terra Santa; and a French engineer, M. Xavier Pascal
Coste, who was later to construct the first telegraph line between Cairo
and Alexandria. They inspected the passage and Giovanni gave them
coffee in his tent. After that the whole European community in Cairo
knew what was going on at the Pyramids and Giovanni had many
visitors.

Probing the forced passage had cost him time and money, but Belzoni
was determined to go on searching for the true entrance. To get a new

perspective on the problem he dismissed the labourers for a day and went to look at the north side of Cheops' Pyramid again. Suddenly he realized that the entrance was not dead centre. The passages inside ran in a straight line from the face to the east end of the King's Chamber. If the internal arrangements of the Second Pyramid were the same, then the entrance would be about thirty feet *east* of the central spot where he had been digging. Back he went to the Second Pyramid and there, thirty feet to the east of the forced passage, Giovanni found the same revealing signs that had encouraged him before. The *débris* was a little less compact and there was a slight concavity in the face above the spot where he calculated the entrance would be.

'This gave me no little delight,' he says, 'and hope returned to cherish my pyramidical brains.' The following day he set the men to work. He had not long to wait for results. On the 28th the workmen came upon a large granite block inclined at the same angle as the Descending Corridor in the First Pyramid. The following day they uncovered three more granite blocks—two of them supporting the third as a lintel and all three inclined at the same angle of approximately twenty-six degrees. Giovanni was jubilant. A few days before he had been visited by a friendly fellow-countryman—Ermenegildo (or Enegildo) Frediani[12]—whom he had met in Thebes. Giovanni persuaded him to stay for the opening of the Pyramid, which now seemed so imminent, and about noon on Monday, 2 March, Belzoni had the tremendous satisfaction of seeing the entrance laid bare. It had taken him three weeks to find what had eluded men for centuries.

From the entrance of the Pyramid—still some fifty feet above the buried pavement—a passage descended through the superstructure. It was lined with rough-dressed red granite blocks of the kind that can still be seen facing the two lowest courses of the Pyramid, and for almost all its length it was choked with stones and boulders that had slid down the ramp. It took the rest of Monday and part of Tuesday to clear this passage, and then, where it levelled out, the workmen came upon a solid granite block that seemed to bar all further progress. When Giovanni examined it, he saw it was a stone portcullis that fitted into vertical grooves in the side walls. Fortunately it had not dropped completely; there was a gap of some eight inches at the bottom through which Giovanni was able to tell that the block was about fifteen inches thick. When he poked a straw up into the crack between the portcullis and the roof, he found there was a cavity there to receive it. The problem was how to raise the portcullis in that confined space, for the passage was only four feet high and three and a half feet wide. If the levers were too long they could not be manœuvred; if they were too short, not enough men could man them. But somehow, inch by inch, the block was raised and supported on stones packed into the side grooves. A very thin Arab was the first to wriggle through. Yanni went next, stripped to the skin. Belzoni had to wait, doubled up under the low roof, until the portcullis could be raised enough to allow his vast bulk to pass through.

Beyond this point the passage was level for a few yards and the roof higher. Then the granite lining ended and the floor dropped away to a lower passage that ran back and downwards under the first one in the direction of the north face. On either side a rough irregular tunnel opened in the rock. That on the right twisted up in the direction of the forced passage which Giovanni had already explored. In front of him across the gap in the floor he could see a straight continuing passage cut through the solid rock. He used a rope to negotiate the fifteen-foot drop to the ramp below, and then, only noticing that the lower passage behind him was half choked with earth and stones, he walked up the slope and on to the level that led towards the centre of the Pyramid.

The walls were covered with feathery incrustations of salt that glittered like hoar-frost in the light of the torches. The passage was about a hundred and thirty feet long and ran direct to the burial-chamber. Giovanni entered it with awe. At first it seemed quite empty. He looked eagerly towards the west end of the chamber, hoping to see there a great sarcophagus like that in the Pyramid of Cheops. There appeared to be nothing except some displaced stones. It was only when he walked to the other end of the chamber that he saw the sarcophagus was sunk in the floor.

'By this time,' says Giovanni, 'the Chevalier Frediani had entered also; and we took a general survey of the chamber, which I found to be forty-six feet three inches long, sixteen feet three inches wide, and twenty-three feet six inches high. It is cut out of the solid rock from the floor to the roof, which is composed of large blocks of calcareous stone, meeting in the centre, and forming a roof of the same slope as the pyramid itself. The sarcophagus is eight feet long, three feet six inches wide, and two feet three inches deep in the inside. It is surrounded by large blocks of granite, apparently to prevent its removal, which could not be effected without great labour. The lid had been broken off at the side, so that the sarcophagus was half open. It is of the finest granite; but, like the other in the first pyramid, there is not one hieroglyphic on it.'

Belzoni's measurements agree tolerably well with the more precise figures of modern Egyptologists, except that he made an error in the length of the sarcophagus, which is nearer nine feet than eight. It is also of much better workmanship than the one in Cheops' Pyramid, but Giovanni paid little attention to it when he saw that it was half full of stones and rubbish. He was more concerned to find some written record of the chamber's history and both he and Frediani searched the walls with care. They found a few faint charcoal scrawls in an unfamiliar script—it may have been Coptic or ancient Demotic—and on the wall at the west end a bolder legend in Arabic. Translated—though not without difficulty—by a Copt brought out from Cairo, it purported to say that the Pyramid had been opened and sealed up again in the time of the 'King' Ali Muhammad.[13]

The following day a young man named Pieri, employed in the counting-house of Briggs and Walmass in Cairo, came out to see the Pyramid and, while rummaging inside the sarcophagus, found a piece of bone. There were other pieces buried in the rubbish, and Giovanni collected them all and sent them to London. There they were examined by Mr. Clift, the gentleman in charge of the Hunterian Museum of Anatomy,[14] who announced that they were specimens of the genus *Bos* and had a very pungent saline flavour. The witticisms this gave rise to on the subject of 'salt beef' infuriated Belzoni, who had not forgotten the innocent cause of them when he came to write his *Narrative*. 'Some consequential persons,' he says with withering contempt, 'who would not scruple to sacrifice a point in history, rather than lose a *bon mot*, thought themselves mighty clever in baptizing the said bones those of a cow, merely to raise a joke. So much for their taste for antiquity.'

Giovanni had many visitors to the Pyramid, and in the intervals of conducting them into the royal burial-chamber he supervised the clearance of the lower passage that ran back towards the north face. It sloped down through virgin rock for a distance he calculated as forty-eight and a half feet; then for another fifty-five feet it continued on the level. Half-way along, another passage descended on the left to a chamber that measured about thirty-five feet by ten. Although it was cut out of solid rock, it had a ridged roof like the other. But the chamber was empty except for some small limestone blocks. At the end of the level section of the main passage Belzoni found another place for a granite portcullis, but the slab had been broken and lay in fragments on the floor. Beyond this the passage ascended again. Giovanni followed it for nearly fifty feet to the point where it was blocked by a series of large stone plugs that had evidently been slid down the ramp from above. Belzoni's calculations showed correctly—though he did not verify the fact by digging—that the second entrance to the Pyramid lay outside the base.[15]

The Count de Forbin had left Cairo a few days before the opening of the Pyramid. With an eye to publicity, even in the enemy camp, Giovanni had promised to send him a plan of the interior, and this he now hastened to do. In due course the Count published it in his *Travels in Egypt* and, after a note about Giovanni's previous achievements, added: 'Mr. Belzoni's labours of the present year are likely to be still more gratifying and successful. Without any powerful patronage, unassisted by subscriptions or with the zeal of fellow-labourers, he has very lately made an opening into the second pyramid of Gizeh.' However, the Count—who seems to have been what the Elizabethans would have called 'a magotie-headed fellow'—had some grievances. He insisted that the lion-headed goddesses at Karnak had been found by the French. He declared that Belzoni had not discovered Abu Simbel. (Giovanni indeed made no such claim.) He said that Salt had spent five hundred guineas on getting the Young Memnon head to Alexandria. He accused Giovanni of taking away a colossal arm he had found at Thebes. He bemoaned the 'prodigal expenditure of some English gentlemen' which had 'excited the cupidity of the Orientals'. But he did at least say: 'The world is under obligation to Mr. Belzoni.'

Unfortunately, long before this somewhat equivocating tribute appeared in print, the French press had reported the Count's return home. 'On the 24th of April'—the translation is Giovanni's—'Mr. Le Comte de Forbin, Director General of the Royal Museum of France, landed at the lazaretto of Marseilles. He came last from Alexandria, and his passage was very stormy. He has visited Greece, Syria, and Upper Egypt. By a happy chance, some days before his departure from Cairo, he succeeded in penetrating into the second pyramid of Ghizeh. Mr. Forbin brings the plan of that important discovery, as well as much information on the labours of Mr. Drovetti, at Carnak, and on those which Mr. Salt, the English consul, pursues with the greatest success in the valley of Beban el Malook, and in the plain of Medinet Aboo.' The Count's passage was nothing like so stormy as Giovanni's brow when he read this. He refused to believe it was merely an incompetent reporter that had muddled the story. From now on the Count de Forbin was his sworn enemy.

Meanwhile Henry Salt, who had found nothing at all in the Valley of the Kings but had had some luck elsewhere, was wondering what had happened to the man he employed. The 'little private business' had taken an unconscionably long time—almost two months. Rumours reached him at last of what Belzoni had been up to and as there were consular matters to attend to in Cairo—an English ship had arrived at Suez—Salt set off down the Nile at the end of March.

The Earl of Belmore and his *entourage* had left shortly before. Their journey to the Second Cataract had been a great success. Although one of their number had been shot at in Aswan, they had proved that a family party could safely travel into Nubia. Indeed, the sight of Miss

Brooks, Lady Belmore's maid, tittuping round the ruins of Thebes in
a rose-coloured spencer, with a parasol in her hand, had caused the
Count de Forbin to declare that there was no adventure left in Africa.
He himself had never been further than Thebes.

Lord Belmore and his family were the first British travellers to enter
Chephren's Pyramid, as they had been the first to see the tomb of Seti.
Belzoni was delighted to have this noble patronage again. The family
had already visited Giza on their way up the Nile, and the earl had
inscribed his own name, his lady's and that of her ladyship's lap-dog
Rosa on the top of Cheops' Pyramid. Now they were able to show a
connoisseur's interest in the new discovery. The earl had made a large
collection of antiquities during his stay in Egypt. In due course the
party set off for Jerusalem, bearing—we hope—a loving message for
Sarah. Giovanni decided it was time he returned to Thebes.

Salt arrived in Cairo on the evening of 7 April and went straight to
the consulate. There is no record of what passed at his first meeting
with Belzoni, but perhaps the conversation was a little inhibited by the
arrival, half an hour after Salt, of Lieutenant-Colonel Fitzclarence, later
the Earl of Munster. The officer was on his way home to England from
India with dispatches from Lord Hastings. He had crossed the Eastern
Desert from Qusair to Qena and there missed Salt by one day. He had
pursued the consul all the way down river but never caught him up.
It was dark when he entered Cairo and the street gates were closed. At
last, very tired, he reached the consulate and jumped off the donkey that
had brought him from Bulaq. He passed through a narrow passage into
a small courtyard and there, as he says, 'from the extraordinary figures
against the walls around me, should have fancied I was in the catacombs,
had I not recollected that I was in the sanctum sanctorum of an inveterate and most successful antiquarian'. The light of the lantern shone
on the seated statues of the goddess Sekhmet, sinister in black granite.
At the door a life-size wooden figure of Ramses I stepped forward to
meet him, one arm crooked, like a well-trained butler.

Salt was still at the supper table when the colonel was shown in. A
little later Belzoni made an appearance. 'He was the handsomest man
I ever saw,' records the colonel, fascinated by his great height and his
long beard and the easy debonair way in which he wore Turkish
costume. He listened intently to Giovanni's sober account of his discoveries while Salt tried to capture the conversation with his own eulogy
of Thebes. On the following day the colonel had an audience with
Muhammad Ali, but the morning after the three men set off for Giza.

Fitzclarence was quick to understand Belzoni's character. 'Fame
appears to be the object for which he is most desirous,' he noted in his
diary, and there to confirm it was his name carved above the entrance

to the Second Pyramid and a gang of workmen already digging at the Third. 'I have had a long conversation with Belzoni,' he added later. 'He professes that his great anxiety is to become known to the various antiquaries of Europe, and to be taken by the hand by them. . . . He said he looked upon it as a fortunate circumstance I had passed through Egypt, and trusted I should be able to speak of him in England, so as to bring his merits before a nation to which he declares himself to be most devotedly attached.' Fitzclarence offered to publish an account of the opening of the Second Pyramid, which Giovanni hastily wrote for him in Italian and Salt translated. The colonel included it with a plan and drawings in his *Journal of a Route across India, through Egypt, to England* (1819). He was particularly impressed by Giovanni's uncanny knack of knowing exactly where to dig. Evidently at this time he was speaking somewhat mysteriously of an *index* that guided him. 'In my opinion,' concluded the colonel, 'he is too valuable a man for us to permit to labour for any other nation.'

Giovanni basked in the warmth of the colonel's appreciation. He pressed upon him a handful of bones from the sarcophagus as a souvenir. When Fitzclarence said he would present them to the British Museum, he gave him the lot. But after the colonel had gone and Giovanni was left *tête-à-tête* with Salt, the prospect suddenly seemed less bright. The consul had taken Giovanni's defection on 'a little private business' in good part, since it had resulted in such a brilliant discovery. He was even willing to pay the expenses of the operation, which had amounted to just under one hundred and fifty pounds. But Belzoni would not surrender any of his rights in the Pyramid and refused to accept the money. Had he done so, he could have continued digging at the Third Pyramid and would probably have succeeded in opening it, for the entrance again was on the north side, east of centre, and below a cavity on the surface. It was left for Colonel Howard Vyse[16] to discover—in a reflective mood—nineteen years later, after that advocate of gunpowder archaeology had unsuccessfully bored and blasted his way half through the Pyramid.

Giovanni grew more and more restive as the time came for him to return to Thebes. He made no attempt to conceal the resentment he felt that all those splendid pieces of antiquity that filled Salt's courtyard and overflowed into the grounds of the Austrian consulate now passed out of his hands for ever. If any of them did reach the British Museum, it would be in another man's name. He had worked hard, not sparing himself, for nearly two years; his only return—apart from some small private transactions—had been the first hundred pounds and a part of the proceeds of the two statues which he had sold to the Count de Forbin. (Salt's promise of a monthly allowance of twenty-five pounds he had brushed aside as irrelevant.) Yet money was not his main concern, and the consul's argument that *he* had already spent two thousand pounds out of his own pocket without having had any return simply missed the point. Salt was patient and forbearing, but a little obtuse; Belzoni was unreasonably jealous, but had much right on his side. Neither knew how to manage the personal relationship. In consequence feeling simmered till at last it boiled over. There was another angry scene and then a new agreement was drawn up.

'Whereas it appears that some erroneous ideas had been entertained by Sig. Giovanni Baptista Belzoni, with respect to the objects collected under the auspices and at the expense of Henry Salt, Esq. in Upper Egypt, as being intended for the British Museum; and whereas it has since been satisfactorily explained to Sig. Belzoni that such ideas were altogether founded on a mistake'—so ran the preamble. Salt undertook to pay Belzoni, over and above his expenses, five hundred pounds within the next twelve months. He gave him another statue of Sekhmet like the two already sold to the Count de Forbin. He recognized Belzoni's right to the lid of the sarcophagus 'given' him by Drovetti and promised to concede 'such other objects as he may be able to spare'. Furthermore, Salt agreed that Belzoni should receive half of whatever sum the alabaster sarcophagus made in excess of two thousand pounds, the consul undertaking to offer it to the British Museum at a fair valuation within three years. (Little did either of them realize then what a legacy of trouble there would be in this clause.) And finally Salt promised to assist Belzoni 'in making a collection on his own account, during the present season, at Thebes'.

In return, Giovanni—acting 'under the auspices of' the consul and no longer 'in his employ'—undertook simply 'to go to Thebes, and to do all in his power to bring down, for the said Henry Salt, Esq. at the expense of the latter, the two sarcophagi now remaining under Mr. Beechey's charge at Thebes, and to give such other assistance to Henry Salt Esq.'s agent there, as may appear to him, Sig. Belzoni, advisable'. This was indeed a handsome way of putting it. The agreement was to be considered 'as a final settlement between the said parties', and it was signed and sealed at the consulate on 20 April 1818.[17]

The two men parted with great goodwill. 'I hope,' said Giovanni, as he shook the consul by the hand, 'we shall continue the best friends.'

CHAPTER XII

I saw a modern geographer, a man of classical education, and a great traveller, take the pen in his hand, and, in order to make the newly discovered Berenice fall on the spot where it ought to be, and accord with the description of the ancient geographer, scratch out a large cape that incumbered him, being on the south of the supposed Berenice, and with the same coolness as if it had been a piece at draughts or chess, place it on the north. . . .

G. B. BELZONI, *Narrative*, 1820

GIOVANNI stopped on his way south to renew his *firman* with the Daftardar Bey. When he reached Thebes, Dr. Ricci had already been there two and a half months, diligently copying the reliefs in the New Tomb. Giovanni brought with him a quantity of wax and at once began to take impressions of the principal figures that he needed for his model. Summer was advancing and the wax ran; he had to stiffen it with a mixture of resin and fine dust, and a messy job it must have been.

Giovanni now had authority to dig on his own account on either side of the Nile. In practice, there were few spots on the east side, in the Thebes of the Living, that had not been claimed by the French. On the west side, for some reason, Giovanni no longer backed his researches in the Valley of the Kings. (Salt had dug there unsuccessfully for four months and later Giovanni was to write with some malice: 'What he has found he will of course describe himself with more minuteness than I could do.')

Giovanni tried one or two other places without success. The site he favoured was just behind the two seated Colossi on the plain. He had long ago marked it down as a promising spot. Drovetti had dug there and found only a few broken statues of the lion-headed goddess. Salt continued hopefully when he realized it was the site of a very large temple, but he did not find much of interest. Belzoni now set some men to work here in spite of Beechey's protests that this spot was reserved for the consul. He did however write to Salt and explain what he was doing; he pointed out that the ground would soon be covered by the rising Nile and he thought it advisable to finish the work that was half done. It was now Salt's turn to be touchy and he took it ill. It so happened that on the very second day of digging Giovanni came upon a fine seated statue of Amenhetep III in black granite, nearly ten feet high and almost perfect. Giovanni was sensible enough to recognize Salt's claim and only remarked ruefully: 'See how lucky I am excavating for others, and how unlucky when for myself!' But he could not resist the temptation to carve his name in large letters on the base, where it can still be seen in the British Museum. There were fragments of many other colossal statues in this area, and Giovanni was not far wrong when he said, 'These ruins appear to me to have belonged to the most magnificent temple of any on the west side of Thebes.' Before it was despoiled by Merenptah for his own selfish purposes, the mortuary temple of Amenhetep III must have been even more magnificent than the Ramesseum.[1]

After this, Giovanni gave up digging and concentrated on the work in the tomb. It was certainly a formidable task he had set for himself and Ricci. According to Giovanni's reckoning there were a hundred and eighty-two life-size figures and not less than eight hundred smaller ones, varying between one and three feet. 'The hieroglyphics in this tomb,' he adds, 'are nearly five hundred, of which I took a faithful copy, with their colours; but they are of four different sizes, from one to six inches; so that I have been obliged to take one of each size, which makes nearly two thousand in all.'

The work continued throughout the summer. Life in the tomb was certainly more tolerable than in the burning arid bowl of the valley above. But the concentration involved, the painstaking attention to detail, the effort to reproduce line for line, colour for colour in every chamber and every passage, all by candlelight, must have imposed a great strain. Dr. Ricci's devotion to his strange parergon is something of a mystery;[2] Giovanni, we know, was sustained by the thought of the dazzling impression his model would create when he erected it in London.

He had time now to think about the future. His intention was to join Sarah later in Jerusalem when the work was finished and then to return to Europe to exhibit his model of the tomb and enlist support for further research from antiquarian bodies and museums. He was also anxious to see his family again; it was seventeen years since he had left Italy. He had kept up a desultory correspondence at intervals of many months. But now, in the quietness of the tomb, he sat down to write a long letter to his brothers, Antonio and Francesco. It was headed: 'The Valley of Biban el-Muluk near Thebes. 15 August 1818. Latitude 25° 44' 31" North. Longitude 32° 36' 31". Shade temperature 124° Fahrenheit.'

Giovanni had evidently received from his brothers a letter written in the previous March. He was happy to learn from them that there were people of influence in Padua who thought well of him. Already it seems there were offers of help with the publication of his travels and discoveries—offers more polite perhaps than seriously intended. Giovanni told his brothers he was still being misrepresented and confused with other people, particularly in the press of France and Malta. And then he devoted the rest of his letter to a long *résumé* of his operations since he had first suggested he should bring down the head of Young Memnon from Thebes.[3]

By September the work in the tomb was nearly finished. Giovanni had also acquired, without digging, a choice collection of small antiquities that had been brought to him by his friends among the *fellahin* of Qurna. He was perhaps beginning to feel a little bored and in need of new worlds to conquer when the chance arrival of a sick man put thoughts of Sarah and Jerusalem right out of his head and turned an idea that had long been teasing him into sudden and energetic action.

Frédéric Cailliaud, the young French mineralogist with the appropriately stony-sounding name—the man whom Giovanni suspected of having smashed his reliefs at Philae—had a romantic, questing spirit. He had arrived in Egypt about a month before Belzoni[4] and in the winter of 1815–16 had travelled up the Nile with Drovetti and Rifaud as far as the Second Cataract. (It was then that Drovetti had tried unsuccessfully to persuade Dawud Kashif to open the temple of Abu Simbel.) On their return to Cairo they found that the Pasha was looking for a European to survey the sulphur mines which were reported to exist in the southern part of the Eastern Desert. Drovetti recommended Cailliaud for the job and in November 1816—shortly after his first meeting with Belzoni at Thebes—the ex-jeweller of Nantes set out to explore one of the oldest trade routes of the ancient world that ran through the Red Sea Mountains.

Two months later Cailliaud was able to inform the Pasha that he had not only seen the sulphur mines at el-Ranga—which he did not think, however, were an economic proposition—but he had also discovered emeralds in some long-forgotten workings of Mount Zabara, seven leagues distant from the Red Sea and forty-five to the south of Qusair. This emerald mine was known then only from classical writers and the romances of Arab story-tellers. Muhammad Ali was impressed. He knew that the ancient Egyptians had mined gold in this region. If there were still emeralds, might there not also be gold? An expedition was fitted out during the summer of 1817 and miners were recruited from Syria, Greece and Albania. Cailliaud went with them in November and a few months later—on the eve of Giovanni's opening of the Second Pyramid—he was back in Alexandria with a present of ten pounds of emeralds for the Pasha. Many of the stones were clouded and flawed, but undoubtedly they were emeralds.

South of Zabara Cailliaud had discovered other small emerald mines and near them—though Muhammad Ali was not interested in this—the ruins of what he described as 'a little Greek town', to which the desert tribesmen gave the name of Sakait.[5] Cailliaud's somewhat romantic and exaggerated account of these ruins, together with his elegant drawings and the fact that he had discovered a mutilated Greek inscription containing the name Berenice, half persuaded some of the antiquaries in Cairo that the Frenchman had really found the lost city of Berenice, Egypt's main *entrepôt* for trade with India and the Persian Gulf in Ptolemaic times. Cailliaud himself made no such claim and admitted that Sakait was eight hours' journey from the sea. But visions of a new Pompeii rose like a mirage to tempt all those antiquaries who found no room to dig in Thebes.

It was about the middle of September 1818—when Cailliaud was in Cairo, thinking of returning to France—that a miner who had come down to the Nile Valley to buy provisions fell ill and, hearing of a Frank physician in the tombs of Biban el-Muluk, went there to ask him to prescribe. While Ricci doctored the man, Belzoni questioned him searchingly about the ruined city in the desert. Whatever his answer, Giovanni's mind was already made up: he would go and see the place for himself. Beechey did not need much persuading to join in, and with the doctor, Yanni, another Greek, the miner and two Arab boys from Qurna, Belzoni soon had a sizable party.

They locked up Seti's tomb—Giovanni had taken the precaution of putting a stout door on it some time before—and left it under a guard. They had first to go to Edfu by boat. That year there was a phenomenally high Nile; the river had risen three and a half feet above the previous year's highest level. Whole villages disappeared: cattle, corn, women and children were swept away while the mud houses dissolved into their parent mud. The plain of Thebes became a vast lake eight miles across, in which Karnak and Luxor were islands and the twin Colossi of Amenhetep III rose like rugged lighthouses above the swirling brown waters.

At Armant the travellers used their boat to rescue a number of stranded villagers. At Esna, Giovanni received from the governor a *firman* to dig for antiquities and a warning not to touch emeralds. He was also given a janissary to protect the party. At Edfu they were moved on from their first mooring-place lest their boat should breach the protective fence of earth and reeds and let in the waters to drown the village. Here Belzoni hired camels and men and a *shaikh* to guide them through the desert.

In ancient Egypt the main starting-point of the roads that ran from the Nile Valley to the Red Sea was Koptos, the modern Quft. There the colossal phallic statues of Min, decorated with reliefs of Red Sea *Pterocera* shells, testified to a traffic that was already well-established five thousand years ago. The shortest route to the coast followed the Valley of Qusair. But another longer road struck out south-east across the desert and through the mountains to the latitude of Aswan. A more southerly route left the Nile Valley near Edfu and intersected the Koptos highway. Many rare and precious stones were found in the Eastern Desert—agate and amethyst from predynastic times, green and red jasper during the Middle Kingdom, emeralds under the Ptolemies. Here were the porphyry quarries of Imperial Rome and a source of *breccia verde*, fine granite and serpentine. Further south there was gold. From the mines and quarries of this region a steady flow of wealth vitalized the old arteries of Egypt and encouraged trade with other countries. Along these roads came the precious products of Punt—ivory, ebony and sweet-smelling woods, rich spices and myrrh, leopard-skins, gold-dust and dog-headed apes.[6]

It was Ptolemy II (Philadelphus) who in the third century B.C. built the port of Berenice in the shelter of a little spur that jutted into Foul Bay (*Sinus Immundus*) five hundred miles south of Suez. His ships, beating up the Red Sea against a northerly wind nine months in the year, could if they wished go through the canal he had built from Arsinoe (near Suez) to the Nile, and unload their cargoes at Alexandria. But many preferred to save time and avoid bad weather by discharging at Berenice, even if the port facilities were not as good. Ptolemy improved the road between Koptos and Berenice and constructed watering stations along it for the convenience of travellers. From Berenice his elephant-carriers sailed to Somaliland and brought back the great beasts that lumbered over the desert hills to their depot in the Thebaid. And along the same road, but in the opposite direction, went the unhappy labour battalions drafted into the emerald mines at Zabara and Sakait.

A tablet found behind a guard-post at Koptos shows the kind of traffic over this road and the dues levied on it in the ninth year of the reign of the Emperor Domitian (A.D. 90). An able seaman paid five drachmas, a skilled artisan eight. For a soldier's wife—a relative luxury —the toll was twenty, but a prostitute coming into the country had to pay over a hundred drachmas; such was the protective tariff erected against those 'frail goods'—the phrase is Sir Frederick Henniker's— whose later exemplars the worthy baronet saw at Qena—ten miles from Quft and now, as Qus was in the Middle Ages, the terminus of the Red Sea route.

If the road had frayed a little at the Nile end, it was still possible that

it led direct to Berenice. Several ancient writers—Pliny and the authors
of the Antonine Itinerary and the Theodosian Table[7]—list the watering
stations that existed along the route and give the distances between
them. Although their accounts do not tally in detail, they agree pretty
well that the total distance from Koptos to Berenice was about two
hundred and fifty-eight Roman miles. Cailliaud had seen a number of
these stations—rough stone enclosures usually with a sand-choked well
in the middle—and had noticed that those on the Koptos road were
bigger and better-defined than the ones on the transverse route he had
followed first from Edfu.

Belzoni's caravan—sixteen camels, twelve men and two boys—set off
on 23 September along a good level road through a valley dotted with
sunt and sycamore trees and occasional clumps of camel-thorn. On the
second day, in the Wadi Miah, they reached a small rock-cut temple
which Cailliaud had seen and described. There were two colossal statues
under the portico and some painted reliefs which Giovanni thought
'not of the worst execution'. He made a drawing of the temple, while
Beechey copied a Greek inscription on one of the columns, but did it so
badly that he could not read it afterwards. It gave the names of thirteen
soldiers who had once been quartered in the station opposite—a bored
little group of men in a desert outpost with nothing to do but scratch
their names on a thousand-year-old ruin.

How happy Giovanni would have been to know that the little temple
and the ruined caravanserai had been built by the Pharaoh whose tomb
he had lovingly occupied for so many months! Seti I had needed gold
for his ambitious programme of temple restoration. But he was a humane
man and thought of those who must travel through the desert to and
from the mines in the mountains. Even a limited tour of the region left
him appalled at the hardships involved. Seti recorded his reactions and
the steps he took on a tablet that was placed in the little temple which
he built a day's journey from the Nile: 'His Majesty inspected the hill
country as far as the region of the mountains, and he said: "How evil is
the way without water! A traveller's mouth is parched. How shall his
throat be cooled? How shall his thirst be quenched? For the Low Land
is far away and the High Land is vast. The thirsty man in this fatal
country cries aloud. Make haste then, and take counsel for their needs.
I will make a supply to preserve their lives so that in after years they will
thank God in my name." ' By Pharaoh's orders a well was dug 'and the
water flooded it plentifully like the two caves of Elephantine. Then His
Majesty said: "God has answered my prayer; he has brought forth water
for me upon the mountain." '[8]

Giovanni's own feelings after forty days in the wilderness were not unlike Pharaoh's, when he contemplated the horrors of thirst. 'What a situation for a man, though a rich one, perhaps the owner of all the caravans! He is dying for a cup of water—no one gives it to him—he offers all he possesses—no one hears him—they are all dying—though by walking a few hours further they might be saved,—the camels are lying down, and cannot be made to rise—no one has strength to walk—only he that has a glass of that precious liquor lives to walk a mile farther, and perhaps dies too.'

On the third day out from Edfu, Dr. Ricci was taken ill. His disorder was so violent, says Giovanni, that it was decided he must go back. The following day they split the caravan into three parts. The baggage train went east; Ricci returned towards the Nile; while Beechey and Belzoni rode off in a south-easterly direction to see something that the Ababda tribesmen wanted to show them. It turned out to be another ancient station at Bir Sammut.

From there they took the road to the east through several beautiful and romantic valleys—'if so they may be called,' says Giovanni. The colours of the rocks fascinated him. He noticed a splendid outcrop of granite—as fine as that of Aswan—and wondered whether the ancients had used it. These aesthetic and speculative moods were not even interrupted by the harsh realities of desert life. Beechey fell ill through drinking bad water. Belzoni remained obstinately fit.

He was interested in the wild Ababda[9] who after their first suspicion of the strangers showed themselves very friendly. These nomadic tribesmen lived in tents of mats and went almost naked. They spoke a kind of Arabic but were much more like the Nubians in appearance, with their chocolate skins, long frizzy hair, good teeth and fine eyes. Fortunately Giovanni had no sense of smell; otherwise he might have been bothered by their habit of putting lumps of mutton-fat in their hair and letting it melt malodorously for days.

On 29 September the travellers saw the Red Sea at a great distance and entered a region of mountains. On the 30th they reached Gebel Zabara, the *Mons Smaragdus* of the ancients, Emerald Mountain. The fifty miners encamped at its foot were a dour, dejected lot—Syrians, Greeks and a few Albanians who had come there ten months before in high hopes of making their fortunes. Conditions were very bad. All their food had to be brought from the Nile Valley—a week's journey. There were two small wells but they were half a day's march from the camp. The work itself was difficult and dangerous. So far they had done no more than clear some of the ancient adits in the mines of the *débris* that choked them. These workings were like rabbit holes, and the men crawled through them in constant fear of being buried alive. They had mutinied against their overseers and two men had been killed. They went in dread of an attack by the Ababda, for some of the miners had tried to rape their women and steal from their tents. Worst of all, there were no emeralds—or none worth speaking of—for the great veins of mica-schist that ran through the mountain now produced only a low-grade commercial beryl. Yet the vast heaps of spoil in the valley testified to the zeal—and perhaps the thoroughness—with which the ancients had searched for, presumably, true emeralds.

Belzoni questioned the miners about the ruined city in the desert. Some had been with Cailliaud when he saw it, but their recollections were hazy and to them one ruin in the desert was very much like another. However, Giovanni found an old man among the Ababda who knew the place, and with him as guide they set off early the next morning.

The path climbed through a steep and craggy pass where the camels suffered as much as horses would have done on soft sand. They circled the Emerald Mountain to the south, and at the top of the pass Giovanni strained his eyes to catch some sight of ruined towers and broken columns beyond. Belzoni's account of this part of his journey is written with heavy sarcasm at Cailliaud's expense. They had planned, he says, how to make best use of the limited time they could spend at the lost city. Beechey 'was to take drawings of all the beautiful edifices, monuments, figures, paintings, if any, sculptures, statues, columns, &c. I was to run all over the vast ruins like a pointer, as fast as I could, to observe where any thing was to be found or discovered, to take measures of all the beautiful monuments, and plans of every stone in that great city.' When the old man halted the caravan near some scattered low ruins and said that this was the place where the other Christian had been, Giovanni flatly refused to believe him. He pushed on for another four hours till they were overtaken by darkness. 'By this time,' says Giovanni, 'we were without water, and though in the proximity of a great town according to Monsieur Caliud, no water could be had at less than fifteen miles distance.' That was rather hard on Cailliaud who—in print, at least—claimed no more than that he had found a miners' town.

There was still a suspicion in Giovanni's mind that the old man might be playing them false. Perhaps he wanted to wait till their provisions were nearly exhausted and then drive a hard bargain. But that was not characteristic of the Ababda, who only wished to be left in peace. Belzoni, however, had good reason to be worried about their supplies. They had lost their only sheep, there was biscuit for not more than twenty days, and the little stock of water in the skins was putrid.

The following morning he climbed with Beechey to the top of a peak that commanded a wide view. Giovanni had with him a small pocket telescope and D'Anville's map of the Red Sea coast, published in 1766.[10]

The cartographer had tried to combine the statements of classical writers like Ptolemy and Strabo with the information given in early Portuguese charts. The result was highly conjectural but some of the data was sound. Giovanni decided that, as he could not see any ruins corresponding to Cailliaud's description, he would try to find Berenice Trogloditica where D'Anville placed it on the map.

Accordingly, as soon as the camels had returned with water, he told the drivers that they were going further south. There was great consternation at this and only a mixture of threats and promises carried the day. Their direction at first was north-east, down the Wadi Gemal towards the sea. At sunset they passed through a narrow cleft in the rocks; the Ababda called it Khurm el-Gemal, the Camel's Hole. By noon the next day they had reached the sea, and Giovanni and Beechey plunged in 'like the crocodiles into the Nile'. When they came out, with appetites increased, they calculated that they had biscuit now for only seventeen days.

From here their way lay south along Pliny's Troglodytic Coast to the point where D'Anville hopefully placed the ruins of Berenice, immediately beyond Cape Lepte Extrema, just below the 24th degree of latitude. The camel-drivers jibbed again. In the end Giovanni had to allow them two days to go to a well to fetch an adequate supply of water. Meanwhile he and Beechey began to explore the coast, which was fringed here with curious coral and madrepore formations. They found that a little bay shown to the north on D'Anville's map did not exist—no good augury for their search for Berenice.

They met some fishermen who sold them their catch, and Giovanni ate an inordinate quantity of shell-fish which he picked off the rocks. This helped to solve the food problem, but it gave them a raging thirst which was only relieved when the camels came back with the water on the 6th. Giovanni now divided the caravan into two parts. The baggage and most of the camels went inland with Giovanni's Greek servant and the janissary to wait at a spring. The rest—Beechey, Yanni, the four drivers and the two boys—were to go south along the coast with Giovanni and five camels.

Later that day they saw more of the inhabitants. An old woman was broiling fish over a fire and putting them into an upturned tortoise-shell; her daughters were fishing from a boat inshore. Yanni tells how the old woman fled with loud cries as soon as she saw the strangers' Turkish costume. They called her back, but she would not come, so they sat down and ate her fish—all, that is, except Beechey, who with proconsular punctilio left some money in the tortoise-shell, which one of the camel-drivers tried to steal. Later the old woman sent more fish after them and the following morning they were pursued by a breath-

less small boy with yet another catch. This was Strabo's Land of the
Ichthyophagi.

On the 7th the travellers stopped to look at the sulphur mines of el-
Kabrit, near the mouth of the Wadi Abu Husun. The earth was yellow
and red with ore washed out of the workings. That night they reached
the root of the long pointed peninsula of Cape Lepte Extrema, Belzoni's
'el Galahen', which Arab sailors called 'Cape Nose'. Already their store
of water was getting low.

About noon on the 9th they came to the sea again on the other side
of the peninsula. According to D'Anville's map Berenice was still some
way to the south. But to Giovanni's amazement and delight they suddenly found themselves on a sandy shore covered with regular mounds
that clearly indicated an ancient occupation site.

While the camel-men wondered that one dusty ruin should excite the
Franks so much more than another, Giovanni and his companions
eagerly hurried up and down the straight criss-cross streets of the little
town. The buildings—or what they could see of them under hummocks
of sand and clumps of bushes—were made of soft madrepore[11] blocks,
in which strange writhing shapes of seaweed and coral were petrified in
a timeless immobility. Two rows of taller mounds further apart than
the others showed where the main street ran towards the sea.

In the middle of it, at the highest point, stood a small limestone
temple. The sand had drifted against it in dunes and its walls were pitted
and eroded by the salt air. Giovanni measured the temple and made it
one hundred and two feet long by forty-three feet wide. The whole
town he estimated at some one thousand six hundred feet from north
to south and two thousand feet from east to west—not large, but very
different from the huddle of miners' huts at Sakait.

There was a staircase leading to the roof of the temple and from that
vantage-point Giovanni could take in the whole scene. 'The situation
of this town is delightful,' he wrote. 'The open sea before it is on the
east, and from the southern coast to the point of the cape is like an
amphitheatre of mountains, except an opening on the north-west plain,
where we came from. The Cape el Galahen extends its point nearly
opposite the town on the east, and forms a shelter for large ships from
the north and north-east winds. Right opposite the town there is a very
fine harbour entirely made by nature; its entrance is on the north, it is
guarded on the east by a neck of incrusted rock, on the south by the
land, and on the west by the town; the north side, as I said before, being
covered by the range of mountains which forms the cape, protects the
harbour also. Its entrance has been deep enough for small vessels, such
as the ancients had at those times, but no doubt was deeper. It has at
present a bar of sand across, so that nothing could enter at low water;

but a passage could be easily cut, and the harbour rendered useful.'

There was not much time to examine the ruins, for the water problem was now becoming acute. The camel-men had exhausted their own supply—or at least they said they had—and Belzoni and his companions were not disposed to share theirs. The drivers wanted to return at once, but this would have been intolerable to Giovanni after making such an effort to get there. Such was his strength of personality that he at last persuaded the camel-men to wait till noon the next day. Fortunately there was a moon that night and Belzoni was able to explore the ruins after dark. Judging the largest buildings to be about forty feet by twenty, he calculated that the square of one thousand six hundred by two thousand feet would contain four thousand houses. But as half the area seemed to be without buildings, he reduced this estimate to two thousand—'that I might not be mistaken for another Caliud'. Lieutenant R. Wellsted, I.N., who made a survey of Berenice nearly twenty years later, estimated the number of houses at between one thousand and one thousand five hundred.[12] But he also reckoned a mile for the town's circumference, which is very close to Giovanni's figures.

Belzoni's faith in D'Anville as a geographer was such that he still felt a little worried because the map showed Berenice further south than the actual position of the ruins. Determined not to be laughed at, as Cailliaud would be, he set off before sunrise the next morning with Beechey and the Ababda guide to explore a few miles further south. When the sun came up he saw there was no mound or elevation anywhere in the plain as far as the mountain wall. Giovanni was convinced at last that he had found Berenice.

Before leaving in the morning he had set one of the bright little Arab boys from Qurna to dig in the temple mound. By some strange oversight Belzoni had not included a spade in their equipment, but, nothing daunted, young Musa began to scoop away the soft sand with a large shell. When Giovanni and Beechey returned they found the boy had cleared down to a depth of about four feet at a spot near the north-east corner of the sanctuary. He had uncovered some bas-reliefs and part of a hieroglyphic inscription on the upper part of the wall. Musa also found in the sand a stele or tablet of red breccia engraved with hieroglyphs and figures. 'We took it away,' says Giovanni, 'as a memorandum of having seen an Egyptian temple on the coast of the Red Sea; a circumstance that, as yet, no antiquarian has had any idea of.' Some years later Sir Gardner Wilkinson partly excavated the temple at Berenice and discovered a Greek inscription which showed that it was dedicated to Serapis—that fusion of Osiris and Apis whose cult became universal in Egypt under the Ptolemies. A number of ex-voto statuettes were found, some of them no doubt offered by grateful sailors and merchants using the port of Berenice. The name of the emperor Trajan, carved in hieroglyphics, proved that the little temple had continued to function at least until the end of the first century A.D.[13]

The travellers left Berenice in the late afternoon and Giovanni relented so far as to give the camel-drivers half a pint of water each. Their direction was now north-west through a gap in the mountains. They passed another ancient station in the moonlight—the first on the road to Koptos. By midnight they had reached the well at el-Haratra, where, almost as welcome as the water, was the presence of some 'chocolate nymphs'—Ababda girls watering their flocks. Giovanni was 'gallant with them, for the sake of devouring some of their lambs'. They bought a sheep and ate it there and then.

Giovanni's intention was to take another look at Sakait, which he had passed so contemptuously on the outward journey. A day and a half brought them to Um Sueh, where they found the rest of the caravan comfortably idling at the spring, whose abundant flow Giovanni—with the trained eye of an hydraulic engineer—pronounced sufficient 'to make a jet of about one inch diameter'. The water gushed out of a granite cleft in the rocks and was pure and wholesome.

After resting and refreshing themselves here the travellers continued on their way to Sakait. There, in order to dispel any last lingering doubt, Giovanni insisted on going down to the sea again by the route Cailliaud had taken. The journey occupied nine hours; Cailliaud later said in print that it took him eight, but either he had been incautious in his statement before or else he was misreported, for Giovanni taxes him with having said three.

They spent the 16th searching the coast north of the spot where they had been at first. The Ababda could make even less of this manœuvre, but Giovanni was taking no chances. On the 17th they returned to Sakait.

The rough stone huts of the ancient mining village were scattered over two slopes of the mountain with a dry watercourse running between them. Unlike those at Berenice, the buildings were not buried, but they were much smaller and of cruder construction. No roofs remained, only low walls of hewn stone. Most of the houses had a single large room and several smaller ones; sometimes also there was a store-cellar cut in the rock. But Cailliaud had been able to wander in and out of these places, and it was this that had so worked upon his romantic imagination. 'It was highly amusing to me,' he says, 'to stroll from house to house, from chamber to chamber. In these deserted dwellings, various instruments, utensils, &c., were to be seen, with lamps of burnt earth, and fragments of vases of a beautiful form, both of earth and glass; also stones, hollowed and fluted, that served for mills to grind their grain.

With unbounded satisfaction I greeted and hailed a town, hitherto un-known to all our voyagers, which had not been inhabited, perhaps, for 2,000 years, and almost entirely standing.'[14]

Giovanni counted the houses; there were eighty-seven, according to his reckoning. Cailliaud in his book gives the figure as 'about 500' and Belzoni accuses him of having spread reports of eight hundred. Cailliaud's own sketch is illuminating; it shows the houses dotted about the slopes like currants in a cake. But, exaggerated as his description is, he could at any rate claim that he had found three temples—shrines or chapels would be a better name—partly built out of hewn stone, partly hollowed out of the rock. Here the miners, doomed to a miserable, hazardous life, offered up their prayers and vows to Serapis and the Mnevis bull, to Apollo and 'Our Lady Isis of Senskis'.[15] Giovanni copied the pathetic, half-obliterated *graffiti* from what he scornfully describes as a 'niche' in the rock and later published them in his book.

Now at last the caravan headed for home. The camels had been so sorely tried by the rough going over the mountains that they could scarcely crawl; four out of the sixteen died on the journey. On the even-ing of the 22nd they reached the little temple of Seti I and it seemed like civilization. The day after, they came to the last well before the Nile. Giovanni says feelingly: 'The water of this place tasted to us very bad on our going up, but it appeared pretty good on our return.'

They got aboard their boat the same night. The following morning they met the Shaikh of the Ababda, who was held a hostage by the Nile for the safety of the miners at Zabara. Giovanni complained of the bad-ness of the camels he had provided, to which he answered that none of the Ababda had ever undertaken such a journey as this with forced marches. The camels had only cost a piastre a day each and their drivers half that amount; out of this they had to find food for both. Giovanni gave the Shaikh of the Ababda a present of a gun and some ammunition to make up for the loss of the camels. Their guide he rewarded in the same way, for he had served them well.

In their month's absence from the Nile the floods had gone down; 'all the lands that were under water before were now not only dried up, but were already sown; the muddy villages carried off by the rapid current were all rebuilt; the fences opened; the Fellahs at work in the fields, and all wore a different aspect.' The age-old miracle of death and resurrection was again performed.

At Qurna, Giovanni found two letters waiting for him from his family. There had been sickness at home[16] and he hastened to reply. But he was full of his own exciting Red Sea adventure and told them as much of it as he could. Two things, it seemed, had impressed him greatly: the existence of an Egyptian temple so far from the Nile and the composition of the ruined buildings. '*L'intiera Città: L'intiera Città è fabricata con non altro materiale che belissime pietrificazioni del Mare.*' . . . 'The whole city—the whole city—is made of nothing but the most beautiful petrifications of the sea!' And he came near to falling into the same sin as Cailliaud when he told his brothers that he reckoned there were three thousand houses; caution overtook him later before he prepared his manuscript for the press.

'I have made a little map of all the places we passed through and all the coast for 80 miles. I have put the town in the right place and the mountains at the proper distance. Hunger and thirst forced us to return quickly and forty days after we entered the desert we came back to the Nile with the full intention of returning as soon as possible to explore these ruins and giving a more exact account of them, which I shall not fail to send you on my return.'[17]

So Giovanni rattled on to his brothers, but long before they read this letter he had changed his mind not once but several times. The desert had got hold of him and now he thought of going off to the Great Oasis of el-Kharga, west of Thebes, which Cailliaud had visited the year before. Perhaps there was something the Frenchman had missed there too. Giovanni even went up as far as Esna to collect information about the route, but when he got back to Qurna Salt had arrived with a large party and other projects were afoot.

Then there had been the unsettling business of the story put about by Rosignano. Giovanni heard it first a few days after his return from Berenice. It was being said in Thebes that Belzoni had not discovered the new tomb in Biban el-Muluk by himself. A native of Qurna, who knew of its existence, had offered the information to one of Drovetti's agents for a hundred piastres. The agent—so the story went—did not want to buy and eventually the secret was sold to Belzoni for the sum named.

This put Giovanni in a cold fury. He wrote at once to Drovetti,[18] who was in Luxor, asking abruptly whether he had heard the story. That was on Thursday, 29 October. Drovetti answered the same day, apparently suggesting they might discuss the matter when Salt came. This was not good enough for Giovanni. Back went another letter by return on the Friday: the truth could not wait for Salt's uncertain arrival; what had been written or said was utterly false and nothing could be proved more easily. If there was a native at Qurna who had received a hundred piastres from Belzoni for showing him the tomb, let Drovetti produce him. When would it suit him to come over?

Drovetti was not going to be bothered. He made some excuse that Rosignano was not available. The matter could be investigated when he came back. But Giovanni would not let it go like that. His honour had been impugned and he wanted the slander killed immediately. He was ready, he said, in a third letter written on Saturday, to pay five hundred piastres to any man who would state that he had received a hundred piastres for showing him the tomb.

The question haunted the week-end. When Drovetti replied, it was with tact and cunning to stop the bombardment from Biban el-Muluk. Giovanni wrote his fourth and final letter, in a much mollified tone, on Monday. '. . . I cannot understand why you did not realize from my two previous letters of 29 and 30 October that what I wanted cleared up was, not what was offered to your agent but the fact that you had been made to believe that the tomb in question was sold to me. . . . I was not a little surprised when you were good enough to tell me that you had this in writing from your agent, Signor Rosignano, who as far as I can tell seems to be a young man of character, incapable of asserting such a falsehood. I have no doubt that when he arrives he will not fail to do me justice by telling the truth about what you have heard on this subject.— As for my claim to have found the tomb myself, I certainly want the world to know the truth and not to suppose that someone else showed me what they had found. But that's not the main point, it is that you stop making it appear that I bought the tomb and wanted to claim the credit of finding it for myself.—Thank you very much for your congratulations about the Pyramid, I assure you I don't look for honour or immortality but only to live in peace, far removed from mischief and slander.' The letter ends with Giovanni's warmest expressions of regard.

Could there have been any truth in the story that someone showed him the tomb? It seems most unlikely, on the face of it, that Rosignano or any other collector of antiquities would have turned down the offer without making investigations first. Yanni makes no mention of it and he had no love for Belzoni; he would certainly have used this story to belittle him, as he tried to do so often, if he had reason to think it would be believed. Giovanni's own account of finding the tomb emphasizes the reluctance of the workmen to dig on a spot which they considered hopeless because of the torrent. Yanni confirms that the entrance was completely buried under tons of earth and stones; the Arabs could not have *known* about it, even if they suspected that something was there. Moreover the story was circulated a whole year after the event to which it referred. It came to Giovanni's ears just after his return from Berenice. Can it have been that his scornful remarks about Cailliaud prompted Rosignano to put out this *canard*, knowing that nothing else would wound him more and provoke him to such violent reaction? That seems the likeliest explanation.[19]

At any rate the episode is very revealing. Those four letters written by Giovanni in five days, the mounting tide of anger, as Drovetti replied promptly but evasively, the sudden change in the last letter after the disarming reference to the Pyramid—belated congratulations indeed!— all these things show clearly the motives that urged Belzoni to take upon himself, like Hercules, one labour after another. Money had very little to do with it, scientific interest only so much. The desire to collect was there, but subordinate. Fame indeed was the spur.

CHAPTER XIII

Nile-land was then, as now, a field for plunder; fortunes were made by digging, not gold, but antiques; and the archaeological field became a battle-plain for two armies of Dragomans and Fellah-navvies. One was headed by the redoubtable Salt; the other owned the command of Drovetti. . . .

RICHARD F. BURTON, The Cornhill Magazine, 1880

SALT had arrived in Thebes with an even more oddly assorted party than the Belmores. There was William John Bankes, Byron's old college friend, a brilliant *amateur* of antiquity and a yet discreet homosexual. In the Holy Land he had enlisted the ever-ready services of Captains Irby and Mangles for another excavating adventure, this time in secret outside the walls of Jerusalem. Disguised as an Albanian, he had entered the Mosque of the Dome of the Rock on the site of Solomon's Temple; he had also penetrated to the ruins of Petra. Now with the faithful Finati and his French and Portuguese adherents he was back in Egypt for a second assault on the Nile. Then there was Baron Sack,[1] an elderly Prussian nobleman, chamberlain to King Frederick William III and a dedicated naturalist; he had been warmly recommended by Government, and Salt was looking after him well. Lastly there was a young French midshipman, Louis Maurice Adolphe Linant de Bellefonds.[2] He was not quite nineteen. He had served in the frigate *Cléopatre* that brought the Count de Forbin to the Levant with a team of draughtsmen to record the great discoveries that were then being made. When a painter died and the architect had an accident, Linant volunteered to replace them. Afterwards, in spite of his youth, he carried out some commissions for the Pasha in connection with harbour works at Alexandria and the Mahmudiya Canal project.[3] Then Salt engaged him for his trip to Upper Egypt and Nubia. Half a century later, after a lifetime of service under the Egyptian Government, Bellefonds Bey was to become Minister of Works and Privy Councillor to the Khedive Ismail.

The party travelled in a small fleet. There was a large *kanjia* with fourteen oars hired by the month for Mr. Bankes, a more roomy but less manageable *maash* for the consul, an inferior sort of boat for the baron, and another craft to bring up the rear with a cargo of sheep, goats, fowls, donkeys, pigeons and turkeys and anything else that might

help to make them virtually self-supporting on their leisurely trip up-
stream. Belzoni joined the party with alacrity when he heard their plans,
but he was rather contemptuous of their luxurious way of living; 'even
at table,' he says with heavy sarcasm, 'we had not ice to cool ourselves
after the hot repast, which was concluded with fruits, and only two sorts
of wine. . . . To be sure, some travellers will say, Why should I starve
myself, while I am in a plentiful country? O! then, but you should not
make the world believe you are starving, while you live like Sir John
Falstaff.'

Beechey and Ricci added two more to the party. The doctor had now
completed his work in the tomb of Seti I. Some time previously
Giovanni had cleared the first descending passage of the earth and
stones that encumbered it almost to the ceiling. This was necessary in
order to uncover the reliefs near the entrance. But Giovanni was also
concerned about the removal of the sarcophagus. With this in mind he
had the well filled up with earth so that the precarious wooden bridge
that spanned it was no longer necessary. In doing so he strangely overlooked one of the two original purposes of the well, which he had
already noted: besides being a trap (in more senses than one) for intending tomb-robbers, it took the water that occasionally cascaded down the
steps when Thebes had one of its rare but regular rainfalls. Giovanni did
at least begin to dig a channel outside the entrance to divert the torrent
when it flowed. But Salt's arrival put it right out of his head and he left
it unfinished.

The consul was in good spirits. Happy he that could leave his work
for several months in the year and devote himself to a pleasant cruise
upon the Nile in such agreeable company! As he wrote home to a
friend, 'Mr. Bankes is one of the most delightful companions I ever met
with, high-bred, well informed, and possessing an inexhaustible fund of
humour; the Baron Sack full of little anecdotes . . . of armadilloes,
flamingoes, field mice, and monstrous snakes, which he had collected in
the course of a long residence at Surinam; withal very credulous, and
permitting himself to have a goose's egg foisted upon him for a crocodile's, yet infinitely amusing and *good-humoured*.' They had moved from
temple to temple as inclination prompted them, digging here, sketching
there. 'All but the baron, who was chiefly engaged in killing frogs,
snakes, beetles, and such like game, were enthusiastically fond of the
arts, and really vied with each other who should produce the best
sketches.'[4] Beechey, Ricci and Belzoni made the competition even
keener, when *they* joined the party. But in the early stages of the voyage,
before the travellers reached Thebes, the most active and successful
researcher was undoubtedly William John Bankes.

At Abydos, digging in the small temple of Ramses II, he uncovered a tablet in a wall that had inscribed upon it a series of cartouches, each enclosing a number of hieroglyphics. Even at that date he guessed that this could be nothing else but a list of kings, for it had generally been accepted that these ovals contained royal names. Bankes had already identified the hieroglyphic name of Cleopatra on the obelisk at Philae. He was, of course, unable to read the characters, but in England the redoubtable Thomas Young had worked out an evaluation of a number of signs and this very year (1818) had drawn up a considerable word-list which was published in a Supplement to the *Encyclopædia Britannica*. A list of kings would be invaluable in extending knowledge of the hieroglyphics, for the names could be compared with the Greek versions given by classical writers. This was a most important discovery and Bankes made a careful and complete transcript.[5]

Bankes had more enlightened views than many of his contemporaries about the despoiling of ancient monuments, especially when they were entire or nearly so and could be preserved. He therefore left the tablet *in situ*—part of it indeed, giving the earliest names, had already been lost—but Mimaut, the French consul general who succeeded Drovetti, was less scrupulous and removed it. After his death it was sold to the British Museum. The temple itself was almost entirely destroyed by the local population in their search for building-stone.[6]

Bankes had fewer compunctions about the removal of free-standing objects, however big these might be. He had set his heart on the obelisk at Philae—which he intended for his own country seat and not for the British Museum—and Salt freely waived any claim. Belzoni was asked now to undertake the transport of the obelisk as far as Alexandria and this commission he gladly accepted. It was a challenge again and a tribute to his unique powers.

But Giovanni had already been grumbling to the consul that he was not making any headway with his own collection; there were no good places left to dig since Salt and Drovetti had parcelled out all Thebes between them. Salt recognized the force of this argument and suggested a new agreement: Belzoni might dig on any site not allocated to the French and a third of what he found would be his; the consul would continue to pay all expenses. This was a much more satisfactory arrangement, and indeed some partnership like this should have been worked out at the beginning. Not much was said about Berenice. The expedition had cost Salt several thousand piastres and produced no returns except part of a tablet; Giovanni, through some strange quirk of independence—no doubt to secure his title-deeds to fame—had paid for his own camel—at the rate of sixpence a day!

But now something happened that gave Belzoni great pleasure and encouragement. Salt refers to it in a letter which he wrote to Sir Joseph

Banks on 16 November. He says: 'I had the delight of receiving a few days back your very kind and obliging letter respecting the Memnon, for which I beg leave to return my sincerest thanks. Since the receipt of it, I have had an opportunity of showing that part of the contents which refers to your idea of collecting for the British Museum to Mr. Belzoni, who feels very grateful for this notice of him, and has begged me to remit for him a letter containing his proposals to the Trustees of the British Museum'. Salt enclosed this and asked for an answer at the first opportunity since, as he said, 'Mr. Belzoni proposes to leave Egypt in April next if his services should not be required'.

Giovanni's memorandum to Salt begins: 'As I understand it is the wish of Sir Joseph Banks that I should enter into an arrangement with the Trustees of the British Museum to employ myself in excavating and collecting antiquity in Egypt, I take this method of acquainting you that I should feel myself highly honored in engaging with the said Trustees for the periode of two years, promising that I would endeavour to the best of my knowledge to employ the above time in the most minute researches.' He goes on to say that after calculating the expenses necessary 'on a scal equal to that of Individuals who have lately been very successful,'—obviously he had Salt and Bankes in mind—'I find that, on the most economical system, they would amount to the sum of one Thousand five hundred Pounds per annum, including the necessary presents to the Beys, Hasheffs and Kaimakams of the Country, leaving it to the Trustees to decide on whatever recompenses they may think propur for my own exertions on this occasion. . . .'[7]

Before they left Thebes, Belzoni and Salt went over to Karnak and there with Drovetti checked the position of the few enclaves that were still reserved to the English on that side of the river. As they walked along, Drovetti tried to pull Belzoni's leg by telling him about a mysterious stranger who frequented the ruins; he dressed exactly like Belzoni, and Drovetti thought he was up to no good. Salt laughed at this, but Giovanni took it very seriously. He believed it was an attempt to exculpate in advance anyone who might be tempted to loose off a shot at him from behind a wall; the man could then say in his defence that he thought it was the sham Belzoni. Giovanni seems very humourless over this, but future events came near to proving him right.

Later, as the French ex-consul gave them sherbet and lemonade in his hut among the ruins, Giovanni let fall a word about the obelisk at Philae. Drovetti pretended astonishment: those rogues at Aswan had deceived him; they had many times promised to bring down the obelisk for him and had obviously done so only to extort money. Salt and Belzoni explained their prior claim and added that the obelisk now belonged to Bankes. Drovetti graciously bestowed it on him with much the air, Giovanni thought, that he had used when he gave *him* the cover of a sarcophagus.

Salt's party left Thebes on 16 November. (Giovanni had celebrated his fortieth birthday just eleven days before.) They reached Edfu on the 21st and found Drovetti's men in occupation of the temple. They also heard a disquieting story that one of his agents had gone off post-haste to Philae in response to an urgent message from the ex-consul.

At Gebel el-Silsila, where the river ran through a narrow granite gap in the mountains, they overtook Drovetti's agent, the Piedmontese ex-*gendarme*, Antonio Lebolo. They hailed him, but he would not stop. A few miles further on, at Kom Ombo, Belzoni left the party and hurried after him in a *kanjia*. At Aswan Lebolo tried to persuade the Agha that he must not allow the English to remove the obelisk. But the Turk pointed out that Belzoni had already taken possession of it two years before and had left money to pay for a guard. Lebolo thereupon resorted to bribery and secured an affidavit before the Qadi that Drovetti was the owner. Then he disappeared.

Giovanni heard of Lebolo's activities as soon as he arrived in Aswan. When he remonstrated with the Agha and reminded him of the thirty dollars he was to receive after the obelisk was safely shipped, the Turk admitted unabashed that Drovetti's men had already made several attempts to remove it; the last one failed because there was too little water in the Cataract. It was this that disturbed Giovanni most; the season was already late and the high Nile had subsided rapidly. He hurried off at once to Philae and was there met by an old man who handed him a note. It was written in French and said: 'M. Drovetti's *chargé d'affaires* begs European travellers to respect the bearer who is guarding the obelisk in the island of Philae, the property of M. Drovetti.' It was signed 'Lebolo' and dated a week earlier.

By now the main party had reached Aswan. There was no difficulty with the Agha, who admitted that Giovanni had been the first to lay claim to the obelisk. Fortunately too there was a boat available, but the *reis* of the *shallal*, the 'captain' of the Cataract, looked askance at the idea of lowering it through the rapids with such a load when the water was low. Two months before he had refused the French when the level was much higher. However, there was one compelling argument, and with half the amount paid in advance the *reis* promised to do what he could. The Agha was also given a gold watch, worth nearly four pounds, in the name of Mr. Bankes.

Giovanni had even less equipment for moving the obelisk than he had when he tackled the Young Memnon. There was scarcely any wood to be had at all. But with the old primitive method of roller and lever he managed to get the fallen obelisk down to the water's edge—a matter of a few dozen yards. The pedestal gave more trouble; it was almost buried and had to be dug out. But eventually this too was in position for loading into the boat.

Meanwhile the Agha had received a letter from Drovetti, warning him not to allow anyone to remove the obelisk. Salt, nettled at this, told the Agha to send his compliments to M. Drovetti and say that the English were taking it.

For what happened next Giovanni blamed only himself. He had gone down to look at the *shallal* and plot a course through the sleek elephant shapes of the rocks that lay in the channel. The Barabras in his absence were building a pier of stones out into deep water. On his return he did not inspect the work closely. When the time came to embark the obelisk, the twenty-two-foot-long monolith was levered and rolled out along the pier to the waiting boat. Suddenly—to Giovanni's horror—the whole structure began to disintegrate. The obelisk slewed round and then with a slow majestic motion slid into the river.

The cause was all too clear. The men, instead of bedding the foundations in the mud, had laid the stones on the sloping underwater surface of the bank so that the weight of the obelisk had simply pushed them apart. Some of the workmen laughed. A few thought of the money they would lose. Then they drifted away to their other occupations.

For an awful moment Giovanni thought the obelisk was lost. He heard the triumphant jeers of Lebolo and Drovetti. But only for a moment. As he sat transfixed on the bank, he was already working out the salvage operation.

Bankes said little, but he was not very pleased. He and the rest of the party set off up the Nile, leaving Belzoni to extricate himself and the obelisk as best he could. (Finati also stayed behind for a while. He had taken it into his head to marry a black Berberine beauty and the wedding ceremonies and the consolation of his bride occupied three or four weeks.)[8]

Giovanni's method of recovering the obelisk from the river was classically simple; not so his English. 'I caused a great quantity of stones to be brought to the water-side. I then desired several men to enter the water, and to make a heap of stones on the side of the obelisk opposite to [i.e. further from] the shore, and to form a solid bed for the levers to rest upon. I accordingly placed the levers under the obelisk, one at the basis, and the other near the leaning point [i.e. the beginning of the pyramidion or cap], so that by the pressure of the levers, the obelisk must turn round upon its axis: the men could not put down the lever under water as they do on shore, but by seating themselves on the extremity of the levers, the pressure of their own weight produced the effect. Two ropes were passed under the obelisk: that end which was from under it was fastened to some date-trees, which happened to be on the bank, and to the ends which came from above I put as many men to pull as I thought were sufficient. At the side where the levers were I put some good divers, who were ready to put large stones under the obelisk when it rose, so that it might not return back to its former situation.' Then with the men hauling on the ropes the obelisk was turned over and over, largely by its own weight, so that it advanced up the bank almost a breadth at a time, till it reached dry ground. The whole operation took less than two days.

Next, by means of a palm-tree bridge such as he had used for the Young Memnon, Giovanni got the obelisk aboard the boat. The base had already been carried across to the mainland and left on the bank, since the vessel could not take both at the same time. The following day came the tricky job of lowering the boat down the Cataract. A cable was fastened to a tree up-stream, ready to be paid out from the boat. Naked Nubians stood on rocks in the water, holding guide-ropes fastened to the gunwales, by which they hoped to control the boat's passage. But the cable was not strong enough to stop the boat once it had started—and indeed, had it stopped, the swift rush of water would have instantly overwhelmed and sunk it. Everything depended on split-second instinctive co-ordination by the men holding the ropes, for there would be no time to give orders. The captain of the boat was almost in tears. He had only accepted the commission because he had waited so long for a cargo; now he would have paid handsomely to be rid of the contract, for he thought his boat was lost.

When all was ready, Giovanni gave the signal. The boat leapt forward towards the edge of the *shallal*, then gathered speed as it slid over into the broken water among the rocks. 'It was one of the greatest sights I have seen,' says Giovanni. The Nubian boatmen played their part superbly, using the backward drive of the eddies to check the boat's onward rush. Finati was full of admiration. There was 'the great boat wheeling and swinging round, and half filling with water, while naked figures were crowding upon all the rocks, or wading or swimming between them, some shouting, and some pulling at the guide ropes, and the boat-owner throwing himself on the ground, scattering dust upon his head, and hiding his face'.

But at last the boat with its precious burden reached calmer water. The *reis* was overjoyed, the Nubians laughed and shouted with pleasure, and Giovanni breathed a thankful prayer. There were still other rapids to be negotiated but none as difficult or dangerous as this.

Later that day Belzoni saw the Agha of Aswan and discharged his obligations. Then he set off in the boat for Thebes but, as the wind was against them, he presently left it and continued by land. On his arrival he went straight to Biban el-Muluk, where, waiting for him steadfast among the tombs, he found the faithful Sarah.

Sarah had had a hardly less adventurous year than Giovanni, though she had made no great discoveries. After a slow start—she was delayed two months at Rosetta—she reached Jerusalem on 12 March, just in time for the celebration of Easter. Finati had now left her to join Bankes, and James Curtin, who wanted to return to England, was presently allowed to enter the service of Mr. Legh. On 1 May she set off for Jordan, defying the regulations that forbade pilgrims to leave before the appointed time. When a guard tried to stop her, she struck at him with her whip. He drew his sword, but she slipped off her mule and dared him to touch her. Then she walked boldly past the barricade and the guard in amazement let her go.

Later she joined the vast throng of pilgrims, mostly Greeks, who were going to bathe in Jordan. There were English travellers too, but she preferred to be independent of them, especially as someone—it may have been Bankes—had hinted broadly that he could not understand 'people being so romantic as to travel about, who had no fortune to support it'.[9]

But the Belmores were kind and friendly, and Sarah joined them later for an excursion to Nazareth. On her own again—except for a servant provided by the convent there—and still dressed as a Mamluk youth, she stayed in Arab tents and Turkish villages and was villainously bitten by fleas.

In Jerusalem once more she made a determined effort to enter the Mosque of the Dome of the Rock—risking death or conversion to Islam for her pains—but only succeeded in seeing the neighbouring Mosque of al-Aqsa.[10] Then, knowing that Giovanni was not able to join her in Palestine, she booked a passage on a boat leaving Jaffa. When she got aboard, she found the cabin full of melons and the deck full of Albanian soldiers—a combination that distressed her more than any previous *contretemps*. To make matters worse, she was suffering from a bad bilious attack. Eventually she got rid of the melons and was befriended by two Italians, who looked after her during that uncomfortable thirteen days' voyage.

At Cairo she waited two months for Belzoni. Once, with a curiosity born of the old fair-ground days, she went to see Abdallah, the captured Wahhabi chief, who had been brought in irons to Cairo before being sent to Constantinople for execution. Sarah found him a young man of 'about twenty-eight or thirty, of a very expressive and interesting countenance'.

Finally she decided to go to Thebes. Taking with her as escort a genuine Mamluk—a deserter from Dongola who had met Belzoni at Abu Simbel—Sarah hired a *kanjia* with two small cabins and left Cairo on 27 November. At Luxor she learned that Giovanni had gone up to Philae, so she crossed the river to wait for him in the Valley of the Kings. There the guards on the tomb of Seti told her that the torrential rain of the previous week-end had flooded the place in spite of all they could do. When she went inside to look at the damage she saw that a great deal of mud had been brought in and the dampness had already made some of the fine flaky limestone crack and fall from the walls. There was nothing she could do but get the Arab boys to remove the mud. Then she sat down to wait for Giovanni. He arrived triumphantly a week later on 23 December.

The damage dashed him a little. It was the jambs of the doorways that had suffered most, but in one of the chambers the upper part of a relief involving three figures had come away from the wall; in another a whole figure had fallen and broken in three pieces, but Giovanni was able to save it from further injury.[11]

Christmas came, and he and Sarah spent it together in the quiet solitude of a valley that was already old and remote when the Christian era began. 'On earth peace, good will toward men.' But not among rival collectors of antiquity in the inexhaustible ruins of Thebes. It was now that Giovanni found himself entering upon what he later called, in a sombre and self-dramatizing mood, 'new contests with evil beings'.

On Boxing Day Giovanni mounted his donkey in Biban el-Muluk and trotted off to the Nile with the intention of crossing over to inspect the English enclaves at Karnak. A French visitor, Édouard de Montulé,[12] who was sketching in the Memnonium, saw him pass. But we have only Belzoni's version of what happened later that day. On the way from Luxor, he says, an Arab warned him not to go where the other Europeans were, but he took no notice of this. Coming to Karnak, he found some of Drovetti's men digging in a spot near the two small lakes which had definitely been reserved for the English. There were no Europeans with them and Giovanni's Greek servant wanted to intervene, but he would not let him and they rode past. Belzoni looked at some digging grounds at the northern end of the temple area and then started back. They were riding through the ruins not far from the grand First Pylon of the temple of Amun when Giovanni suddenly saw a crowd of Arabs hurrying towards them. At their head, shouting and gesticulating, were the two Piedmontese, Lebolo and Rosignano. Giovanni heard Lebolo asking in an angry voice what he meant by taking the obelisk from Philae. (The boat had arrived on Christmas Eve and the tantalizing present that was not for them was stuck tactlessly under their very noses.) In a moment they were all round him. Lebolo seized the bridle of his donkey with one hand and grabbed Giovanni's waistcoat with the other. Rosignano levelled a gun at him and swore violently. The Arabs overpowered the Greek and relieved him of his pistols. Rosignano said it was time Belzoni paid for all he had done to them, and Lebolo declared that he was to have had one-third of the proceeds from the obelisk if Belzoni had not stolen it.

'My situation was not pleasant,' says Giovanni, mildly understating. 'I have no doubt that if I had attempted to dismount, the cowards would have despatched me on the ground, and said that they did it in defence of their lives, as I had been the aggressor. I thought the best way was to keep on my donkey, and look at the villains with contempt.'

Then, as they glared at each other, another party of Arabs came hurrying up with Drovetti in the lead. Why, he wanted to know, had Belzoni stopped his men from working? Giovanni indignantly denied that he had done any such thing and protested at the way he was being treated. Drovetti ordered him to dismount and Giovanni refused. But the next moment a pistol went off behind his back and he slipped smartly to the ground. Then, according to Belzoni, Drovetti seemed to realize that his henchmen had gone too far, and he tried to smooth things over.

It was now there appeared someone whom Giovanni for reasons of delicacy refers to throughout as 'the stranger'. He admits, however, that he was an old acquaintance, 'neither English nor French', who had come to Egypt 'not to see antiquities, but to purchase some if he could'. He was returning to 'one of the capitals of Europe', and Giovanni had asked him to take four of the lion-headed statues in his name as a present 'to a certain high personage'. From these hints and some clues given by de Montulé it is clear that the stranger was an Italian named Sylvestre, in whose company the Frenchman had arrived in Thebes. Sylvestre had bought a cargo of antiquities which he intended shipping to Rome, and on the day of the fracas he had been with Drovetti in Karnak. As soon as he appeared Giovanni told him what had happened; Drovetti said they had 'only had a few words, and that was all'. But Sylvestre, according to Giovanni, declared that he had seen the Arabs pick up their arms and rush out of the huts, and he recalled that Drovetti had said he must run after them and prevent trouble. Giovanni believed he had here an important witness to the fact that a premeditated attack had been made upon him.

He went back to Biban el-Muluk angry and perhaps a little afraid. He had no doubt that there had been an attempt on his life[13] and, though it seems likely that Rosignano—if it was he—discharged his pistol only to frighten Belzoni, tempers were roused and anything might have happened. There is some corroboration of the seriousness of the affair in de Montulé's account of it. He admits that he was not an eye-witness of the quarrel, but he says that the following day Lebolo spoke to Mustafa, his interpreter, and tried to get him to go across with him to Qurna. De Montulé suspected a further attempt on Belzoni's life and would not let his man go.

De Montulé is a reasonably unbiased observer and he seems to have assessed the situation pretty well, for he says: 'I firmly believe that Messrs. Drovetti, Salt and Belzoni are not to blame, but their Agents, who are frequently rewarded in proportion to the value of the discoveries which they make, and consequently nourish mutual animosities against one another.' The Frenchman is also illuminating on another point. Giovanni says that many of the Arabs of Karnak were horrified at Rosignano's outrageous behaviour and took his part. But he had always found the Arabs on that side of the river very different from the men of Qurna, over whom he seemed to exercise a peculiar fascination. De Montulé recalls that the night before this incident took place he saw and heard a number of Arabs in Drovetti's headquarters under the First Pylon passionately inveighing against 'the colossus of the left bank'.

Giovanni was concerned now only to pack up and get out. Yet it took him another month to make all ready. The wax moulds and drawings of the tomb—representing almost a year's work—had to be made secure for their long journey. Then there was the delicate problem of moving the alabaster sarcophagus—poised precariously as it was above the entrance to the tunnel—up the narrow steps, through the chambers and corridors, out into the valley. One careless step by a workman and the precious, fragile shell might have been shattered. It was put into a strong crate—how Giovanni made or found that in Thebes he does not say—and then conveyed on rollers for more than two miles over rough, uneven ground and for another mile over soft sand and small stones to the water's edge. There was also the lid of the other sarcophagus to be taken out of the tomb of Ramses III. This, Giovanni says, was the best piece he ever acquired on his own account. Drovetti, who had seen it lying near the sarcophagus, half-buried under *débris*, did not realize how fine it was when he offered it to Belzoni at the outset of his career as a collector. The red granite cover lay reversed; it was only when Giovanni cleared it and turned it over that he saw the splendid figures of the king and the two attendant goddesses, Isis and Nephthys, carved in relief upon it. The lid was broken at the foot, but above the knee the figures were perfect.[14]

Belzoni left Thebes for the last time on 27 January 1819. 'I must confess,' he says, 'that I felt no small degree of sorrow to quit a place which was become so familiar to me, and where, in no other part of the world, I could find so many objects of inquiry so congenial to my inclination. I must say, that I felt more in leaving Thebes, than any other place in my life.'

Sarah was less sorry to go. She was just recovering from a bad bout of jaundice and had been very frightened by the attack on her husband. Yet to an Englishman they met on their journey down the Nile she seemed a very angel of sweetness and grace. It was that strange character Nathaniel Pearce, the sailor who had deserted the ship in which Salt and Lord Valentia once explored the Red Sea coasts, to become the first English resident in Abyssinia. He had been a person of great influence with the Ras of Tigré, but on that ruler's death and the outbreak of civil war Pearce left Abyssinia to join Salt in Egypt. He had come down to Cairo and was now anxiously making his way up the Nile again in search of the consul like a faithful dog looking for its master. Sarah was the first Englishwoman he had seen for over fifteen years. He had almost forgotten his own language. But his gratitude for Sarah's cordial and Giovanni's kindly interest are touchingly recorded in the pages of his journal.[15]

The Belzonis took their assorted cargo—obelisk, sarcophagus, mummies and moulds—direct to Alexandria. There Giovanni found a letter from Salt, who was still in Nubia. He had told him about the incident at Thebes, and the consul now advised him to take legal action against his assailants. Giovanni learnt that the vice-consul, Mr. Lee, had already instituted proceedings on his behalf and taken the matter up with the French consul, M. Roussel. He therefore decided to wait for Salt's return.

Meanwhile Sylvestre had arrived in Alexandria but was no longer willing to give the kind of evidence Belzoni had supposed he would in Thebes. He had, in fact, come to an understanding with Lebolo. He also went back on his promise to take four of Giovanni's statues 'as a present to a certain court' and departed instead with a large collection bought from Belzoni's rivals for re-sale.

Giovanni now resolved to send two of the statues as a gift to his native city. On 12 March he wrote to the civic authorities at Padua, offering them a pair of black granite Egyptian figures, 'having the body of a woman and the head of a lion', the best of their kind in his collection. He added rather diffidently that some people thought they represented the combined zodiacal signs of Leo and Virgo. But he was quite positive and precise about the place the statues should occupy; he wanted them to go just inside the east door of the *Gran Salone di Padua*, the thirteenth-century Town Hall, on pedestals two feet high.[16]

The pride and pleasure of public benefaction were muted a little by private grief. Giovanni's brother Antonio—the gay, wine-loving Antonio—had died recently, and he wrote now—belatedly, it seems—

to comfort his mother and say that he would be with her soon. He sent her money—four hundred thalers—and urged his brothers Francesco and Domenico to take a little house on the river which would not cost them much more than they were paying at present. In the same letter he told them about his offer to the municipal authorities and asked them to be certain to deliver the enclosure to the right person. There was a postscript in which Giovanni said he wanted it known that the family came originally from Rome and had been settled a long time in Padua. Could his brothers therefore look in the baptismal registers of Santa Sofia and tell him when their name Belzoni became corrupted to Bolzon because of the Venetian accent?

It was impossible for Giovanni to sit idle in Alexandria and wait for Salt's return. The difficulty was to know what to do. He thought of excavating in Lower Egypt, but Drovetti was back in Alexandria, and he was sure there would be opposition. His thoughts turned again to the desert, which had such a powerful attraction for him since his expedition to Berenice. Some months before he had considered the idea of going to the Kharga Oasis, which Cailliaud had visited in the summer of 1818. There was another small oasis west of that—el-Dakhla—from which Drovetti had just returned and was later to claim—if he had not done so already—that he was the first European in modern times to explore it. But Giovanni had met a young Scotsman, Archibald Edmonstone,[17] travelling up the Nile with two companions in January of that year. As they intended visiting el-Kharga Giovanni told them of the smaller oasis beyond, and Edmonstone's party was in fact the first to reach it. On their way *back* in February they met Drovetti on his way *towards* it. Yet he persisted in claiming that he had been there at the end of 1818— a circumstance that throws new light on the character of Drovetti and must have infuriated Belzoni beyond words if he ever knew about it.

But el-Kharga and el-Dakhla were too remote for Giovanni now; both were in the latitude of Thebes. It occurred to him, however, 'that the temple of Jupiter Ammon had been an object of search for a long time, and by more than one traveller but that the true spot where it existed had not been fixed'. He considered also 'that the Faioum was a province as yet little explored' and that he might 'make an excursion in it perhaps undisturbed, and from thence proceed to the western desert'. To avoid letting people know where he was going, he did not bother to apply for a *firman*, but as soon as he had settled Sarah in a house at Rosetta, kindly lent by an English merchant of Alexandria, with a man to call each day to buy her food as the plague had begun to show, he set off for the Faiyum.

Two stories have invested the name of Ammon with romantic adventure and stark horror. It was in the temple of Re-Amun at Siwa—the most remote and inaccessible of all the ancient oracles—that a fawning Egyptian priest, mumbling bad Greek, is said to have addressed the young Alexander of Macedon by mistake as 'son of Zeus' and filled him with dreams of world conquest.[18] It was against the Ammonians that the Persian King Cambyses, already expiating *hubris*, sent an army of fifty thousand men, recklessly ill-provided, that disappeared in the desert and was never seen again; a wind arose from the south as they were at their midday meal and the sand overwhelmed them all.[19] But Giovanni was on the wrong tack this time. He did not come within a hundred and fifty miles of the Siwa Oasis and the temple of Jupiter Ammon, whose inconspicuous ruins William George Browne had already discovered in 1792, though he hesitated to confer on them so famous a name.[20] Hornemann visited the Oasis in 1798.[21] Cailliaud was to go there[22] only a few months after Belzoni thought that he might have found the temple of Jupiter Ammon—perhaps tit for tat for Berenice. In 1820 a new Macedonian, Muhammad Ali, added Siwa to his conquests; Drovetti, Linant and Ricci were among his peaceful camp-followers.[23]

Giovanni had with him on this expedition a Sicilian servant whom he engaged in Alexandria and a Moorish pilgrim returning from Mecca; this man had asked for a passage on their boat and 'he proved very useful'. They reached Beni Suef—eighty miles above Cairo—on 29 April and, leaving the boat there, engaged donkeys for the journey into the Faiyum.

This great depression is itself virtually an oasis, though it lies only a dozen miles from the river Nile. That evening the travellers reached the gap in the low hills, through which the ancient channel known as the Bahr Yusuf—Joseph's Canal—brings water into the Faiyum, and camped not far from the nearer of two pyramids, by the bridges of Lahun.

The next morning Giovanni climbed the ruined brick pyramid that Senusret II—Sesostris of the Greeks[24]—built for himself in the Twelfth Dynasty round about 2000 B.C. A good deal of it was buried under sand and stones, for Giovanni says the length of the base appeared to be only eighty feet. But in fact the true base line is almost 350 feet long. Petrie and Brunton, excavating there between the two enclosure walls, found in 1913 a magnificent treasure in the tomb of a princess: a golden crown and pectorals, necklaces of gold, amethyst and cornelian, toilet jars of obsidian overlaid with gold. There was no hint of that buried splendour below as Giovanni stood on the crude brick mound.[25]

Six miles away to the north-west, at Hawara, is another brick pyramid—that of Amenemhet III, a later king of the Twelfth Dynasty. He it was who largely created the Faiyum province by draining the eastern part of Lake Moeris and regulating the flow of Nile water through a system of canals and sluices. But Amenemhet III is even more famous as the builder of the Labyrinth. Of this wonder of the ancient world— oddly enough not numbered among the Seven—Herodotus says: 'Though the Pyramids were beyond description and every one of them a match for many of the great monuments built by the Greeks, the Labyrinth surpasses even the Pyramids.' It stood, he says, 'a little beyond Lake Moeris, near the city called after the crocodiles,' and he adds that 'at the far corner of the Labyrinth is a pyramid 240 feet high'.[26] Now Strabo says that the town of Arsinoe was formerly called Crocodilopolis, and Belzoni knew that Madinet el-Faiyum, which he could see a few miles off, was close to the ruins of Arsinoe. By collating his ancient authors, he might have deduced that, despite the absence of a lake, the site of the Labyrinth was in that neighbourhood and near a pyramid. Indeed, Giovanni crossed over to the Pyramid of Hawara and just before he reached it made the following observation: 'We entered a place 600 feet square, surrounded by high earthen dikes, apparently to protect the above ground from the inundation of the canal. This spot had no doubt been the seat of some ancient town, of which nothing remained but a few blocks of stone, and the appearance of some brick-work.'

So Belzoni passed on to search for the Labyrinth elsewhere near the shores of the Birket Qarun, that shallow expanse of water in the north-west corner of the Faiyum which is all that is left of Lake Moeris. Seventy years later Petrie cleared the site in front of the Pyramid of Amenemhet at Hawara and discovered under a bed of limestone chips the foundations of an enormous building. The whole area measured about one thousand feet by eight hundred. It was big enough to take all the temples of Karnak and Luxor and the Ramesseum as well. Probably the building—the mortuary temple of Amenemhet III—consisted of rows of courts and small chapels without a single central shrine. But of the fifteen hundred chambers above ground that Herodotus saw and the other fifteen hundred below ground that the priests told him of—courts and colonnades and yet more courts, with pillars of a dazzling white stone—nothing is left but those limestone chips.[27]

At Madinet el-Faiyum, celebrated for its rose-water that disguised, if it did not dispel, the lingering stenches of Cairo, Giovanni obtained a *firman* and a guide. Leaving the ruins of Arsinoe to look at later, he set off north through a fertile countryside towards the Birket Qarun. Presently he passed what he thought was the site of another ancient town and casually noted 'two parts of the wall, the only remains of which are composed of large blocks of stone, without hieroglyphics'.

They were in fact two massive plinths, originally with pyramidal sides, on which sat monolithic statues of the king who had made this corner of the land prosper. Here were the two 'pyramids' that Herodotus saw rising out of the flood, each surmounted by a colossal statue of Amenemhet III. There are fragments of these colossi in the Ashmolean Museum at Oxford.

On 1 May Belzoni and his party came down to the desolate shores of the brackish Birket Qarun, a hundred and thirty feet below sea-level. Near the outfall of the Bahr Yusuf their guide engaged an ancient man with his equally ancient boat. 'The outer shell or hulk was composed of rough pieces of wood scarcely joined, and fastened by four other pieces, wrapped together by four more across, which formed the deck: no tar, no pitch either inside or out, and the only preventive against the water coming in was a kind of weed moistened, which had settled in the joints of the wood.'

In this crazy contraption they sailed westwards across the lake by moonlight. Giovanni for once was in a relaxed happy mood and full of poetic fancies. It pleased him to pretend that this was Acheron and the old man Charon and their boat the bark that ferried souls over to Elysium.

They landed the next day near the south-west corner of the lake, and Giovanni explored the ruins of Qasr Qarun, which probably represents the ancient Dionysias.[28] He was startled when a hyena rushed out of a vault and showed its teeth in a hideous roar before making off. The town, he decided, must once have had considerable importance but the Labyrinth that he sought was not there.

For the next two days they skirted the northern edge of the lake while Giovanni scanned the barren hills and wadis for signs of ancient habitation. Near the eastern end of the Birket he decided to follow a clue in D'Anville's map and go up into the mountains. His guide and the crew were horrified; there was nothing there, they said, *except a few houses in ruins, and a high wall*. Delighted, Giovanni dragooned them all into showing him the way. Nearly two miles from the lake he came to the place that the Arabs called Dimai. Belzoni believed he had found the ancient Bacchias, but that lies some seventeen miles further east.[29] Instead he had lit upon the ruins of another Ptolemaic town known as *Nesos Soknopaiou*, the Island of Soknopaios.[30]

'There are a great number of houses, half tumbled down, and a high wall of sun-burnt bricks, which incloses the ruins of a temple.' So begins Giovanni's description. 'The houses are not united, nor built in any regularity as streets, but only divided by narrow lanes, not more than three or four feet wide, and all built of sun-burnt bricks. There is a causeway, or road, made of large stones, which runs through the town to the temple, which faces the south. In the centre of the city I observed several houses, or rather cellars, underground, as they appeared from their tops, which were covered with strong pieces of wood, over which there were some cane, and above that a layer of bricks, on a level with the surface, so that one might walk over without perceiving that he was treading on the top of a house. As the fishermen had brought their hatchets, I caused two or three of the houses to be uncovered. After removing the layer of bricks, we found a layer of clay, then a layer of canes, which were nearly burnt, and lastly, under the canes some rafters of wood, forming the ceiling. The wood was in good preservation, and of a hard quality. The inside of the hut, or cellar, was filled up with rubbish; but they had evidently been habitations, as we saw a fire-place in every one of them. They were not more than ten or twelve feet square, and the communication to each house was by a narrow lane, not more than three feet wide, which was also covered.'

This was interesting, but it was still not the Labyrinth. The following day, at Tirsa on the south side of the lake, Giovanni saw many large limestone blocks and pieces of red granite that suggested they must have come from some imposing edifice. But a search revealed nothing more informative, though the fragments of columns were everywhere, on the roadside and in the huts of the *fellahin*. Giovanni thought that if only he could trace the source of these fragments he would discover the Labyrinth. Yet he reflected that it might never be found, for it was not a building of great height. It might be buried under the vast quantities of silt brought into the Faiyum each year by the Bahr Yusuf.

At Fidimin, on the road back to Madinet el-Faiyum, Giovanni heard the legend of the three hundred churches that were said to have existed once in this town of many Copts. Three hundred churches—three thousand chambers. Giovanni's tired brain, going round in circles in search of a Labyrinth, wondered whether there could be any connection here. Then he gave it up and turned to something new.

He wanted a guide to take him through the desert to the oasis west of Lake Moeris. The Bedouin camp where he inquired knew only of the Great Oasis to the south. But then an old man remembered that there *was* an oasis in the west; he knew a *shaikh* who had a daughter who was married to another *shaikh* who lived there. Giovanni hurried off at once to Beni Suef to see his old friend Khalil Bey, who was now governor of that province. Through him it was arranged that Shaikh 'Grumar' should be Giovanni's conductor. (Cailliaud used the same man as guide a few months later, and he gives his name as 'Kouroum'.) He was almost as tall and broad as Belzoni himself, and he had 'a countenance that bespoke a resolute mind, and great eagerness after gain'.

The caravan left on 19 May and entered the desert from the southern edge of the Faiyum. On the fourth day out, as they were crossing a high level plain, Giovanni saw a number of 'tumuli, nearly in the form of a parallelogram, from twenty to thirty feet long. There were, I believe, nearly thirty, and some of them I calculated were large enough to contain a hundred corpses.' He concluded that these were the graves of Cambyses' men and argued later with a learned critic who said that the Persians left their dead unburied.

They reached the Wah el-Bahariya—the Little Oasis of the Romans —on 25 May. While they watered their camels, which had not drunk for three days, Giovanni noticed that Shaikh 'Grumar' was showing some uneasiness. He had said that no European had ever been to this oasis and had hinted more than once that Belzoni should pretend to be a Muslim, which he did not want to do. As they approached the village of Zabu, a chocolate-coloured dwarf suddenly sprang out of the bushes and pointed a gun menacingly. 'Grumar' advanced and addressed him in the local dialect, inquiring after the health of his son-in-law. The dwarf at once became friendly and welcomed 'Grumar' and the Moorish *hajji*. But he still looked askance at the two Franks, Belzoni and his Sicilian servant, especially when 'Grumar' said they had come in search of old stones. After a while he ran off to acquaint the village elders with this strange phenomenon.

Presently 'Grumar' went forward and he too disappeared into the compound. As neither of them returned, Giovanni became impatient and walked into the village by himself. The Arabs rose and stood in silence as he entered the dusty square. Giovanni sensed that they were divided; some were willing to be friendly, but others were deeply suspicious. He therefore spread out a new mat he had brought with him, sat down majestically and invited the elders to join him. A few did so with alacrity, but the rest stood and glowered.

What finally won them over was a cup of coffee. Giovanni's Sicilian servant and the Moorish *hajji* made a large pot as soon as they arrived and served it to the shaikhs sitting on the mat. 'The sight of such a treat,' says Giovanni, 'brought the other rusty fellows to sit down also and share the same dainty, as they could not resist the attraction of a cup of coffee, a luxury which they perhaps taste only once a year, on the first day of the arrival of the caravan of Bedoweens, who come there for the purpose of carrying dates to Cairo or Alexandria.'

There was still a reluctance however to let the stranger look at the local stones. The people assured him there were others far better in the next oasis, four days' journey to the north-west; by this Giovanni understood they meant Siwa. Finally the shaikhs agreed that he might see the stones, provided he gave them the treasure that he found in them. They led him to some rock-cut tombs outside the village, in one of which he saw a number of crude *terra cotta* coffins. They were too heavy for a camel to carry, but Giovanni broke some of the flat lids and took away the upper part of each that had a head modelled on it.[31] The villagers also showed him, with greater pride, a spring of water which turned white woollen cloth black in twenty-four hours.

There was a ridge of sandstone rock separating Zabu from the much larger village of el-Qasr, the capital of the oasis. As the name Qasr is analogous to *castra*, Giovanni expected to find there some considerable ruins. On the 27th the paramount Shaikh of the oasis and the Qadi, or justice, came over to see the stranger. They were even more suspicious than the villagers of Zabu, and they only agreed to Giovanni's visiting el-Qasr on condition that he kept away from the ruins, did not touch or take anything away and refrained from writing a single word that might have some magical effect upon the stones. Giovanni accepted this, prepared to advance one step at a time. At el-Qasr the coffee gambit was tried with the same success, and Giovanni presently learnt from the Shaikh one reason for the Qadi's mistrust. His father was a wealthy date-merchant, who was popularly supposed to keep his dollars hidden in the ruins; not unnaturally the Qadi feared that the Frank's magic might discover them.

'On the morning of the 29th,' says Giovanni, 'a great consultation took place, and the great difficulty was to persuade the father of the Cady to let me walk to the ruins.' Finally it was agreed they should go together. Off they went, and the whole of el-Qasr followed at a respectful distance. The old man led the way to the north side of the village, where on a raised platform of rock Giovanni saw a stone arch flanked on either side by a high wall and approached from the lower level by a flight of stone steps. (Belzoni supposed it was a Greek temple, but in fact the building is Roman.) Fifty yards from the ruin the old man stopped and flatly refused to allow Giovanni to go any further. Already the top of the wall was crowded with sight-seers who had rushed ahead to get a vantage-point for any entertainment that might ensue. Giovanni calmly pulled out his pocket telescope, extended it to its full length and trained it on the wall. At once the rubbernecks fell off their perches as if they had been shot. Giovanni handed the telescope to the old man, who was torn between his wonder at the marvel and his fear that the Frank, in spite of his promises, was bringing the stones towards him by magic.

Though Giovanni was not allowed any closer inspection of the ruins,[32] he did prevail upon the people—bribing them by peeps through his telescope—to show him some ancient tombs. They were like those at Zabu. What interested him more was the well of warm and cold water that 'Grumar' talked about. This so obviously suggested the Fountain of the Sun, mentioned by classical writers as a feature of the Oasis of

Ammon, that Giovanni was determined to see it and test its qualities. According to Herodotus, the water was tepid at sunrise, colder when the market-place began to fill up, and coldest of all at noon; it became warmer during the afternoon, was hot in the evening and boiled at midnight.[33]

Giovanni realized he must not show too much interest in the well, so he merely expressed a desire for a bath, and the place was pointed out to him. He says that the water bubbled up from a great depth in a shaft some eight feet square. When he first put his hands in the water—after sunset—it felt warm. He returned to the house where he was staying and at midnight slipped away again with the Sicilian and the *hajji*. The water then was apparently much warmer, but as Giovanni had broken his thermometer he could not be certain. Again, a little before sunrise, he went to the well on the pretext of bathing. The water now seemed warmer than it had been the night before, but cooler than at midnight. On a fourth and final visit at noon he found it quite cold.

Belzoni saw that the phenomenon was easily attributable to the comparative stability of the water's temperature and the wide variations in atmospheric temperature. Gardner Wilkinson, who visited the Little Oasis a few years later, found the temperature of the water to be about 93° Fahrenheit.[34] Giovanni confused what Herodotus had said, but it made no great difference; he was only concerned to know if the existence of this well identified the oasis as the home of the oracle. It seemed to him, from the descriptions given by Browne and Hornemann, that Siwa had as much claim as Wah el-Bahariya to be considered the site of the temple of Ammon; 'the only objection I have against Siwah is, that the ruins in that place are surrounded by water, of which we have no account from the ancient authors, yet it might have formed a lake since that time'. It is a pity, therefore, in view of his cautious attitude here, that the title-page of Belzoni's *Narrative* should assert so positively that he made a journey *to the Oasis of Jupiter Ammon*.[35]

Giovanni wanted to go on to Siwa, but neither offers, promises nor entreaties would persuade 'Grumar' to take him there. He had to be content with visiting the much smaller Oasis of el-Farafra—really a dependency of the Wah el-Bahariya and two days' journey from it to the south-west. He found there only the ruins of a Coptic convent and church and a few suspicious inhabitants. Giovanni returned to the Wah el-Bahariya on 4 June.

The people were now much more friendly and the Qadi at one point took him aside and made him a proposition. He and his father and the Shaikh were agreed that if Giovanni would turn Muslim, they would give him a share of their lands and he might choose four wives from among their daughters and 'be happy there without going about so much after stones'. Giovanni had some difficulty in extricating himself from this situation without causing offence.

On the way over the ridge to Zabu, Belzoni's camel stumbled and rolled down the rocks with him. Fortunately there were no limbs broken, but Giovanni's side was badly bruised—he may even have cracked a rib or two—and he had to lie up for three days. His bed was placed in a narrow passage 'constantly crowded with people, who occasionally trod on my feet, or gave me a kick on the head'. Worse still, there were passing cows, buffaloes, donkeys, sheep and goats that treated the man on the ground with scant consideration. To crown all, a funeral feast was going forward on the day of the accident, with much ululation on the part of the women. The widow, who saw Giovanni trying to write up his notes, later came to him in tears and begged for two pieces of magic paper—'one to get another husband, as soon as possible, and the other to make use of for the same purpose if he should die'. She was very displeased at Giovanni's refusal to encourage such superstitious practices.

By the 8th Giovanni was able to ride his camel again, though his ribs were still black and sore. On the journey back to the Nile the water supply ran low and he knew all the agonies of thirst. He reached Beni Suef on 15 June and from there returned to Cairo. Salt meanwhile had arrived from the south, having been obliged to leave his jovial party in Nubia because of another of those recurring bouts of illness that troubled him all his life. The plague was still raging in Cairo and Giovanni had to visit the consulate secretly by night.

The meeting was quite friendly. The two men went through their accounts together and it was found that Salt still owed Belzoni one hundred and sixty-nine pounds out of the five hundred promised to him over a year before. The consul made this up to the round figure of two hundred pounds. He also picked out a number of items in his collection, which he thought he could spare, and gave them to Belzoni. Salt says he 'seemed quite a satisfied man, and expressed a hope in parting that we should continue friends'.

Off went Giovanni to Rosetta where Sarah was patiently waiting for him, beguiling the time with her pet chameleons. By now he had probably received a letter from the Trustees of the British Museum, declining his offer—solicited by them—to collect antiquities on their behalf.[36] There remained only the Karnak affair to settle. But this proved utterly frustrating. Drovetti wanted the charges to be preferred against himself by Salt; Belzoni insisted that his accusations were made only against Lebolo and Rosignano. Then M. Roussel was recalled to France, and the vice-consul, who took over the case, wished Belzoni to put down twelve hundred dollars immediately to cover his expenses in going up to Thebes with a boat-load of lawyers and lawyers' clerks. However, this was circumvented and eventually Lebolo and Rosignano were brought down to Alexandria. But another loophole was soon found. The men accused were both Piedmontese and not French subjects. So the vice-consul ruled—probably under pressure from Drovetti—that the case against them could only be heard in Turin.

Giovanni gave up in disgust at this and prepared to leave. 'At last, having put an end to all my affairs in Egypt, in the middle of September, 1819, we embarked, thank God! for Europe: not that I disliked the country I was in, for, on the contrary, I have reason to be grateful; nor do I complain of the Turks or Arabs in general, but of some Europeans who are in that country, whose conduct and mode of thinking are a disgrace to human nature.'

THE *podestà* of Padua was a puzzled man. A certain Belzoni, calling himself a native of the city, had written to say he was sending two ancient Egyptian statues which he would like to have set up in the Palazzo della Ragione on either side of the east door. In due course this unusual gift had arrived through the agency of the British consul in Venice and the donor's brothers in Padua. Not daring to cross the unknown benefactor's wishes, Signor Venturini had nervously placed the two black barbaric statues of Sekhmet under the high roof of the Salone, where they faced the huge wooden horse that commemorated a tournament held in 1466, and were flanked by the frescoes of Giusto Menabuoi and Niccolò Moreto with their symbolic figures of the months. Startled by their strangeness, knowing nothing of Egyptian art or religion and not much more of Belzoni, the *podestà* was anxious not to seem unworthy of his position as the civic head of an ancient seat of learning. Accordingly he addressed himself to Professor Meneghelli, Librarian and Keeper of the Numismatic Museum in the University of Padua, for enlightenment on the two savage feline goddesses that had invaded his Town Hall.

The professor knew little more than the *podestà* about ancient Egypt. But he took a hint from Belzoni's own letter and perhaps added a cautious gloss of his own. The *podestà* was delighted with his explanation. How appropriate it all was! How well the new comers now fitted in with their civilized surroundings in the Palace of Reason! An astrological theme inspired both. The letter that Signor Venturini composed with the help of his secretary Macoppe was a little masterpiece of its kind, combining as it did a dignified acceptance of the gift, a little homily on the virtues of the Good Citizen, a ray of light from Padua's 'lamp of learning' for the benighted wanderer in Egyptian darkness, and a useful note on the changed political situation in Italy.

The letter, dated 16 June 1819, began thus: 'The character of a true citizen who loves his native country is seen in the man who remembers and cherishes it, however long he may be absent, however far away he may be. You are that praiseworthy citizen who, after an absence from Padua of some nineteen years, living in far-off places as you now are in Egypt, have not forgotten your own country, but rather wish to em-

bellish it with a new glory by sending together with your kind letter of
12 March in this present year 1819 two most valuable Monuments of
ancient Egypt.'

Then came the gentle reminder that time had not stood still in Padua
while the traveller was away. Giovanni had addressed his letter 'To the
Illustrious Heads of Government' in his native town. Signor Venturini
discreetly pointed out that Padua was now 'a Royal city under Austrian
rule, represented by its *Podestà* and four *Assessori*, who together com-
prise the Municipal Assembly'.

Lastly, to reassure the traveller that he had not wasted his time but
had really found something of importance, the letter declared—in a
tone that brooked no argument—that the two statues 'represent in point
of fact Isis with the head of a Lion, symbolizing the two signs of the
zodiac, Leo and Virgo, as in the two months of July and August the
Nile overflows and waters the land of Egypt with its fertilizing flood'.
What Giovanni thought of this last gratuitous piece of information is
not on record, but as Sekhmet embodied the principle of the sun's
destructive heat, the *podestà*'s presumption was perhaps not so very
wide of the mark.

The two figures, however, posed a more pressing practical problem.
There was the question of the customs. As the statues had been imported from abroad, they were liable to duty, and this could be heavy.
The *podestà* did not want to evade his responsibilities towards his
Austrian overlords; on the other hand he wished to show that he was a
man of taste who knew when he was dealing with works of art and not
with common merchandise. Anyway he was reluctant to pay. Fortunately the Viceroy Rainieri was accommodating, two experts were found
who valued the statues at fifty *lire* each, and honour was satisfied all
round.[2]

The Belzonis arrived in Venice some time in November and after
completing their period of quarantine reached Padua just before
Christmas. There was a civic reception awaited the barber's son who had
become a famous traveller and antiquary. It must have been a proud
moment for Giovanni—shorn now of his flowing beard and compressed
into stiff European clothes—when he saw his two statues in the Salone
as he had imagined them and heard the formal tributes of his fellow-
citizens. And then there was the first ecstatic meeting with his family.
What joy there must have been at that reunion! What happiness for
Teresa, widowed and now bereft of a son, still a martyr to those
migraines that the baths at Battaglia could not cure, to see Gio Batta
return safe and to meet the indomitable Sarah! Francesco and Domenico
were both there, the former now back from his wanderings in Europe
but by no means disposed to settle down. There was Toni's widow to

meet for the first time, and her little girl, and many remembered cousins and aunts to see after such long years of absence.

But Giovanni's stay in Padua was brief; important projects summoned him to London and Paris. Perhaps he had time to see his family installed in the large and commodious house at Monselice to which he induced them to move for the sake of his mother's health. It lay a dozen miles from Padua near the Euganean hills and there was a garden for the gazelles—presumably a pair—that Giovanni had brought from Egypt as pets for the family.

Meanwhile the *podestà* was searching for some signal honour to bestow upon this illustrious son of Padua. It occurred to him presently that the city could hardly do better than strike a medal to commemorate the occasion. The Assembly approved the idea and after some delay, in June 1820, the *podestà* signed an agreement with the engraver Manfredini, who was then employed by the mint at Milan.

The decision to strike the medal was communicated to Giovanni before he left Padua. By the end of March he must have been in London, for *The Times* announced on the 31st, not altogether accurately: 'The celebrated traveller Mr. Belzoni has arrived in this metropolis after an absence of ten years, five of which he has employed in arduous researches after the curious remains of antiquity in Egypt and Nubia. The famous sarcophagus of alabaster, discovered by him in Thebes, is safely deposited in the hands of the British Consul in Alexandria, waiting its embarkation for England along with the obelisk, 22 feet long, taken by Mr. Belzoni from Philae, above the first cataract of the Nile. Mr. Belzoni's Journal of his discoveries in Egypt and Nubia and the Oasis will be published as soon as possible. The model of the beautiful tomb discovered by Mr. Belzoni in Thebes will be erected as soon as a convenient place shall be found for its reception.'

It was in fact only six or seven years since Giovanni had left London, but many changes had taken place in that time. There were three new bridges over the Thames. Southwark and Vauxhall gave their names to two utilitarian structures of cast iron, while the third, which Giovanni must have noted with approval was made of granite—'the noblest bridge in the world', according to Canova, and in Baron Dupin's words 'a colossal monument worthy of Sesostris and the Caesars'—linked the Strand with Lambeth Marsh. Together with its approaches the bridge had cost more than a million pounds, and the Duke of Wellington had opened it on the second anniversary of the battle of Waterloo, after which it was named.

A little south of the bridge a new theatre had sprung up to rival the old Surrey. It was called the Coburg, but presently was to change its name to Victoria in honour of a young princess. The theatre was built on a swamp, and a lurid marsh-gas glow of putrescence seemed to illumine its early years. 'Jew' Davis, Belzoni's old fellow-trooper from the Wells, was a popular draw here—and he was coarse even by Regency standards. Hazlitt, who saw a performance at the Coburg in the month that Giovanni returned to London, wrote that 'you felt yourself in a bridewell, or a brothel, amongst Jewboys, pickpockets, prostitutes and mountebanks, instead of being in the precincts of Mount Parnassus or in the company of the Muses. The object was not to admire or to excel, but to vilify and degrade everything.'

Across the river there was more refinement of taste, if no better morals. In 1820 Nash was re-designing the front of the Opera House in the Haymarket and about to build another theatre almost opposite with a fine Corinthian portico. Indeed Nash was changing the face of London for his patron the Prince. In the seven years of Giovanni's absence he had given the metropolis a new north-to-south axis by creating a broad and elegant thoroughfare from the Regent's residence at Carlton House to the Regent's park beyond Marylebone village.

London's centre of gravity—and levity—was shifting west and the line of Regent Street offered a new demarcation of a more exclusive West End, whose nodal points were somewhere in Old Bond Street and St. James's. The 'Bond Street loungers' were matched by those who took their ease in the famous bay window at White's. The gambling rake-hells of Boodle's and Brooks's had their counterpart in the patrons of 'Gentleman' Jackson's boxing saloon in Bond Street or Angelo's fencing rooms in St. James's. Tom and Jerry, Kate and Sue and all the other raffish characters of Pierce Egan's *Life in London*[3] were no less real than the fantastic 'Poodle' Byng, 'Teapot' Crawfurd and 'Kangaroo' Cooke who actually existed.[4] They merely moved like engaging cogs in different circles.

Outside this small world England was stirring uneasily after the long years of war. Deep-rooted agricultural distress, short-lived booms in trade followed by sudden slumps, mass unemployment, the shrinking purchasing power of money—all these bred a disillusionment that made men question whether they were indeed the victors. Industrial unrest and a demand for political reform went hand in hand together. In the hot summer of 1819 strikes, protest meetings and the secret arming of workers culminated in the massacre of Peterloo. The Government tightened the law and screwed down the safety-valve.

When the authors of *The Annual Register* came to chronicle the events of 1820 from the safe distance of 1821, they deemed it a 'comparatively quiet' year. Yet in January the old mad king George III died at Windsor and the Duke of Kent predeceased him by five days, leaving an eight-months-old daughter, Victoria. Her grandfather had lost the

American colonies; she was to become Empress of India. In February a desperate gang of men, operating from a stable off the Edgware Road, planned to murder the entire Cabinet while they were attending a dinner in Grosvenor Square; they were to carry away the heads of Castlereagh and Sidmouth in a bag, start fires in several places and set up a provisional government in the Mansion House.[5] Later in the year another bag became famous—the green one said to be filled with scabrous details of the Queen's persistent adultery with an Italian servant in her household. For five years Caroline had romped about the Continent and the Middle East, the unwanted hoydenish wife of a fat fornicator and fribble. But now that he was King of England, Caroline of Brunswick was not going to forgo her rights. She was furious when she heard that her name had been excluded from the Book of Common Prayer. She landed at Dover in June and came to London amid the acclamations of the mob, who saw in her a symbol of their own grievances and wrongs. The Ministers were faced with the alternatives of the King's being forced to abdicate or themselves having to resign, if they did not get rid of the Queen quickly. Accordingly they brought in a Bill of Pains and Penalties against her. Her trial in the House of Lords began in August and lasted till November. For three months the nation was titillated by the bedroom and bathroom indecencies of the whole squalid story. In the end the Bill was abandoned—and so, said the current *bon mot*, was the Queen. Altogether it was not an uneventful year.

Belzoni's first concern when he arrived in London in March was to arrange about the publication of his book. He therefore called upon Mr. John Murray at his house in Albemarle Street. The choice was an obvious one. Murray had not only made that famous front room of his on the first floor the meeting-place of the literary giants of his day —Byron and Scott foremost among them—but he had also given great encouragement to the less than literary, whose chief merit was that they had travelled in unfamiliar places. There was yet a further reason why Belzoni should approach the house in Albemarle Street. John Murray was the founder of *The Quarterly Review*, whose editor, William Gifford, had already given Giovanni such good publicity. Belzoni's book was not an easy proposition but, as Samuel Smiles says of it in his Memoir on the publisher, 'nothing daunted Mr. Murray when a new and original work was brought under his notice'. Moreover he knew that the colossal head of Memnon would be there in the British Museum as a constant advertisement for the book. Other Egyptian antiquities were on their way to England and soon London would have an opportunity to see a replica of the new tomb discovered at Thebes.

Beechey had written home—probably to his father, the Royal Academician—a glowing description of the colours in Egyptian tomb paintings. He had also vouched for the accuracy of the drawings and models made by Ricci and Belzoni and this tribute was enshrined in a Supplement to the *Encyclopædia Britannica*.

Narrative of the Operations and Recent Discoveries within the Pyramids, Temples, Tombs, and Excavations, in Egypt and Nubia; and of a Journey to the Coast of the Red Sea, in search of the ancient Berenice; and another to the Oasis of Jupiter Ammon was published before the end of the year. Smiles says: 'Although only 1,000 copies were printed, the payments to Belzoni and his translators, as well as for plates and engravings, amounted to over £2,163. The preparation of the work gave rise to no little difficulty, for Belzoni declined all help beyond that of the individual who was employed to copy out or translate his manuscript and correct the press.' How well we know that obstinacy, and how disarmingly Giovanni justifies it in his Preface to the book! 'As I made my discoveries alone, I have been anxious to write my book by myself, though in so doing, the reader will consider me, and with great propriety, guilty of temerity; but the public will perhaps gain in the fidelity of my narrative, what it loses in elegance. . . . If I am intelligible, it is all that I can expect.'

Belzoni cannot have taken very long over the writing of his book. Copies of it—or proofs at least—were in his hands by the beginning of August and he was already arranging then for the French and Italian editions. Giovanni was helped, of course, by the fact that he had kept a very full and detailed journal—probably in a mixture of English and Italian—from the day when he first left Cairo to go into Upper Egypt. Parts of this were incorporated in the book just as they were; others were amplified in the light of later knowledge or embroidered with some of his more mature reflections and theories. But the whole shows little evidence of having been properly worked over and revised. There are errors and contradictions that Belzoni could easily have removed if he had taken the trouble. Much of the description, particularly of locality, is vague and imprecise. Sometimes the English is so odd as to be almost meaningless. The quarrels with the French, his rumbling suspicions of Salt, the jealousy and the bitterness are all left in. Yet the narrative moves forward with the nervous strength that was one of the chief characteristics of Belzoni himself. The style reveals the man. M. Depping,[6] who made the translation for the French edition, says sadly: 'In France people are ready to forgive a traveller for tampering with the truth a little, so long as his story grips. With Belzoni the interest lies in facts or ultimately in things; form is almost ignored.' How thankful we should be that he was not improved upon by some dull conscientious pedant like the chronicler of the Belmores, Dr. Richardson!

Giovanni was certainly not so immersed in his book that he neglected the social world around him. On the contrary, he was very conscious of the need to find influential friends if his further ambitions were to be satisfied. Murray was a great help; the two men were the same age, almost to the day, and each found the other congenial company. But outside the literary circle that Giovanni now touched tangentially there was Society itself with its High Priestesses presiding over the rites at Almack's Assembly Rooms in King Street, St. James's. The hostesses who conferred the *cachet* of fashion from that exclusive club required each season a suitable supply of 'lions'. Belzoni with his fine commanding appearance, the traveller newly returned from the East who promised to amuse London in the near future with a unique exhibition of his discoveries, was just the kind of celebrity to lend distinction to a ball or rout. The Lady Patronesses of Almack's saw to it that he did not lack invitations.

There was one occasion when the Countess of Cork and Orrery, that diminutive but determined hunter of 'lions', had collected a whole pride for the evening. There was the Quaker James Lancaster, founder of a new system of education for the masses that included hanging recalcitrant pupils in a cage from the class-room ceiling; William Betty, the actor, the former Infant Roscius, who at the age of thirteen had rocked the London theatres to hysteria with his Hamlet and his Lear, now making occasional appearances on the stage before he settled down to a comfortable fifty years of retirement; Walter Scott, the poet and the laird, the publisher and the sheriff, also reputed author of the 'Waverley' novels, visiting London in the spring of 1820 to receive his baronetcy at the hand of George IV; and the traveller Belzoni. Scott felt a little superior to the indiscriminate sort of admiration that could turn itself so easily from one object to another. He wrote afterwards to his friend the Earl of Dalkeith: 'If you are celebrated for writing verses, or for slicing cucumbers, for being two feet taller or two feet less than any other biped, for acting plays when you should be whipped at school, or for attending schools and institutions when you should be preparing for your grave, your notoriety becomes a talisman, an "open sesame" which gives way to everything, till you are voted a bore and discarded for a new plaything.'[7]

Scott was glad to escape from London, which he found 'incredibly tiresome'. But Giovanni evidently made an impression on him, for he told John Morritt in a letter from Edinburgh dated 19 May 1820: 'The great lion—great in every sense—was the gigantic Belzoni, the handsomest man (for a giant) I ever saw or could suppose to myself. He is said completely to have overawed the Arabs, your old friends, by his great strength, height, and energy . . .'[8]

Scott, with his interest in the theatre, may well have seen Belzoni play Orson, the she-bear's fosterling, ten years earlier in Edinburgh. If he did, he would have been wise not to mention it when he met Belzoni in London. For Giovanni had put that world far behind him. Yet there must have been many people who remembered his appearances at Bartholomew Fair and Sadler's Wells, at Astley's and the old Royalty, though his *milieu* was now so much further West. It is unlikely that he went back to any of those once-familiar haunts. But he must have known that Sadler's Wells had changed hands. Grimaldi was there for his last season, not far now from cracking up under the tremendous physical strain of a Clown's business. Dibdin had got into debt and was confined within the Rules of the King's Bench Prison. But he could afford to pay for a private lodging in St. George's Fields and from there he continued to pour out his facile effusions. He had just written an extraordinary piece for Edmund Kean to appear in at Drury Lane. In it Kean, who had played Othello in February and Lear in April, was to sing, dance, fence and harlequinade. This omnibus vehicle was appropriately entitled *The Admirable Crichton*. But Kean was no longer the lithe lad who had tumbled in a monkey-skin at Bartholomew Fair. On the opening night (12 June) he twisted his ankle during the first act and retired hurt. The piece had to be withdrawn. Dibdin quickly furbished up an old tragic opera *David Rizzio* with some new comic scenes.[9] But the season at Drury Lane ended triumphantly that month with a production whose billing could only have given innocent pleasure to Belzoni. It was a musical extravaganza called *Giovanni in London*.

Early in June Giovanni wrote to his family, asking them to do what they could to prepare the way for an Italian edition of his book. He complained that Francesco had not told him when the ship had left with his cases of antiquities. And he had another grumble, which he put in English, so that it might not be seen by the wrong eyes: 'It is long time that I see a parfect silence about a certain decoration that the city of Padova has volontirly promised to do for me but I begin to think it has gone out of memmory. . . . However I am surprised you self did not mention anything about it as I thought that been a mater wich would have done honour to our famely. . . . When you see Jappelli you may inquire as if from yourself and let me know. You should have done so without my teling you wot to do, you bloked head.'[10]

By the time this brotherly rebuke reached Padua the *podestà* had already commissioned the medal and Jappelli the engineer could probably give Francesco a reassuring answer. Giovanni wrote again to his family in August, but now it was to give them elaborate instructions about finding a translator for his book. He was very worried in case there should be a pirated edition. He told his brothers he was sending them the two volumes, text and plates, which they were to deliver to his friend Lazara. He in turn would pass them on to the Cavaliere Papafava. From these two influential citizens of Padua Giovanni clearly hoped he would receive a favourable judgment on his work. And in a postscript to the letter he wondered whether his long-suffering family could get a thousand copies of the Italian edition subscribed for, before publication, in Padua and Venice, Rome, Florence and Milan.

Although Giovanni made these large demands on his relations, he was always concerned on their behalf, and indeed saw in the success of his book the chief means of retrieving the family fortunes. He had very little money to spare at present, but he sent them what he could. He was sorry for Domenico who had to shoulder the main burden. Domenico now had a wife and baby son to support as well as his old mother. Then there was Anna and her little girl living with them; it was unlikely that Antonio had provided enough to make them independent. Teresina was now about six years old and her uncle Giovanni was most anxious when he wrote in August that she should be sent to a good school. Were they still living in Monselice, he wanted to know, and how were the animals—the gazelles? Francesco—poor Francesco!— must look after them properly and see that they were not exposed to sudden changes of temperature.

About the beginning of September Giovanni went to Paris to find a publisher and translator for the French edition of his work. He was indignant at having to pay over a pound to the customs at Calais for bringing in three sets of his lithographed plates. Galignani,[11] a fellow-countryman who had started an English newspaper in Paris, undertook to publish the book and Georges Bernard Depping completed the translation in two months. He added a few notes, mostly drawn from the works of other travellers and from Burckhardt's in particular, and he drastically cut down Sarah's 'Trifling Account', which he thought too trivial for the French. One problem was the extremely anti-French tone of some of the passages in Belzoni's *Narrative*. Depping took advice on this and decided to leave them substantially as they were, though he softened a few expressions and omitted repetitions. Giovanni, full of suspicion, saw in this as well as in the notes a subtle attempt to minimize the importance of his discoveries. He wrote sharply to Depping, but the translator exercised great tact and succeeded in persuading him that these minor changes left the spirit of the original unchanged and improved the chances of the book's sales in France. In the end Belzoni was mollified; indeed, he liked Depping's translation so much that he sent it to Italy to have the Italian version made from it. The German translation was also based on the French.[12]

The English edition appeared shortly before Christmas as a handsome quarto volume priced at two guineas and a separate folio volume containing forty-four coloured plates that sold for six guineas.[13] The book was well received by the serious journals. They appreciated the fact that Belzoni had literally unearthed a mass of new evidence about the civilization of ancient Egypt. They were impressed by his devotion to England. 'This extraordinary and intrepid foreigner'—'indefatigable traveller'—were the phrases used; 'love of antiquity'—and 'skill and persevering research' were his constant attributes. *The Quarterly Review* rightly took credit for having brought Belzoni's name before the public and in the course of a thirty-page notice offered this estimate of his work: 'Mr. Belzoni makes no pretension to classical literature or science of any kind. "I must apologize," he modestly says, "for the few humble observations I have ventured to give on some historical points: but I had become so familiar with the sight of temples, tombs, and pyramids, that I could not help forming some speculation on their origin and construction. The scholar and learned traveller will smile at my presumption; but do they always agree themselves in their opinions in matters of this sort, or even on those of much less difficulty?" It is not to him, therefore, that we are to look for erudite historical disquisitions, or antiquarian elucidations; but, what is probably of more real value and importance, we may implicitly trust his pen and his pencil in what he has described and delineated. But though no scholar himself, he may justly be considered as the pioneer, and a most powerful and useful one, of antiquarian researches; he points out the road and makes it easy for others to travel over. . . .'[14]

This was highly discerning—more than *The Quarterly Review* could realize at the time. By contrast the French were inclined to complain of Belzoni's spleen and to suggest that he did not acknowledge his debt to his predecessors. Letronne, writing in the *Journal des Savans*, said: 'We are justified in protesting at the prejudice he shows against the French, from whom he has had nothing but kindness, esteem and enlightenment. He never, or hardly ever, mentions their work. European research in Egypt seems to date from the consulate of M. Salt. . . . Yet M. Belzoni studied and consulted the text and plates of the *Description* in Cairo; it was the work of the French that he used as a guide. . . . If in some ways he has seen further than they did, that is because he stood on their shoulders.'[15]

The solid worth of Belzoni's book lay in its vigorous first-hand account of five or six major achievements: carrying away the colossal head from Thebes, excavating Abu Simbel, discovering what is still

19. GIOVANNI BATTISTA BELZONI

20. THE EGYPTIAN HALL, PICCADILLY

21. BELZONI'S EXHIBITION

the finest royal tomb in Egypt, establishing the site of Berenice, penetrating the Second Pyramid. When he ventured on theory, Giovanni sometimes fell into ludicrous errors.[16] But if his opinions were backed by his own close and accurate observation, they deserved attention. For example, he noted in a royal tomb at Thebes that one of the mummies 'had new linen, apparently, put over the old rags; which proves, that the Egyptians took great care of their dead, even for many years after their decease'. We know from the Abbott Papyrus (B.M. No. 10221) that there was regular inspection of the tombs, and the finding of the *cache* of royal mummies at Deir el-Bahari in 1881 amply confirmed the practice which Belzoni had presumed; dockets on the mummies gave the dates of their re-wrapping by their pious successors. Again, in the Faiyum Belzoni came to the conclusion that the Birket Qarun was a natural lake used by the ancients to produce a second local inundation. This is contrary to the account given by Herodotus, who said that the lake was artificial and had been constructed by King Moeris. Modern opinion has accepted the view put forward by Belzoni.[17]

These and the few other speculative advances made in *Narrative* do not much affect Belzoni's stature; that was determined by his major discoveries. But they indicate a more inquiring mind than some of the brief notices of his career have hitherto allowed. They more than atone for his unscholarly errors, such as confusing Herodotus with Diodorus; any schoolboy could have put him right there. The truth is that Belzoni's tentative probings into the past were based on the most assiduous field-work then possible. It was from such efforts eventually that the science of Egyptology was born.

Long before the publication of his book Giovanni was busy with plans for his exhibition. Here he had a splendid stroke of luck. Right in the middle of the West End, in Piccadilly almost opposite the bottom of Bond Street, stood the Egyptian Hall. It had been built in 1812 to house the natural history museum of Mr. William Bullock of Liverpool.[18] The architect, G. F. Robinson—perhaps in a riot of inspiration induced by the plates in the great French work on Egypt—designed for it an 'Egyptian' façade. Tilted mouldings helped to detach it from its staid Georgian neighbours and suggested the slight rakish batter of a pylon. The same *motif* was evident in the windows which—on the ground floor, at least—also borrowed from the Step Pyramid. But it was the temple of Dendera that contributed most. A huge cornice dominated the whole front. Below it were sphinxes and a winged disk and two very un-Egyptian colossal nude statues representing Isis and Osiris. The door was flanked by squat lotus columns, and hieroglyphs,

17

even more meaningless than their originals, were freely sprinkled on every lintel and jamb.

Taste apart, no other building could have been more suitable for Belzoni's exhibition, and fortunately he was able to secure it for the summer of 1821. Bullock's museum of curiosities, which displayed most of the known quadrupeds in realistic attitudes around an Indian hut, reached oddly enough through a replica of Fingal's Cave, was sold up in 1819.

In the following year, when Belzoni returned from Egypt, the painter Benjamin Robert Haydon had taken the big room upstairs to exhibit one of his vast canvases, 'Christ's Entry into Jerusalem'. Belzoni succeeded him as tenant. Thereafter through the years the Egyptian Hall housed with scant discrimination monsters and masterpieces. The Siamese Twins and 'General' Tom Thumb, a Murillo and more Haydons, a fake Japanese mermaid and a machine for composing Latin hexameters all drew their sadly discrepant followings.[19]

The central attraction of Giovanni's exhibition was to be his model of the tomb of Seti I. He had now given up calling it the Tomb of Apis, since Dr. Thomas Young, grappling with the problem of the hieroglyphs, had assured him that he had identified the names of the Pharaohs in the two royal cartouches found in association throughout the tomb. ⟨cartouche⟩ and ⟨cartouche⟩, the divine and dynastic names of the king, Men-maat-Re and Merenptah-Seti, were wrongly construed by Young to mean 'Psammis [son of] Necho.' Necho was the Biblical Pharaoh who led an army into Palestine in 609 B.C. and defeated Josiah, king of Judah, at the battle of Megiddo. His son Psammetichus II—Psammis and Psammuthis are variants of the name—had a short and unimportant reign, but he made a raiding expedition into Nubia and we have seen how Salt and Bankes found an inscription left by his soldiers on one of the colossal statues of Ramses II at Abu Simbel. Seven hundred years separated Seti and Ramses from Necho and Psammetichus, but the long papyrus of Egyptian history had still to be unrolled.

However—Psammis or Seti—his tomb was to be the principal feature of the exhibition in Piccadilly. It was not possible to make an exact replica, for the whole rock-cut excavation is three hundred and twenty-eight feet long. Belzoni decided to concentrate on two of the most impressive chambers; these he would reproduce full size from his wax impressions and set up in the main hall under the dome. But he would make a model of the entire tomb, showing the sequence of chambers, stairs and corridors, on a smaller scale of one to six and put this in the galleries upstairs; it would still be over fifty feet long. Then there were the moulds he had made of the portico in the temple of Isis at Philae; that would mean another model. Abu Simbel and the Second Pyramid must also be represented. And dispersed about the exhibition would be the statues and the mummies, the idols and the scarabs, the papyri and the vases and all the other miscellaneous small objects that Giovanni had collected during his excavations.

What help Giovanni had and how he paid for it are not recorded. Ricci was no longer with him to colour the plaster casts and arrange the panels in their correct order. James—poor timid James, who had broken his leg in the water-wheel and had to be sent back from Qurna in the first season because he could not stand the climate—was now in the winter of 1820 penetrating deep into Ethiopia, an experienced dragoman, with Waddington and Hanbury.[20] Giovanni's brother was presently to be summoned from Italy to lend a hand, but he did not arrive till after the exhibition was open. One cannot help feeling that the indefatigable Belzoni and his faithful Sarah probably did most of the work themselves.

At the end of the year Giovanni seems to have been lodging at No. 4 Craven Hill, Bayswater. But he must have spent a good deal of his time in the small orbit bounded by John Murray's house at the bottom of Albemarle Street and the Egyptian Hall just round the corner in Piccadilly. Giovanni was capable of the same immense concentration in Mayfair as he was in the middle of a desert.

There were not many people out of his old life that he still cared to see, though one good friend turned up unexpectedly while he was working on the exhibition. It was Cyrus Redding, the journalist who had come to his help ten years before in his dispute with the manager of the Plymouth theatre. Redding was delighted to see his old acquaintance famous in a new role. And he was especially sympathetic about his quarrel with Salt. Later he referred in the most disparaging terms to H.B.M.'s Consul General in Egypt. Salt had been 'a sort of clerk or secretary to an Irish peer, Lord Valentia'. He was described in an article in *The New Monthly Magazine* as 'Valentia Salt', and even more rudely as 'Mr. Valentia Secretary Salt'. Redding saw in him, as in the manager of the Plymouth theatre, someone ready 'to screw the Italian too hardly in his bargains'. As a witness to Giovanni's character Redding is as biased in his favour as Yanni the Greek was against him.

Belzoni had an odd experience one day in Redding's company. The journalist had been dining with the poet Campbell,[21] who expressed a desire to meet the great traveller. A day or two later Redding saw Giovanni in Piccadilly, just as he was coming away from the Egyptian Hall. He suggested they should go and call on the poet; Belzoni agreed and the two men set off up Bond Street. Redding himself was very tall and the pair might well have attracted some attention. Giovanni was used to being stared at in the street, but now suddenly he became aware that they were being followed by a crowd—a hostile crowd that began to jeer and call after them. Presently he heard the name Bergami being tossed from one to another. It was a name calculated at that moment to arouse all the worst passions of the mob. Queen Caroline was then the subject of judicial proceedings in the House of Lords, and the most scandalous details of her alleged misconduct with Bergami, a courier promoted chamberlain, were being made public every day. A cloud of unsavoury Italian witnesses buzzed like blow-flies about the head of the unfortunate queen. Bergami, or any like-sounding name, was enough to start a riot, for Caroline was as popular with the people as George was disliked. . . . When Belzoni and Redding realized their danger they quickened their pace. 'We had better get out of this,' said Giovanni. They slipped through into Conduit Street and by devious back ways reached Hanover Square, almost running now to shake off their pursuers. A dozen of the more persistent followed them across Oxford Street to the poet's lodging, but there the chase petered out. Giovanni was considerably annoyed.[22]

Work on the exhibition continued throughout the early months of 1821. It was scheduled to open on Tuesday, 1 May and the preview was held the previous Friday. No list of those who attended seems to have survived, but with Belzoni's flair for showmanship and John Murray's standing in society the net must have been cast pretty wide. Some time before this Giovanni had invited a number of distinguished doctors to witness the unwrapping of a particularly fine mummy; this was shrewdly-aimed advertisement, calculated to bring in a large body of professional men. But all the omens were good. London was filling up for the Coronation, the book was selling well, the print-shops in Piccadilly displayed the coloured plates, the façade and even the very name of the Egyptian Hall had acquired a new significance. Of the exhibition itself *The Times* wrote after the preview: 'Every eye, we think, must be gratified by this singular combination and skilful arrangement of objects so new and in themselves so striking. . . . The mechanical ingenuity and indefatigable diligence by which Mr. Belzoni has been enabled thus to transport to the arena of European controversy the otherwise immoveable excavations of Egypt reflect no less credit upon him as an artist than his sagacity and success in discovering the subject matter of this extraordinary exhibition has distinguished him above all European travellers in modern times.' After delivering itself of that weighty judgment *The Times* added that the main exhibit of the tomb was surrounded by a 'multitude of collateral curiosities', which it particularized as 'mummies, papyri, medals, and female ornaments'.[23]

The First of May was cold and cloudy—not pleasant enough to entice people into the parks. All day the carriages were setting down and picking up at the junction of Old Bond Street and Piccadilly and no less than one thousand nine hundred persons paid half a crown admission money to see 'Belzoni's Tomb'. Giovanni had erected in the middle of the hall replicas of what seemed to him two of the most important features of the tomb—the first pillared hall beyond the well and the so-called 'Room of Beauties'. The catalogue explained that these two apartments were not immediately contiguous in the tomb, but had been selected for exhibition 'the one for its great beauty, and the other for the instructive character of its emblematical representations'.

The models were made of plaster of Paris, cast in sections from the wax moulds taken by Belzoni and coloured after his own and Dr. Ricci's drawings. The visitor first entered the 'Room of Beauties'. It was just over twenty feet long and almost fourteen wide. On either side, as if reflecting each other in mirrors, were the splendid dyads of the Pharaoh and his gods: Seti kilted and serene before the jackal-headed Anubis; Seti offering to Isis; Seti and the hawk-faced Horus; Seti bearing gifts to a Hathor wearing a magnificent 'moony tire'; Seti at the last before Osiris in majesty. The contours were fine and delicately traced, the colours rich and glowing. Deep ochrous reds and royal blues lapped the beholder in a warm tide; bright yellows and greens flamed exotically about him. The low roof and the lamp-light sought to re-create Belzoni's first impressions as he entered the tomb.

Beyond this was the so-called 'Entrance Hall'—the first pillared chamber that Giovanni entered after he had crossed the well. This was considerably larger than the other room. On the far wall facing the door was what *The Gentleman's Magazine* described as 'the finest painted group of the whole sepulchre'. Here Osiris enthroned, with Hathor-Isis behind him, welcomed the king whom a Leslie Henson-like Horus led forward with a friendly hand upon his shoulder. But to reach this group the visitor had first to pass the nightmare creatures of the under-world— twelve gods carrying a snake with human heads projecting from it; more snakes intricately coiled in patterned loops and whorls; ibis-headed gods and demons without arms; mummies endlessly stretched upon a serpent-headed couch.

Outside the 'Room of Beauties' Giovanni had placed two lion-headed statues of the goddess Sekhmet, found not at Karnak in the temple of Mut but behind the Colossi of Memnon. (Were they got while poaching on Salt's preserves?) When Lady Blessington visited the exhibition she noticed between these granite grislies 'an elderly man, in the act of masticating tobacco, whose countenance bore a strong likeness to them'.[24]

There was a model of the Second Pyramid in wax and another that showed it in section with the passages and tunnels laid open like the galleries in a molehill. The scale was one to a hundred and twenty, so that the model was nearly four feet high. Abu Simbel was displayed on a scale of one to thirty.

The most remarkable of the 'models', apart from the two reconstructed chambers, was the reproduction in miniature of the whole tomb —or rather, of its decorations. Ricci's drawings, on a linear scale of one-sixth the originals, were mounted on canvas frames and arranged in an upstairs gallery so that the visitor could see the whole lay-out of the tomb and follow the sequence of passages and chambers from the entrance to the burial-vault.[25]

Dispersed about the exhibition were a dozen or more glass cases containing a strange medley of objects: the mummy unwrapped by Belzoni before the physicians; another of late date, thought wrongly by Giovanni to be that of a priest because of the red and white 'geometric' bandaging; *shabti* figures in wood and *faience*; 'vases, containing the bowels of mummies'—the so-called Canopic jars; a papyrus roll twenty-three feet long, said then to be the longest in Europe; 'fragment of a sarcophagus of terra cotta, from the Oasis of Ammon'; fragments of breccia from Berenice; ancient shoes and the ancient palm-tree rope found in the well of Seti's tomb; 'fallen portions of the tomb of Psammis'—the sad result of damp; and—as a token of wonders yet in store—'the toe of a colossal figure, the head and arm of which are coming to England'.[26]

Horace Smith, who had once vied with Shelley to produce a sonnet on Osymandias, now found new inspiration in the Egyptian Hall. 'An Address to the Mummy in Belzoni's Exhibition' soon flowed from his facile pen:

> And hast thou walk'd about (how strange a story!)
>   In Thebes's streets three thousand years ago,
> When the Memnonium was in all its glory,
>   And time had not begun to overthrow
> Those temples, palaces, and piles stupendous,
> Of which the very ruins are tremendous?

After another verse the business man asked some shrewd questions:

> Tell us—for doubtless thou canst recollect,
>   To whom should we assign the Sphinx's fame?
> Was Cheops or Cephrenes architect
>   Of either pyramid that bears his name?
> Is Pompey's Pillar really a misnomer?
> Had Thebes a hundred gates, as sung by Homer?

But the mummy was silent and the stockbroker turned sentimental:

> If the tomb's secrets may not be confess'd,
>   The nature of thy private life unfold:—
> A heart has throbbed beneath that leathern breast,
>   And tears adown that dusty cheek have roll'd:—
> Have children climbed those knees, and kissed that face?
> What was thy name and station, age and race?

Still there was no answer, but the poem remained a favourite recitation for years with those who loved its mixture of the facetious and the philosophical.

There was only one thing needed to make the exhibition complete from Belzoni's point of view. That was the precious alabaster sarcophagus which Salt sent home in the summer of 1821. With its arrival a new and somewhat sordid chapter began in the annals of Egyptology.

CHAPTER XV

I cannot allow myself to doubt that the Trustees of the British Museum will, as they ought, act handsomely by Mr. Salt and Mr. Belzoni also.

THE RT. HON. CHARLES YORKE
in a letter to Bingham Richards, 1821

The conduct of the Trustees of the Museum was worthy of low shopkeeping.

CYRUS REDDING, Past Celebrities Whom I Have Known, 1866

THROUGHOUT 1820 and 1821 Henry Salt was forwarding the greater part of his *first* collection of Egyptian antiquities to the British Museum. Bingham Richards, his agent in London, had instructions to deposit them with the Museum as Salt's property, pending negotiations for their eventual sale.[1]

Salt, as we have seen, had been given very positive encouragement to collect, particularly from Sir Joseph Banks, who was one of the Museum's Trustees. It might have been thought too that the gift of the Memnon head would stimulate interest in extending the nation's then modest collection of Egyptian antiquities. But in fact the reception accorded to the Young Memnon was only lukewarm. There was even some delay in acknowledging its safe arrival. Salt heard from William Hamilton in the early summer of 1818 that it was proposed to place the head in the courtyard of the Museum. The consul deprecated this because of the injurious effect the English climate would inevitably have on the polished granite. But Montague House was proving too small to hold the British Museum and even the Elgin marbles, acquired in 1816, had to be accommodated for a time in a wooden shed.

Salt was more worried still by hints he received about this time that Sir Joseph Banks had changed his views. It was said he was using his influence with the other Trustees to persuade them *against* acquiring Egyptian antiquities. The consul had by then engaged in several expensive projects. He had partly financed Caviglia's excavations around the Sphinx. He had also paid for Belzoni's two expeditions to Abu Simbel and his operations at Thebes, besides sharing with Burckhardt the cost of removing the Memnon head. Salt had inherited five thousand pounds by his father's death in 1817, and this had solved his immediate financial problems. But it also encouraged him to plunge more deeply into his search for antiquities. Within a year he reckoned he had spent half his father's money on forming a collection.

It was this that made Salt write privately to Hamilton in June 1818—as to a friend rather than to the Under Secretary of State for Foreign Affairs—frankly explaining his position and asking for advice. He said he was anxious to recover what he had spent and to make something more that would enable him to retire in six or seven years' time; 'otherwise,' he declared, 'I must be for ever condemned to remain here, which you will allow is no very desirable lot, since saving out of my salary is totally out of the question, so long as a due regard is paid to keeping up the respectability of the Consulate.'

Salt suggested that the Government should take his collection—the alabaster sarcophagus for the British Museum and the statues for the Royal Academy—at a valuation to be put upon it by Hamilton himself or by any other expert the Government might name. He enclosed a list of the principal items and marked against each what he thought it might be worth. But he admitted that this was only 'a rough calculation' and he might easily be mistaken, as he did not know at all how such antiquities would sell; their like had not been seen in Europe before.

The colossal head of Thothmes III, dug up by Belzoni at Karnak, Salt valued tentatively at five hundred pounds; the arm that went with it, in the same finely-polished red granite, he thought might be worth fifty pounds. Two figures of the lion-headed goddess Sekhmet were priced at four hundred pounds the pair. The white seated statue of Seti II holding the shrine with the ram's head—one of Giovanni's first finds at Thebes—was marked £800, while the figure of five hundred pounds was suggested for the so-called 'altar with the six divinities', which the French had so greatly admired. But the most important item of course was the sarcophagus of Seti I. Salt hesitated here; 'impossible for me to estimate,' he said, 'but I should think between three and four thousand pounds, being in alabaster, of unequalled workmanship.'[2]

Salt's total came to something in the neighbourhood of eight thousand pounds. It was not a very realistic figure, and indeed he admitted—unprompted—in a later letter to Hamilton that he had perhaps been over-optimistic. 'I have no doubt,' he said, 'that in our fit of enthusiasm we have greatly exaggerated the value of these remains, but still they are such as will do honour to any Collection.' However, by then, the damage was done. It was useless for Salt to say that he had laid out sums of money which, with interest, would amount to over three thousand pounds. The impression most people got was that he was trying to make a very large profit. The fact that this happened while he was in a Government post and that he devoted more of his time to archaeology than to affairs of state caused no comment in pre-Reform England. But when one remembers that, had it not been for Belzoni, most of the items in this collection would never have been discovered or, if they were already known, would have defied all ordinary efforts to remove them, Salt's attitude towards Belzoni seems rather less excusable, and Giovanni's own return for all his efforts and ingenuity pitifully inadequate. In three years he received from Salt only six hundred pounds,[3] apart from the statues and the other pieces that he gave him. It is true that Belzoni lived at the consul's expense for most of this time, but for months he had no contact with civilization and his wants were very few.

Still, Belzoni had had some monetary reward; Salt, so far, had had none. He sent off his annotated list to Hamilton, who—rather incautiously, as he afterwards confessed—showed it to Sir Joseph Banks and other interested persons. It would seem that the old man had changed his mind again, for he had recently written to Salt, congratulating him on the Young Memnon and suggesting that Belzoni might collect for the Museum. It was this letter that Salt showed to Giovanni at Thebes in November 1818. A few days later Belzoni submitted his application to the British Museum. It was turned down by the Trustees at their General Meeting on 13 February 1819. By that time Sir Joseph had seen Salt's list.

There was a loud outcry against the consul. Banks, tetchy and irritable with the gout, exploded in anger. He cared little for art or antiquity; he was a naturalist, a scientist, and had sailed with Captain Cook. He had just seen the Museum pay thirty-five thousand pounds for the collection of sculpture brought back from Greece by Lord Elgin. The city still echoed with the noise of *that* controversy: the sneers of those who doubted the antiquity of the marbles, the indignation of those who considered Lord Elgin a sacrilegious Goth, the cries of disparagement, the paeans of praise. Perhaps Sir Joseph did not go so far as to say, as some did, that Salt was a Jew, a dealer, another Elgin, but he had no wish to see the already overcrowded and overspent Museum involved in another art *imbroglio*. He wrote a cool, sarcastic letter to Salt the day after the Trustees turned down Belzoni's application:

'Though in truth we are here much satisfied with the Memnon, and consider it as a *chef-d'œuvre* of Egyptian sculpture; yet we have not placed that statue among the works of *Fine Art*. It stands in the Egyptian Rooms. Whether any statue that has been found in Egypt can be brought into competition with the grand works of the Townley Gallery[4] remains to be proved; unless however they really are so, the prices you have set upon your acquisitions are very unlikely to be realized in Europe.'

Hamilton wrote tactfully in a covering letter: 'I can only unite with Sir Joseph in recommending to you not to dig too deep in search of the hidden treasures of Egyptian sculpture, for in these economical times,

John Bull may be easily induced to withhold his purse-strings, even at the risk of losing the unique monuments you have discovered.'

Salt was deeply distressed to receive these letters. He wrote off at once to Sir Joseph Banks, Lord Mountnorris, William Hamilton, the Right Honourable Charles Yorke, telling them all at some length that his 'foolish list' had been no more than a privately-expressed hope; that he had in fact agreed in advance to accept the Government's valuation. He now offered the whole of his collection, apart from a few items intended for Lord Mountnorris, to the British Museum unconditionally. And even before he heard of the storm that his list had aroused in London, he had told Hamilton he would be satisfied if the Museum gave him four thousand pounds.

THE YOUNG MEMNON

The storm subsided after some further rumblings from Sir Joseph, who, though he forgave Salt, could not understand what had induced him to circulate such a list. Charles Yorke told the old man it would be 'an indelible disgrace' if the collection were allowed to go to a foreign museum or became '*a ruinous charge* and a *subject* of *regret* and mortification' to those who had had the enterprise to form it. William Hamilton hoped the Trustees would ask the Government for a transport to bring home from Alexandria whatever Salt was ready to send.

The first of Salt's statues to arrive—the white limestone figure of Seti II—reached England in the autumn of 1819. Sir Joseph went to see it where it was stored in a cellar in the City, but because of his gout and his girth he could not get down the steps. However, he reported that Taylor Combe, who went with him from the Museum, considered it by far the best Egyptian work he had seen, the Memnon alone excepted. Thereafter for the next two years antiquities continued to arrive from Egypt, were checked by Bingham Richards and piled up in the British Museum. Banks died; Salt's offer was almost forgotten. It was only in the late summer of 1821 that Richards received advice of an alabaster sarcophagus arriving by the frigate *Diana* and found the even tenor of his duties interrupted by the sudden appearance on the scene of Mr. Belzoni.

For Giovanni the season had gone well. The exhibition continued to draw the crowds—at a shilling a head—and his book had run into a second edition. In May his fellow-citizens of Padua had produced the long-awaited medal, commemorating—Belzoni was quick enough to notice—not his discoveries themselves but, with a touch of parochialism, only his gift to the city.[5] The medal for himself was of gold. Six others of silver he asked should be distributed to His Royal Highness '*il Duca di Sucsess* [the Duke of Sussex], President of the Society of Arts and 'my patron and friend'; the Universities of Oxford, Cambridge and Edinburgh; William Gifford, the editor of *The Quarterly Review*; and 'my good friend Sir Walter Scott, the most celebrated poet of the day'. There were also twenty-four medals in bronze for various '*professori di arti e Scienze*'. It is doubtful whether Scott's friendship went beyond occasional encounters at 'lionizing' parties. Nor is it clear how far royal patronage had been extended, though the Duke of Sussex and Belzoni were both members of the same Masonic Lodge, and Giovanni presented His Royal Highness with a portfolio of his drawings of Egyptian hieroglyphics for the splendid ducal library.[6]

In June Giovanni was able to send the *podestà* of Padua and his own admiring friends and family copies of another medal which had been struck in London on English initiative. This showed a portrait head of

Belzoni on one side; on the other it commemorated Giovanni's opening of the Second Pyramid in March 1818.[7]

July brought the Coronation. Murray had tickets for Westminster Hall and invited Belzoni to go with him. For this occasion the door-keepers appointed by the Lord Chamberlain were reinforced with professional boxers under the supervision of 'Gentleman' Jackson. Tom Cribb ('the Black Diamond'), Eales, Spring and Harry Harmer were all there to see that the Queen did not carry out her declared intention of being present at the Coronation. She did in fact try to get into the Abbey with Lord Hood, but was resolutely refused admission by the door-keeper on the grounds that she had no ticket.[8] Her unwelcome appearance with a mob of supporters threw the authorities into something of a panic and all the doors were closed. Murray and Belzoni arrived to find themselves debarred from entering even though they had tickets. Giovanni quietly pushed past the door-keepers in their scarlet frock-coats and gold lace and came face to face with the bruisers. They tried to hold him but he prised them apart and put his shoulder to the door. Murray quickly slipped through and Belzoni followed him into Westminster Hall.[9]

Giovanni was sought after on many social occasions about this time, and some of his refusals and acceptances still survive to give us tiny glimpses of the popular and celebrated traveller. He writes from the Egyptian Hall less than a week after the Coronation: 'Mr. Belzoni's Compliments to Mr. and Mrs. Ullerson will do himself the honor to attend their Oblidging Invitation on Saturday next the 28th at the appointed time.' But two days later he has to say: 'Mr. Belzoni's Compliments to Mr. and Mrs. Marryat, his excedingly sorry he cannot have the honor to attend their Oblidging Invitation on Thursday the 2nd August.'[10]

One invitation came from Longman the publisher, evidently suggesting that Belzoni might like to meet another celebrity who owed his fame to his wanderings. 'I should be most happy to be of the little Party of Travelers all, on Friday next,' wrote Giovanni, 'not been engaged on that evening, but not having the pleasure to be parsonaly aquinted with that gentleman, it would be an Intrusion on my parte was I to accomplay with your wishes. an other occasion I shall be glad to meet you.' Belzoni was not often given to such airs. The fact that he feared competition showed that he was already bored with being a London 'lion'. Soon he would be restless and anxious to be off on his travels again.

It was some time in August that the Egyptian frigate *Diana* arrived in the Port of London with the alabaster sarcophagus on board. Belzoni at once called on Bingham Richards and showed him the agreement made with Salt which gave him a contingent interest in this particular piece of antiquity. It was clear that half of whatever it made over and above the sum of two thousand pounds would be his, and Belzoni said he had already had an offer of three thousand. He therefore asked Richards not to deliver the sarcophagus to the British Museum unless the Trustees put a value on it at least equal to the sum he had been offered. Giovanni also approached the captain and the agents of the *Diana* and got them to delay the unloading while he petitioned the Trustees to allow him to show the sarcophagus in his exhibition. Samuel Briggs of Alexandria was then in London, and his standing as a merchant and his personal knowledge of Belzoni were a good enough guarantee.

But Bingham Richards was worried. He had explicit instructions from Salt to deliver the sarcophagus to the Museum, yet he was reluctant to compromise Belzoni's interest by letting it go without a valuation. He decided to ask Salt's friends for advice. He wrote to Hamilton at the Foreign Office, who answered briefly that he could not authorize *any* deviation from Salt's instructions and knew nothing about Belzoni's claim. He tried Charles Yorke. The ex-Minister agreed with Hamilton, but introduced another element of doubt. He said he thought the Trustees would act generously and take account of the offer already made to Belzoni, provided it was not from a foreign source. Lord Mountnorris saw further complications. He gave it as his opinion that duty was remitted on the sarcophagus only because it was intended for the national collection. If Salt and Belzoni violated the agreement, then they might have to pay more than the difference between the Trustees' valuation and the three thousand pounds already offered. Finally Richards had consulted his father, who wrote back: 'It is *possible* that the whole may be a forgery to obtain possession of the article; and although it may not be probable, yet there is no reason that you should run the least shadow of risk for the advantage of any correspondent whatever. Indeed I go farther and suppose even that if Belzoni should bring the three thousand pounds in bank notes and take your bill of lading, I do not think you would be justified in deviating from your instructions, and you might be liable to an action for damages by the Trustees of the British Museum.'

At this moment the tide of success began to turn against Belzoni. From now on nothing went quite right. On 10 September, while Bingham Richards was conscientiously seeking advice from Salt's friends, Giovanni addressed a simple and humble memorial to the Trustees of the British Museum on the subject of the sarcophagus.[11] He said that 'in order to obviate any difficulty which might occur from my eventual claim to share in its proceeds, & happy in seeing my original wishes accomplished of its being secured to England, I am willing to wave such eventual interest if I might be allowed the benefit of exhibiting it in the Tomb erected by me at the Egyptian Hall in Piccadilly, for the space of Twelve or even six months previous to its final removal to the British Museum'.

'Such a concession,' he went on, 'even did no pecuniary claim exist on my part, might perhaps be considered not unfavourably by the enlightened and liberal Institution to which I am addressing myself. . . .' It seems a reasonable enough request from a man whose enterprise had already enriched the Museum with the Memnon head, and through whose efforts a unique collection was being offered to the nation. But the Trustees did not consider the memorial for another two months. Then at their General Meeting on 8 December they bleakly resolved that a letter should be sent to Salt, 'requesting him to specify the Persons to whom any Article in the Collection not intended for the Museum may belong; and also that he will have the goodness to transmit to the Trustees the Valuation of such part of the Collection as he proposes offering for Purchase'. Salt, after his previous experience, must have been terrified at this command.

What immediate answer, if any, Belzoni received to his request is not known. Richards, however, told Briggs that he had heard from the Museum the application would not be granted. Briggs agreed there could be no further grounds for delay and on 28 September Richards delivered the sarcophagus to the Museum. He was beginning to hate the whole business and when Belzoni wrote a tart little letter complaining that he had slandered him to Hamilton, Richards did not bother to reply but merely relieved his feelings by scribbling on the cover:

> *Picciol' anima fece monna natura*
> *In corpo di grandissima statura.*

The exhibition closed for a few weeks during the summer and opened again in the autumn. Giovanni had now persuaded his brother Francesco to come to London again, probably to take over some of the routine duties of management and leave him free to travel. He was already planning to take his exhibition to Paris and other European capitals. Financially he was better off than he had ever been before, which was just as well, for Domenico's wife had brought another addition to the family. Giovanni was trying to persuade them to buy a piece of land and he offered to put down anything up to twenty thousand *lire* in hard cash. About this time, too, he and Sarah moved from their lodgings in Bayswater to No. 46 Half Moon Street, just off Piccadilly—more because of its nearness to the Egyptian Hall and John Murray's than because it was a fashionable address.

Yet Belzoni was still inordinately ashamed of his showman's past, even though most people now knew about it and *The Gentleman's Magazine* and other periodicals had given garbled accounts of his 'strong man' days. His sensitiveness caused an embarrassing scene at a party in Murray's house on the last day of 1821. All the D'Israeli family were there, and they and the young Murrays had been playing a cheerful, noisy game of Pope Joan. Afterwards their host gave each of the guests a pocket-book as a New Year's gift. It was then the incident occurred that Crofton Croker, the Irish antiquary, describes in Willis's *Current Notes*.[12] 'Murray was engaged, at a side-table, making the punch, upon tasting the excellence of which he uttered something like the sounds made by a puppet-showman, when about to collect an audience. The elder D'Israeli thereupon took up my pocket-book, and wrote with his pencil the following impromptu:

> Gigantic Belzoni at Pope Joan and tea,
> What a group of mere puppets we seem beside thee;
> Which our kind host perceiving, with infinite zest,
> Gives us Punch at our supper, to keep up the jest.

Indifferent as the epigram itself was, I smiled at it and observed "Very true—excellent." Which Belzoni perceiving said: "Will you permit me to partake of your enjoyment?" "Certainly," I replied, handing him the book. Never shall I forget his countenance after he had read the four lines. He read the last line twice over, and then his eyes actually flashed fire. He struck his forehead and muttering "I am betrayed" abruptly left the room.' D'Israeli's feeble doggerel had seemed to Giovanni an insulting reference to his early life as a showman. He told Croker so when he met him next and insisted on his going with him at once to Murray to explain the matter. The publisher's surprise was probably more tactful than real, though Croker seems to have been taken in.

Early in the New Year Giovanni wrote to Salt about the sarcophagus. He reminded the consul of his promise to offer it to the British Museum at a fair valuation within the space of three years. It was now three years and nine months since that agreement had been signed. Belzoni said he had an offer from the Continent of three thousand pounds, but he would prefer to see the sarcophagus in the British Museum. However, the Trustees would not make up their minds until they had Salt's formal offer of his collection. Would he therefore please take the necessary steps so that the matter could be considered before Parliament rose for the summer recess? Giovanni also begged Salt to inform Bingham Richards that the red granite cover of a sarcophagus belonged to him. It had gone with the other antiquities to the British Museum, where it

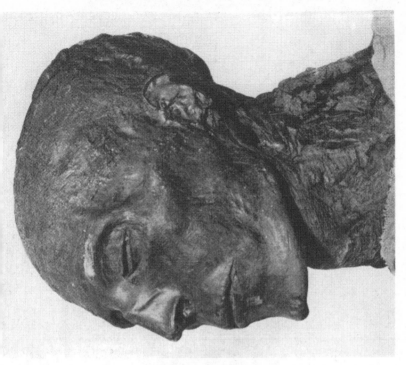

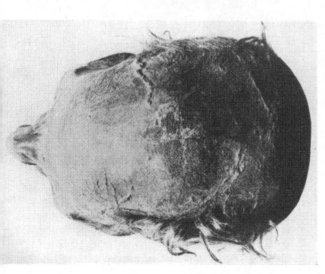

22. (*Above*) THE HEAD OF RAMESES II

23. (*Right*) THE HEAD OF SETI I

24. THE SAR-
COPHAGUS OF
SETI I IN SIR
JOHN SOANE'S
MUSEUM

lay in the courtyard, as visitors to the Egyptian Tomb in Piccadilly were informed in their catalogue.

Giovanni's movements during the next couple of months have not been accounted for, but in April—astonishingly enough—he was writing to Murray from St. Petersburg! Probably he had gone there to prospect for a new exhibition centre to follow Paris. But a Leningrad winter lasts long and on 6 April Giovanni wrote to say he had had 'a severe attack of inflamatory fever which brought me nearly to the gates of heven, but providence ordered otherwise and hope to be able to quit the dreadful horrible climate for hever'. He was worried by the delay his illness had caused, for the exhibition was due to close on 1 April and most of its contents were to be sold by auction. He hoped Murray would give an eye to it, if the sale took place before his return; his brother Francesco, he said, would be happy to take his advice.

On the 18th Giovanni wrote again to the publisher. 'Thank God I am out of danger and much better than I have reason to expect. I hope to be able to leave this for Dear England on the 22nd of this month and to be in London before the sail of the Tomb will take place. . . . I have marked out several articles in my letter to my Brother which I wish rather to remain in my possession rather than they should be disposed of under the price I put on them.'

Giovanni's casual unconcern about his wife is here once more apparent, for it seems he did not bother to write to her. Murray passed on his own letter from Belzoni and Sarah thanked him for it,[13] adding: 'I must confess I was surprized yesterday at not receiving one myself. The last I received from you I sent on the moment to his brother, but my feelings are not considered by this disinterested Relation.' Evidently there was some coolness now between Francesco and his sister-in-law.

Giovanni travelled back fast *via* Finland and Sweden and reached Copenhagen in twelve days. There he was delayed long enough to be able to see some of the attractions of that city and to meet the Danish journalist Andreas Andersen Feldborg, who was impressed by his enormous vitality and interest in everything he saw. Belzoni visited the ruined palace of Christiansborg and was shown the king's library and pictures by friendly Danes eager to entertain the distinguished traveller. Feldborg took him along to the Academy of Arts, where he held forth to the men of learning and letters in Italian, French and English. Danish he had none, but this did not prevent him from going to the theatre to see Holberg's *Berselstuen*, a satire on the old custom of annoying a woman with troublesome visits during her confinement. When Feldborg asked what possible enjoyment he got out of hearing a play in a language he did not understand, Giovanni answered with portentous gravity: 'I make it a point when I travel in foreign countries to plunge at once into the midst of some large assemblage of people when the opportunity offers. I seldom fail to come away with some idea of the national character.' Giovanni had been too long in cities, too long the 'lion', and was beginning to play the part expected of him. His real instinct had always been—and was still to be—to get away from crowds. But he rewarded Feldborg with a medal for his persistent efforts as a cicerone.[14]

On 24 May—probably just after Giovanni's return to London—*The Times* reported that 'Belzoni the traveller has had the honour of being presented to the Emperor of Russia in a private audience. His Majesty conversed a considerable time with him on his extensive travels.' What *The Times* did not mention was that the Tsar Alexander I had given Belzoni, as a mark of his esteem, a magnificent ring containing twelve diamonds and an oriental topaz.[15]

This honour was in sharp contrast to the indignity put upon him soon after his arrival in London. On 30 May a grand charity ball was given at the Opera House in the Haymarket 'for the relief of the distressed Irish'. Giovanni was too late to get a ticket from the usual sources, but he heard through friends that Mr. Ebers, the owner of the theatre, had some to dispose of at ten guineas each. Accordingly he sent and obtained one; Sarah, it seems, was not going to accompany him. On the night, Giovanni entered the theatre and was half-way upstairs when he was asked by a checker for his ticket. There was a sudden secret colloquy over the piece of pasteboard, and then Belzoni was told he could not enter. Two police officers appeared from nowhere and he found himself under arrest. For a quarter of an hour, as he said later in an indignant letter to *The Times*, he was exposed to public contempt, 'as if I had been in a pillory'. Presently one of the organizers of the charity, the Earl of Ancram, came up and told Belzoni that the ticket he presented was one that had been lost; but he took him for an honest man and gave him his own to enter the assembly. Half an hour later, when Belzoni was beginning to recover from his ill humour, three Bow Street runners appeared and haled him before the chief magistrate, Sir Richard Birnie, who was then in the concert room. Birnie began in a hectoring tone: 'I will not hear anything from you, Sir; you entered with a wrong ticket and you must go out.' Only the intervention of the Earl of Ancram, who explained that Mr. Ebers now remembered having sold the ticket, saved Belzoni from more humiliation. But his evening was thoroughly spoilt and many must have sympathized with him when, at the end of his long letter to *The Times*, he wrote: 'I leave the reader to consider if I had not reason to be disgusted, having met with some of the grossest ill-treatment that could be conceived.'[16]

It was just over a week after this painful episode in the Haymarket that the contents of Belzoni's exhibition in Piccadilly came under the auctioneer's hammer. A copy of the sale catalogue, marked with the prices fetched by some of the main lots, is in the British Museum.[17] Lot 1 is described as a 'Fac simile, executed in Plaster of Paris, of the two principal apartments in the Tomb of Psammis, including the four pillars'. With some additional pieces there was a 286-foot run of bas-reliefs from seven to eight feet high, containing fourteen life-size figures and over three hundred and sixty others ranging in height from four and a half feet to eighteen inches, the whole 'highly coloured in Imitation of the Original'. This unique piece of work was knocked down at £490. Two imperfect lion-headed statues of Sekhmet went for £380, and another, perfect, fetched £300. Even the wax models made a good price. The Second Pyramid, cross-section and complete structure, realized thirty-four guineas, the porticoes of the temple of Isis at Philae £28 and Abu Simbel £24. We are not told how much was made by the contents of the glass cases or even if they were all sold. A granite head of Sekhmet, apparently left over from the sale, is still to be seen above the portico of Sotheby's building in New Bond Street.

Meanwhile Salt had replied to the British Museum's request for a formal offer of his collection. His need for reimbursement was now even greater than before. Soon after Belzoni's departure from Egypt this sad, frustrated, lonely man had married a young Italian girl whom he met in Alexandria and carried off in a lightning courtship.[18] In the summer of 1821 she bore him a daughter. The responsibilities of a family and the knowledge that his health was very precarious weighed heavily upon him, and he was greatly disappointed when the uncertainty of the situation in the Eastern Mediterranean, where the Greeks had rebelled against their Turkish overlords, prevented him from taking leave in England. At the same time that he wrote to the Trustees the consul replied to Belzoni's letter of 24 January, pointing out that in accordance with the terms of their agreement he had offered the sarcophagus to the British Museum as far back as 1819, and so Belzoni had nothing to complain about on this score. A fortnight later he wrote to Bingham Richards, urging him to do all he could to further the sale of his collection and adding: 'It may be right to tell you in confidence, that I hope to get four thousand pounds from the Government, or otherwise I shall feel myself aggrieved. Should it be five thousand, I shall be highly satisfied. You know, I believe, that I was offered for the sarcophagus ten thousand dollars *in Egypt*, by Mr. Drovetti; and the same offer was repeated to me by a Prussian traveller, Baron Minutoli. . . .'

But already the British Museum had rejected the alabaster sarcophagus. On 11 May 1822—the day after Salt wrote to make the formal offer that Belzoni had told him was required—the Trustees met under the chairmanship of the Archbishop of Canterbury. Henry Bankes, the father of William John, laid before them a letter that his son had received from Salt, dated 6 January. This said that the whole of his collection had now arrived in England and he hoped the Museum would decide on its purchase. The Trustees agreed that young Mr. Bankes should ask Salt to appoint someone to value his collection, but they declined the offer of the sarcophagus out of hand—in the words of the Minute—'on account of the very high value put upon it by Mr. Belzoni'. However, it was not until September that Bingham Richards heard of this decision. Then it was only a day or two before Bankes told him he had advised Salt to make over the sarcophagus to Belzoni at once 'for the sum which he has professed himself ready to deposit in payment for it, as not only the sole means of silencing so troublesome and vexatious a claimant, (who I am very sure would be capable, should it be otherwise disposed of, of harassing Mr. Salt with lawsuits that might lead into great expense,) but also as looking legitimately to his own interests, since I happen to know that the utmost value set upon the sarcophagus in a meeting of the Trustees, assembled for the purpose, was *considerably under one thousand pounds*.' Bankes's low opinion of Belzoni seems ungracious after the effort Giovanni had expended and the risks he had run in transporting William John's obelisk from Philae to Alexandria. It now lay at Deptford waiting to be removed to the lawns of the Bankes home at Kingston Lacy in Dorset.

Bingham Richards thought he saw his way clear at last. He wrote to Belzoni on 1 October, asking him for the name and address of the prospective purchaser who had offered three thousand pounds for the sarcophagus. He addressed the letter to Paris where, as he later informed Bankes, Belzoni was now 'fixing his tomb'. Giovanni returned to London at once but, according to Richards, was convinced that the Trustees would not surrender the sarcophagus; or if they did, he said, the Government would not allow him to export it. He wanted a formal guarantee that the sarcophagus would be delivered to him immediately on payment of the money. This seemed reasonable enough, for Richards remembered the trouble there had been over a sarcophagus intended for Lord Mountnorris which had found its way into the British Museum and could not lightly be disengaged. The Trustees, as Richards pointed out to William John, had declined the sarcophagus, but they had not placed it at the disposal of Mr. Salt. This aroused Belzoni's worst suspicions. As no guarantee seemed to be forthcoming, since no Trustee could take action without the others, Giovanni wrote to Richards from his hotel in the Rue de Helder with a hint of legal proceedings. 'I cinciarly wish that this matar may comes to an end in a friendly maner, but I fear it will not be so oweing to the eroneous prociding taken by the honorable Messrs. Bankes against me. I hope also it will not be necessary to Inforce the Low to obtain what is justly due to me, for such Mass of facts would apear before the publick, that would rise the Indignation of every onest Inglishman, and I am realy astonished how an honorable body of Men like the Trustees of the British Museum can late themselfs be persuaded away by the wrong sugestions of two or three Indiuduals, whose motiues for so doing are euident, I hope Mr. Bankes will reflect that the low in Ingland is administrated for a Stranger on the sam scole with an Inglishman, though he may be related to poiple of influence, as he, Mr. B——, boast to be. I shall wait your answer to this as early as posible that I may act acordingly.'

Poor Belzoni! His patience was as fretted as his spelling. The trouble he had had with Kashifs and Qaimaqams was nothing to the frustration he felt now as he tried to get a great British institution to alter its deliberate and predestined course. The next General Meeting of the Trustees was scheduled for 14 December, but as there was not a quorum no business could be transacted and the matter of the sarcophagus and Salt's collection generally had to stand over till the middle of February. Richards was still hopeful that the Trustees might change their minds about the sarcophagus, and his correspondence with Lord Mountnorris and others encouraged him to think that it might even be bought by public subscription to save it from going abroad.

At the end of the year Belzoni came over from Paris for a few days. He wrote to Bingham Richards on New Year's Eve: 'I am just arrived to pay my last visit to Ingland, at least for some time, I am sorry I have not the pleasure to meet you in Town to settle, as far as we can, the affair of Alabaster Surcophagus, which must come to a determination in one way or the other. I leave the choice to the Trustees to pursase it, or to let other have it, on more advantagious Termes than what they offer themselves, and if their Precident is still obstinate in refusing to retourn the properiety of other, I am ditermined to troy how far the low of Ingland can be inforced against injustice and harogance.'

To this Bingham Richards replied on New Year's Day: 'I have received the favour of your note of yesterday which has met me on my return home from a visit to Lord Mountnorris, at Arley Hall, near Bewdley. He is paving the way, to the utmost of his power, to bring the Trustees of the British Museum to purchase the sarcophagus. . . . I hope to be in town next week. Should you leave before that, pray let me have *your address*, that I may inform you of anything interesting. I return your kind wishes for a happy new year, which is better than a merry Christmas.'

For Giovanni it was to be the last new year of all.

CHAPTER XVI

Britains farewell my friends adieu
I must far away from the happy shore
My hart will remain hever with you
Should I the dear land see no more
I scoff at my foes, and the Intrigoni
If my friends remember their true Belzoni.

G. B. BELZONI in a letter to John Murray,
2 September 1822 [1]

THERE is a laconic entry in Thomas Moore's diary for 24 October 1821.[2] 'Called upon Murray: Belzoni there: mentioned a Dutchman,[3] who has just arrived from the Mountains of the Moon in Africa, and came through Timbuctoo: says Mungo Park was executed there.' The poet had left his dear Betsy in Paris—Betsy whose own recollections of Belzoni went back to the pantomime at the Crow Street Theatre, Dublin, twelve years before, when she was Columbine and Giovanni so disastrously mismanaged the water-works—and he had gone to see John Murray about the sale of the Byron Memoirs. Whether Belzoni or Murray mentioned the Dutchman is not clear, but Timbuktu was a name of powerful magic in those days. To Giovanni it brought back poignant memories of Burckhardt who had spent so many years preparing for the journey that was to have had that fabulous city as its goal. The man he had loved and respected more than any other had died with his mission unaccomplished, leaving a debt of honour to be paid by the strongest and boldest of his friends.

Precisely when Belzoni made up his mind that he would try to trace the mysterious Niger to its source is not known. Certainly it was not to be expected that he would settle in England. After the Paris exhibition there might be others—in Copenhagen or St. Petersburg—but soon he must find fresh fields to conquer. By the autumn of 1822 his plans were maturing, for he wrote in a letter to a business acquaintance: 'I shall leave Europe as soon as I have see Ingland and arranged the shameful affair of the sarcophagus.'

Even without the memory of his friend Burckhardt to inspire him, no other enterprise could have commended itself more to a seasoned traveller like Belzoni than Britain's efforts in those years to explore and exploit the country south of the Sahara. The genesis of the movement was the founding of the African Association in 1788 with Sir Joseph Banks as its first president. In that year the American John Ledyard undertook, on behalf of the Association, to cross Africa from Egypt to the Niger, but, like Burckhardt later, he died in Cairo before he could start. In 1789 Lucas[4] pushed south from Tripoli as far as the Fezzan but prudently decided to go no further. In 1790 Major Houghton set out from the Gambia with some Moorish merchants and was robbed and murdered in the desert. Such was the choice of routes. It was left to Mungo Park—a Scottish ship's surgeon with a taste for botany—following Houghton's trail, to make the first real contribution to our knowledge of the Niger. On 20 July 1796 he saw the river 'glittering to the morning sun, as broad as the Thames at Westminster, and flowing slowly *to the eastward*'.[5]

The evidence brought back by Park started a controversy that raged for years. Did the Niger flow eastwards into what the armchair geographer Rennell called 'the great sink of Africa' and there evaporate? Did it double round and find an outlet to the sea through the vast delta between the Bights of Benin and Biafra, as the German Reichard correctly reasoned? Was the Niger after all a tributary of the Nile—the theory another German, Hornemann, gave his life to prove? Or were the Congo and the Niger really one and the same river—the view Maxwell maintained? Park himself inclined to this last theory and thought he could prove Maxwell right. In 1805 he was given command of a large expedition that was to attempt what single-handed men had so far uniformly failed to achieve. But less than seven months after setting out from the West Coast Mungo Park wrote his last letter to the Secretary of State, Lord Camden, with these terrible words: 'I am sorry to say that of forty-five Europeans who left the Gambia in perfect health, five only are at present alive, viz. three soldiers (one deranged in his mind) Lieutenant Martyn and myself.' Mungo Park finally reached the Busa rapids eight hundred miles beyond Timbuktu, but nothing more was heard from him and his exact fate was never known.

That disaster and the Napoleonic wars discouraged further exploration for a time. But in 1816 the British Government sponsored another attempt to establish the identity of the Congo and the Niger. Major Peddie was to lead an expedition overland from the West Coast to the Niger and then descend the river to meet Captain Tuckey with another party ascending the Congo. Both parts of the project ended in utter tragic failure.

Men on their own had failed; large parties of Europeans had been equally unsuccessful. It seemed now to the British Government that the least dangerous and difficult way to tackle the problem of the Niger was to attach small groups to Arab caravans crossing the Sahara. In 1818 Ritchie and Lyon set out from Tripoli, but Ritchie died and Lyon had to return. Still the friendliness of the Pasha of Tripoli encouraged the

Government to make another attempt and in 1821 Major Dixon Denham, Lieutenant Clapperton, R.N., and Doctor Oudney assembled at their starting-point in the North African port. However, they were unable to begin their journey across the desert before November 1822. By then Belzoni—original as ever—was planning to make his own attempt by a new northern route through Morocco.

Giovanni may have been influenced in his choice of a route by the fact that one of the few non-Africans who claimed to have seen Timbuktu had apparently made his way north-west from that legendary city to the Moroccan port of Mogador. This was the American seaman Robert Adams, whose strange story Murray had published in 1816. Adams maintained that when his ship the *Charles* was wrecked off the West African coast in 1810 he was taken into slavery by Arabs of the Great Desert and captured from them by negroes who sent him to Timbuktu; eventually, after a series of escapes, re-captures and ransomings, he reached Morocco. Adams's story was doubted at first by many people who were reluctant to see in his description of flat-topped houses built of 'sticks, clay, and grass' the magnificent gold-roofed city of the legends. But the African Association accepted it, and the myth and reality came closer.

Although Belzoni proposed to risk his life on an enterprise that was said to be dear to the heart of the British Government, he had no financial backing from the Treasury. Even if such assistance had been forthcoming, it would probably have been on a very meagre scale. Richard Lander, who finally solved the mystery of the Niger's mouth in 1830, was directly commissioned by the Government. But they did no more than promise to pay his wife twenty-five pounds a quarter for a year and to give him a further hundred pounds when he returned! Belzoni seems to have had help from his old friend, Samuel Briggs, whose disinterested support at all times he so warmly acknowledges.[6] And we know from *The New Monthly Magazine*—the periodical edited by Cyrus Redding —that a subscription was started in Cambridge to defray the cost of Giovanni's journey to Fez.[7]

How much that raised we are not told: it is not easy even in university towns to find money for causes that are lost almost before they are begun. Yet Cambridge had particular reason to be grateful to Belzoni. Early in 1823, before he left England for the last time, he presented the red granite cover of the sarcophagus of Ramses III to the Fitzwilliam Museum. It was the finest piece in his collection, he had acquired it only by great labour and ingenuity, and it was typical of his open-handed generosity that he should give it to a newly-founded museum in an ancient university, where he must have hoped it would be appreciated and his name remembered. Today the three-ton cover of the sarcophagus is still one of the principal treasures of the Fitzwilliam. But few visitors who have seen it in modern times can have realized the romantic story behind it.[8]

At Cambridge Giovanni found a friend in the person of the Reverend George Adam Browne, a Fellow of Trinity.[9] Although this mild and retiring don seems to have had no special qualifications for the task, Belzoni gave him power of attorney to deal with his affairs and drew him willy-nilly into the complicated controversy over the other sarcophagus.

In Paris, James Curtin, now back from Ethiopia, was left in charge of Giovanni's exhibition. Francesco had returned to Italy after some quarrel with his brother, perhaps due to a certain fecklessness in his character. But the exhibition was not a success, partly because of the cramped quarters in which it was held, partly because it had so few genuine antiquities now left in it. Belzoni offered to make casts of the reliefs in his Egyptian tomb for various museums in Europe, but according to Depping he did not get many orders. The giant energy of the man no longer had enough material to work upon; it was time he got to grips with a bigger problem.

In a letter written on 14 February 1823, after he had left Paris, Giovanni told his family not to expect to see him for another three months because he had to make a journey to the North. (Probably there is a mistake here and we should read 'to North Africa'. Three months was an impossibly short time for his journey, but obviously he did not want to disappoint his family too much or alarm them unnecessarily.) He shows himself in this letter still concerned to give them advice about money, as if he were the most practical man of affairs himself. 'Tell me if you have had the hundred pounds from Messrs. Schichers in Venice. Don't neglect to pay my aunt's rent as usual and be sparing with what you have. Buy your provisions wholesale and when they are cheap. I hope you'll have enough to last you some time. . . .' And in a postscript he adds: 'Send the children to school, Teresa must learn to read and write now. If my mother is tired of staying in town, she could take a little cottage in the country and spend the summer there as it will be better for her health. . . .'[10]

Five weeks later Giovanni was at Gibraltar. From there he wrote to John Murray, thanking him for certain letters of introduction which he had forwarded from Robert Wilmot, Under Secretary of State for War and the Colonies. He also announced his plans: 'I intend to pass over to the Kingdom of morocco and indeavour to penetrate southly, at least as far as I can on that Direction, I presented myself to the Earl of Chatum at Gibraltor with a Letter from Mr. Wilmot, and found his Lordship Disposed to Do all in his power to facilitate my wishes and has given me letters of Introduction to Mr. Douglas Cons¹ Gen¹ in Tangier, from whence I shall aquint you of my farther success.' But already funds were running low. 'My pairce scrink very much at the have expences I am obliged to encounter particularly as it is suposed that I am suported by some quarter or other and of course all charges are accordingly. . . .' Giovanni said he hoped 'to hear soon on the result of the surcophagus' and told Murray he regretted having refused an offer of a thousand dollars for his share made by Salt at Thebes.[11] Belzoni was spared the indignity of knowing that a week earlier the Secretary of the British Museum, Henry Ellis, had sent a little note to Bingham Richards, telling him he might remove the sarcophagus whenever he wished, but adding that it could 'remain as a deposit quite as long' as he chose. Oh, the offensiveness of that 'quite'!

The truth was that the Trustees—old Bankes, Lord Aberdeen and the Solicitor General among them—had been rather cunning. Noting at their February meeting that Richards, on behalf of Salt, had asked for five thousand pounds for the whole collection and accepting for the nonce Belzoni's statement that he had a buyer willing to pay three thousand pounds for the sarcophagus alone, though they had previously valued it at well under one thousand pounds, they now blandly offered two thousand pounds for the rest. Richards saw the trap but was not clever enough to avoid it. He accepted the meagre two thousand pounds for Salt and sadly addressed himself to the Reverend G. A. Browne of Cambridge. Unfortunately he had to do so *through the Solicitor General*, who was actually in possession of Belzoni's power of attorney. This gentleman, Sir John Copley, sat on Richards's letter for some months, and by the time the Rev. G. A. Browne heard of the Trustees' decision, he knew that his friend Belzoni had long since left Tangier heading south.

With the help of Douglas, the British consul in Tangier, and by gracious permission of the Emperor of Morocco, Giovanni reached Fez early in May. Sarah—strong-minded woman!—had insisted on accompanying him so far, but this, as he informed Browne, was to be his 'better half's' *non plus ultra*. Sarah, it was agreed, should wait in Fez until she heard of Giovanni's departure with a caravan from Tafilet, some eighteen to twenty days' journey away across the Atlas Mountains; then she would return to Europe. On the 4th Giovanni was presented to the Emperor and was delighted at his reception. The fact that he had met the Prime Minister, Sidi Benzelul, in Cairo was a great advantage. The Emperor's agent at Gibraltar, Judah Benalish, had also written to his Government on Belzoni's behalf. But, as Sidi Benzelul told Giovanni in a letter, that was unnecessary. 'It is quite enough to say that you are the man I knew in Egypt.'[12]

The omens therefore seemed propitious, although, as Giovanni told Browne, the Jewish interests that controlled the trade into the interior were not pleased at European attempts to penetrate any further into Africa. Still, Belzoni had received the Emperor's permission to join a caravan leaving for Timbuktu in a month's time. 'Should I succeed in my attempt,' he wrote to Browne, 'I shall add another "votive tablet" to the Temple of Fortune; and if on the contrary, my project should fail, one more name will be added to the many others which have fallen into the River of Oblivion.'[13]

Giovanni appreciated the odds against him and in the weeks of waiting he made his will. By this whatever might accrue from the sale of the sarcophagus was to be added to the proceeds of the Paris exhibition and the sum realizable from a few *objets de vertu*—a marble Bacchante, a picture of Silenus (copy of a Rubens) and two more of the inexhaustible supply of lion-headed goddesses that had been left at Mr. Bullock's Hall in Piccadilly—and the total amount, after all debts had been paid, was to be divided into three equal parts. Of these one share was for his mother, with the residue after her death to go to little Teresina, 'only daughter of my dear brother Antonio'. Another share was for Sarah and the third for his brother Domenico, who again might have to be the family's main prop. But Giovanni had no illusions about the amount he was likely to leave them. If the money is not as much as it might be, he says with a touch of wry humour, 'I hope my relatives will accept my good wishes and live happy.' He appointed Briggs Brothers and Company of 15 America Square, London, to be his executors.[14]

In a letter to his family written at this time Belzoni asked that his mother, who was ill again, should be kept from all disturbing thoughts and unnecessary worries. 'Don't listen to "old women", male or female, keep yourselves to yourselves as you have no friends outside the family, and as for Francesco, I'll see he is not the loser, though he has brought the trouble on himself.'[15] What *had* Francesco been up to?

Giovanni was soon to have enough worries of his own. With that sudden change of political weather that can blow up in the Arab world, Belzoni now found ways that had been open closed against him. The Emperor revoked his permission for him to go forward with the caravan. He gave as his reason the unsettled state of the country beyond.[16] But Giovanni suspected intrigue and opposition, particularly from the Jewish merchants. In a letter to Browne he speaks of persons in office who vent their spleen on those who do not pay court to them. Giovanni had already spent several hundred pounds and wasted some months on this project. He decided to cut his losses and start again from a different quarter.

By the middle of June he was back in Gibraltar. From there he travelled by way of Madeira to Tenerife in the Canaries, where he waited weeks for a passage to West Africa. H.M.S. *Swinger*, taking out Captain Filmore, R.N., to command the African station, called at the island in September and was glad to be of help to the well-known explorer.[17] Giovanni's intention was to land at St. Jago (São Tiago) in the Cape Verde Islands and from there proceed to the mouth of the Gambia; but as he learnt there was no chance of another ship he decided to go still further south.

Early in August Sarah had written what must have been one of *her* last letters to Giovanni. We do not know if it ever reached him; a copy only, in Sarah's hand, survives in a notebook which she kept for odd memoranda, now preserved in the City Museum at Bristol. This is the only letter between husband and wife that we possess. It shows a tenderness one had not perhaps suspected. The letter is written from London and begins: 'My Dear jovanni, I arrived here on thursday night 24th july after a voyage of twenty days. much troubled in mind on your account the manner we parted in so unexpected neither saying farewell.' Then follow details of a meeting with Samuel Briggs. 'I cannot express the intrest that Mr Briggs taks. he has opened you Credit for two hundred pounds which is to be forwarded to timbuctou in case of your arriving there . . .' There is various advice for Giovanni. 'remember the rains in sept and oct likewise do not forget the powder used by the negroes, called suso, from the tree called the Baobab, the fruit of which you bought from the Nubians merchants it tis good to prevent fever, dysentery, spitting of blood by sucking continually during the wet season.' The letter ends: 'God protect you once more do not be too ventursome recollect poor Mungo Park if you find too many difficulties turn before it is too late write by all Caravans. I am far from happy we must hope for the best God will I hope and trust either prosper you in your undertaking or cause your safe return once more farewell be catious. May God Bless and Protect you trust in him my dear jovanni and happy return to England.'

From 'Latitude 21° North in Africa' on 25 September Belzoni wrote what was probably his last letter to his family.[18] In it he assured them that not a day passed without his thinking of them all. 'Remember me to all who you think are my friends, about the others I care little. Remember me to the aunts and look after the education of the children as much as you can. Don't fill your heads with any sad thoughts, for there's no reason to do so: consider how God has protected me till now, and reflect that he will still protect me in the future.'

On 15 October H.M.S. *Swinger* arrived at Cape Coast Castle, the British fort and trading-post some eighty miles west of Accra. Captain Filmore had taken a great liking to the explorer and on his instructions

Belzoni was conveyed in H.M.S. *Swinger* to the British factory at the
mouth of the Benin river. He was also given as guide and interpreter a
native seaman from H.M.S. *Owen Glendower*. This man came from the
Hausa country and seems to have called himself at one time Abu Bekr.
But he was now known as William Pascoe and we find him later appearing in the pages of Clapperton and Lander as an inevitable adjunct to
any English mission.[19] He was a rogue in many ways and was constantly
getting into trouble, but he seems to have had his own kind of devotion
to the white men he served. Pascoe had asked for his discharge because
he wanted to return up-country and get married; his own plans and
Giovanni's to a point marched in step.

On 26 October, just before he left Cape Coast, Belzoni wrote to his
friend Browne. 'I am only now able to tell you,' he said, 'that I am going
to take a northern direction from the kingdom of Benin straight up to
Haussa. . . . If God please I hope to meet the Niger on the east of
Houssa.'[20]

The Times was watching Giovanni's progress. A report, taken from
a West African newspaper and dated 23 October, announced: 'Mr.
Belzoni embarked in His Majesty's brig *Swinger* this morning. . . . He
has with him only one man, who is a native of Houssa. Mr. Belzoni has
assumed Moorish costume, which does not ill become him, having five
or six months' beard and mustachios. We sincerely hope that this enterprising traveller may succeed in the grand object of exploring the Niger,
but we fear he will encounter numberless difficulties, as he takes an
entirely new route.' Still, there were some, it seems, who had unbounded
confidence in him, for *The Times* reported on another day that an
express dromedary had been sent from Fez to Timbuktu with money
and letters to await Belzoni's arrival. The paper understood that this
had been done 'through the interest of the Moorish minister at Fez'.
Perhaps there was less hostility towards Belzoni there than he thought.

Early in November Giovanni arrived in the Benin river and transferred to the brig *Castor* of Liverpool. Her supercargo, William Fell,
gave him a friendly welcome, and indeed everyone in that small community of skippers, agents and traders seemed eager to help the explorer
in his great enterprise. Belzoni had letters of introduction to a merchant
named Houtson, who was well acquainted with Benin and its king.
While he waited for him to finish some business he made a short trip
inland to Warri. This town actually stands on one of the western arms
of the Niger Delta, and is linked by creeks with the Benin river. So near
unwittingly did Giovanni come to his real objective.

On 22 November Belzoni and Houtson set off up-river in a Fanti
canoe. Before he left, Giovanni distributed presents to the crew of the
Castor; they lined the sides to see him off and gave him three rousing

cheers. He was a little overwrought, now that the actual moment of departure had arrived, and he answered with emotion: 'God bless you, my fine fellows, and send you a happy sight of your country and friends.'[21] But he was glad to leave the steaming miasmal marshes of the coast behind him and to feel that his journey really had begun.

They reached Gwato on the 24th and Benin two days later. King Oddi or Odalla gave the traveller a friendly reception, out of regard for Houtson, and appeared to believe the story that Belzoni was a native of the interior who had gone to England as a youth and was now returning to his own country. It was arranged that he should have an escort and carriers to take him as far as Hausaland.

But the day after his arrival in Benin Belzoni went down with dysentery. Almost from the first he lost heart. He dosed himself heavily with opium and castor oil, and in his drugged and debilitated condition soon felt that the hand of death was upon him. Houtson had gone back, but Captain John Hodgson of the brig *Providence*, who came up to see him on the 28th, found him very weak and exhausted. On 2 December he begged to be taken down to the coast for a breath of sea air. They carried him as far as Gwato in a roughly-constructed litter, and there he rallied a little and ate some bread and drank a cup of tea.

Before he left Benin he struggled to write two letters. The first was to Samuel Briggs. It ran:

My dear, dear Sir and true friend,

God has pleased that I should not survive to see my friends again: a violent attack of dysentery has brought me to the hour of death. All I can say is that I am fully resigned to my fate, and I beg pardon of any one I may happen to have offended in my past life, begging their prayers for my next. All the travelling apparatus will be carried to Liverpool by the brig *Castor* now in the river Benin, I believe belonging to Mr. Bold of that place. The next is what I feel most deep in my heart: console my poor Sarah; tell her I cannot write to her; she has been to me a most faithful and dutiful wife upwards of twenty years. I die at last a beggar; and if my friends should agree to do anything for her and my family, I wish it to be divided between my wife and my mother. God bless you, my good sir; may He reward you for all your goodness to me.

Yours, most truly,
G. Belzoni [22]

In a second letter that was almost illegible he asked William Fell to carry out some last requests. His provisions and his medicines were to go to Houtson, his pistols to the worthless Pascoe who was caught trying to steal from his dying master. There was also three hundred and fifty pounds in money and the amethyst ring that the Tsar Alexander had given him; this was to go to Sarah with his tender affection and regrets that he could not write to her.[23]

Belzoni's life came to a quiet end in the afternoon of 3 December, shortly before three o'clock. He was buried that night under the spreading branches of an arasma tree on the outskirts of Gwato. The crew of Houtson's canoe fired a salvo over the grave. William Fell had his carpenter make a wooden tablet that recorded the date and manner of Belzoni's death, to which was added the sentence: 'The gentlemen who place this inscription over the grave of the celebrated and intrepid traveller, hope that every European visiting this spot will cause the ground to be cleared and the fence around repaired, if necessary.'

Nearly forty years later, when Richard Burton visited the place, the old men of Gwato still remembered the gigantic stranger with the huge black beard, who had spent such a short time among them. 'Belzoni's tree' was still pointed out, but of the grave itself and the tablet once placed upon it not a trace remained.[24]

It took five months for the news of Belzoni's death to reach England. Shortly before it came, *The Times* had reported[25] that his exhibition had not been a success in Paris; in fact, it had run at a loss. Mrs. Belzoni was proposing to sell the casts and models in France. If she could not do so, she would take the exhibition to Edinburgh or Dublin and after that to St. Petersburg! When the Tomb had been opened in the Russian capital, this indomitable woman would then travel right across Europe and the Mediterranean to Egypt and ascend the Nile as far as Shendi in the Southern Sudan, where she would hope to hear of Belzoni's movements through caravans coming from the west.

For sheer lion-hearted courage one wonders which to admire most— Sarah or Giovanni. But while Sarah moved independently in her own orbit, she always felt the gravitational pull of the larger body whose light she reflected. Without Giovanni her life lost direction. She could only try to preserve the memory of him in the place where he looked most for recognition. In June 1824—a month after the news of his death was announced—Sarah was back at No. 5 Downing Street, where she had once lodged with Giovanni. She was having a new engraving of the explorer prepared, that would show him surrounded by the principal antiquities with which his name was linked. In the spring of 1825 she opened a new exhibition of the Egyptian Tomb at 28 Leicester Square. James Curtin constructed the model chambers, and *The Times* announced[26] that it was 'for the support of Mr. Belzoni's aged mother and numerous relatives at Padua' that Mrs. Belzoni was now exerting herself.

But there were too many rival attractions in London at the time: the new Diorama in the Regent's Park, constructed in four months at a cost of ten thousand pounds, where the spectators sat in a circular hall that revolved inside illuminated scenes; the Cosmorama in Regent Street; the 'Apollonicon' which provided mechanical music in St. Martin's Lane; the 'Magic Cave' in the Lowther Arcade; and many other shows. Before long the exhibition ran into debt. Poor Haydon, the saviour of the Elgin marbles, who had himself been dunned and hounded into prison by his creditors, wrote in his journal on 18 October: 'Called on Mrs. Belzoni,—found her full of energy and misery. An execution on Belzoni's property;—his models, casts and all seized.' A morning newspaper observed that 'the afflicted widow of the most eminent traveller that modern times have produced, is left in a state of destitution'.[27]

There were not wanting friends to take up her case. Letters appeared in the press, like this in *The Times* from 'A Friend of Belzoni's'.[28] 'The English,' it said, 'take care of their navy and army; because if they did not, no rational being would risk his life for their comfort and security. They take care also of the widows of the officers'—no mention of the widows of the men!—'who fall in their service; but it is painful to think that a man may sacrifice his life to advance science and knowledge, he may be the means, the principal means, of enriching England with the most curious and stupendous monuments, and his widow (if he die in any future enterprise) may be left for support to the pity of her countrymen!—Is this just? Is it common sense? Is it English?' Donations began to flow in. John Murray gave fifty pounds. A committee was set up to administer the fund. But there was no response from the Government, except that the Treasury graciously allowed Sarah two hundred pounds against the same sum that she had sent out two years before to the Moorish Minister at Fez with the request that it be forwarded to Timbuktu. The Government decided that this money could now be made available to Major Laing or Captain Clapperton, both of whom were soon to lose their lives in Africa.

With Giovanni dead there was not much hope of retrieving the Belzoni family fortunes. Though two-thirds of his estate went to his mother and his niece, it must have been a desperately small sum; almost all his money had gone on that last expedition. The city fathers observed Teresa's plight and proposed to grant her a small pension. But this was overruled by higher authority, which could not understand why the municipality should want to give a pension to the family of *one who had never done even a day's service*. Eventually the council appealed to the Viceroy of Lombardy-Venetia, and he understood. Teresa Belzoni was granted a pension of five hundred *lire*. The first payment was made in July 1827. But no receipts are traceable after that year, and it is likely that Teresa did not live long enough to enjoy the practical recognition of her son's services to archaeology.[29]

But Teresa did live to see the monument erected to Giovanni's memory by the proud citizens of Padua. It took the form of a large medallion in Carrara marble, carved by Belzoni's fellow-citizen, Rinaldo Rinaldi, who was a pupil of Canova. They placed it above the east door in the Palazzo della Ragione between the two lion-headed statues of Sekhmet. Bearded and be-turbanned, the explorer's profile in high relief gazes majestically over the head of the goddess on his right, frozen in time like Ramses III upon the cover of his sarcophagus. Around his head is wreathed the serpent of immortality—or can it be a snake from Seti's tomb?

This was not the only memorial planned in Padua. Half a century later Richard Burton saw in the same *Salone* a plaster statue of Belzoni —still uncast in metal—bearing on its base the name of the artist, Sanavio Natale. The Orientalist is scathingly frank.[30] 'It is of heroic size, at least ten feet tall, and habited in a very fancy costume: large falling collar, doublet buttoned in front, sash round waist, shorts, long stockings, and "pumps" with fancy arabesques. . . . The right hand holds a roll of manuscript; the left controls a cloak, or rather a fringed cloth, a curtain, which is, I presume, the picturesque and poetical phase of cloak. This work of art has two merits. It shows the explorer's figure exactly as it never was, and it succeeds in hiding his face from a near view; the rapt regard is so "excelsior", so heavenwards, that the spectators see only a foreshortened nose based upon a tangled bush of beard.' Somewhat oddly the inscription commemorated Belzoni as NATVRALISTA IDRAVLICO ARCHEOLOGO. Burton hoped that the final monument might be worthier than this. But the plaster cast has since disappeared and nothing more permanent has taken its place.

Belzoni had left England on his last journey with the fate of the alabaster sarcophagus still unsettled. Bingham Richards had been told he might remove it from the British Museum and was ready to offer it to Belzoni's unknown bidder for three thousand pounds. But by then it was too late; Browne's letters to Giovanni asking for the name of the would-be purchaser never reached him. In the spring of 1824 Richards sensed that some of the Trustees were against the idea of letting the sarcophagus go out of the country and accordingly he reopened negotiations. In the meantime Mr. John Soane, architect and art collector,[31] came forward with an offer of two thousand pounds and was generously agreeable to surrendering his purchase at any time within the next two years if Belzoni turned up with a better offer. Richards gave the British Museum a last chance. They did not want the sarcophagus at that price and so on 12 May 1824—only a few days after the news of Belzoni's death reached London—the sarcophagus of Seti I found its present resting-place in Mr. Soane's pleasant house in Lincoln's Inn Fields. Salt got his two thousand pounds; neither Belzoni nor his widow received a penny.[32]

A week before the opening of Sarah's exhibition in Leicester Square, Soane, with a commendable solicitude for the traveller's widow, organized three evenings at his tall, treasure-filled house in the Fields for the fashionable and learned worlds to meet and marvel at the sarcophagus. He had had to breach an outer wall to bring it into his basement. 'The rank and talent of this country, to an immense number', and 'many foreigners of distinction' crowded down the steep stairs among the marble urns and statuary. On Saturday evening His Royal Highness the Duke of Sussex graced the assembly. Sarah received 'every attention from the guests'. And when the lights were dimmed in the alcoves and galleries round the well and a single lamp placed in the sarcophagus revealed its warm translucent beauty to the admiration of all, Sarah's thoughts must have gone back to that day almost seven and a half years before when Giovanni and she had first come upon the splendid relic in the depths of the tomb.

Salt's bitterness against Belzoni never abated. The feeling that he had been badly treated by the British Museum, combined with his belief that Belzoni had taken all the credit for the discoveries, soured his memory of the man who had served him so well. Towards the end of the six-year argument over the sarcophagus, Salt had lost patience with poor Richards (who was doing his best) and blamed him for taking the wrong line with the Museum. 'Nothing vexes me so much,' he wrote, 'as the circumstances that you should have, by this line of acting, given the Trustees reason to suppose that I have been in collusion all the time with that prince of ungrateful adventurers [Belzoni]—God knows, on the contrary, that I have always believed his offer to be a fictitious one, and that I have but one wish, never to have my name coupled with his.'

That letter was written under the stress of great emotion, for Salt's young wife had died of puerperal fever only a short time before, leaving him with a three-year-old daughter and the new-born infant, which did not survive long. These misfortunes and his own shattered health brought him near to breaking-point. He tried to find consolation in writing and study. He had worked at various times on a long descriptive poem to be entitled *Egypt*. It was published now in Alexandria with a foreword that said: 'This Poem was printed with a view to divert the Author's attention whilst suffering under severe affliction, as well as to give encouragement to a very worthy man, the Printer.' It had no other merit. But Salt deserves credit for his modest contribution to the study of hieroglyphics. With Champollion's *Lettre à M. Dacier*[33] before him he had set out to apply the phonetic system first adumbrated by Young to the decipherment of royal names. Unfortunately the publication of his work was delayed by his private misfortunes, and Salt had the chagrin of seeing Champollion's *Précis du Système Hiéroglyphique* of 1824 anticipate many of the conclusions in his own *Essay on Dr. Young's and M. Champollion's Phonetic System of Hieroglyphics* which, though written earlier, did not appear in print till 1825.

Salt still continued to collect antiquities—in spite of professing to find it so ruinous to his pocket—and had made three large collections before he died. For the first he had received—from Soane and the British Museum—the sum of four thousand pounds. The second, got together between 1819 and 1824, when the jealous and servile Yanni had supplanted Belzoni as Salt's agent, was sold to the King of France for ten thousand pounds. The third collection, made between 1824 and Salt's death in 1827, was auctioned at Sotheby's in a seven-day sale, in which the 1,083 lots fetched £7,168 18s. 6d.[34] Salt's estate thus benefited by well over twenty thousand pounds from his eleven years spent in spoiling the Egyptians. Yet Giovanni ended his days a beggar.

Salt died of an infection of the intestinal tract, and by some ghastly joke of Fate his funeral was attended by the officers and men of that stomachic vessel H.M.S. *Pylorus*. Macabre names dogged his end. Dr. Madden wrestled with him in his delirium, and Coffin was by him at the last. His body was buried in Alexandria and for his tombstone his friend and cousin, the Reverend Thomas Butt, wrote:

His ready genius explored and elucidated
the Hieroglyphics and other Antiquities
of this Country.
His faithful and rapid pencil,
And the nervous originality of his untutored verses,
conveyed to the world vivid ideas
of the scenes which delighted himself.
In the midst of his important duties and useful pursuits,
he was, in the forty-eighth year of his age,
and after a short illness, summoned, as we trust,
to his better and eternal home, on the
twenty-ninth day of October,
in the year of our Lord 1827

His rival Drovetti survived him by many years. In 1821 the Piedmontese again became French consul general in Egypt. When he retired for reasons of health in 1829, he had spent twenty-seven years in that country. He too had difficulty in disposing of his collection of antiquities. For three years he negotiated with the French Government. It was not only that the price was in dispute. There was considerable lobbying by the clergy against the purchase of the collection on the grounds that the study of Egyptian antiquities would destroy fundamentalist belief in the Bible; in particular, it was thought that Egyptian history might upset the established view as to the date of man's first appearance on the earth. While they argued for and against, Drovetti had offers from England and Germany. He refused them all and finally in 1824 sold his collection to the King of Sardinia, Carlo Felice, for four hundred thousand *lire* (over £13,000). It became the nucleus of the justly famous Museum of Egyptology at Turin.

So by the strange irony of Fate, after all the fierce nationalistic antagonisms that divided men in the scramble for Egyptian antiquities during the early days of the nineteenth century, it was the British consul Salt who enriched the collection in the Louvre, the French consul Drovetti who founded Italy's superb collection, while the galleries of the British Museum owe most to the Italian Belzoni.

William John Bankes eventually set up the Philae obelisk outside the doors of Kingston Hall. The pedestal—abandoned by Belzoni on a Nile mud-bank—was salvaged by Yanni Athanasiou, while at Bankes's request the young French midshipman Linant brought down from Maharraqa in Nubia a great limestone platform to serve as a base. The obelisk—the first complete specimen to reach England[35]—was re-erected in 1839 in the presence of the Duke of Wellington. By then knowledge of the ancient Egyptian language had advanced so far that Bankes's own small contribution to its decipherment was almost forgotten.

A new generation of Egyptologists took the place of merely curious or acquisitive collectors. With the key of the language in their hands, men like Champollion, Rosellini, Gardner Wilkinson and Lepsius began a systematic study of the monuments. Robert Hay and James Burton— a brother of Decimus, the architect—Joseph Bonomi and Edward Lane followed in the footsteps of Rifaud and Gau and filled vast portfolios with detailed drawings of temple and tomb. Most of their work has never been published.[36] Superseded now by later surveys and modern photography, these drawings still remain an invaluable source of information about the monuments of ancient Egypt as they were in the early nineteenth century. For, although a new respect for ruins was growing and there was a desire to preserve rather than to pillage, the temptation to carry off some particularly fine fresco or bas-relief was very strong, especially when it could be shown—often with some truth—that to leave it *in situ* was to expose it to ultimate destruction.

The tomb of Seti I provided a good example of this. In 1829 Joseph Bonomi, an English draughtsman working at Qurna, heard that Champollion was proposing to cut out some of the more striking reliefs and remove them to the Louvre. Bonomi wrote in a tone of high moral indignation: 'If it be true that such is your intention I feel it my duty as an Englishman and a lover of antiquity to use every argument to dissuade you from so Gothic a purpose at least till you have permission from the present Consul General or Mohammed Ali.' To this Champollion replied with equal *hauteur*: 'I am also performing a duty as a Frenchman in telling you that, as I do not recognize any authority in Egypt but the Pasha's, I have to ask no other permission, much less that of the British consul, who certainly does not make the ridiculous claims that you put forward for him. If I succeed in obtaining better workmen than those they have sent me from Cairo, to whom I can entrust this delicate operation, rest assured, Sir, that one day you will have the pleasure of seeing some of the beautiful bas-reliefs of the tomb of Osirei in the French Museum. That will be the only way of saving them from imminent destruction and in carrying out this project I shall be acting as a real lover of antiquity, since I shall be taking them away only to preserve and not to sell.'

Champollion clearly meant to do what he said. Rosellini, who was working with him and had similar designs on other reliefs for the museum at Florence, told Bonomi that the tomb would be ruined in less than five years if the rain got in again. Bonomi accepted this view and wrote unblushingly to James Burton: 'I therefore proposed that they should cut also a fine bas relief out for the British Museum to which they agreed. The Sawyers are now at work.' Burton was horrified, but it was too late to stop the vandalism. He comments sadly on the letter: 'It is true enough that if the rain *does* get in it will ruin the place, but it might be kept out by very simple means and at little expence.'[37]

Belzoni has been criticized for battering down the door of a tomb and ripping open mummies in search of papyri. But at least he did not hack out sculptures from an almost perfect tomb. Giovanni's methods were no worse than those of his age. In aesthetic appreciation he was sometimes ahead of his fellows. And if he was born too soon to understand the exacting needs of archaeology, that was not his fault. Scientific Egyptology may almost be said to date from the winter of 1899–1900, when Flinders Petrie began patiently to comb through the cemetery at Abydos—which Amélineau had ransacked for everything of value that he could take away—and from the fragments and *débris* recovered a new kind of evidence that had not been known or sought before.

For years Belzoni's achievement stood like a high peak to challenge those who found in Egyptology a new and exciting field for exploration.

But not until Mariette discovered the tombs of the Apis bulls at Saqqara in 1851 was there anything on a scale to rival Giovanni's Herculean labours. In 1846, when George Long came to write a survey of ancient Egyptian civilization based on the antiquities in the British Museum, Belzoni's *Narrative* was still 'a most valuable supplement to previous descriptions'. But, unhappily for Giovanni's reputation, Long had to admit that 'though Belzoni was an accurate observer, he was not always a very good describer, at least in the English language; and we not unfrequently find passages in his book which are very difficult to comprehend'. Yet as the story of a great and thrilling enterprise the book had an enormous success. It ran into a third edition by 1822. It was translated into French, German and Italian. The English version was reprinted at Brussels in 1835. And that was not all.

Soon after the original publication of *Narrative* in 1820, a popular juvenile version appeared, by arrangement, from the egregious pen of one Sarah Atkins, author of *The India Cabinet opened: or, Natural Curiosities rendered a source of amusement to Young minds*. The full title of the new little volume was *Fruits of Enterprise Exhibited in the Travels of Belzoni in Egypt and Nubia; Interspersed with the Observations of a Mother to her Children*. The children were as odious a collection of little prigs as one could imagine, but we were now heading for the Victorian Age and Sarah's book rode triumphantly into its ninth edition by 1841.[38] Industry and enterprise, humble beginnings and self-improvement, patience under adversity and courage in the face of danger—these were all elements in the life of Belzoni that made him an ideal subject for a mid-century hero. Magazine writers in search of uplifting copy took a hint from Sarah Atkins, so that in the end the man whose odd skills and practical knacks made him a pioneer in a new field was buried under a pyramidal load of moral virtues and high purpose.[39]

And yet strangely enough the memory of Belzoni still persisted sharp and clear in the world of popular entertainment. Even as late as 1846 a stage magician named Anderson, who billed himself as 'The Wizard of the North', appeared at Covent Garden with a mammoth show that exploited both Belzoni's reputation as a conjuror and his association with Egypt. After 'various Astounding Experiments', encouraged by a band of sixty musicians, the illusionist reached the climax of his performance with 'the Grand Egyptian Feat, called The "Belzonian" Creation! Water, Fruit, Flowers, Birds, Quadrupeds & Fish, in their Chrystal Fountains—all produced from Nothing!' A playbill preserved in the Enthoven Theatre Collection at the Victoria and Albert Museum shows the magic production of doves and rabbits from under a cloth; vignettes of crocodiles and temples set the Egyptian scene. . . . Years passed, and the Wizard of the North was still a popular draw at the

Egyptian Hall in Piccadilly. Few recognized in those days the old man who acted as Anderson's black-faced assistant. What memories the name Belzoni must have evoked for *him* after sixty years! But who would have seen in that shambling, pathetic figure, waiting to drop and die in harness, the once shining kingfisher of a man, the Harlequin Jack Bologna?

Meanwhile Belzoni's widow struggled on, fighting the unequal battle against poverty and oblivion. Again and again she petitioned Parliament for some help in recognition of her husband's services and the sacrifice of his life. In 1834 *The Times* reprinted from *The Cambridge Chronicle* the news that 'some notice will at last be taken of the services of the late celebrated traveller Belzoni, and . . . a pension will be granted to his exemplary and long-suffering widow'. But this was premature—by seventeen years! It was not until February 1851 that the Government announced the grant of a civil list pension of one hundred pounds a year to Mrs. Belzoni. And that was only after an indignant correspondence in *The Times* had drawn attention to her distress and roused some sense of national shame.

Sarah was now nearly seventy. For over twenty years she had been living in Brussels, where she rented a large house near the *Boulevard de Waterloo* and sub-let most of it. An American, Dr. John Weisse, met her there in 1849 and for a time became her medical adviser. But she was still strong and energetic and went for walks, winter and summer, in all kinds of weather. She took a lively interest in everything that was going on, but travel and antiquities were still her abiding passion. She told Weisse she wanted to go to America to see Niagara Falls and the ruined cities of Mexico. She talked to him a good deal about her stay in Egypt, and when she discovered that he was interested in Freemasonry brought out some old papers and drawings of Giovanni's and something that she said she had written herself. This, according to Weisse, put forward the theory that the tomb of Seti I was in fact not a tomb at all, but a Masonic Temple. The scenes represented on the walls were obviously initiation ceremonies; there, for all to see, was the King in his Triangular Masonic Apron. How much of this was Sarah's own idea and how much of it was written up by Weisse when he came to publish the theory thirty years later it is impossible to say.[40] But by then he had expanded this hint of Masonic mysteries in ancient Egypt into a quaint farrago of nonsense which he entitled *The Obelisk and Freemasonry according to the discoveries of Belzoni and Commander Gorringe*. It was Lieutenant-Commander H. H. Gorringe, U.S.N., who transported to New York the companion to 'Cleopatra's Needle' that now stands on the bank of the Hudson River.

Sarah survived another twenty years. Evidently she left Brussels and retired to the Channel Islands, perhaps to enjoy her little pension more comfortably on English soil and in a milder climate. According to Frederick Boase's *Modern English Biography*, she died in Bellozanne Valley, Jersey, on 12 January 1870 at the advanced age of eighty-seven.

One by one the links with Belzoni were broken. He left no child. His grave was swallowed up in Africa. Copies of his book became harder to find. The commemorative plaque is still in the Palazzo della Ragione between the lion-headed goddesses, and the street where Giovanni was born is now named after him. But it is not in Padua that we should expect to find his ghost. In Egypt his name is carved on the Second Pyramid and 'Belzoni's Tomb' still means something in the Valley of the Kings. There are times when we may get a glimpse of his tall, bearded figure striding majestically over the desert or emerging triumphantly from tomb or pyramid. But it is in London, in Bloomsbury, that his presence really can be felt.

Go and sit in the Egyptian Galleries of the British Museum and look up at the bland smiling face of the Young Memnon when the afternoon sun through the west windows is playing strange tricks with those mobile features. The slightly parted lips still seem to express pleasure 'at the thought of being taken to England'. On your left are those half-figures of the Pharaoh's queens from Abu Simbel, maggot-white and a little repellent as though they had been too long in the dark. On either side there are black granite figures of Sekhmet, though these are not all that the Museum possesses. Down the long vista you can see the colossal head and arm of Thothmes III, and beyond in the vestibule are the wooden statues of Ramses I taken from his tomb. These are only a few of the items in that vast collection of antiquities brought down the Nile by the boat-load by the indefatigable Belzoni. Yet his name is seldom recorded here—conspicuously absent from the Young Memnon, defiantly carved on the base of the black statue of Amenhetep III—while Salt's name and initials abound. Belzoni never knew if the Museum had taken the collection he always hoped would rest there. But his spirit may be happier now that so many of the fine pieces that he wrested from the hard Egyptian earth, under the pitiless Egyptian sun, are together under one roof. No better memorial is needed for the man who laid the foundations of an English school of Egyptology. Of no one could it be more truly said: 'If you seek his monument, look around you.'

NOTES

CHAPTER I

1. Charles Dibdin Senior (1745–1814), composer and dramatist, author of hundreds of ballads and sea songs, including the famous 'Tom Bowling', formed a liaison with Harriet Pitt, an actress at Covent Garden. By her he had two sons—Charles Isaac Mungo (1768–1833) and Thomas John (1771–1841). They were brought up by their mother's uncle, a prosperous business man, away from the theatre atmosphere, but heredity proved stronger than environment. Tom threw up his City apprenticeship at eighteen, and at twenty-five was stage manager at Sadler's Wells. Charles presently followed his example. He worked at the Royalty and Astley's Amphitheatre before going to the Wells. Both brothers took their father's name, although they had no legal right to it.

2. John Fawcett's adaptation from the German of Kotzebue, produced at Covent Garden in 1801.

3. In a letter written many years later from Clerkenwell workhouse. A copy of this letter, full of pungent comment on the personalities of the Wells, is preserved in the Percival Collection, Vol. IV (British Museum press-mark Crach. 1. Tab. 4. b. 4).

4. *Past Celebrities Whom I Have Known*, Vol. II, 1866. But in *Fifty Years' Recollections, Literary and Personal*, Vol. I, 1858, Redding, who was rather a slapdash journalist, says that Giovanni was 'nearly seven feet' and Francesco 'six feet six inches'.

5. Reproduced by Prof. Luigi Gaudenzio in *Giovan Battista Belzoni alla luce di nuovi documenti*, Padua, 1936.

6. *Auto-biography*, 1850.

7. The principal portraits are: (1) M. Gauci's half-length drawing (in Turkish costume), lithographed by C. Hullmandel and used as a frontispiece to Belzoni's *Narrative* in 1820; (2) a three-quarter face drawing (artist unknown), published in *The European Magazine* in 1822; (3) a pencil sketch profile by William Brockedon, engraved and published in 1824 after Belzoni's death; and (4) a painting in oils by the same artist, now in the National Portrait Gallery.

8. Charles Le Brun (1619–90) was for many years *le premier peintre du roi* at the Court of Louis XIV. His Academy lectures on the delineation of the passions were famous. They were published in 1698 and an English version appeared in 1791. He is not to be confused with Marie Élisabeth Louise Vigée Le Brun (1755–1842), the fashionable portrait-painter who married his grandson, and did in fact come to London in 1802.

9. *'donna di maestose sembianze, e di statura eccedente l'ordinaria al suo sesso'*, according to the Abbé Lodovico Menin, who edited the Italian version of Belzoni's *Narrative* and knew the family well. Teresa's migraines are frequently mentioned in Giovanni's letters.

10. The four sons were Domenico, Giovanni Battista, Francesco and Antonio. *The Book of Days*, edited by Robert Chambers, 1863–4, is responsible for the statement: 'There was little room for this novel addition to an impoverished family of fourteen.'

11. The baptismal entry in the records of the Episcopal Court of Padua says: 'Born on 5 November at the eleventh hour of the preceding night.' This presumably means that the night hours were reckoned from sunset to sunrise. Most of the reference books wrongly give the date of birth as 15 November.

12. *The Imperial Dictionary of Universal Biography*, 1857–63.

13. *The Book of Days*, entry for 3 December.

14. *Ibid.*

15. *Cenni biografici*, Lodovico Menin's Preface to *Viaggi in Egitto ed in Nubia . . . di G. B. Belzoni*, Leghorn, 1827.

16. Egidio Bellorini in *Giovan Battista Belzoni e i suoi viaggi*, Turin, 1930, says that Belzoni first went to Holland in the *entourage* of a French general.

17. *Giovan Battista Belzoni alla luce di nuovi documenti*, Luigi Gaudenzio, 1936.

18. A handbill in the Percival Collection, Vol. III, f. 107, which reproduces Van Assen's full-length engraving of the Patagonian Sampson (1804), says that Belzoni 'first exhibited his wonderful strength in public in Holland'. It may well be that the idea suggested itself to him at a Dutch fair when he had little or nothing to sell. The same handbill also says that Belzoni 'was for a short time in the Prussian service, and held the rank of a Subaltern'.

19. Years later the dramatist Frederick Reynolds wrote of the 'dog star' Moustache: 'I see him now, in his little uniform, military boots, with smart musket and helmet, cheering and inspiring his fellow soldiers, to follow him up scaling ladders, and storm the fort.'

CHAPTER II

1. Here, as in the other quotations from *The Prelude*, the authorized text of 1850 is used in preference to the original one of 1805. There are no significant differences in the passages quoted.

2. The Reverend Thomas Maurice (1754–1824) became Assistant Keeper of Manuscripts at the British Museum in 1798. He was the author of *Indian Antiquities* (in seven volumes) and other monumental works, as well as of some miscellaneous verse. In 1803 he wrote a poem, *The Crisis of Britain*, which he addressed to Pitt. Byron referred to his *Richmond Hill* as 'the petrifactions of a plodding brain'.

3. For much interesting detail on this see *The History of Clerkenwell*, William J. Pinks, 1881.

4. *England and Napoleon in 1803*, Oscar Browning, 1907.

5. *Histoire de la Louisiane*, François de Barbé-Marbois, 1829; *Years of Victory*, Arthur Bryant, 1944.

6. John Hatfield came to Keswick in 1802, calling himself Alexander Augustus Hope, M.P. He imposed upon tradesmen and courted a local heiress before bigamously marrying Mary. Coleridge was very interested in her story and wrote three pieces for *The Morning Post* (see *Essays on His Own Times*, 1850, edited by his daughter). But the poet admitted that Mary was no beauty, being 'rather gap-toothed, and somewhat pock-fretten'. A novel, *James* (sic) *Hatfield and the Beauty of Buttermere* was published by Henry Colburn in 1841.

7. No. 143 in *The Letters of Charles Lamb to which are added those of his Sister Mary Lamb*, edited by E. V. Lucas, 1935.

8. The original drawing is in the Percival Collection, Vol. III, f. 106.

9. Mr. Willson Disher in *Pharaoh's Fool* makes *Fire and Spirit* end with a

'Grand Hydraulical Performance'. There is no evidence however to suggest that the 'Magical Cataract' of the advertisements involved the use of real water. In fact, the name is almost a proof that it consisted merely of that 'Wood, Canvass and Whalebone, painted', which enabled them, as Dibdin says, to 'produce *artificial* water, or wrap up our rivers when not used, in tarpaulins'. Dibdin is positive about the introduction of hydraulics later in the season (see the letter referred to below in note 12). According to the *Memoirs* the tank in the roof (for producing real waterfalls) was not installed until after the inauguration of the Aqua-drama in 1804.

10. The author was Peter Longueville, who used the pseudonym Edward Dorrington.

11. The pantomime 'book' is in the Percival Collection.

12. Percival Collection, Vol. III, f. 104. The letter is addressed to D. Hill, Esq., Queenhithe, who had evidently asked for details of the programmes.

13. The fact that Belzoni presented 'a most curious Exhibition of Hydraulicks' at the Royalty Theatre the following January does not prove that he was the inventor of *Fire and Water* at the Wells, as Mr. Willson Disher, *op. cit.*, seems to suppose. It is difficult to follow the latter's apparent argument that Jack Bologna was given the credit for the hydraulic display because 'he was capable of expounding marvels fluently'. Surely *Fire and Water* needed very little explanation!

14. Dibdin says in his *Memoirs* that 'beneath the Stage of Sadler's Wells, there are two springs, or currents from springs, the one of ferruginous chalybeate, and the other of pure sweet water'. See also E. W. Brayley's *Historical and Descriptive Accounts of the Theatres of London*, 1826.

15. The pantomime 'book' is in the Percival Collection.

CHAPTER III

1. *Memoirs of Bartholomew Fair*, Henry Morley, 1859.

2. Before the change the Fair was proclaimed on the Eve of the Saint's Day.

3. So called, according to Morley, after that Lady Holland who secretly entertained actors in her home and encouraged them to perform plays there when they came under the Commonwealth ban. But the Holland family also had the right to collect tolls from the Fair.

4. The details are given in the Proceedings of Smithfield Piepowder Court, 1790–1854 (Guildhall MS. 95). 133 licences were granted in all.

5. *The Old Showmen, and the Old London Fairs*, Thomas Frost, 1874.

6. The Catalogue suggests that the plate was made in 1817. Some pencil studies for it are preserved in *Sketches and Studies by George Cruikshank*, Vol. I (Nos. 10 and 11) in the Department of Prints and Drawings at the British Museum. A pencilled note on No. 10 says 'for Belzoni's Travels never published'. Belzoni would certainly not have allowed such a shameful record of his past to appear in his own book.

7. This was a court of summary jurisdiction set up at fairs to deal with minor disputes among those who attended them. The origin of the name in *Pieds Poudreux* is confirmed by an old Scots borough law quoted by Sir John Skene, the sixteenth-century lawyer: 'Gif any stranger marchand travelland throw the realm, havand no land, no residence nor dwelling within the sheriffdome, but vagand from ane place to ane other,—qwha therefore is called pied poudreux or Dustifute . . .'

8. Edmund Kean (1787–1833) was the son of the actress Anne Carey. As Master Carey he was engaged by Charles Dibdin to recite 'Rollo's Address to the Peruvians' from Sheridan's *Pizarro* at Sadler's Wells in the summer of 1801.

CHAPTER IV

1. The 'Amazonian' reference may be due, as Mr. Willson Disher suggests, to the misunderstanding of a phrase in *Nouvelle Biographie Générale*, where the writer pays tribute to Sarah's courage. But Mr. Willson Disher himself speaks of Belzoni as 'taking an old warhorse for his bride'. As Sarah was only about twenty at the time, the description seems a little harsh, however plain she may have been. It does of course help to support Mr. Willson Disher's theory that Belzoni was secretly in love all his life with the famous opera singer Angelica Catalani.

2. During these years he visited India and Abyssinia.

3. Belzoni spells his name 'Curtain'.

4. I find that Mr. Colin Clair had the same impression from his own study of the subject.

5. John Fawcett, the actor, was stage manager at Covent Garden in 1803. It was he who with the dramatists Frederick Reynolds and Thomas Morton had been negotiating for Sadler's Wells when Dibdin and his friends stepped in.

6. Mr. Willson Disher, *op. cit.*, makes Belzoni responsible not only for the introduction of hydraulics at Sadler's Wells, but also for the invention of the Aqua-drama. There is no evidence to support this and, as has been shown, the chronology is entirely against it. A full and fascinating account of the installation of the water at Sadler's Wells is given in Dibdin's *Memoirs*. Their editor, Mr. George Speaight, has challenged Mr. Willson Disher's views on this in *The Times Literary Supplement* (19 April, 3 and 24 May 1957).

7. Press cuttings in the Enthoven Collection, Victoria and Albert Museum.

8. Mr. Willson Disher relies on the evidence of one of Skelt's coloured prints for the Juvenile Drama, which shows the characters in 'Monk' Lewis's horrific play *The Wood Demon: or, The Clock Has Struck*. The Giant Hacko is confidently identified as Belzoni by his luxuriant growth of whiskers.

9. *The Drama in Perth*, Peter Baxter, 1907.

10. *The English Fleet in 1342* was composed by Tom Dibdin for Covent Garden in 1803.

11. Leigh Hunt said of Elliston that he was 'the only genius that has approached that great man [Garrick] in universality of imitation'.

12. Written by John Fawcett and first produced at the Haymarket in June 1800. It told the story of a runaway slave from the plantations of Jamaica who sought revenge.

13. *The Old Showmen, and the Old London Fairs*, Thomas Frost, 1874. There is a copy of *Valentine and Orson* in the British Museum (press-mark 841. e. 21).

14. What a combination Madame Tussaud and Belzoni would have made! There is no evidence however that they ever even met. But it is strange that Belzoni's effigy never appeared in the celebrated waxworks.

15. Cyrus Redding (1785–1870) was born at Penryn in Cornwall. After some London training as a journalist he returned to the West Country in 1808 to edit *The Plymouth Chronicle*. In 1810 he started and edited *The West Briton*

and Cornwall Advertiser. Later he went to France and from 1815 to 1818 edited *Galignani's Messenger,* an English-language newspaper published in Paris. Between 1821 and 1830 he ran *The New Monthly Magazine,* though Thomas Campbell, the poet, was its nominal editor. Redding was a prolific writer. Perhaps his best claim to fame is that he did much to educate English palates in the use of French wines.

16. A relation of Samuel Foote, the comedian.

17. *Giovan Battista Belzoni alla luce di nuovi documenti.*

18. *Ibid.*

19. *Edward Webbe, Chief Master Gunner, his Travailes, 1590,* edited by Edward Arber, 1868.

20. *A History of Fireworks,* Alan St. H. Brock, 1949.

21. *Annals of Industry and Genius,* C. L. Brightwell, 1863. 'Gibraltar' must be a nickname, but the agent is so called in a letter from Colonel Missett, consul general in Egypt, to Lord Liverpool, dated 20 May 1812 (Public Record Office, W.O.I/349/37). Captain Ismail visited England in 1811. It was this officer that Muhammad Ali was so anxious to send round the Cape in a corvette (see chapter V, note 14).

22. Abusir is the ancient Taposiris Magna. The ruined pylon, probably of a late temple to Osiris, and the remains of a Roman watch-tower are still conspicuous from the sea. The modern town of Burg el-Arab close by perpetuates the traditional name of 'Arabs' Tower'.

23. 'Pompey's Pillar' may have formed part of a late temple of Serapis, but even this attribution is uncertain; at any rate, it is not older than the fourth century A.D. 'Cleopatra's Needles' were both set up originally by the Pharaoh Thothmes III (*c.* 1500–1450 B.C.) in front of his temple at Heliopolis. They were moved to Alexandria by the Emperor Augustus in 13–12 B.C. One of them was thrown down, probably by the earthquake of A.D. 1301. In 1820 Samuel Briggs suggested that Muhammad Ali should offer it to the King of England. He was moved to do so, having 'witnessed the stupendous labours of the celebrated Mr. Belzoni, and received from him the assurance that he could confidently undertake the removal to England of one of the granite obelisks at Alexandria'. However it was not until 1878 that the 'Needle' was finally brought to London and set up on the Thames Embankment. Its twin was re-erected in New York's Central Park in 1881.

24. A familiar though inexact transliteration of the Arabic word for 'fifty'. It is the name given to the hot south wind in Egypt that is reputed to blow, off and on, for fifty days in early summer.

CHAPTER V

1. *The Principal Navigations,* Richard Hakluyt (1904 edition), Vol. VI.

2. *Macbeth,* I. iii. 6–7.

3. *The Travels of certaine Englishmen into Africa, Asia,* etc., by Theophilus Lavender. For the character of this man see *The Travels of John Sanderson,* edited for the Hakluyt Society by Sir William Foster, 1931.

4. Norden had studied ship construction in Denmark and art in Italy. His drawings are more accurate than his maps.

5. Richard Pococke (1704–65), afterwards Bishop of Meath.

6. See *A History of the Levant Company,* Alfred C. Wood, 1935; also *An Organ for the Sultan,* Stanley Mayes, 1956.

7. In Arabic *mamluk* means 'that which is bought or owned', hence 'a slave'. From the middle of the thirteenth century Egypt was ruled by a succession of Sultans who rose from the ranks of a military slave-corps, the Mamluk guards. When the Turks conquered Egypt in 1517, Selim abolished the monarchy but left an aristocracy of Mamluk Beys.

8. 'Essai d'histoire de l'Institut d'Égypte et de la Commission des Sciences et Arts' by Gabriel Guémard in *Bulletin de l'Institut d'Égypte*, Vol. VI, 1924.

9. William Richard Hamilton (1777–1859), the son of a cleric, was accidentally lamed for life while he was at Harrow. In 1799 he became secretary to Lord Elgin when the latter was appointed ambassador in Constantinople, and in 1801 was sent by him on a mission to Egypt. In 1802 he superintended the removal of the Elgin marbles. Hamilton was Under Secretary of State for Foreign Affairs from 1809 till 1822. His *Remarks on Several Parts of Turkey: Part I, Ægyptiaca*, published in 1809, remained for many years the standard English work on Egyptian antiquities.

10. They included two black basalt obelisks bearing the names and titles of Nectanebo II, the last native Pharaoh of Egypt (*c.* 350 B.C.); his immense agglomerate sarcophagus, used for many years as a bath at Alexandria (note the holes drilled in it to let out the water); a black granite statue of the lion-headed goddess Sekhmet; and the left fist of a colossal red granite statue of Ramses II from Memphis. These are all in the British Museum.

11. The preceding night was known as the Night of the Drop, because it was believed that a miraculous drop fell into the Nile then and so caused it to rise.

12. Drovetti was replaced after a time by M. Roussel, who remained in Egypt as French consul general until 1819.

13. W.O.I/349/37 *et seq.*

14. Missett had reported in November 1811 that Muhammad Ali's ambitions 'embrace no less than the immediate conquest of the whole of the Yemen; and such is the presumptuous arrogance of that man, that he has frequently expressed to his confidential advisers a determination to expel the English from their Indian possessions, which, with characteristic ignorance, he says belong of right to the Porte'.

15. William Turner's *Journal of a Tour in the Levant* (3 vols.) was published by John Murray in 1820, the same year as Belzoni's *Narrative*. Turner went back to Constantinople in 1824 as secretary to the ambassador and later became minister plenipotentiary. In 1829 he was appointed envoy extraordinary to the republic of Columbia.

16. George Pardalis served Turner faithfully and accompanied him to England. He died in 1818 and was buried in Yarmouth churchyard.

17. The bones may have belonged to men killed in the Battle of Alexandria under Sir Ralph Abercromby in 1801.

18. Turner spells his name Lensey, but he was certainly an Italian.

CHAPTER VI

1. The Canal (*Khalig*) left the Nile at Old Cairo and ran through the city to Ezbekiya. In summer it was a dusty, sunken lane, in winter a stinking ditch. The occasion of cutting the dam was a public holiday, and there are good descriptions of the ceremony in Edward Lane's *Modern Egyptians* (1836) and Robert Curzon's *Visits to Monasteries in the Levant* (1849).

2. A form of mosque, usually cruciform, designed to house the theological schools and introduced into Egypt by Salah al-Din.

3. The Association for Promoting the Discovery of the Interior Parts of Africa was founded in 1788 with Banks as its first President. In 1831 it was absorbed by the Royal Geographical Society.

4. Stanley Lane-Poole in *The Dictionary of National Biography* credits him with having been the first European to visit Mecca. This is difficult to prove and rather unlikely. But Burckhardt was certainly more thorough in performing the duties of a pilgrim than many of the faithful.

5. *The Travels of John Sanderson*, edited for the Hakluyt Society by Sir William Foster, 1931.

6. Karl Richard Lepsius (1810–84) commanded a Prussian expedition sent out by Friedrich Wilhelm IV to catalogue the monuments of Egypt and Nubia.

7. Here is a small example of how Belzoni's lack of English sometimes obscures the sense. He says 'the soldier gave me such a blow with his staff' and adds: 'The staves of the Turks, which are like shovels, cut very sharp'. This gives an odd picture until one remembers that *staffa* is the Italian for 'stirrup'.

8. Turner's chronology is more accurate here. Belzoni was not keeping a diary at the time.

9. Various accounts of the massacre are given, but see especially *Histoire de l'Égypte sous le gouvernement de Mohammed-Aly* by F. Mengin, Paris, 1823, and for a useful description of the atmosphere in Cairo at the time *Narrative of the Life and Adventures of Giovanni Finati* (1830).

10. Ibrahim was in fact Muhammad Ali's adopted step-son—the son of his first wife.

11. 'Why, I can smile, and murder whiles I smile . . .' *Third Part of King Henry VI*, III. ii. 182.

12. *Il Corpo Epistolare di Bernardino Drovetti*, Vol. I. Giovanni Marro, Rome 1940.

13. *Ibid.*

14. A shocking incident mentioned by most travellers in Egypt about this time was the murder of a young girl, the daughter of the Swedish consul general Bokty, who was shot dead in the street by a Turkish soldier. Sir Robert Henniker offers a plausible explanation of this apparently motiveless crime. He suggests that either the Turk thought she was a light woman, because she was unveiled, and became resentful when his advances were rejected, or else he was genuinely affronted by her European immodesty.

Belzoni himself was shot at one day when he cracked his whip across the shoulders of a Turkish subaltern who struck him in a crowded street. The bullet singed his hair and killed one of the Turkish soldiers. The officer was disarmed by his own men before he could fire again.

15. The Step Pyramid, built about 2750 B.C., represents the transition from the *mastaba*-tomb to the true pyramid. *Mastaba*, the Arabic word for the low stone bench outside an Egyptian house, is the term conveniently used by archaeologists to denote the rectangular superstructures of many Archaic and Old Kingdom tombs.

16. Old Kingdom inscriptions show that Sneferu built himself two Pyramids. One of these has been identified with the Pyramid of Meidum on the strength of the Eighteenth Dynasty *graffiti* scribbled on the walls of the Mortuary Temple. In 1894–5 de Morgan discovered *mastaba*-tombs belonging to members of Sneferu's family and his Court near the Pyramid at Dahshur

which stands a little to the north of the Bent Pyramid. This encouraged the belief that it was Sneferu's other Pyramid. However in 1947 stone blocks bearing the name of Sneferu were found in the Bent Pyramid, which suggests that this and not the northern stone Pyramid at Dahshur belonged to that Pharaoh.

17. The Bent Pyramid—so called because the angle of its slope changes abruptly from about 54° to 43°—was tentatively assigned to Huni, the last king of the Third Dynasty, until Sneferu's name was found in it. See preceding note.

18. Mit Rahina is close to the site of the great temple of Ptah, the most important in Memphis. Badrashain is on the river.

19. The Book of the Prophet Jeremiah, xlvi. 19. Noph was the Hebrew name for Memphis.

20. *Il Corpo Epistolare di Bernardino Drovetti.*

21. See Lane's *Modern Egyptians* (1836) and Sir Gardner Wilkinson's *Modern Egypt and Thebes* (1843) for descriptions of the magic mirror of ink.

22. The capsular fruit of the gumbo or okra (*Hibiscus esculentus*), known also as *bamies*.

23. Charles Nicolas Sigisbert Sonnini de Manoncourt (1751–1812), a French naturalist sent out to Egypt in 1777 to report on the country. His book *Voyage dans la Haute et la Basse Égypte* was not published till 1799. An English translation appeared in 1800.

24. *Voyage dans la Basse et la Haute Égypte*, 2 vols., Vivant Denon, 1802. Arthur Aikin's English version was published the following year.

25. *Notes during a visit to Egypt, Nubia, the Oasis, Mount Sinai, and Jerusalem*, Sir Frederick Henniker, Bart., 1823.

26. Zulfur Carcaja, according to Belzoni in *Narrative*, but in a letter published by Marro he calls him Gulfurkar Kaya. The last part evidently represents the title *Kiaya*, meaning Steward or Deputy.

CHAPTER VII

1. Charles Philip Yorke (1764–1834), Secretary for War in the Addington administration till August 1803, when he was transferred to the Home Office. He was elected a Fellow of the Royal Society in 1801.

2. *The Life and Correspondence of Henry Salt, Esq., F.R.S. &c.*, Vol. I, J. J. Halls, 1834.

3. Briggs was a good friend of English travellers and a generous patron of research. He later helped both Caviglia and Belzoni.

4. For all its authority it is a dull book and the accompanying volume of plates made from the drawings of Major Hayes, R.E., is disappointing.

5. Public Record Office, F.O. 24/6.

6. A plate in the *Description de l'Égypte* (Vol. II, No. 32) shows the head broken off from the shoulders, perhaps as the French intended it to be.

7. Byron describes him as leader of a college set at Cambridge that included Hobhouse and himself. Bankes represented Truro in Parliament from 1810 to 1812, when he began his eastern travels with letters of introduction from Byron. He was a great talker. Samuel Rogers says he sometimes outshone even Sydney Smith.

8. Letter from Burckhardt to William Hamilton, dated 20 February 1817 and quoted in the Preface to the former's *Travels in Nubia*.

9. The 'Statement' is dated 10 October 1821. Salt intended only to communicate it to a few friends. It was published after his death by his biographer, J. J. Halls, in *The Life and Correspondence of Henry Salt*, Vol. II.

10. *Ibid.*, Vol. I.

11. He had once promised to get some mummies for a friend of Drovetti's. See *Il Corpo Epistolare di Bernardino Drovetti*.

12. *Travels in Egypt, Nubia, Holy Land, Mount Lebanon, and Cyprus, in the year 1814*, Captain Henry Light, R.A., 1818.

13. *Narrative of a Journey in Egypt and the Country beyond the Cataracts*, Thomas Legh, Esq., M.P., 1816.

14. It was begun probably towards the end of the second century B.C., but not completed for another two hundred years.

15. Baron Dominique Vivant Denon (1747–1825), a connoisseur who had once been entrusted by Louis XV with the task of cataloguing a cabinet of antique gems and coins that had belonged to the Pompadour, accompanied Napoleon on his Egyptian campaign. Denon's fine minuscule drawings are one of the chief charms of his book, which captivated the French and English publics long before the ponderous *Description de l'Égypte* got into its stride.

16. Published in 1766. See chapter XII, note 10.

17. *Notes*, Henniker.

18. Hamilton gives a number of these inscriptions in his *Ægyptiaca*.

19. Strabo appears to have visited Upper Egypt in 25–24 B.C.

20. Diodorus travelled in Egypt between 60 and 57 B.C.

21. The name Sesostris in the Greek writers also seems to refer sometimes to the Middle Kingdom Pharaoh Senusret III or his father Senusret II. They lived about eight hundred years before Ramses II.

22. Norden visited Egypt in 1737–8. The head is shown in his *Drawings of some Ruins and Colossal Statues at Thebes in Egypt* (1741).

23. *Travels in Egypt*, etc.

24. Ramses II tried to recover the territories in Syria once conquered by the energetic Thothmes III and then lost again under the indolent Akhenaten. In or about the year 1288 he advanced as far as Kadesh on the Orontes and there fought an indecisive battle against the Hittites. A poem was written to commemorate this supposed Egyptian victory—the so-called Poem of Pentawer—and Ramses' imaginary triumph was carved on the walls of his temples at Karnak, Luxor and Abu Simbel as well as on those of the Ramesseum.

25. Phamenoph is a corruption of Amenhetep, which the Greeks rendered as Amenophis.

26. A Turkish military rank equivalent to lieutenant-colonel.

27. *The Ramesseum*, J. E. Quibell (Egyptian Research Account), 1898.

28. Horace Smith (1779–1849) and his elder brother James had a *succès fou* with their collection of parodies published in 1812 under the title of *Rejected Addresses*. Horace was a member of the Stock Exchange. One of the most popular of his later poems was 'An Address to the Mummy in Belzoni's Exhibition'.

CHAPTER VIII

1. Burckhardt's journey through Nubia began in February 1813. He saw Abu Simbel a month later.

2. This is very puzzling. Belzoni's description does not suggest at all that he was now in the tomb of Ramses III—a properly constructed sequence of chambers and corridors. Nor is it easy to understand how the Arabs could have hidden the entrance of such a well-known tomb from a man like Drovetti or prevented him, once inside, from realizing where he was. Again, Belzoni speaks of returning 'from the king's tombs' to find the Kashif causing trouble with his working party at Qurna. It would be tempting therefore to suppose that the sarcophagus, or its lid at least, was no longer in the tomb of Ramses III, but had been removed by the Arabs to a *cache* of their own.

There are even greater difficulties, however, in the way of accepting this theory. It is unlikely that the Arabs could have moved even the lid by themselves. Bruce certainly saw the sarcophagus with the lid still on it, though broken, when he entered the tomb in 1769. Thirty years later the French, according to the *Description*, thought that the lid was missing. But Belzoni specifically says when he comes to describe his removal of the cover: 'It had been thrown from its sarcophagus when it was forced open, and being reversed it remained buried by the stones, and unnoticed by any visitor.' If we accept the view that both were *in situ* when Belzoni found them, we must also believe that the tomb of Ramses III communicated with a labyrinth of tunnels that probably extended right through the mountain to Qurna. Giovanni says of the operation of getting out the cover that it 'cost much trouble, as may be supposed, to remove a heavy piece of granite from those abysses, through a place scarcely high enough to allow a man to sit on the ground'. That certainly does not describe the tomb of Ramses III.

Salt later removed the sarcophagus and it went with his second collection to the Louvre.

3. Part of the temple was cleared by Muhammad Ali in 1842 to provide better accommodation for an underground powder magazine.

4. The temple of Edfu took the relatively short time of 180 years in the building (237–57 B.C.). It has therefore a more uniform style and plan than most Egyptian temples.

5. Now at Kingston Lacy in Dorset.

6. Traces of two other Greek inscriptions were later found on the base. One was Ptolemy's answer to the priests of Isis. The other was a copy of the orders he sent to Lochus, the general commanding the Thebaid, telling him that the nuisance must cease.

7. Bankes observed that a Greek inscription on a pylon at Hu, the ancient Diospolis Parva (between Abydos and Dendera) offered the only instance then known where the name Cleopatra preceded that of Ptolemy. The sculptures also showed a female figure taking precedence over a male. Bankes saw that the cartouche of Ptolemy, identified by Dr. Young on the Rosetta Stone, exactly corresponded to the cartouche above the male figure. There was therefore a presumption that the cartouche for the female figure contained the name of Cleopatra. Confirmation was obtained when Bankes discovered this same cartouche on the obelisk at Philae, standing in the same relationship to the other as the name Cleopatra to Ptolemy in the Greek inscription on the base. See *Essay on Dr. Young's and M. Champollion's Phonetic System of Hieroglyphics*, published by Salt in 1825.

8. See 'Mrs. Belzoni's Trifling Account' at the end of *Narrative* for her very engaging description of her pets.

9. *Narrative of the Life and Adventures of Giovanni Finati*. See chapter IX, note 17.

10. The temple was constructed by Ramses II and dedicated to the goddess Hathor.

11. This is Re, the Sun-god, in his aspect as Horus, Lord of the Two Horizons.

12. A generic term for grain. This would probably have been *Sorghum vulgare*, which is grown extensively in Upper Egypt and Nubia for making meal. It is sometimes known as Indian millet or Guinea corn.

13. This may have been the so-called Porch of Nectanebo, a restoration by Ptolemy II Philadelphus of the original fourth-century structure, or the temple of Arsnuphis, built by Ptolemy IV Philopator and Ptolemy V Epiphanes, now almost completely destroyed.

14. Jean Jacques Rifaud (1786–c. 1845) spent over twenty years digging, drawing and collecting in the countries of the Eastern Mediterranean. It is said that he bore on his face and body the scars of the bullet-wounds he received while defending his treasures. Many of these are now in the Drovetti collection at Turin. In 1829 Rifaud announced the publication of *Voyages en Égypte, en Nubie . . . depuis 1805 jusqu'en 1827* in five volumes of text with a large folio volume of plates. Only the plates appeared.

15. Frédéric Cailliaud (1787–1869) arrived in Egypt just before Belzoni. William Turner evidently had his company from Damietta to Alexandria, for he mentions as travelling companion 'a French goldsmith, a native of Brittany, going to settle for a time in Cairo, in the hopes of finding work'. Turner thought him 'a diminutive effeminate fop, but as he had travelled in Italy and Holland, his conversation was not uninteresting'. In 1816 Cailliaud ascended the Nile with Drovetti and Rifaud as far as the Second Cataract. For his subsequent employment with the Pasha see chapter XII. Jomard, chief editor of the French *Description*, helped with the publication of his *Voyages à l'Oasis de Thèbes et dans les déserts à l'Orient et à l'Occident de la Thébaïde* (1821), which covered the years 1815–18. In 1819 Cailliaud returned to Egypt and undertook a further survey of the Oases before accompanying Muhammad Ali's son, Ismail Pasha, on an expedition to Sennar. The fruits of these travels appeared in *Voyage à Méroé, au Fleuve Blanc . . . à Syouah et dans cinq autres oasis*, 4 vols. with 3 vols. of plates, 1826.

16. Mut was the consort of Amun-Re. The temple was mainly built by Amenhetep III about 1400 B.C., but Seti II (*c.* 1200 B.C.) made some additions. It is now in a very ruinous condition.

17. Sekhmet was a Fire-goddess who represented the destructive heat of the sun. Amenhetep III dedicated a large number of statues to her at Thebes, but some were usurped by Shesank I (*c.* 935 B.C.)—the Shishak of I Kings xiv. 25 —who put his own name on them.

18. *The Quarterly Review*, Vol. XIX, page 409, says incorrectly that Mrs. Belzoni found this statue while her husband was in Nubia. It may have been that it turned up while Sarah was supervising the dig at Karnak and Giovanni was busy among the tombs.

19. In the north-east corner of the court to the north of the Seventh Pylon in the temple of Amun.

20. A kind of annexe to the main Valley of the Kings and even more desolate.

21. This is No. 23 in the official numbering. The Arabs call it the Tomb of the Apes from the cynocephali on the walls of the burial-chamber.

CHAPTER IX

1. A juvenile version of Belzoni's *Narrative* that ran into nine editions by 1841.
2. Louis Nicolas Philippe Auguste (Comte de) Forbin (1779–1842) succeeded Denon as Director General of Museums in France after the fall of Napoleon. A year or two later he visited the countries of the Eastern Mediterranean to acquire antiquities for the Louvre. In Egypt he employed Rifaud to collect for him. His *Notes d'un voyage fait dans le Levant, en 1817 et 1818* was published in Paris in 1819.
3. Giovanni Battista Caviglia (1770–1845) used Malta as a home port and regarded himself as a British subject. His enthusiasm for Egyptian exploration on behalf of the country of his adoption was second only to Belzoni's. He worked at Giza with Colonel Howard Vyse as late as 1836, but eventually quarrelled with that explosive explorer. The following year he retired to Paris and became a protégé of Lord Elgin.
4. Nathaniel Davison had explored the 'well' as far as he could in 1764, but his account was not published till 1817, the year of Caviglia's activities in the Great Pyramid.
5. See chapter VI, note 15.
6. In 1821, after his return to England, Beechey was sent out by the Colonial Office to examine and report on the antiquities of Cyrenaica, while his brother, Captain Beechey, R.N., was surveying the coast from Tripoli to Derna. Henry William eventually emigrated to New Zealand and died there about 1870. He remains an elusive, shadowy figure.
7. *A Brief Account of the Researches and Discoveries in Upper Egypt made under the Direction of Henry Salt, Esq.* 'I come with an inexpressible satisfaction, to declare to that gentleman's fellow countrymen that Mr. Belzoni was but the servant of Mr. Salt' is a fair sample of Athanasiou's cringing style and mischievous manner.
8. One of a pair representing Ramses II.
9. *Viaggi*, 1650.
10. *The Travels of John Sanderson.*
11. A *vade-mecum* for the under-world. By reciting its chapters the dead acquired new powers in the after-life.
12. Sometimes the jars were placed in a chest.
13. *Shabti* and *ushabti* are derived from *usheb*, 'to answer', the sense being that these figures are substitutes for the dead man, who answer when he is called upon to perform any duties in the under-world. But the form *shawabti* is also found. This is connected with *shawabt*, 'acacia', and many of the early New Kingdom figures were in fact made of acacia-wood. It is possible that the Egyptians themselves changed the form of the word as these figures evolved from being a representation of the dead man to becoming his servants.
14. Irby and Mangles saw this particular tomb a few months later and the latter was especially enthusiastic about the girl musicians. 'The preservation of this group is astonishing,' he says, 'the colours being perfectly fresh, and no part whatever in the least defaced. What would not the French have given for such a specimen to put in their splendid work? there is nothing throughout Egypt to be compared to it.' Salt is said to have cut out these figures for his collection.
15. These are now in the British Museum. They probably belonged to a colossal statue of Thothmes III (*c.* 1500–1450 B.C.).
16. This red granite monument 'of uncertain description', as the British Museum still calls it, may have been the pedestal to support a sacred boat.

Carved in high relief round the four sides of a solid block are the figures of Hathor, Mentu (the oldest god of Thebes) and Thothmes III. Each is duplicated and the figures join hands.

17. His story is given in *The Life and Adventures of Giovanni Finati*, which William John Bankes translated from the version Finati dictated in Italian; it was published by John Murray in 1830. Mr. Willson Disher believes that Bankes wrote the book himself. Bankes unfortunately never settled down to write his own book. His manuscript notes and drawings are mostly in the Griffith Institute at the Ashmolean Museum, Oxford; there are also two albums in the British Museum.

18. Charles Leonard Irby (1789–1845) was a younger son of the second Lord Boston. He afterwards married a sister of Mangles. James Mangles (1786–1867) became a Fellow of the Royal Society in 1825 and was one of the original members of the Royal Geographical Society. In 1853 he published a guide to the navigation of the Thames estuary. He was also author of *The Floral Calendar*, a little book that extolled the virtues of town and window gardening.

Apart from the exploit which they shared with Belzoni, these two young men made other useful contributions to Egyptology. They discovered (at el-Barsha) the splendid Middle Kingdom tomb of Thut-hotpe with its wall-painting showing how a colossus was moved. They also observed, while helping Caviglia at Giza, that on the night of 21 March 1817 (the vernal equinox) the Pole Star was visible from the Descending Corridor of the Great Pyramid.

19. The Arabic name for the inhabitants of Nubia.

20. *Travels in Egypt and Nubia*, Irby and Mangles (privately printed), 1823.

21. The cynocephali are called in Egyptian religious texts 'watchers for the dawn'.

22. See Appendix A for details of these Abu Simbel finds, which are now in the British Museum.

23. An inscription in the temple is dated to the thirty-fifth year of the reign of Ramses II. Probably the temple was completed about 1260 B.C.

24. If Egypt's projected High Dam is ever built a few miles south of Aswan it will create a vast lake 400 miles long. Both temples at Abu Simbel and many other ancient monuments in Nubia will be completely submerged. UNESCO undertook in 1956 to make a final survey of the antiquities.

CHAPTER X

1. Possibly Mr. Bidwell of the Foreign Office.
2. Strabo, *Geography*, XVII. i. 46.
3. Diodorus Siculus, *Bibliotheca Historica*, I. 46.
4. *Ægyptiaca*.
5. The tomb is No. 22 in the official numbering.
6. *The Pyramids and Temples of Gizeh*, W. M. F. Petrie, 1883.
7. At Lahun, Hawara and Dahshur.
8. Tomb No. 38.
9. Tomb No. 20.
10. A late priest-king of the Twenty-first Dynasty, who died about 950 B.C.
11. Thothmes' tomb is of interest now only for its place in the history of tomb-development. Ineni's own tomb—still well-preserved—is No. 81 at Qurna.
12. Either No. 24 or No. 25.
13. Tomb No. 19.

310 THE GREAT BELZONI

14. Nos. 21, 27 and 28.
15. Tomb No. 16.
16. These wooden figures are in the British Museum. For over a hundred years the one with the damaged nose (No. 854) has been ascribed to Seti I, largely because Samuel Birch of the Department of Antiquities saw a similarity in the treatment of the hair here and in the figures of Seti on the walls of his tomb (see *Gallery of Antiquities selected from the British Museum*, F. Arundale and J. Bonomi, 1842). There is no doubt however that the statue was found in the tomb of Ramses I and presumably it represents that king. Belzoni, for once, is quite explicit about the circumstances of its discovery. A similar wooden figure (No. 883), which has had part of one leg and the whole of the other restored, is described by the Museum as representing an unknown king of the thirteenth or fourteenth century B.C. This is almost certainly the companion figure found by Belzoni in the tomb of Ramses I. A third wooden figure (No. 882) shows completely different workmanship. Here both legs have been restored. This also came from the Salt Collection, but there is no evidence to show where it was found. Birch, *op. cit.*, thought from the shape of the nose and the style of the head-dress that it probably represented Ramses II. Salt is known to have cleared part of his tomb, which was choked with *débris*. It is possible however that Belzoni found this statue in the tomb of Seti I; see note 20 below.

Belzoni also found in the tomb of Ramses I 'a number of little images of wood, well carved, representing symbolical figures. Some had a lion's head, others a fox's, others a monkey's. One had a land-tortoise instead of a head. We found a calf with the head of a hippopotamus.' Nine such figures are exhibited together in a case in the Third Egyptian Room. They are of wood covered with cartonnage and painted with a black resinous substance. Their significance is not clear, but they are thought to represent gods and demons of the under-world. Two of these figures are reputed to be from the tomb of Seti I and the rest, it is said, possibly came from that of Thothmes III. In the light of Belzoni's statement, however, there is a strong presumption that some at least came from the tomb of Ramses I. The tortoise-, monkey- and hippopotamus-headed creatures are there just as Giovanni describes them.
17. No. 74.
18. For a complete set of line drawings of the scenes and texts in this tomb see *Memoires publiés par les membres de la Mission Archéologique Française du Caire 1882–1884*, Vol. II, *Les Hypogées Royaux de Thèbes*, Part I, *Le Tombeau de Seti Ier*, by Eugène Lefébure in collaboration with U. Bouriant and V. Loret, Paris, 1886.
19. There are three pieces now in the British Museum and others with the sarcophagus in the Soane Museum in Lincoln's Inn Fields.
20. See note 16 above. There is also in the British Museum a small seated wooden figure, No. 2321, cut off at mid-thigh, that is believed to represent Seti I and to have come from his tomb. For what such evidence is worth, the features are not unlike those of the life-size wooden figure (No. 882) described above in note 16.
21. A gold cock frequently appears in the stories of fabulous treasure recounted by early Arab writers in Egypt. Perhaps there is some folk-memory here of a golden statue of Horus the falcon. At Abydos hollow gold figures of the children of Horus, one of whom was falcon-headed, were filled with sand, barley and precious stones and then buried as part of an elaborate ritual of death and resurrection.

22. See his *Travels along the Mediterranean and parts adjacent; in company with the Earl of Belmore, during the years 1816–17–18*, 2 vols., 1822.
23. Hamilton was Secretary of the African Association.

CHAPTER XI

1. In his *Journal of a route across India, through Egypt, to England, 1817–1818*, published in 1819.
2. Edmé François Jomard (1777–1862) devoted the best part of a long life to publishing his own and other people's work on Egypt.
3. Seti's tomb is in fact 328 feet long, but it is exceeded in mere length by four other royal tombs that were known to the French at the time of their occupation, namely those of Ramses III, Ramses VI, Tausert (usurped by Setnakht) and Amenhetep III.
4. Evidently the Major Edward Moore who later became a Fellow of the Society of Antiquaries.
5. Herodotus, *Histories*, II. 127.
6. Diodorus Siculus, *Bibliotheca Historica*, I. 63.
7. Pliny, *Natural History*, XXXVI. 16.
8. The story is told by Abu Abdallah Muhammad Ben Abdurahim Alkaisi.
9. Bernhard von Breydenbach, Canon of Mainz, visited Egypt in 1483.
10. For extracts and summaries from the authors mentioned in this and the previous paragraph see *Operations carried on at the Pyramids of Gizeh in 1807*, by Colonel Howard Vyse, 1840.
11. Letronne in *Journal des Savans* for December 1820 says: 'The discovery of the entrance to this Pyramid is not as new as Mr. Belzoni thinks it is. Not only did the Arabs find their way into it in the twelfth century, but it is certain that Pietro Della Valle went all through it in 1615.' This repeats an error made by Colonel Grobert, who misread Letter XI in Della Valle's *Viaggi*. There it is clear from the internal arrangement of the chambers that Pietro is describing the Bent Pyramid, which he calls the 'Second' at Saqqara.
12. Ermenegildo (or Enegildo) Frediani (1783–1823) arrived in Egypt in 1817. For a while he seems to have been engaged as a kind of private tutor to Ismail Pasha. In 1820 he attached himself, together with Drovetti, Linant and Baron Minutoli, to the expedition which Muhammad Ali sent to impose his authority on the people of the Siwa Oasis. Later (with Cailliaud) he accompanied Ismail Pasha to Sennar in the southern Sudan. Frediani fell a victim of a progressive insanity. In a fit of madness he destroyed many of the notes he had made— 'no great loss', according to Salt, though this was probably a harsh judgment. Cailliaud used some of Frediani's material in his own four-volume *Voyage à Méroé*.
13. The inscription, as given by Belzoni, is corrupt, but attempts to amend it have not been very successful. The writing had disappeared by the time Howard Vyse made his survey of the Pyramids in 1837. One reading—by Professor Francis Lee—made out the name to be 'El Melek Othman'. Sir Gardner Wilkinson pointed out that this, if correct, would assign the opening of the Pyramid to the year 1200, during the short reign of al-Malik al-Aziz Othman, the second son and immediate successor of Salah al-Din. 'King' Ali Muhammad cannot be identified, but this may conceal the name of one of the Abbasid Caliphs of the mid-ninth century, which would then bring the date nearer to Mamun's opening of the First Pyramid.

14. It stood, appropriately enough, near the site of the present Windmill Theatre.
15. Colonel Howard Vyse uncovered this entrance in 1837.
16. See his *Operations carried on at the Pyramids of Gizeh in 1837*.
17. *The Life and Correspondence of Henry Salt*, Vol. II.

CHAPTER XII

1. '. . . an everlasting fortress of fine white sandstone, wrought with gold throughout; its floor is adorned with silver, and all its doors with electrum . . .' So Amenhetep himself described his temple. Allowing for a little kingly exaggeration we can still see that this vast temple, when the Colossi in front of it were perfect, must have been a splendid sight.

2. Ricci's journal has not been published. It was found in Cairo by Verrucci Bey, together with other papers belonging to the doctor, who died in Egypt of a scorpion bite in 1832. Professor Angelo Sammarco undertook to edit them, and the miscellaneous papers appeared as Volume II of *Alessandro Ricci e il suo Giornale dei viaggi* in 1930. The first volume however was not published and the manuscript of the Journal is believed to be still in Cairo. Unfortunately the other papers throw little light on the relationship between Ricci and Belzoni.

3. *Giovan Battista Belzoni alla luce di nuovi documenti*.

4. See chapter VIII, note 15.

5. Cailliaud spells the name Sekket, Belzoni less accurately Sakiet. The latter is a common Arabic place-name, but is derived from *saqiya*, a water-wheel, and so unlikely to be found in the desert. See note 15 below.

6. They are shown in the splendid reliefs of Queen Hatshepsut's mortuary temple at Deir el-Bahari. Punt seems to have been roughly the country we now know as Somaliland, at the southern end of the Red Sea.

7. *Itinerarium Provinciarum Omnium Imperatoris Antonini Augusti* was a register of distances and stations along the roads of the Roman empire. It may be named after the Antonine emperor Caracalla, but the part that survives is dated to the time of Diocletian, *i.e.* the end of the third century A.D. The Byzantine emperor Theodosius II (408–450) is recorded as having sent out surveyors in the fifteenth year of his reign to map the roads.

8. See J. H. Breasted's *Ancient Records of Egypt*, Vol. III, for the full inscription. The reference to 'the two caves of Elephantine' is to an imaginary source of the Nile in that island. This little temple of Seti I is sometimes called after the village of Redesiya, which lies on the Nile about five miles above Edfu.

9. These are one of the two main races inhabiting the Eastern Desert, the other being the Bisharin. Both are Hamitic in origin, ultimately coming from the Caucasus. Physically the Ababda seem to have much in common with the tall, slender, long-haired Amratians of Egyptian prehistory.

10. Jean Baptiste Bourguignon d'Anville (1697–1782) re-mapped most of the ancient civilized world. His great contribution to cartography was that he broke away from the tradition of merely copying older maps and repeating their errors.

11. An organic limestone formation.

12. 'Notes on the Ruins of Berenice', read to the Bombay branch of the Royal Geographical Society on 28 March 1836.

13. *Modern Egypt and Thebes*, 2 vols., Sir Gardner Wilkinson, 1842.

14. *Voyages à l'Oasis de Thèbes et dans les déserts à l'Orient et à l'Occident de la Thébaïde*, Frédéric Cailliaud, edited by E. F. Jomard, Paris, 1821 (English translation, 1822).

15. 'Senskiti' (dative) in the Greek. This is evidently the origin of the name Sakait.

16. Presumably it was his brother Antonio who was ill, for we know that he died some time during the next few months, before Giovanni wrote home again in March. Their father was already dead and probably had been for some years.

17. *Giovan Battista Belzoni alla luce di nuovi documenti.*

18. This and the following three letters are in *Il Corpo Epistolare di Bernardino Drovetti.*

19. It is true that Sir Gardner Wilkinson in *Modern Egypt and Thebes* says with reference to 'Belzoni's Tomb': 'The sinking of the ground at this part, from the water that had soaked through into the tomb, led the peasants to suspect the secret of its position, which was first mentioned to Dr. Rüppell, and afterwards to Belzoni.' Wilhelm Peter Eduard Simon Rüppell (1794–1884), a German traveller and zoologist, visited Egypt and Nubia in 1817. He became friendly with Irby and Mangles, but Belzoni makes no mention of him.

CHAPTER XIII

1. Mr. Willson Disher, *op. cit.*, says that the person known to Belzoni as Baron Sack 'seems to have been the French Orientalist, Baron de Sacy, but may have been Baron Menu von Minutoli, the German Egyptologist, there at the time'. Sylvestre de Sacy, however, was in Paris—and in any case he was a philologist, not a naturalist. Heinrich Karl Menu Minutoli (1772–1846), an officer in the Prussian army though of Neapolitan origin, did not arrive in Egypt till 1820 when he led a scientific expedition to Siwa. The eccentric naturalist in Salt's party was in fact Baron Albert von Sack, who had spent nearly three years collecting livestock in Dutch Guiana and had published a book about it in London in 1810.

2. For details of the remarkable career of this young man see Jean Mazuel's *L'Oeuvre géographique de Linant de Bellefonds*, Cairo, 1937.

3. Muhammad Ali built this canal in ten months in 1819 by the ruthless exploitation of forced labour. According to Cailliaud, 12,000 *fellahin* died of sickness or privation while engaged in this work. This figure may be exaggerated, but most Europeans in Egypt who have left contemporary accounts speak of the enormous death-roll. The canal, which partly followed the old Canopic branch of the river, enabled boats to reach the Nile from Alexandria without having to negotiate the dangerous bar at the Rosetta mouth. G. Marro in a paper, 'Il canale Mahmudieh e B. Drovetti', *Atti del XV Congresso Geografico Italiano*, Turin, 1950, claims that Drovetti inspired the project. Belzoni himself says that Samuel Briggs 'was the person who suggested to the Bashaw of Egypt to cut the canal from Foua to Alexandria'. R. R. Madden makes a similar statement in his *Travels in Turkey, Egypt, Nubia, and Palestine* (1833). But there is no inherent difficulty in supposing that both Briggs and Drovetti saw the advantages of such a water-way and recommended its construction to the Pasha.

4. *The Life and Correspondence of Henry Salt.*

5. It was lithographed for private circulation and eventually published in Salt's

Essay on Dr. Young's and M. Champollion's Phonetic System of Hieroglyphics (1825). In the meantime Cailliaud had made a copy and sent it to Champollion, who reproduced it in his *Lettres à M. le Duc de Blacas d'Aulps*, Paris, 1822.

6. Regrettably enough towards the end of the nineteenth century. But even by 1841 (see *An Appeal to the Antiquaries of Europe* by George R. Gliddon) many of the limestone blocks had been burnt by the *fellahin* who wanted lime for their fields.

7. The letter is with the MS. catalogue of the Salt Collection in the British Museum's Department of Egyptian Antiquities.

8. *Narrative of the Life and Adventures of Giovanni Finati.*

9. See 'Mrs. Belzoni's Trifling Account' at the end of *Narrative*. Bankes, Legh, Irby, Mangles and the whole of the Belmore *entourage* were in Jerusalem for Easter.

10. Sarah did *not* confuse the mosques, as Finati says.

11. There is in the British Museum (No. 884) a fragment of a relief from the right-hand jamb of the entrance to the 'Room of Beauties', showing the arm of the goddess Maat and hieroglyphics. This was presented by Colonel T. P. Thompson in 1864 and may have been a part damaged at the time of the flooding.

12. See his *Travels in Egypt during 1818 and 1819*, published in *New Voyages and Travels*, Vol. V, edited by Sir R. Phillips, 1821.

13. Oddly enough, there was a rumour in England about this time that Belzoni was dead. The July number of *The Quarterly Review* and the November number of *The Gentleman's Magazine* both carried brief announcements to this effect. However, in its issue for May 1819, *The Gentleman's Magazine* was able to publish a denial. 'Lord Belmore', it said, '. . . has received letters from Mr. Belzoni dated from Thebes in Upper Egypt, of the 27th of October.' The origin of the rumour is uncertain. It started too early to be a garbled version of the fracas of Boxing Day, 1818. On the other hand it was slow-moving if, as has been suggested, it was due to a confusion of Belzoni with Burckhardt, who died in October 1817.

14. It is now in the Fitzwilliam Museum, Cambridge.

15. *Narrative of the Life and Adventures of Nathaniel Pearce*, edited by J. J. Halls, 2 vols., 1831.

16. 'Il Comune di Padova e Gian Battista Belzoni,' Camillo Manfroni, *Atti e Memorie della R. Accademia de Scienze, Lettere e Arte in Padova*, Vol. XL, 1924.

17. Archibald Edmonstone (1795–1871) succeeded to a Scottish baronetcy in 1821. His *Journey to two of the oases of Upper Egypt* was published in 1822.

18. So Plutarch tells the story. *O Paidion*=My son; *O Pai dios*=Son of Zeus.

19. Herodotus, *Histories*, III. 26.

20. *Travels in Africa, Egypt, and Syria, from the Year 1792 to 1798*, W. G. Browne, 1799.

21. *The Journal of Frederick Hornemann's Travels, from Cairo to Mourzouk*, edited by Sir W. Young, 1802.

22. He reached the oasis on 1 January 1820. See his *Voyage à Méroé . . . à Syouah et dans cinq autres oasis*, Vol. I, 1826.

23. See *Voyage à l'oasis de Syouah, d'après les matériaux recueillis par M. Drovetti . . . et par M. Frédéric Cailliaud pendant leurs voyages dans cette oasis en 1819 et en 1820*, E. F. Jomard, Paris, 1823.

24. See chapter VII, note 21.

25. The core of the pyramid is a knoll of rock; above that is a framework of retaining stone walls with mud bricks packed between them.
26. Herodotus, *Histories*, II. 148.
27. See *Hawara, Biahmu and Arsinoe*, W. M. F. Petrie, 1889, for the Labyrinth and also for the colossal plinths mentioned in the next paragraph.
28. The principal temple—late Ptolemaic—was devoted to the ram-headed Amun-Khnum. Dionysias marked the extreme Western limit of the Roman province of Egypt.
29. At Kom el-Asl, called Kom el-Qatl by Hogarth and Grenfell, who excavated there in 1896.
30. About five miles to the north of Dimai at the foot of a deep descent into the Libyan desert G. A. Schweinfurth discovered in 1884 a small temple (Qasr el-Sagha) and the remains of an ancient quay.
31. These coffins are of Roman date. There are two such broken lids in the British Museum, both from the Salt Collection. It suggests that Belzoni was magnanimous enough to offer them to his rival, unless indeed Salt got them from some other source such as Cailliaud.
32. Cailliaud had little difficulty in approaching the Roman arch—part of the ancient forum—when he visited the oasis seven months later, though the owner of a house built in the ruins was furious and terrified when he found Cailliaud installed there by the Shaikh and actually sketching. Cailliaud observes correctly that the Greek letters which Belzoni saw on some of the blocks were only masons' marks. For a fuller description of the ruins see *Visit to the Great Oasis of the Libyan Desert; with an account . . . of the other oases*, G. A. Hoskins, 1837.
33. Herodotus, *Histories*, IV, 181.
34. *Modern Egypt and Thebes*.
35. In the Preface to the second edition (1821) Belzoni comes down more firmly in favour of the Little Oasis being the seat of the oracle. This, he says, is in view of the fact that Linant and Ricci—no mention of Drovetti!—'found but scanty and insignificant remains of antiquity' when they visited Siwa in 1820. Belzoni at any rate did not confuse the two oases, as some writers have said.
36. The decision was taken by the Trustees at a General Meeting on 13 February 1819 (Minutes of General Meetings, Vol. V, 1806–28).

CHAPTER XIV

1. In *A Publisher and His Friends: Memoir and Correspondence of John Murray*. Murray sent Byron a copy of Belzoni's *Narrative*, and it was probably on this that he made his judgment. It is unlikely that the two men ever met.
2. 'Il Comune di Padova e Gian Battista Belzoni', Camillo Manfroni, *op. cit.*
3. *Life in London: day and night scenes* was first published in 1821.
4. These were all notable dandies. Byng, who wore his hair long, received his nickname from Beau Brummell. Cooke was for many years private secretary to the Duke of York.
5. The so-called Cato Street Conspiracy.
6. Georges Bernard Depping (1784–1853) was of German origin but became a naturalized Frenchman. He wrote the article on Belzoni in *Annales Biographiques* for 1827.
7. Quoted in *The First Gentleman of Europe* by Lewis Melville.

8. Morritt was more familiar with Turks than Arabs, having travelled in Greece and Asia Minor.
9. *Professional and Literary Memoirs of Charles Dibdin the Younger*.
10. 'Il Comune di Padova e Gian Battista Belzoni'.
11. Jean Antoine Galignani was born in London in 1796. His father opened an English bookshop in Paris in 1800. *Galignani's Messenger* was founded in 1814 and for a time Cyrus Redding was its editor.
12. Depping says (in *Annales Biographiques*, 1827) that the 'Dutch' version was made from the French. This is probably a slip of the pen for 'German'.
13. Thirty-three out of the forty-four plates bear Belzoni's name, seven—illustrating the tomb of Seti I—that of Ricci, and four are unsigned. Ricci was certainly the better draughtsman and copyist, but Belzoni's sketches of scenery and architecture are vigorous and effective. Six additional plates by Belzoni were published in 1822.
14. *The Quarterly Review*, October 1820.
15. *Journal des Savans*, December 1820.
16. As, for example, when he supposes that 'granite and other stones were less hard at the time of the Egyptians, than they are at present'. Or again when he argues that the 'windows' in the walls of temples must have been made by people who lived much later than the original builders and were of a different religion, because they interrupted the sculptured scenes.
17. The vast retaining walls built by Amenemhet III helped to give the impression that the lake was man-made.
18. Bullock was a fairly indiscriminate collector of 'curios'. But he also had a shrewd showman's instinct and one of his most profitable ventures was the purchase of Napoleon's travelling carriage, captured at Waterloo. This later went to Madame Tussaud's and survived until 1925.
19. 'Tom Thumb had 12,000 last week, B. R. Haydon 133½ (the ½ a little girl). Exquisite taste of the English people.' Benjamin Haydon in his Journal, shortly before his suicide in 1846.
20. The Reverend George Waddington (1793–1869) and the Reverend Barnard Hanbury (1793–1833) left a record of their travels in *Journal of a visit to parts of Ethiopia* (1822).
21. Thomas Campbell was nominal editor of *The New Monthly Magazine*, for whom Redding devilled assiduously. The poet lived then in Margaret Street, just off Cavendish Square.
22. *Past Celebrities Whom I Have Known*, Vol. II.
23. *The Times*, 30 April 1821.
24. Lady Blessington wrote an account of the exhibition—or rather of the people she met there—for her sketches of London life, published anonymously in 1823 under the title *The Magic Lantern*.
25. By great good fortune these drawings have survived. For details of their discovery see Appendix B.
26. Catalogue in the Percival Collection, British Museum.

CHAPTER XV

1. The greater part of the transactions with the British Museum is published as an appendix to Vol. II of *The Life and Correspondence of Henry Salt*. It runs to ninety-two pages of small print.

2. The list is in the MS. catalogue of the Salt Collection in the British Museum's Department of Egyptian Antiquities.
3. To be precise, £606.
4. Charles Townley (1737–1805) formed a famous collection of classical antiquities. On his death the marbles and terra-cottas were purchased by the British Museum for £20,000. A new gallery was built to house them and opened in 1808. The Townley bronzes, gems, coins and drawings were acquired in 1814 for a further £8,200.
5. It is true that the reverse of the medal referred to the Second Pyramid, Berenice and 'the tomb of Apis'. But the obverse bore a representation of the two lion-headed goddesses and the inscription 'OB DONUM PATRIA GRATA'.
6. *Hierogliphics found in the Tomb of Psammis, discovered by G. Belzoni . . . Copied from the originals in the said tomb and presented by the author to His Royal Highness Augustus Frederick Duke of Sussex.*
7. There is an example of this medal in the Petrie Collection at University College, London.
8. *The Annual Register*, 1821.
9. *A Publisher and His Friends.*
10. B.M. Additional MS. 18204, f. 57; 35230, f. 65.
11. British Museum Letter Books, Vol. IV.
12. Quoted in *The Book of Days*.
13. Sarah's letter and the two letters written by Belzoni from St. Petersburg are in the possession of Sir John Murray.
14. *Denmark Delineated*, A. Andersen Feldborg, 1824.
15. Mentioned in Belzoni's will. See chapter XVI, note 14.
16. *The Times*, 3 June 1822.
17. Percival Collection.
18. Signorina Pensa, daughter of a merchant from Leghorn who was visiting Alexandria with his family. She was only about sixteen at the time and died in childbirth five years later.

CHAPTER XVI

1. Belzoni had just met the novelist Jane Porter in Paris and claimed to be inspired by reading some of her poetry.
2. Moore had seen Belzoni's *Narrative* and the volume of plates at Galignani's bookshop in Paris. He was particularly interested in Egypt at the time as a subject for a poem.
3. I have not been able to identify him.
4. Lucas—his first name is uncertain, but it was probably William—had spent a number of years in North Africa, some of them as a slave in Morocco and some as British vice-consul in Tripoli.
5. *Travels in the interior districts of Africa*, Mungo Park, 1799.
6. 'God bless you, my good sir; may he reward you for all your goodness to me' were Belzoni's last words to Samuel Briggs, and almost the last words of his life.
7. *The New Monthly Magazine*, October 1823.
8. Belzoni also visited Oxford about this time, but he does not appear to have been so generous to the Ashmolean Museum. I.W., the unknown correspondent who recorded Giovanni's triumphant variety performance at the Blue Boar in 1813, adds this about the later visit in his communication to *Notes and*

Queries for 16 July 1864: 'He [Belzoni] was taken ill at an hotel, and sent for an eminent medical practitioner resident in the place, who told me the circumstance, to prescribe for him. The medical adviser was naturally surprised, and his curiosity much excited, by his patient's uncommon stature and appearance. When he had considered the case, and written the necessary prescription, he said "What name shall I add?" There was no answer. Supposing the question had not been heard sufficiently, he repeated it. After some little hesitation the reply was "Belzoni". "*The* Belzoni?" "Yes." ' That must have been balm to a man who was probably stricken with shame lest his earlier appearances in Oxford should be remembered.

9. Browne was a Freemason and this may have been the link between them. According to *Records of the First Hundred Years of the Royal Arch Chapter of St. James*, W. Harry Rylands, 1891, a Masonic jewel of great interest and beauty that had once belonged to Belzoni later passed into the hands of the Reverend George Browne. The same source says that Belzoni's ordinary R.A. jewel is in the Grand Lodge collection and bears the date 1821, presumably the year when Giovanni became a Mason.

10. *Giovan Battista Belzoni alla luce di nuovi documenti.*

11. Letter in the possession of Sir John Murray. Robert John Wilmot (1784–1841) was married to the subject of Byron's 'She Walks in Beauty'—Anne Beatrix Horton, whose name he later added to his own. Wilmot-Horton was one of those responsible for the destruction of the Byron Memoirs in that famous room at John Murray's. Thomas Moore had had them copied for security and there is still perhaps a remote chance that they may turn up one day.

12. The letter was published by Redding in *The New Monthly Magazine* for January 1824. 'Benzelul' and 'Benalish' may be only approximate forms of the Moroccan names.

13. Letter from Fez, dated 5 May, published in *The New Monthly Magazine* for August 1823.

14. See 'Due lettere inedite e il testamento di G. B. Belzoni', Egidio Bellorini, *Atti e Memorie della R. Accademia di Scienze, Lettere e Arte in Padova*, Vol. XL, 1924.

15. *Giovan Battista Belzoni alla luce di nuovi documenti.*

16. Certainly Mulay Abd ar-Rahman, who had succeeded his uncle only the year before, found himself at the beginning of his reign faced with a serious revolt of the tribesmen in the Central Atlas.

17. Reported by a Sierra Leone newspaper and copied by *The Times*.

18. *Giovan Battista Belzoni alla luce di nuovi documenti.*

19. See *Narrative of Travels and Discoveries in Northern and Central Africa*, Denham, Clapperton and Oudney, 1826, and *Records of Captain Clapperton's last expedition*, Richard Lander, 1830.

20. He would, of course, have reached the Niger before he came to the Hausa country.

21. In a letter from 'a young gentleman of Liverpool'—probably William Fell—to Mr. A. Hodgson, published in *The Times* of 4 May 1824.

22. Sarah Belzoni gave a copy of this letter to Cyrus Redding, who published it in *The New Monthly Magazine* for April 1825.

23. Summarized in William Fell's letter of 20 January 1824 to Messrs. Briggs Bros. and Co., London.

24. Article on Belzoni by Richard Burton in *The Cornhill Magazine* for July 1880.

25. 26 April 1824.

26. 11 December 1824.

27. Newspaper cutting of October 1825 in Percival Collection, Vol. III, f. 108.

28. 24 October 1825.

29. 'Il Comune di Padova e Gian Battista Belzoni', Camillo Manfroni, *op. cit.*

30. *The Cornhill Magazine*, July 1880.

31. Sir John Soane—as he later became—is chiefly remembered for his noble screen in front of the Bank of England and his house of treasures in Lincoln's Inn Fields.

32. It is astonishing how many writers have said that *Belzoni* sold the sarcophagus for £2,000. James Baikie in *Egyptian Antiquities in the Nile Valley*, E. A. Wallis Budge in *Cook's Handbook for Egypt and the Sudan* and Leonard Cottrell in *Lost Pharaohs* are amongst those who have fallen into this error. C. W. Ceram in *Gods, Graves and Scholars* says that the sarcophagus was one of the chief attractions of Belzoni's exhibition.

33. In this monograph, published in 1822, Champollion made use of the alphabetic values of the hieroglyphics discovered by Thomas Young in the names of Ptolemy and Berenice, and with their help worked out the names and titles of a number of Greek and Roman rulers of Egypt.

34. Yanni Athanasiou (D'Athanasi) helped to draw up the catalogue, which is published in *A Brief Account*.

35. Two small black basalt obelisks were taken from the French in 1801 and brought to London the following year. See chapter V, note 10.

36. There are in the British Museum sixty-three volumes of notes and drawings made by James Burton between 1820 and 1829 (Additional MSS. 25613–25675). There are another fifty compiled by Robert Hay and his artists between 1826 and 1838 (Additional MSS. 29812–29860, 31054).

37. See British Museum Additional MS. 25658, f. 50, for this correspondence. Champollion and Rosellini removed the two splendid reliefs of Seti and the goddess Hathor from the right and left sides of the doorway at the foot of the steps leading down from the upper pillared hall. These were sent respectively to the Louvre and the Museum at Florence. Bonomi told Burton in his letter that Rosellini had undertaken to cut a relief for the British Museum from 'one of the two pillasters in the chamber of the Divan where the wooden figures were'. This is clearly Giovanni's 'Sideboard Room', *i.e.*, the large annexe on the left of the burial-chamber. The left-hand pillar lacks a relief on the side facing the entrance and it was presumably from here that Bonomi obtained what is now No. 568 [855] in the British Museum (not at present on exhibition); the relief, much damaged, shows part of the figure of Osiris, but the colours are badly faded. The right-hand pillar has collapsed and A. Henry Rhind in *Thebes: its Tombs and their Tenants* (1862) repeats the charge that Lepsius and the Prussian Commission (1842–5) were responsible for the damage. Lefébure, *op. cit.*, denies this and blames tourists and Arabs, though he admits that Lepsius took reliefs from the second pillar on the left and from the end of the left-hand wall in the lower pillared hall; these went to the Berlin Museum. Even as early as 1821 Linant de Bellefonds described the tomb—with some exaggeration—as being 'quite spoilt' and got Yanni Athanasiou to remove a damaged relief for Salt. See Gliddon's *Appeal to the Antiquaries of Europe*, 1841, for an account of the damage done to Egyptian monuments by that date.

Osirei or Ousirei was the name preferred by Champollion to Psammis or Psammuthis. Mariette was the first to call the tomb correctly after Seti I.

38. There was even a French version of this—*Entretiens d'une mère avec ses enfants sur les voyages de Belzoni*, Victor Houzé, Avesnes, 1838.

39. Belzoni was also neatly pigeon-holed in such works as *The Lives of Celebrated Travellers*, James Augustus St. John, 1831; *Annals of Industry and Genius*, Cecilia Lucy Brightwell, 1863; *Biography of Self-Taught Men*, Bela Bates Edwards, 1869; and *The Triumphs of Perseverance*, Thomas Cooper, 1879.

40. Sarah had a latent streak of mysticism in her which Giovanni's death seemed to bring out. She began to refer to him as 'my sacrificed Belzoni'. She was also inclined to be 'psychic' in later years. She told Dr. Weisse that she had an intimation of Belzoni's death at the moment it occurred. She was wakened during the night, she said, by a sudden stirring of the wind in her bedroom in Paris. In fact, Belzoni died in the afternoon.

BIBLIOGRAPHY

A. PRINTED BOOKS

1. General

ASHTON, JOHN. *The Dawn of the Nineteenth Century in England.* 2 vols. London, 1886.

ATKINS, SARAH. *Fruits of Enterprise Exhibited in the Travels of Belzoni in Egypt and Nubia; Interspersed with the Observations of a Mother to her Children.* London, 1821.

BANKES, VIOLA. *A Dorset Heritage.* London, 1953.

BELLORINI, EGIDIO. *Giovan Battista Belzoni e i suoi viaggi.* Turin, 1930.

BRIGHTWELL, CECILIA LUCY. *Annals of Industry and Genius.* London, 1863.

BRITTON, JOHN. *Auto-biography.* London, 1850.

CHANCELLOR, E. BERESFORD. *The Pleasure Haunts of London during four centuries.* London, 1925.

CLAIR, COLIN. *Strong Man Egyptologist.* London, 1957.

COLERIDGE, SAMUEL TAYLOR. *Essays on His Own Times.* Ed. by his daughter. London, 1850.

COOPER, THOMAS. *The Triumphs of Perseverance.* London, 1879.

DISHER, M. WILLSON. *Pharaoh's Fool.* London, 1957.

EDWARDS, BELA BATES. *Biography of Self-taught Men.* London, 1869.

FELDBORG, A. ANDERSEN. *Denmark Delineated.* Edinburgh, 1824.

[GARDINER, MARGARET, Lady Blessington.] *The Magic Lantern.* London, 1823.

GAUDENZIO, LUIGI. *Giovan Battista Belzoni alla luce di nuovi documenti.* Padua, 1936.

HALLS, J. J. *The Life and Correspondence of Henry Salt, Esq., F.R.S., &c.,* 2 vols. London, 1834.

HAYDON, BENJAMIN ROBERT. *The Life of Benjamin Robert Haydon.* Ed. by Tom Taylor. 3 vols. London, 1853.

LAMB, CHARLES and MARY. *The Letters of Charles Lamb to which are added those of his sister, Mary Lamb.* Ed. by E. V. Lucas. London, 1935.

MALCOLM, J. P. *Londinium Redivivum.* 4 vols. London, 1803.

MARRO, GIOVANNI. *Il Corpo Epistolare di Bernardino Drovetti.* Vol. I. Rome, 1940.

MELVILLE, LEWIS. *The First Gentleman of Europe.* 2 vols. London, 1906.

MENIN, LUDOVICO. *Cenni biografici* (Preface to *Viaggi in Egitto ed in Nubia . . . di G. B. Belzoni*). Leghorn, 1827.

PINKS, WILLIAM J. *The History of Clerkenwell.* London, 1881.

REDDING, CYRUS. *Fifty Years' Recollections, Literary and Personal.* Vol. I. London, 1858.

— *Past Celebrities Whom I Have Known.* Vol. II. London, 1866.

RYLANDS, W. HARRY. *Records of the First Hundred Years of the Royal Arch Chapter of St. James.* London, 1891.

ST. JOHN, JAMES AUGUSTUS. *The Lives of Celebrated Travellers.* London, 1831.

SMILES, SAMUEL. *A Publisher and His Friends: Memoir and Correspondence of John Murray.* London, 1891.

SMITH, JOHN THOMAS. *A Book for a Rainy Day.* London, 1905.

SOANE, Sir JOHN. *Description of the House and Museum on the North side of Lincoln's Inn-Fields, the residence of Sir John Soane.* London, 1832.

TAYLOR, TOM. *Leicester Square, its Associations and its Worthies.* London, 1874.

TIMBS, JOHN. *Curiosities of London.* London, 1855.

WILKINSON, ROBERT. *Londina Illustrata.* London, 1819.

WORDSWORTH, WILLIAM. *Wordsworth's Prelude.* Ed. by Ernest de Selincourt. London, 1950.

2. History and Geography

BALL, JOHN. *The Geography and Geology of South-Eastern Egypt.* Cairo, 1912.

BARBÉ-MARBOIS, FRANÇOIS DE. *Histoire de la Louisiane.* Paris, 1829.

BROWNING, OSCAR. *England and Napoleon in 1803.* London, 1907.

BRYANT, ARTHUR. *Years of Victory, 1802–1812.* London, 1944.

— *The Age of Elegance, 1812–1822.* London, 1950.

DIODORUS SICULUS. *Bibliotheca Historica.* Book I.

DODWELL, HENRY. *The Founder of Modern Egypt: A Study of Muhammad Ali.* Cambridge, 1931.

HERODOTUS. *Histories.* Books II, III and IV.

MAZUEL, JEAN. *L'Œuvre géographique de Linant de Bellefonds.* Cairo, 1937.

MENGIN, FÉLIX. *Histoire de l'Égypte sous le gouvernement de Mohammed-Aly.* Paris, 1823.

MUSTAFA SABRI. *L'Empire Égyptien sous Mohamed-Ali.* Paris, 1930.

PLINY. *Natural History,* Book XXXVI.

SHAFIK GHORBAL. *The Beginnings of the Egyptian Question and the Rise of Mehemet Ali.* London, 1928.

STRABO. *Geography.* Book XVII.

WESSELINGIUS, PETRUS. *Vetera Romanorum Itineraria.* Amsterdam, 1735.

3. Theatre and Fair

BAXTER, PETER. *The Drama in Perth.* Perth, 1907.

BEAUMONT, CYRIL W. *The History of Harlequin.* London, 1926.

BRAYLEY, E. W. *Historical and Descriptive Accounts of the Theatres of London.* London, 1826.

DIBDIN, CHARLES, Junior. *History and Illustrations of the London Theatres.* London, 1826.

— *Professional and Literary Memoirs of Charles Dibdin the Younger.* Ed. by Robert Speaight. London, 1956.

DIBDIN, JAMES C. *The Annals of the Edinburgh Stage.* Edinburgh, 1888.

DISHER, M. WILLSON. *Clowns and Pantomimes.* London, 1925.

— *Greatest Show on Earth.* London, 1937.

— *Blood and Thunder.* London, 1949.

— *Melodrama.* London, 1954.

FINDLATER, RICHARD. *Grimaldi King of Clowns.* London, 1955.

FROST, THOMAS. *The Old Showmen, and the Old London Fairs.* London, 1874.

GILLILAND, THOMAS. *The Dramatic Mirror.* London, 1808.

LAWSON, ROBB. *The Story of the Scots Stage.* Paisley, 1917.

MORLEY, HENRY. *Memoirs of Bartholomew Fair.* London, 1859.

NICOLL, ALLARDYCE. *A History of Early Nineteenth Century Drama.* 2 vols. London, 1930.

NIKLAUS, THELMA. *Harlequin Phoenix.* London, 1956.

WILSON, A. E. *Pantomime Pageant*. London, 1946.
— *The Lyceum*. London, 1952.

4. *Travel*

ANNESLEY, GEORGE, Viscount Valentia, later Lord Mountnorris. *Voyages and Travels to India, Ceylon, the Red Sea, Abyssinia, and Egypt in the years 1802–6*. Includes Salt's Journal. 3 vols. London, 1809.

ATHANASI, GIOVANNI D' (YANNI ATHANASIOU). *A Brief Account of the Researches and Discoveries in Upper Egypt made under the Direction of Henry Salt, Esq. To which is added a detailed Catalogue of Mr. Salt's collection of Egyptian Antiquities*. London, 1836.

BAEDEKER, KARL. *Egypt. Handbook for Travellers*. London, 1929 edition.

BROCKEDON, WILLIAM. *Egypt and Nubia*. Illustrated by David Roberts. 3 vols. London, 1846.

BROWNE, W. E. *Travels in Africa, Egypt and Syria, from the year 1792 to 1798*. London, 1799.

BRUCE, JAMES. *Travels to discover the Source of the Nile*. With Life of Bruce by Henry Salt. 8 vols. Edinburgh, 1815 edition.

BUDGE, Sir E. A. WALLIS. *Cook's Handbook for Egypt and the Sudan*. London, 1908.

BURCKHARDT, JOHN LEWIS. *Travels in Nubia*. London, 1819.

CAILLIAUD, FRÉDÉRIC. *Voyage à l'Oasis de Thèbes et dans les déserts situées à l'Ouest et à l'Occident de la Thébaïde*. Paris, 1821.

—*Travels in the Oasis*. English edition, in *New Voyages and Travels*, Vol. 7, ed. by Sir R. Phillips. London, 1822.

— *Voyage à Méroé, au Fleuve Blanc . . . à Syouah et dans cinq autres oasis*. 4 vols. of text and 3 of plates. Paris, 1823.

— *Recherches sur les Arts et Métiers . . . des Anciens Peuples de l'Égypte, de la Nubie et de l'Éthiopie*. Plates only. Paris, 1831.

CARRÉ, JEAN MARIE. *Voyageurs et Écrivains Français en Égypte*. 2 vols. Cairo, 1932.

CURZON, ROBERT. *Visits to Monasteries in the Levant*. London, 1849.

DELLA VALLE, PIETRO. *Viaggi*. Rome, 1650–8.

DENHAM, DIXON. *Narrative of Travels and Discoveries in Northern and Central Africa in the years 1822–23–24 by Major Denham, Capt. Clapperton and the late Doctor Oudney*. London, 1826.

DENON, DOMINIQUE VIVANT. *Voyage dans la Basse et la Haute Égypte, pendant les Campagnes du Général Bonaparte*. 2 vols. Paris, 1802.

— *Travels in Lower and Upper Egypt*. English translation by A. Aikin. London, 1802.

Description de l'Égypte: ou recueil des Observations et des Recherches qui ont été faites en Égypte, pendant l'Expédition de l'Armée Français. 10 vols. of text and 14 of plates. Paris, 1808–25.

EDMONSTONE, Sir ARCHIBALD. *Journey to two of the oases of Upper Egypt*. London, 1822.

FINATI, GIOVANNI. *Narrative of the Life and Adventures of Giovanni Finati*. Translated and edited by William John Bankes. London, 1830.

FITZCLARENCE, Lt.-Col. GEORGE, Earl of Munster. *Journal of a Route across India, through Egypt, to England, 1817–1818*. London, 1819.

FORBIN, LOUIS NICOLAS PHILIPPE AUGUSTE (Comte de). *Voyage dans le Levant, en 1817 et 1818*. Paris, 1819.

— *Travels in Egypt.* In *New Voyages and Travels,* Vol. 2, ed. by Sir R. Phillips. London, 1820.

GAU, FRÉDÉRIC CHRÉTIEN. *Antiquités de la Nubie.* Stuttgart and Paris, 1822.

HAMILTON, WILLIAM RICHARD. *Remarks on Several Parts of Turkey: Part I, Ægyptiaca.* London, 1809.

HENNIKER, Sir FREDERICK. *Notes during a visit to Egypt, Nubia, the Oasis, Mount Sinai, and Jerusalem.* London, 1823.

HOREAU, HECTOR. *Panorama d'Égypte et de Nubie.* Paris, 1841.

HOSKINS, G. A. *Visit to the Great Oasis of the Libyan Desert; with an account . . . of . . . the other oases.* London, 1837.

IRBY, CHARLES LEONARD, and MANGLES, JAMES. *Travels in Egypt and Nubia.* Privately printed. London, 1823.

JOMARD, EDMÉ FRANÇOIS. *Voyage à l'Oasis de Syouah: redigé et publié d'après les matériaux receuillis par M.M. Drovetti et Frédéric Cailliaud de Nantes.* Paris, 1823.

LANDER, RICHARD. *Records of Captain Clapperton's last expedition.* London, 1830.

LANE, EDWARD WILLIAM. *An Account of the Manners and Customs of the Modern Egyptians.* 2 vols. London, 1836.

LEGH, THOMAS, M.P. *Narrative of a Journey in Egypt and the Country beyond the Cataracts.* London, 1816.

LIGHT, Capt. HENRY. *Travels in Egypt, Nubia, Holy Land, Mount Lebanon, and Cyprus, in the year 1814.* London, 1818.

MADDEN, Dr. RICHARD ROBERT. *Travels in Turkey, Egypt, Nubia and Palestine in 1824, 1825, 1826 and 1827.* 2 vols. London, 1829.

MONTULÉ, ÉDOUARD DE. *Voyage en Amérique, en Italie, en Sicile et en Égypte.* 2 vols. and atlas of plates. Paris, 1821.

— *Travels in Egypt during 1818 and 1819.* In *New Voyages and Travels,* Vol. 5, Ed. by Sir R. Phillips. London, 1821.

NORDEN, FREDERIK LUDVIG. *Drawings of some Ruins and Colossal Statues at Thebes in Egypt; with an account of the same, in a letter to the Royal Society.* London, 1741.

PARK, MUNGO. *Travels in the Interior Districts of Africa in 1795-6-7.* London, 1799.

PEARCE, NATHANIEL. *The Life and Adventures of Nathaniel Pearce, written by himself during a residence in Abyssinia for the years 1810 to 1819.* Ed. by J. J. Halls. 2 vols. London, 1831.

RICHARDSON, Dr. ROBERT. *Travels along the Mediterranean and parts adjacent; in company with the Earl of Belmore, during the years 1816–17–18.* 2 vols. London, 1822.

RIFAUD, JEAN JACQUES. *Voyage en Égypte, en Nubie et lieux circonvoisins, depuis 1805, jusqu'à 1827.* Plates only, no text. Paris, 1829.

SALT, HENRY. *Account of a Voyage to Abyssinia, and Travels into the Interior of that Country . . . in the years 1809 and 1810.* London, 1814.

— *Twenty-four Views taken in St. Helena, the Cape, India, Ceylon, Abyssinia, and Egypt.* London, 1809.

SAMMARCO, ANGELO. *Alessandro Ricci e il suo Giornale dei viaggi.* Only Vol. II published. Cairo, 1930.

SONNINI DE MANONCOURT, CHARLES NICOLAS SIGISBERT. *Voyage dans la Haute et la Basse Égypte.* 3 vols. Paris, 1799.

— English Edition. London, 1800.

TURNER, WILLIAM. *Journal of a Tour in the Levant.* 3 vols. London, 1820.

WADDINGTON, Rev. GEORGE, and HANBURY, Rev. BARNARD. *Journal of a visit to parts of Ethiopia*. London, 1822.

YATES, Dr. WILLIAM HOLT. *The Modern History and Condition of Egypt*. 2 vols. London, 1843.

5. *Egyptology*

A General Introductory Guide to the Egyptian Collections in the British Museum. New Edition. London, 1930.

A Guide to the Egyptian Galleries (Sculpture). British Museum publication. London, 1909.

A Handbook to the Egyptian Mummies and Coffins exhibited in the British Museum. London, 1938.

ARUNDALE, F., and BONOMI, J. *Gallery of Antiquities selected from the British Museum*. London, 1842.

BAIKIE, JAMES. *Egyptian Antiquities in the Nile Valley*. London, 1932.

— *A Century of Excavation in the Land of the Pharaohs*. London, 1924.

BANKES, WILLIAM JOHN. *Geometrical elevation of an Obelisk . . . from the Island of Philae*. London, 1821.

BELZONI, GIOVANNI BATTISTA. *Narrative of the Operations and Recent Discoveries within the Pyramids, Temples, Tombs, and Excavations, in Egypt and Nubia; and of a Journey to the Coast of the Red Sea, in search of the ancient Berenice; and another to the Oasis of Jupiter Ammon*. London, 1820.

— *Forty-four Plates illustrative of the Researches and Operations of Belzoni in Egypt and Nubia*. London, 1820.

— *Six new plates*. London, 1822.

— *Hierogliphics found in the Tomb of Psammis, discovered by G. Belzoni . . . Copied from the originals in the said tomb and presented by the author to his Royal Highness Augustus Frederick Duke of Sussex*. London, [?] 1822.

BIRCH, SAMUEL. *Remarks upon the Cover of the Granite Sarcophagus of Ramses III in the Fitzwilliam Museum*. Cambridge, 1876.

BONOMI, JOSEPH, and SHARPE, SAMUEL. *The Alabaster Sarcophagus of Oimenepthah I, King of Egypt, now in Sir J. Soane's Museum*, London, 1864.

BREASTED, J. H. *Ancient Records of Egypt*. Vol. III. Chicago, 1906–7.

BRODRICK, M., and MORTON, A. A. *A Concise Dictionary of Egyptian Archaeology*. London, 1902.

BUDGE, Sir E. A. WALLIS. *The Rosetta Stone in the British Museum*. London, 1929.

— *Cleopatra's Needles and other Egyptian Obelisks*. London, 1926.

CHAMPOLLION, JEAN FRANÇOIS, le Jeune. *Lettre à M. Dacier relative à l'Alphabet des Hiéroglyphes Phonétiques*. Paris, 1822.

— *Lettres à M. le Duc de Blacas d'Aulps . . . relatives au Musée royal Égyptien de Turin*. Paris, 1824–6.

— *Lettres et Journaux*, ed. by H. Hartleben. (Vols. 30 and 31 of *Bibliothèque Égyptologique*.) Paris, 1909.

EDWARDS, I. E. S. *The Pyramids of Egypt*. London, 1947.

GLIDDON, GEORGE R. *An Appeal to the Antiquaries of Europe on the Destruction of the Monuments of Egypt*. London, 1841.

GROBERT, Col. JACQUES FRANÇOIS LOUIS. *Description des pyramides de Ghizé*. Paris, 1801.

LEFÉBURE, EUGÈNE, in collaboration with U. BOURIANT and V. LORET. *Memoires publiés par les membres de la Mission Archéologique du Caire 1882–*

1884. Vol. II, *Les Hypogées Royaux de Thèbes.* Part I, Le Tombeau de Seti I. Paris, 1886.

LONG, GEORGE. *The Egyptian Antiquities in the British Museum.* 2 vols. London, 1846.

PETRIE, Sir W. M. F. *The Pyramids and Temples of Gizeh.* London, 1883.
— *Hawara, Biahmu and Arsinoe.* London, 1889.
— *The Making of Egypt.* London, 1939.

PETTIGREW, T. J. *A History of Egyptian Mummies.* London, 1834.

QUIBELL, J. E. *The Ramesseum.* London, 1898.

RHIND, A. H. *Thebes: its Tombs and their Tenants.* London, 1862.

SALT, HENRY. *Essay on Dr. Young's and M. Champollion's Phonetic System of Hieroglyphics.* London, 1825.

VYSE, Col. RICHARD WILLIAM HOWARD. *Operations carried on at the Pyramids of Gizeh in 1837.* With an appendix by J. S. Perring. 3 vols. London, 1840–2.

WEISSE, Dr. JOHN A. *The Obelisk and Freemasonry according to the Discoveries of Belzoni and Commander Gorringe.* New York, 1880.

WILKINSON, Sir JOHN GARDNER. *The Manners and Customs of the Ancient Egyptians.* 3 vols. London, 1837.
— *Modern Egypt and Thebes.* 2 vols. London, 1843.

6. *Encyclopædias and Reference Books*

Biographie Universelle. Paris, 1830–4.
Book of Days, The. Ed. by Robert Chambers. London and Edinburgh, 1863–4.
DAWSON, W. R. *Who was Who in Egyptology.* London, 1951.
Dictionary of National Biography, The. Oxford (since 1917), 1885–
Grande Dizionario Enciclopedico. 2nd Edition. Turin, 1954–
Imperial Dictionary of Universal Biography, The. 1857–63.
Modern English Biography. Ed. by Frederic Boase. Truro, 1892–1921.
Nouvelle Biographie Générale. Paris, 1855–66.
Penny Cyclopaedia, The. London, 1833.

7. *Bibliographical*

GILDER, ROSAMOND, and FREEDLEY, GEORGE. *Theatre Collections in Libraries and Museums.* London, 1936.

LOEWENBERG, ALFRED. *The Theatre of the British Isles, excluding London.* London, 1950.

JOLOWICZ, Dr. H. *Bibliotheca Aegyptiaca. Repertorium über die bis zum Jahre 1857 in bezug auf Aegypten.* Leipzig, 1858.

IBRAHIM HILMY, Prince. *The Literature of Egypt and the Soudan from the earliest times to the year 1885 inclusive.* 2 vols. London, 1886.

PORTER, BERTHA, and MOSS, ROSALIND L. B. *Topographical Bibliography of Ancient Egyptian Hieroglyphic Texts, Reliefs and Paintings.* 7 vols. Oxford, 1927–

B. JOURNALS OF SOCIETIES, PERIODICALS NEWSPAPERS, PLAYBILLS AND EPHEMERAL PUBLICATIONS

1. *General*

Annual Register, The. 1803–24.
Bell's Weekly Messenger. 1803.

Cornhill Magazine, The. July 1880.
European Magazine, The. 1821–3.
Fraser's Magazine. June 1834.
Gentleman's Magazine, The. 1803–24.
Hogg's Instructor. 1852.
Household Words. March 1851.
Monthly Review, The. 1821.
New Monthly Magazine, The. 1821–5.
Notes and Queries. July 1864.
Spirit of the Public Journals, The. 1803.
Times, The. 1803, 1820–9, 1851.

2. Theatre and Fair

British Museum
Astley's Amphitheatre (1791–1843). Theatre Playbills 170.
Bartholomew Fair—prints and cuttings (1687–1849).
Percival Collection of material relating to Sadler's Wells (1683–1848). 14 vols. (particularly Vols. III, IV and XIV).
Sadler's Wells (1740–1866). Theatre Cuttings 49.

Finsbury Public Library
Sadler's Wells collection of playbills, cuttings and prints.

Guildhall Library
Bartholomew Fair—a collection of handbills (1779–1804). Granger 2.1.7.

Victoria and Albert Museum, Enthoven Collection
Royalty Theatre, 1803–4.
Sadler's Wells, 1803.

3. Egypt

BELLORINI, EGIDIO. 'Due lettere inedite e il testamento di G. B. Belzoni' in *Atti e Memorie della Regia Accademia di Scienze, Lettere e Arte in Padova.* Vol. XL. 1924.
BUDGE, Sir E. A. WALLIS. *The Rosetta Stone.* British Museum publication. London, 1950.
DEPPING, GEORGES BERNARD. Article on Belzoni in *Annales Biographiques.* Paris, 1827.
GAUDENZIO, LUIGI. 'Memorie Belzoniane' in *Padova* for February and March 1955.
GUÉMARD, GABRIEL. 'Essai d'histoire de l'Institut d'Égypte et de la Commission des Sciences et Arts' in *Bulletin de L'Institut d'Égypte.* Vol. VI. 1924.
JOMARD, EDMÉ FRANÇOIS. Article in *Journal des Savans* for May 1818.
LETRONNE, JEAN ANTOINE. Article in *Journal des Savans* for December 1820.
MANFRONI, CAMILLO. 'Il Comune di Padova e Gian Battista Belzoni' in *Atti e Memorie della Regia Accademia di Scienze, Lettere e Arte in Padova.* Vol. XL. 1924.
MARRO, GIOVANNI. 'Il canale Mahmudieh e B. Drovetti' in *Atti del XV Congresso Geografico Italiano.* Turin, 1950.
— 'La Personalità di Bernardino Drovetti studiata nel suo archivio inedito' in *Memorie della Accademia delle Scienze di Torino.* Turin, 1951.

SALT, HENRY. *Extract of a letter to W. Hamilton.* London, 1819.

SAMMARCO, ANGELO. 'Per il primo centenario della morte di Giovanni Battista Belzoni' in *Bulletin de l'Institut d'Égypte.* Vol. VI. 1924.

WELLSTED, Lieut. R. 'Notes on the Ruins of Berenice' in *Journal of the Royal Geographical Society.* Vol. VI. 1836.

C. MANUSCRIPT SOURCES

1. *General*

British Museum, Additional MSS. 18,204 and 35,230.

Letters of Belzoni (and one of Sarah's) in the possession of Sir John Murray.

2. *Bartholomew Fair*

Proceedings of Smithfield Piepowder Court, 1790–1854. Guildhall Library, MS. 95.

3. *Egypt*

British Museum, Additional MSS. 25,640–4; 25,658 and 25,661 (James Burton papers). 29,818–23; 29,834–5; 29,840–1; 29,849 and 29,851–2 (Robert Hay papers).

British Museum, Letter Books. Vol. IV.

British Museum, Minutes of General Meetings of the Trustees. Vol. V (1806–28).

British Museum, Salt and Sloane Collections. MS. Catalogue of Egyptian Antiquities and various B.M. Correspondence. (Department of Egyptian Antiquities.)

Griffith Institute, Ashmolean Museum, Oxford. Manuscripts of William John Bankes.

Public Record Office. Foreign Office Records, F.O. 24, Vol. 6; F.O. 78, Vols. 85, 87, 89, 91 and 93.

Public Record Office. War Office Records, W.O.1. Vol. 349, f. 37 *et seq.*

Society of Antiquaries Minute Book. Vol. XXXIV, 1817–23.

APPENDIX A

Egyptian Antiquities in the British Museum

BELOW is a list of the principal antiquities that reached the Museum through the efforts of Belzoni. Many of the small items in Salt's second collection must have been obtained by Belzoni, but they are not included here because they cannot be distinguished from those that the consul found for himself or acquired from other sources.

All objects carry a Registration Number, often in square brackets. Some in addition have a now obsolete Exhibition Number. In this list the Exhibition Number is given first for the sake of easy reference to E. A. Wallis Budge's *A Guide to the Egyptian Galleries (Sculpture)*, 1909, where further information will be found by those interested. The visitor to the Museum may identify an object most conveniently by reference to its location in the Galleries and its Registration Number (in square brackets), both given at the end of each entry. An asterisk indicates that the object is not on exhibition at the time of writing.

The objects are in roughly chronological order, beginning from the Eighteenth Dynasty.

360. Head of a colossal statue in red granite, found by Belzoni at Karnak in 1817. It shows a king wearing the Double Crown of Upper and Lower Egypt, and probably represents the great warrior, Thothmes III (*c.* 1500–1450 B.C.). *Northern Gallery* [15].

361. The left arm of the same colossus. *Northern Gallery* [55].

363. The so-called 'altar with the six divinities', admired by the French and shown in their *Description*. It is a massive block of polished red granite, having in high relief on the sides the figures of the goddess Hathor, Mentu (the oldest god of Thebes) and Thothmes III. Each is represented twice. The block stood originally on a white stone base in the little temple of Mentu at the north-east corner of Karnak. It may have been used to support a sacred boat. Belzoni removed it in 1817. *Northern Gallery, Bay 4* [12].

375. A family group in painted limestone. Athu, priest, palace warden and overseer of the treasury, with his wife, Hentur, priestess of Amun, and their son, Neferhebef. The group was dedicated to the memory of his parents by Neferhebef, who was second priest of Amenhetep II (*c.* 1450–1420 B.C.). Found by Belzoni at Thebes. *Northern Gallery, Bay 11* [31].

413. Colossal seated statue of Amenhetep III (*c.* 1400 B.C.) in black granite. This was found by Belzoni in 1818, when he was digging behind the Colossi on the plain in a place already excavated by Salt and reserved by him for future operations. Belzoni grudgingly admitted Salt's claim to the statue, but not before he had carved his own name in capitals on the base by the left foot. *Northern Gallery* [21].

433. Part of a limestone *stele* inscribed with prayers to the goddess Mut. It was set up in her temple in Asher, an eastern quarter of Thebes, during the reign of Amenhetep III. The arrangement of the text is unusual in that each word is separately boxed and the prayers can be read either from right to left or from top to bottom. Belzoni thought this might be of help to Dr. Young in his task of deciphering the hieroglyphics. *Southern Gallery, Bay 20* [194].

567. Wooden *Ka* figure of Ramses I (*c.* 1320 B.C.), found in his tomb in the Valley of the Kings when it was opened by Belzoni in 1817. Memorials of this king are rare and for over a hundred years this figure has been attributed to his more famous son, Seti I. Belzoni's circumstantial account of its discovery, however, together with his description of the tomb, puts the matter beyond any reasonable doubt. *Northern Vestibule* [854].

685. This is almost certainly the other *Ka* figure of Ramses I, found in his tomb with 567 [854] above. It came from the Salt Collection and is described by the Museum as representing an unknown king of the thirteenth or fourteenth century B.C. Part of one leg and the whole of the other has been restored. *Northern Vestibule* [883].

576. THE YOUNG MEMNON. Upper part of a colossal granite statue of Ramses II (*c.* 1300–1235 B.C.), one of a pair which stood (or rather sat) in the Second Court of the Ramesseum on the west bank of the Nile at Thebes. On the back is the king's Horus name and some of his titles. Brought down the Nile by Belzoni in 1816 and presented to the British Museum by Salt and Burckhardt. Note the hole in the right shoulder and the beginnings of another in the left, believed to have been made by the French with the idea of blasting the head from the body. The piece weighs about 7¼ tons. *Central Saloon* [19].

594. A hawk-headed sandstone sphinx, found in the great rock-cut temple of Ramses II at Abu Simbel in Nubia, when Belzoni opened it in 1817. The stone is very soft and friable. *Central Saloon* [11].

595. A companion piece to 594 [11], found in the same place. *Central Saloon* [13].

601. Upper part of a colossal limestone statue of a queen, probably one of the wives of Ramses II. She wears the headdress of the goddess Hathor. Found by Belzoni in the Great Temple at Abu Simbel. *Central Saloon* [93].

602. Upper part of a similar figure wearing a heavy wig and a crown. From the Great Temple at Abu Simbel. Probably another wife of Ramses II. Brought down the Nile by Belzoni in 1817. *Central Saloon* [948].

604. A kneeling figure in painted limestone. Pa-ser, governor of Nubia in the time of Ramses II. He holds in front of him a pedestal surmounted by the head of a ram, the theophany of Amun. Found in the Great Temple at Abu Simbel. *Southern Gallery, Bay 15* [1376].

*619. Dog-headed ape in sandstone from the Great Temple of Ramses II at Abu Simbel [40].

616. A seated statue of the Pharaoh Seti II (*c.* 1215–1205 B.C.), holding on his knees a small shrine surmounted by a ram's head. The material is a quartzite sandstone, and this is the 'white statue' found by Belzoni among the lion-headed goddesses in the temple of Mut in Asher at Thebes. *Southern Gallery, Bay 16* [26].

763. A massive seated statue of Sekhmet, the lion-headed goddess, in black granite. She wears the solar disk on her head and represents the fierce heat of the sun. Her throne bears the name of Sheshank I (*c.* 935 B.C.), the Shishak of the Bible. This figure came from the temple of Mut in Asher and may be the one given by Belzoni to Lord Belmore, as it was once in the Belmore

Collection. (There is, however, another figure of Sekhmet—409 [518], not on exhibition—which also belonged to Lord Belmore.) *Southern Gallery* [517].

764. A similar figure to 763 [517]. This came from the Salt Collection and was probably one of the many unearthed by Belzoni. (It is impossible to trace the individual history of each of these Sekhmet figures. The Museum has over thirty such statues or parts of statues, most of them not on exhibition. See however 386 [60] and 390 [65] in the *Northern Gallery* for two small seated statues of Sekhmet, dating from the reign of Amenhetep III, which may have been among the score discovered by Belzoni.) *Southern Gallery* [63].

*913. Sandstone coffin and cover of a woman whose name is illegible. It belongs to the Late Period. Belzoni gave it to Lord Belmore, after 'restoring' some of the painted figures, and Lord Belmore presented it to the Museum. [39].

*Two fine large bronze vessels (*situlae*) with cauldron handles, inscribed with hieroglyphics. Belzoni bought these at Qurna. [38212 and 38214].

Wooden figures of gods and demons of the under-world, covered with carton-nage and painted with a black resinous substance. Some of these almost certainly came from the tomb of Ramses I. *Third Egyptian Room, Case 95.*

Among other antiquities mentioned in this book or associated with Belzoni's contemporaries the following may be of interest:

Taken from the French at Alexandria in 1801

*597. Left fist of a colossal red granite statue of Ramses II from the ruins of Memphis. It weighs about $1\frac{1}{4}$ tons [9].

919. A black basalt obelisk bearing the names and titles of Nectanebo II, the last native Pharaoh of Egypt (*c.* 350 B.C.). *Southern Gallery* [523].

920. Similar to 919. *Southern Gallery* [524].

923. The immense agglomerate sarcophagus of Nectanebo II. The outside is covered with texts from *The Book of That Which is in the Other World* and shows the journey of the Sun-god through the hours of night. The sarcophagus was used in Alexandria as a bath for many years; note the holes drilled in the sides to let out the water. *Southern Gallery* [10].

960. THE ROSETTA STONE. *Southern Gallery* [24].

Found by Henry Salt

416. Head of a colossal statue of Amenhetep III in breccia. From the ruins of his mortuary temple behind the Colossi at Thebes. *Northern Gallery, Bay 4* [6].

417. A similar head from the same place. *Northern Gallery, Bay 5* [4].

Found by Lord Belmore and given to Salt

*566. A large wooden door from the tomb of Khensu-Hetep in Western Thebes. New Kingdom [705].

Found by William John Bankes

592. Part of the Second Abydos King List, a series of limestone slabs which showed Ramses II paying tribute to a number of his predecessors. Originally there were fifty-two royal names in cartouches. The slabs were set in a wall of the temple of Ramses II at Abydos, where Bankes discovered them in 1818. He copied the names but left the stones *in situ*. Mimaut, the French consul

general who succeeded Drovetti, was less scrupulous and removed them. After his death they were bought by the British Museum. *Northern Gallery, Bay 8* [117].

Found by Drovetti and given to Salt

720. The massive red granite cover of the sarcophagus of Setau, a royal scribe, steward of the palace and governor of the Sudan, who flourished in the twelfth century B.C. *Southern Gallery, Bay 19* [78].

Found by Sir Frederick Henniker and given to Salt

The painted wooden coffin of Soter, archon of Thebes in the second century A.D. *First Egyptian Room, Cases 48 and 49* [6705].

APPENDIX B

The 'Model' of Seti I's Tomb

WHILE this book was in the press I visited the Griffith Institute at Oxford in search of possible illustrations from among the Bankes MS. drawings. There Miss Rosalind Moss, with her splendid memory for bibliographical detail, recalled a letter she had had in 1936 from Mr. S. R. Stanton of the Bristol Museum. This she found and showed me. It referred to 'a set of drawings and lithographs' in the possession of the Museum, that were evidently part of Belzoni's 'model' of the tomb of Seti I. I wrote to the present Curator in Archaeology, Mr. L. V. Grinsell, found that they had survived the blitz, and in due course went down to see them.

The drawings were given to the Museum in 1900 by a Mr. C. E. Wilson. It is not known how they came into his possession, but Mr. Grinsell thinks he probably got them from Mrs. Belzoni, who died in 1870. (A small memorandum-book of hers was with the collection.) In 1934 the drawings were registered and catalogued by Stanton, who used the 1902 edition of Baedeker's *Egypt* as his guide to the tomb. Until my visit the drawings had not been collated—in this country, at any rate—either with Belzoni's published plates or with the complete survey of the tomb in Lefébure's *Les Hypogées Royaux de Thèbes* (1886). In 1935 the collection was lent to the Palais du Cinquantenaire in Brussels for exhibition during a *Semaine Égyptologique*. Jean Capart, the well-known authority on Egyptian art, praised it highly. After their return the drawings remained in their box at Bristol for over twenty years. Mr. Grinsell, however, has taken a personal interest in them and is concerned about their preservation.

Unfortunately at the time of registration the larger drawings were cut in two in order to make them fit a box measuring 30 inches by 22; the smaller ones were mounted, several together, on stiff paper. When I saw them in September 1958, there were approximately 250 sheets. Some of the drawings still had the original canvas backing, which showed signs of having once been tacked on to a wooden frame. Apart from water-colour copies of the reliefs in the tomb, there were some pencil sketches that had evidently been made on the spot, a few others from Abu Simbel, some colour lithographs from Belzoni's book of plates, and one or two unrelated subjects.

There are, it is clear, two sets of coloured drawings of the tomb,

333

neither of them complete. Stanton distinguished them in his 1934 catalogue as the 'blue' set and the 'yellow' set, since the most striking difference between them lies in the colour of the striped head-dress worn by the king. According to Stanton—I did not have time to check this myself—the 'blue' set is the less complete. However it is not always possible to attribute a particular drawing to either set with certainty, if there is no distinguishing head-dress.

On the whole the 'yellow' set is much less accurate than the 'blue' and was presumably copied from it by someone who had not seen the originals or was merely very careless. The hieroglyphs in the 'yellow' set, for example, are much more crudely drawn than those in the 'blue' and often their essential characteristics are missing. Decorative detail, especially in the costumes, is generally fudged.

It may be that Belzoni or his widow intended to run two exhibitions at the same time. On the other hand we know that, after the failure of the Paris exhibition, Sarah hoped to dispose of the casts and models in France. James Curtin, who was in charge of it, may have made the 'yellow' set then in order to raise money. Certainly he was responsible for making the new casts required for the Leicester Square exhibition in 1825.

It seems reasonable to assume that the 'blue' set was the one used for the 'model' of the tomb in the Piccadilly exhibition; that most of the drawings in it were made by Ricci in Biban el-Muluk; and that the rest are those which, because of their importance, Belzoni chose to do himself. Some of these can be identified by reference to the signed copies in Belzoni's book of plates. We may then conclude that the 'yellow' set was copied from the 'blue' at a later date by some inferior hand— possibly, at a guess, James Curtin's.

At the time of writing—October 1958—it is hoped that a selection of these drawings will shortly be on view in the City Museum, Bristol. Later it may be possible to bring some of them to London. Their survival is not merely a happy link with Belzoni. Despite their imperfections, the drawings still richly evoke the splendour of Seti's tomb, as Giovanni and Dr. Ricci must have known it, before time and the tourists, damp and despoliation had robbed it of much of the glory.

INDEX

INDEX

ABABDA, 215–21
Aberdeen, Lord, 197, 282
Abu Bekr. *See* Pascoe
Abukir Bay, 77, 83–4, 302
Abu Simbel, 11, 12, 132, 141–7, 153, 154, 164, 165–72, 173, 196, 205, 258, 262, 264, 296, 305, 309, 330, 333
Abusir, 73, 301
Abydos, 121, 180, 226–7, 306, 310, 331
Abyssinia, 111, 112, 236
Addington, Henry, 25–6, 34–5
Ægyptiaca (William Hamilton), 114, 115, 121, 174, 302, 304, 305, 309
'Ægyptiana', 65–6
African Association, 91, 118, 142, 278–9, 280, 303, 311
'Aggrescopius', 70
Agha of Aswan, 136, 137–8, 147, 229, 230, 231
Ai, King, 150, 176, 177
Albanians, 73, 96, 97, 101, 126, 127–8
Alexander of Macedon, 238
Alexandria, 73–83, 108, 112–14, 152, 154, 197, 225, 236–8, 246, 301–2, 307, 313, 331
Allmark, engineer, 82, 92, 95–6, 102, 103
Amenemhet III, King, 103, 175, 238, 239, 240, 315, 316
Amenhetep III, King, 122, 136, 150, 174, 177, 209, 210, 212, 307, 329
Amiens, Peace of, 20, 24–6, 33–4, 43, 60, 80
Amsterdam, 23–4
Andrews, Bob, 17, 32, 38, 59
Anderson, 'Wizard of the North', 294–5
Anhapu, Queen, 176, 187
Antiquaries, Society of, 14, 78, 197, 311
Antonine Itinerary, 214, 312
'Apis, Tomb of' (Seti I's tomb), 196–197, 258
Aqua-drama, 59–60, 300
Arabs, 79, 83, 85–6, 89, 93, 99, 100, 102–3, 106–8, 119, 126–8, 129, 130, 132–4, 135, 137–8, 151–2, 158, 160, 161, 162, 175, 193, 198–9, 200–1, 212, 225, 234–5, 240, 241–5
'Arabs' Tower', 73, 301
Armant, 125–6, 129, 150–1, 157

Arsinoe (Faiyum), 239
Arsinoe (near Suez), 213
Ashmolean Museum, Oxford, 14, 240, 309, 317, 333
Astley, John, 60–1
Astley, Philip, 60
Astley's Amphitheatre, 28, 35, 57, 60–1
Aswan, 123, 136–8, 147, 229–31, 309
Asyut, 119–20, 125, 135
Athanasiou, Yanni (Giovanni D'Athanasi), 155, 156, 162–3, 165, 167, 179, 192, 198, 212, 217, 223, 291, 308, 319
Atkins, Sarah, 153, 294
Awalim, 107

BACCHIAS (Kom el-Asl), 240, 315
Badrashain, 103, 104, 304
Baffi, chemist, 103–4
Bahr Yusuf, 238, 240
Bankes, Henry, 276, 282
Bankes, William John: first visit to Egypt, 116; identifies name Cleopatra on Philae obelisk, 139, 306; copies reliefs and wall-paintings at Abu Simbel, 171–2; excavates at Jerusalem, 225; visits Petra, 225; finds Second Abydos King List, 226–7, 331; his ingratitude to Belzoni, 276–7; sets up Philae obelisk at Kingston Lacy, 292; his character, 304; his manuscripts and drawings, 309, 333; translates Finati's manuscript, 309; other references, 141, 163, 164, 193, 228, 229, 230
Banks, Sir Joseph, 91, 112, 115, 227–8, 264–8
Barabras, 165, 309
Barker's Panorama, 118
Bartholomew Fair, 45, 46–55, 61–2, 172, 299
Beauty of Buttermere, 38–9, 298
Bedouin, 92, 241, 242
Beechey, Henry William, 154–5, 156, 158, 161, 162–3, 165, 167, 171, 174, 180, 189, 208, 209, 212, 214, 216, 217, 219, 226, 252
Bellefonds. *See* Linant de Bellefonds
Belmore family, 188, 189, 190, 205–6, 225, 232, 314, 330–1
'Belzonian Creation', 294

337   22